Wonders

ELL Small Group Guide

Strategic Support for English Language Learners

Mc
Graw
Hill

mheducation.com/prek-12

Copyright © 2023 McGraw Hill

Send all inquiries to:
McGraw Hill
1325 Avenue of the Americas
New York, NY 10019

ISBN: 978-1-26-577905-4
MHID: 1-26-577905-8

Printed in the United States of America.

4 5 6 7 8 9 LMN 26 25 24 23 22   A

Contents

UNITS 1-2

Contents

UNITS 3-4

Contents

Contents

Contents

ELL Resources

A variety of resources will help English Language Learners meet grade level expectations. The components provide scaffolded instruction and practice through integrated domains to help students tackle core content and transition to more proficient levels of English.

Components	Differentiate: N = Newcomer B = Beginning I = Intermediate A = Advanced/Advanced-High AL = All Levels	Integrated Domains 📖 Reading ✏️ Writing 👂 Listening 🎤 Speaking	Available Digitally 🖱️
ELL Small Group Guide • Literature Big Book • Interactive Read Aloud • Leveled Reader • Writing	B, I, A	📖 ✏️ 👂 🎤	●
Leveled Readers	AL	📖 ✏️ 👂 🎤	●
ELL Differentiated Texts	B, I, A	📖 ✏️ 👂 🎤	●
Visual Vocabulary Cards	AL	📖 ✏️ 👂 🎤	●

Components		Differentiate: N = Newcomer B = Beginning I = Intermediate A = Advanced/Advanced-High AL = All Levels	Integrated Domains 📖 Reading ✏️ Writing 👂 Listening 🎤 Speaking	Available Digitally
Newcomers • Newcomer Cards • Newcomer Teacher's Guide • Newcomer Online Visuals • Newcomer Interactive Games	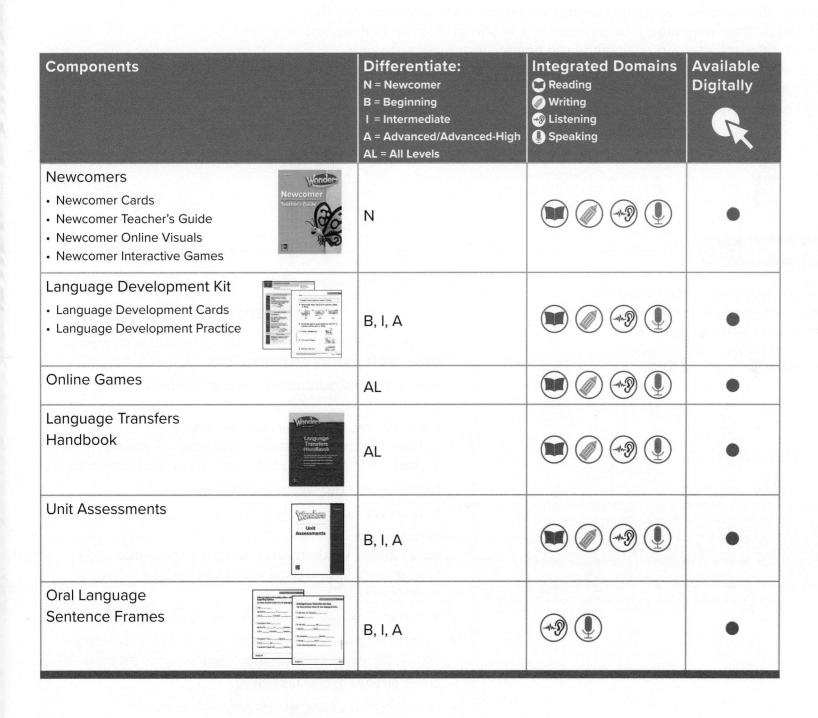	N	📖 ✏️ 👂 🎤	●
Language Development Kit • Language Development Cards • Language Development Practice		B, I, A	📖 ✏️ 👂 🎤	●
Online Games		AL	📖 ✏️ 👂 🎤	●
Language Transfers Handbook		AL	📖 ✏️ 👂 🎤	●
Unit Assessments		B, I, A	📖 ✏️ 👂 🎤	●
Oral Language Sentence Frames		B, I, A	👂 🎤	●

Understanding English Language Learner Levels

The *Wonders* program provides targeted language support for all levels of English language proficiency. The English language learners in your classroom have a variety of backgrounds, each with different ethnic background, first language, socioeconomic status, quality of prior schooling, and levels of language proficiency. They bring diverse sets of academic knowledge and cultural perspectives that can enrich learning.

This overview is designed to help teachers determine the appropriate level of support for their English language learners and understand students' abilities depending on their language proficiencies. It is important to note that students may be at different levels in each language domain (listening, speaking, reading, and writing). Systematic, explicit, and appropriately scaffolded instruction helps English language learners attain English proficiency and meet the high expectations defined in English Language Arts standards.

BEGINNING

At this early stage of language development, students require significant language support. As they gain experience with English, support may become moderate or light for familiar tasks and topics.

The Student...

- recognizes English phonemes that correspond to phonemes produced in primary language;
- initially demonstrates more receptive than productive English skills;
- communicates basic needs and information in social and academic settings, using familiar everyday vocabulary, gestures, learned words or phrases, and/or short sentences;
- follows one- or two-step oral directions;
- answers *wh-* questions (who, what, when, where, why, which);
- comprehends words, phrases, and basic information about familiar topics as presented through stories and conversations;
- identifies concepts about print and text features;
- reads short grade-appropriate text with familiar vocabulary and simple sentences, supported by graphics or pictures;
- draws pictures and writes labels;
- expresses ideas using visuals and short responses.

INTERMEDIATE

Students require moderate support for cognitively demanding activities and light support for familiar tasks and topics.

The Student...

- pronounces most English phonemes correctly while reading aloud;
- communicates more complex personal needs, ideas, and opinions using increasingly complex vocabulary and sentences;
- follows multi-step oral directions;
- initiates and participates in collaborative conversations about social and academic topics, with support as needed;
- asks questions, retells stories or events, and comprehends basic content-area concepts;
- comprehends information on familiar and unfamiliar topics with contextual clues;
- reads increasingly complex grade-level text supported by graphics, pictures, and context clues;
- increases correct usage of written and oral language conventions;
- uses vocabulary learned, including academic language, to provide information and extended responses in contextualized oral and written prompts.

ADVANCED/ADVANCED HIGH

While the English language proficiency of students is advanced, some language support for accessing content is still necessary. If students are requiring little to no support, exiting them from the ELL designation should be considered.

The Student...

- applies knowledge of common English morphemes in oral and silent reading;
- communicates complex feelings, needs, ideas, and opinions using increasingly complex vocabulary and sentences;
- understands more nonliteral social and academic language about concrete and abstract topics;
- initiates and sustains collaborative conversations about grade-level academic and social topics;
- reads and comprehends a wide range of complex literature and informational texts at grade level;
- writes using more standard forms of English on various academic topics;
- communicates orally and in writing with fewer grammatical errors;
- tailors language, orally and in writing, to specific purposes and audiences.

Scaffolding the Literature Big Book

Digital Tools

Children can access the Digital Resource Library for audio recordings of each **Literature Big Book.** The audio can be played on a page-by-page basis.

Wonders provides differentiated instruction for the **Literature Big Book.**

- Linguistically accommodated instruction for all levels offers access to the **Literature Big Books** and the Paired Selections.

- Prereading strategies enhance comprehension for children from different cultural backgrounds; prereading support includes preteaching the vocabulary, using visual and other resources, and providing a summary of the selection while showing photos or illustrations from the selection.

- The Interactive Question-Response routine with leveled prompts focuses on the meaning of the text.

- Oral language is developed through peer interaction.

- Targeted ELA academic language is reinforced through review and guided questions.

- Children have an opportunity to work independently and collaboratively on a variety of activities, including glossary building, role-plays, writing tasks, and peer-to-peer instruction. The routines help children take ownership of their language development.

- Children can also listen to a digital recording of the selections to develop comprehension and practice fluency and pronunciation.

LESSONS 1-2

READING · LITERATURE BIG BOOK · ACCESS THE TEXT

WEEK 1

LEARNING GOALS

We can understand important ideas and details in a story.

We can use photographs to learn new information.

OBJECTIVES

With prompting and support, ask and answer questions about key details in a text.

With prompting and support, identify characters and events in a story.

With prompting and support, retell familiar stories, including key details.

Confirm understanding of a text read aloud or information presented orally or through other media by asking and answering questions about key details and requesting clarification if something is not understood.

LANGUAGE OBJECTIVES

Children will narrate, or tell, what friends do using naming words.

ELA ACADEMIC LANGUAGE

· retell, details

· Cognate: *detalles*

MATERIALS

Literature Big Book, *What About Bear?*

Visual Vocabulary Cards

DIGITAL TOOLS

Have children listen to the selection as they follow along to develop comprehension.

Use the vocabulary activity for additional support.

What About Bear?

Prepare to Read

Build Background Show images of friends doing things together. *The children are friends. Friends play together. Friends do things together. What do friends do?* Help children describe using: *Friends ___ together.*

Focus on Vocabulary Use the **Visual Vocabulary Cards** to review the oral vocabulary words *friend* and *problem.* As you read, use gestures and other visual support to clarify important story words, such as *play, game, grumpy,* and *far away.* Have children add these words to their personal glossaries.

Summarize the Text Before reading, give a short summary of the story. *This book is about Bear and his friends and how they play together.*

Read the Text

Use the Interactive Question-Response Routine to help children understand the story.

Pages 4–11

Pages 4–7 Read the text. Point to the chest of toys. *Bear and Goose have toys. What do Bear and Goose have?* (toys) *What do Bear and Goose want to do?* (play) Point to the puppets. *Bear and Goose are playing with puppets. What are Bear and Goose playing with?* (puppets)

Pages 8–11 Read the text. *Fox wants to play. Fox wants to play with Bear and Goose. What does Fox want to do?* (play) *Who does he want to play with?* (Bear and Goose)

What are Bear and Goose doing? What do Bear and Goose have? Talk to a partner.

Beginning Help partners point to the illustrations and respond using: *Bear and Goose are playing.*

Intermediate Have partners respond using: *Bear and Goose have toys.*

Advanced/Advanced High Have partners respond using: *Bear and Goose are playing. Bear and Goose have toys/puppets.*

Pages 12–23

Pages 18–19 Read the text. Point to Goose and Fox. *Goose and Fox are playing the game.* Point to Bear. *Bear is sitting by himself. Bear is watching Goose and Fox.*

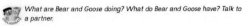

What About Bear?

Literature Big Book

Bear has a problem. He is grumpy. Does Goose want Bear to play? (yes) *How does Bear look?* (grumpy)

What are Goose and Fox doing? What is Bear doing? Talk to a partner.

Beginning Help partners point to the illustration and respond using: *Goose and Fox are playing.*

Intermediate Have partners respond: *Fox and Goose are playing a game. Bear is sitting.*

Advanced/Advanced High Have partners respond and give details about Bear: *Fox and Goose are playing a game. Bear is sitting alone. Bear is grumpy.*

Pages 24–33

Pages 24–29 Read the text. Point to the illustrations of the animals on pages 24–25. *What is Bear doing?* (walking away) *What does Goose tell Bear?* (come back) Point to the illustrations of the animals on pages 28–29. *Goose tells Fox that Bear is a big, old friend and Fox is a new friend. What is Bear?* (old friend) *What is Fox?* (a new friend)

Pages 30–33 *What does Goose ask Fox to do?* (play together) *Does Fox want to play?* (yes) *What is everyone doing?* (playing; jumping rope)

 What kind of friend is Bear? Talk to a partner.

Beginning Help partners point to the illustration of bear and respond using: *Bear is big.*

Intermediate Have partners point to the illustration of bear and respond using: *Bear is big. Bear is old.*

Advanced/Advanced High Have partners respond using: *Bear is big and old. Bear is grumpy.*

 **Retell** Use the **Retelling Cards** for "What About Bear?" to retell the story with children. Display the cards and model retelling using sequence words, such as *first, next, then,* and *last* as you point to the events and actions in the cards. Then help children take turns retelling one part using sequence words.

LESSON 4 Paired Selection: "How to Be a Friend"

Pages 35–40 Read the text on pages 35–37. *Friends can do many things together.* Point to the children in the photographs and describe the them. *Friends can work together/play a game/learn together. What can friends do together?* (help, play, read, learn) Point to the lists on pages 38 and 39 as you describe them. *Friends can get along. Friends listen to each other/ share together/ play fair. You can help a new friend. Say hello. Tell your name. Ask the friend to play.*

 How can you help a new friend? Talk to a partner.

Beginning Help partners point to a photograph and respond: *I can say hello.*

Intermediate Have partners respond: *I can say hello/ my name.*

Advanced/Advanced High How can you get along with a new friend? (*I can share with a new friend.*)

FORMATIVE ASSESSMENT

STUDENT CHECK-IN

Main Selection Have partners retell one thing that friends do.

Paired Selection Have partners share important information they learned from the photograph.

Have children reflect using the Check-in routine.

Independent Time

Talk About It Have children describe what they read in "What About Bear?" and "How to Be a Friend." Ask: *Are the characters in "What About Bear?" friends? What did you learn from "How to be a Friend"?* Have partners describe how the two stories are alike. Help them respond using: *The two stories tell about ___.*

---

2 UNIT 1 WEEK 1

ENGLISH LANGUAGE LEARNERS 3

Scaffolding the Interactive Read Aloud

Wonders provides differentiated instruction for the **Interactive Read Aloud**.

- Linguistically accommodated instruction for Beginning, Intermediate, Advanced/Advanced High children offers access to the grade-level text.

- Prereading strategies enhance comprehension for children from different cultural backgrounds; prereading support includes preteaching the vocabulary, using visual and other resources, and providing a summary of the selection while showing photos or illustrations from the selection.

- The Interactive Question-Response routine is chunked by card and focuses on the meaning of the text.

- Oral language is developed through peer interaction.

- Targeted ELA academic language is reinforced through review and guided questions.

- Children have an opportunity to work independently and collaboratively on a variety of activities.

- Children can also listen to a digital recording of the selections to develop comprehension and practice fluency and pronunciation.

AUTHOR INSIGHT

"Effective teachers understand that English Language Learners are studying complex concepts and processing new content in a new language. These students are capable of meeting high academic standards but require adjustments to the way instruction is presented. Their unique linguistic needs require that additional support be provided. Linguistically accommodated instruction will result in greater participation in class and overall achievement."

—Dr. Jana Echevarria

LEARNING GOALS

We can listen actively to learn how a lion and mouse become friends.

OBJECTIVES

Ask and answer questions about unknown words in a text.

With prompting and support, compare and contrast the adventures and experiences of characters in familiar stories.

With prompting and support, describe the relationship between illustrations and the story in which they appear.

Continue a conversation through multiple exchanges.

LANGUAGE OBJECTIVES

Children will discuss the story and the animals using action words and naming words.

ELA ACADEMIC LANGUAGE

- *problem, illustration*
- Cognates: *problema, ilustración*

MATERIALS

Interactive Read Aloud, "The Lion and the Mouse"

Visual Vocabulary Cards

DIGITAL TOOLS

Have children listen to the selection as they follow along to develop comprehension.

Use the vocabulary activity for additional support.

"The Lion and the Mouse"

Prepare to Read

Build Background Display illustrations of a lion and a mouse and discuss with children the physical and behavioral characteristics of each animal. Ask questions and discuss to help them compare the animals: *What animal is this? What does a lion/mouse have? What does it do? Where does it live? Is it big or small? Is it strong or weak?* Help children discuss using: *The lion/mouse has/is ___.*

Interactive Read Aloud

Focus on Vocabulary Use the **Visual Vocabulary Cards** to review the oral vocabulary words: *rescue, grasped,* and *escape.* As you read, use gestures and other visual support to clarify important story words, for example: *promise, trap, solve, plan,* and *different.*

Summarize the Text This story is about two very different friends: a large lion and a tiny mouse. One day the mouse helps the lion solve a big problem.

Read the Text

Use the Interactive Question-Response Routine to help children understand the story.

Card 1

Paragraphs 1–4 Read the text. Point to the illustration. *The lion was napping. The mouse wakes up the lion. Who was napping?* (the lion)

Paragraphs 5–7 Read the text. *The lion doesn't believe the mouse. But the lion lets the mouse go. What does the lion do?* (let the mouse go)

 What does the lion do for the mouse? Talk to a partner.

Beginning Help partners point to the illustration and respond using: *The lion does not eat the mouse.*

Intermediate Have partners describe what the lion did using: *The lion does not eat the mouse. The lion let the mouse go.*

Advanced/Advanced High Have partners describe the actions of the lion and mouse: *The lion does not eat the mouse. The mouse promises to help the lion.*

Card 2

Paragraphs 1–2 Read the text. *The mouse hears the lion roar.* Point to the lion. *The lion is caught in a net. The lion wants to break free. What did the mouse hear?* (lion roar) *What is the lion in?* (a net)

Paragraphs 3–5 Read the text. Point to the mouse. *The mouse says that he will rescue, or save, the lion. The mouse will solve the lion's problem. What does the mouse tell the lion?* (The mouse will help the lion.)

 What happened to the lion? Talk to a partner.

Beginning Help partners point to the illustration and respond using: *The lion is in a net.*

Intermediate Have partners describe what the mouse tells the lion using: *The lion is in a net. The mouse is going to help the lion.*

Advanced/Advanced High Have partners describe what the mouse tells the lion using: *The lion is in a net. The mouse is going to solve the lion's problem.*

Card 3

Paragraphs 1–3 Read the text. *The lion doesn't believe the mouse can help him. But the mouse has a plan. Does the lion think the mouse can help?* (no)

Paragraphs 4–6 Read the text. *The mouse chews the net and makes a hole. The lion escapes. How does the mouse help the lion?* (The mouse chews the net.)

 How does mouse help the lion? Talk to a partner.

Beginning Help partners point to the illustration and respond using: *The mouse chews the net.*

Intermediate Have partners describe what the mouse helps the lion do using: *The mouse chews the net. The lion goes through the hole.*

Advanced/Advanced High Have partners describe what the mouse helps the lion do using: *The mouse chews the net and makes a hole. The lion goes through the hole.*

Card 4

Paragraphs 1–2 Read the text. Point to the lion and the mouse. *The lion is giving the mouse a ride. They are going up the hill to see the sunset. What are they going to do?* (see the sunset) *Are they friends?* (Yes, they are friends.)

Paragraphs 3–4 Read the text. *The mouse likes to watch the sunset on the hill, too. Each day the lion and the mouse watch the sunset together. What do the lion and the mouse like to do together?* (watch sunset from the hill)

 What do the mouse and the lion do together? Talk to a partner.

Beginning Help partners point to the illustration and respond using: *The lion and the mouse watch the sunset.*

Intermediate Have partners describe what the mouse and the lion do together using: *The mouse and the lion watch the sunset together.*

Advanced/Advanced High Have partners describe what the mouse and the lion like to do together using: *The mouse and the lion watch the sunset on the hill together.*

Retell Use the illustrations on the **Interactive Read-Aloud Cards** to retell the story with children. Display the cards and model retelling using sequence words, such as *first, next, then,* and *last* as you point to the events and actions in the cards. Then help partners take turns retelling one part using the sequence words.

FORMATIVE ASSESSMENT

STUDENT CHECK-IN

Have partners share what each animal does in the story.

Have children reflect using the Check-in routine.

Independent Time

Draw and Label Have partners select one illustration from the **Interactive Read-Aloud Cards** and describe it. Provide a model and sentence frames for them to use: *I see a lion. I see a ___.* Then have them draw one thing they see and help them label it.

Using Leveled Readers

AUTHOR INSIGHT

"Teachers must apply a wide range of effective scaffolding strategies to help ELLs process text at higher and higher levels of complexity and accelerate the development of their English proficiency. Leveled readers with linguistically accommodated texts that also share the same genre, vocabulary, and topic as the main selection have the potential to offer just the right level of ELL support and challenge."

—Dr. Josefina V. Tinajero

The Leveled Readers for English language learners are scaffolded versions of the On Level Readers. Children benefit from reading linguistically accommodated text with the same genre focus and essential question as the other main selections.

- The Build Background section connects to the Essential Question and supports children from different cultural backgrounds.

- Prereading support includes preteaching the vocabulary, using visual and other resources.

- The Interactive Question-Response routine is chunked by section and focuses on the meaning of the text.

- Fluency is reinforced through teacher modeling.

- For the Build Knowledge: Make Connections activity, children work collaboratively to connect with ideas they have read in other selections

- After working through the ELL version, some children may be ready to move on to the On Level text successfully.

- Children can also listen to a digital recording of the selections to develop comprehension and practice fluency and pronunciation.

- As an option, teachers can read aloud the text as children follow along.

LESSONS 4-5

READING • LEVELED READER • ACCESS THE TEXT

WEEK 1

LEARNING GOALS

We can ask and answer questions about the story as we read.

OBJECTIVES

With prompting and support, ask and answer questions about key details in a text.

With prompting and support, identify characters in a story.

With prompting and support, retell familiar stories, including key details.

LANGUAGE OBJECTIVES

Children will inquire, or ask and answer, about characters in a story using naming words and simple sentences.

ELA ACADEMIC LANGUAGE

- details, ask, answer
- Cognate: detalles

MATERIALS

ELL Leveled Reader:
The Mouse and the Moose

Online Differentiated Texts,
"The Friends"

Online ELL Visual Vocabulary Cards

DIGITAL TOOLS

Have children listen to the selection as they follow along to develop comprehension.

Use the vocabulary activity for additional support.

The Mouse and the Moose

Prepare to Read

Build Background We have been reading about friends. Let's think about the Essential Question: How can we get along with new friends? Have children share ways that friends can get along. Provide a model and sentence frames: Friends can share. Friends can work/play together.

Focus on Vocabulary Use the routine on the ELL Visual Vocabulary Cards to preteach share and together. As you read, use images and any labels to clarify important story words, for example: mouse, moose, can.

Read the Text

Use the Interactive Question-Response Routine to help children understand the story.

Pages 2–8

Pages 2–3 Read the text while tracing the words. Have children repeat after you. The mouse and the moose are playing together. The mouse can swing. The moose can push the swing. What can the mouse do? (swing) What can the moose do? (push)

Main Story Elements: Character Help children identify the characters. Use the illustrations to help them describe: The mouse and the moose are playing together. I see two characters in the story. Who are the characters? (the mouse and the moose)

 What can the mouse do? What can the moose do? Talk with a partner.

Beginning Help partners point to the pictures and respond using: The mouse can swing. The moose can push.

Intermediate Have partners describe what the mouse and moose do together using: The mouse can swing. The moose can push. The moose and the mouse are playing together.

Advanced/Advanced High Have partners describe details in the illustrations: The mouse can swing. The moose can push. The moose and the mouse are playing together. The moose is helping the mouse.

Pages 4–5 Read the text while tracing the words. Help children discuss details. The mouse can pick an apple. What can mouse do? (pick an apple) The moose can help the mouse. What can the moose do? (help the mouse)

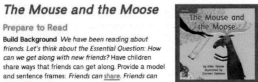
Lexile BR

What can the mouse and moose do together? Talk with a partner.

Beginning Help partners point to the pictures and respond using: The mouse and moose can pick an apple together.

Intermediate Have partners describe what the mouse and moose can share using: The mouse and moose can pick an apple together. The moose and the mouse can share the apple.

Pages 6-8 Read aloud while tracing the words. The mouse can read. What can the mouse do? (read) The moose can help the mouse.

What can the mouse and the moose do together? Talk to a partner.

Beginning Help partners point to the pictures and respond using: The mouse and moose can read together.

Intermediate Have partners describe what the mouse and the moose can share using: The mouse and moose can read together. The mouse and the moose can share the story.

Advanced/Advanced High Have partners describe how the mouse and moose can help each other using: The mouse and moose can read together. The mouse can help the mouse read. The mouse can share the story.

Ask and Answer Questions Help children ask and answer questions. What can the mouse do? (read)

Retell Have partners retell the story. Have them take turns pointing to a picture and describing it each other.

Focus on Fluency

Read pages 2-8 and have children echo read. For additional practice, have children record themselves reading the same text a few times, and then select their favorite recording to play for you.

Build Knowledge: Make Connections

Talk About the Text Have partners discuss how friends get along and work together.

Self-Selected Reading

Help children choose a fiction selection from the online **Leveled Reader Library** or read the Differentiated Text, "The Friends."

LITERACY ACTIVITIES

Have children complete the Literacy Activities on the inside back cover of the book.

FORMATIVE ASSESSMENT

STUDENT CHECK-IN

Have partners dicuss how the mouse and the moose help each other and share with each other. Have children reflect using the Check-in routine.

LEVEL UP

IF children can read The Mouse and the Moose ELL Level with fluency and correctly answer questions,

THEN tell children that they will read a more detailed version of the story.

HAVE children page through The Mouse and the Moose On Level and describe each picture in simple language.

- Have children read the selection, checking their comprehension and providing assistance as necessary.

Writing

Wonders provides differentiated instruction to support targeted sections of the daily core writing activities.

- The Actor/Action routine breaks down the modeled and interactive writing prompts to support understanding.
- Children work collaboratively to respond to the prompts and complete the writing activities in their writer's notebook or **Reading/Writing Companion.**
- Daily scaffolded writing support is provided for all levels.
- The Independent Writing routine focuses on supporting children in accessing and retelling the Literature Big Book or shared read using text and picture evidence, analyzing the writing prompt, and responding to the prompt.
- The self-selected writing activity focuses on revising the activity through teacher modeling and group as well as partner collaboration. The lesson provides an opportunity to review the weekly grammar skill.
- The **Language Transfers Handbook** and **Language Development Cards** provide additional grammar support.

AUTHOR INSIGHT

"The attributes that make text especially complex for ELLs include unfamiliar words and phrases, the complexity of the syntax, the number of referential chains, and the amount of background knowledge required to understand the text. It is important for teachers to understand the attributes that make text complex for ELLs so that they can support ELLs in understanding complex text."

—Dr. Diane August

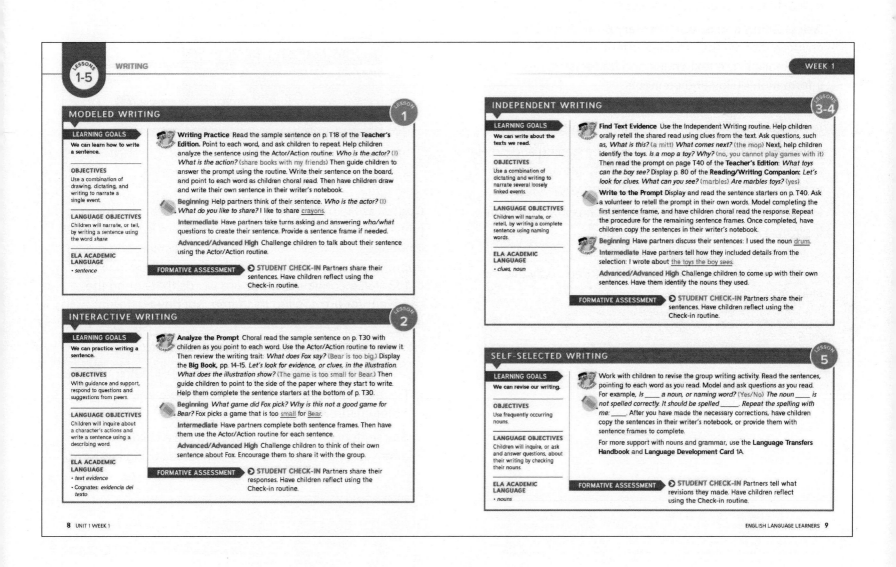

Instructional Routines

The instructional routines provide carefully sequenced steps to scaffold instruction and allow children to focus on learning content. Once children are familiar with a routine, the teacher can use it to teach new skills and content efficiently.

Interactive Question-Response

This routine was designed to provide context and opportunities for English language learners to learn how information builds and connects and to focus on key concepts and vocabulary. The Access the Text lessons incorporate this routine in the instruction.

Read the Text in Chunks Read one section of text at a time so children can focus on the meaning of the text. For each text chunk:

- **Use Visuals and Text Features** Use headings to help children predict what the section will be about and images and other text features to aid children's comprehension.

- **Explain** As you read, explain difficult or unfamiliar concepts and words. Provide background and contextual knowledge, as needed.

- **Ask Guiding and Supplementary Questions** Help children identify the most important information and details in the text chunk and understand how information builds and connects.

- **Scaffold Responses** Provide sentence starters/frames to help children express and communicate their ideas.

- **Reinforce Vocabulary** Reinforce the meaning and point out cognates and false cognates. Ask questions that require children to use newly acquired vocabulary.

- **Retell** Have children retell the most important ideas in their own words.

- **Reinforce Skills and Strategies** Model using skills and strategies. Ask questions to help children apply the skills and strategies.

Vocabulary

Define/Example/Ask Routine Use this routine to help children learn unfamiliar, conceptually complex words they encounter in the texts. The **Visual Vocabulary Cards** provide this routine on the back of the card. Here is an example for *recent*.

1. **Define**: Recent *means something happened a short time ago. En español,* recent *quiere decir "reciente, ocurrido hace poco."* Recent *in English and* reciente *in Spanish are cognates. They sound alike and mean the same thing in both languages.*

2. **Example**: Mary learns about recent events from the newspaper. En español: Mary se entera de los eventos recientes por el periódico.

3. **Ask**: *What word is the opposite of* recent?

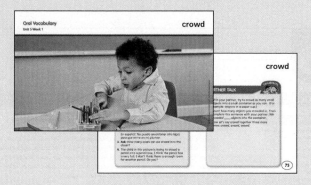

Cognates Help children transfer knowledge from their native language. Explain that cognates are in two different languages, but they look similar, sound similar, and mean approximately the same thing. Remind children to watch out for false cognates, which are words that sound the same and/or are spelled the same, but have different meanings, such as *pie/pie*.

Here is an example for the cognates *cat/gato:*

1. Display and say cognate word pairs and images.

2. Have a native Spanish speaker say *gato* and *cat*. Have other children echo.

3. Say sentences using the word, and have children echo after you or have partners say sentences using the word.

Sentence Analysis

Actor/Action Help children focus on the structure of written language by using this routine with sample sentences. This routine is primarily used in the writing lessons to analyze the models but can be used any time to talk about the text and confirm understanding.

1. Sentences can have an actor and action or an object and a description.

2. Review definitions: the actor/action is a person or thing that a sentence is about and what the person/thing is doing; the actor/description is how a person, place, or thing can be described.

3. Read the sentence while pointing to each word.

4. Ask children to identify actor(s)/action(s) or the action/ description.

5. Then ask follow-up tag questions with *why, what, when,* or *how.*

Independent Writing Routine Use this routine to support the independent writing in Lessons 3 and 4.

Find Text Evidence

1. Review comprehension of the story by helping children orally retell it. Use the images from the selection and ask guiding questions.

2. When children have finished, explain that they are going to write about the selection.

3. Read the prompt found in the **Teacher's Edition** or the **Reading/Writing Companion.** Reword the prompt, and use questions as well as images from the selection to ensure understanding.

Write to the Prompt

4. Display the sentence starters found in the **Teacher's Edition.** Tell children you will use these to help write about the selection. Ask a volunteer to retell the prompt in their own words.

5. Provide a question to help children orally answer the first sentence frame. Model completing the sentence frame on the board, and have children choral read the response. Repeat the routine for the remaining sentence frames.

6. Once completed, ask children to copy the sentences into their writer's notebook or **Reading/Writing Companion.**

7. Have partners work together to read their sentences and talk about them. Provide scaffolded instruction as partners work together to revise their sentences.

Teacher Response Techniques

Throughout the lessons, use these techniques to motivate children's participation and build oral fluency.

- **Wait for Responses** Provide enough time for children to answer a question or process their ideas to respond. Depending on their levels of proficiency, give children the option of responding in different ways, such as answering in their native language that you can rephrase in English, or answering with nonverbal cues.

- **Revise for Form** Let children know that they can respond in different ways, depending on their levels of proficiency. Repeat the children's response to model the proper form. You can model in full sentences and use academic language.

- **Repeat** Give positive confirmation to the answers that each child offers. If the response is correct, repeat the response in a clear voice and at a slower pace to encourage others to participate.

- **Revise for Meaning** Repeating an answer offers an opportunity to clarify the meaning of a response.

- **Elaborate** If children give a one-word answer or a nonverbal cue, elaborate on the answer to model fluent speaking and grammatical patterns. Provide more examples, or repeat the answer using proper academic language.

- **Elicit** Prompt children to give a more comprehensive response by asking additional questions or guiding them to get to an answer.

Planner Units 1-10

Customize your own lesson plans at
my.mheducation.com

20+ mins
Reading
Suggested Daily Time

MATERIALS

- Literature Big Book
- Visual Vocabulary Cards
- Reading/Writing Companion
- Literature Anthology
- ELL Leveled Reader
- Online Differentiated Texts
- Online ELL Visual Vocabulary Cards

Reading

Literature Big Book

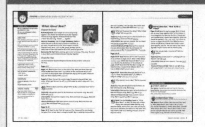

Main Selection
- Access the Text

Prepare to Read
- Build Background
- Vocabulary
- Summarize the Text

Read the Text
 Partner Work

Paired Selection
- Access the Text

Prepare to Read
- Vocabulary

Read the Text
 Partner Work

 Independent Time

 Listen Along to Text

15+ mins
Writing
Suggested Daily Time

MATERIALS

Modeled and Interactive Writing
- Reading/Writing Companion

Independent Writing
- Teacher's Edition
- Reading/Writing Companion

Self-Selected Writing
- Online Language Development Kit
- Online Language Transfers Handbook

Writing

Modeled Writing

Modeled Writing
Write About the Literature Big Book

 Partner Work

Interactive Writing

Interactive Writing
Write About the Literature Big Book

 Partner Work

Learning Goals

Specific learning goals identified in every lesson make clear what children will be learning and why. These smaller goals provide stepping stones to help children meet their reading and writing goals.

Reading

Interactive Read-Aloud

Anchor Text
- Access the Text

Prepare to Read
- Build Background
- Vocabulary
- Summarize the Text

Read the Text
 Partner Work

 Independent Time

 Listen Along to Text

Additional Texts

Leveled Reader
- Access the Text

Prepare to Read
- Build Background
- Vocabulary

Read the Text
 Partner Work

Apply Skill and Strategy

Listen Along to Text

Self-Selected Reading
- Leveled Reader Library
- Differentiated Texts

Writing

Independent Writing

Independent Writing
Write About the Shared Read

Apply Conventions

Independent Writing
Write About the Shared Read

Apply Conventions

Self-Selected Writing

Self-Selected Writing
Revise with Conventions

Check-in Routine

The routine at the close of each lesson guides children to self-reflect on how well they understood each learning goal.

Review the lesson learning goal.
Reflect on the activity.
Self-Assess by showing thumbs up, sideways, or down.
Share with your teacher.

Supporting Newcomers

Components:
Using the Newcomer Kit

Use the online *Wonders* **Newcomer Components** for children with little or no English proficiency. These components provide newcomers with access to basic, high-utility vocabulary. The kit helps children develop language skills to transition to the Beginning level of language proficiency.

Newcomer Cards

Each card introduces a topic through colorful visuals to stimulate conversation to help children develop oral language and build vocabulary.

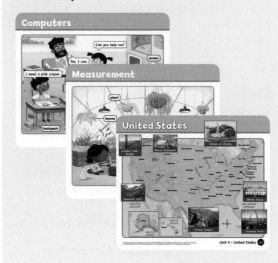

Newcomer Teacher's Guide

Provides three lessons for each Newcomer Card topic and student worksheets with reading and writing activities to help children transition into the English-speaking classroom.

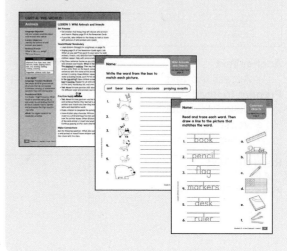

Suggested Planning:
4-Week Learning Blocks

Because newcomers can enter your classroom at any time during the year, the program is designed for flexibility with multiple entry-points for instruction:

- Use the Start Smart materials with new arrivals.
- The four units of instruction can be completed in any order, so new arrivals can join those who are already well underway.
- The Newcomer Teacher's Guide also provides songs and chants, reproducible manipulatives, conversation starters, and games.
- At the end of Start Smart and each unit, use the Progress Monitoring materials to measure children's progress.

UNIT 1: 4 WEEKS

Start Smart for new arrivals
- Alphabet
- Greetings
- Shapes and Colors
- Numbers

Unit 1: Life at School
- In the Classroom
- Computers
- A Day at School
- Calendar
- Weather

Materials
Newcomer Cards Start Smart, Unit 1
Newcomer Teacher's Guide
- Start Smart pp. 1-25
- Unit 1 pp. 26-57
- Optional Materials 154-T38
- Progress Monitoring T39-T45
Newcomer Visuals Start Smart, Unit 1
Newcomer Interactive Games

UNIT 2: 4 WEEKS

Start Smart for new arrivals
Unit 2: My Family and Me
- My Body
- Clothing
- Feelings
- My Family
- My Home

Materials
Newcomer Cards Start Smart, Unit 2
Newcomer Teacher's Guide
- Start Smart pp. 1-25
- Unit 2 pp. 58-89
- Optional Materials 154-T38
- Progress Monitoring T39-T45
Newcomer Visuals Start Smart, Unit 2
Newcomer Interactive Games

Newcomer Visuals

Provides additional opportunities for vocabulary building and oral language development for each topic through prompts and words and phrases children can use.

Newcomer Interactive Games

Online Interactive Games provide independent practice to build vocabulary.

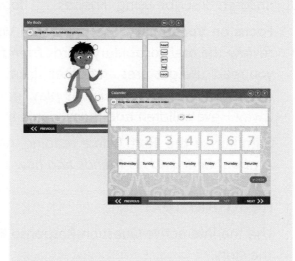

UNIT 3: 4 WEEKS

Start Smart for new arrivals
Unit 3: Community
- My Community
- Park
- Transportation
- Food and Meals
- Shopping

Materials
Newcomer Cards Start Smart, Unit 3
Newcomer Teacher's Guide
- Start Smart pp. 1-25
- Unit 3 pp. 90-121
- Optional Materials 154-T38
- Progress Monitoring T39-T45
Newcomer Visuals Start Smart, Unit 3
Newcomer Interactive Games

UNIT 4: 4 WEEKS

Start Smart for new arrivals
Unit 4: The World
- Measurement
- Animals
- Growth and Change
- United States
- My World

Materials
Newcomer Cards Start Smart, Unit 4
Newcomer Teacher's Guide
- Start Smart pp. 1-25
- Unit 4 pp. 122-153
- Optional Materials 154-T38
- Progress Monitoring T39-T45
Newcomer Visuals Start Smart, Unit 4
Newcomer Interactive Games

LESSONS 1-2

LEARNING GOALS

We can understand important ideas and details in a story.

We can use photographs to learn new information.

OBJECTIVES

With prompting and support, ask and answer questions about key details in a text.

With prompting and support, identify characters and events in a story.

With prompting and support, retell familiar stories, including key details.

Confirm understanding of a text read aloud or information presented orally or through other media by asking and answering questions about key details and requesting clarification if something is not understood.

LANGUAGE OBJECTIVES

Children will narrate, or tell, what friends do using naming words.

ELA ACADEMIC LANGUAGE

• *retell, details*

• Cognate: *detalles*

MATERIALS

Literature Big Book, *What About Bear?*

Visual Vocabulary Cards

DIGITAL TOOLS

Have children listen to the selection as they follow along to develop comprehension.

Use the vocabulary activity for additional support.

What About Bear?

Literature Big Book

Prepare to Read

Build Background Show images of friends doing things together. *The children are friends. Friends play together. Friends do things together. What do friends do?* Help children describe using: *Friends ___ together.*

Focus on Vocabulary Use the **Visual Vocabulary Cards** to review the oral vocabulary words *friend* and *problem.* As you read, use gestures and other visual support to clarify important story words, such as *play, game, grumpy,* and *far away.* Have children add these words to their personal glossaries.

Summarize the Text Before reading, give a short summary of the story. *This book is about Bear and his friends and how they play together.*

Read the Text

Use the Interactive Question-Response Routine to help children understand the story.

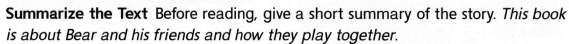

Pages 4–11

Pages 4–7 Read the text. Point to the chest of toys. *Bear and Goose have toys. What do Bear and Goose have?* (toys) *What do Bear and Goose want to do?* (play) Point to the puppets. *Bear and Goose are playing with puppets. What are Bear and Goose playing with?* (puppets)

Pages 8–11 Read the text. *Fox wants to play. Fox wants to play with Bear and Goose. What does Fox want to do?* (play) *Who does he want to play with?* (Bear and Goose)

 What are Bear and Goose doing? What do Bear and Goose have? Talk to a partner.

Beginning Help partners point to the illustrations and respond using: *Bear and Goose are* playing.

Intermediate Have partners respond using: *Bear and Goose are* playing. *Bear and Goose have* toys.

Advanced/Advanced High Have partners respond using: *Bear and Goose are* playing. *Bear and Goose have* toys/puppets.

Pages 12–23

Pages 18–19 Read the text. Point to Goose and Fox. *Goose and Fox are playing the game.* Point to Bear. *Bear is sitting by himself. Bear is watching Goose and Fox.*

Bear has a problem. He is grumpy. Does Goose want Bear to play? (yes) *How does Bear look?* (grumpy)

 What are Goose and Fox doing? What is Bear doing? Talk to a partner.

Beginning Help partners point to the illustration and respond using: *Goose and Fox are* <u>playing</u>.

Intermediate Have partners respond: *Fox and Goose are* <u>playing a game</u>. *Bear is* <u>sitting</u>.

Advanced/Advanced High Have partners respond and give details about Bear: *Fox and Goose are* <u>playing a game</u>. *Bear is* <u>sitting</u> *alone. Bear is* <u>grumpy</u>.

Pages 24–33

Pages 24–29 Read the text. Point to the illustrations of the animals on pages 24–25. *What is Bear doing?* (walking away) *What does Goose tell Bear?* (come back) Point to the illustrations of the animals on pages 28–29. *Goose tells Fox that Bear is a big, old friend and Fox is a new friend. What is Bear?* (old friend) *What is Fox?* (a new friend)

Pages 30–33 *What does Goose ask Fox to do?* (play together) *Does Fox want to play?* (yes) *What is everyone doing?* (playing; jumping rope)

 What kind of friend is Bear? Talk to a partner.

Beginning Help partners point to the illustration of bear and respond using: *Bear is* <u>big</u>.

Intermediate Have partners point to the illustration of bear and respond using: *Bear is* <u>big</u>. *Bear is* <u>old</u>.

Advanced/Advanced High Have partners respond using: *Bear is* <u>big</u> *and* <u>old</u>. *Bear is* <u>grumpy</u>.

 Retell Use the **Retelling Cards** for "What About Bear?" to retell the story with children. Display the cards and model retelling using sequence words, such as *first, next, then,* and *last* as you point to the events and actions in the cards. Then help children take turns retelling one part using the sequence words.

 LESSON 4 **Paired Selection: "How to Be a Friend"**

Pages 35–40 Read the text on pages 35–37. *Friends can do many things together.* Point to the children in the photographs and describe the them. *Friends can work together/play a game/learn together. What can friends do together?* (help, play, read, learn) Point to the lists on pages 38 and 39 as you describe them. *Friends can get along. Friends listen to each other/ share together/ play fair. You can help a new friend. Say hello. Tell your name. Ask the friend to play.*

 How can you help a new friend? Talk to a partner.

Beginning Help partners point to a photograph and respond: *I can say* <u>hello</u>.

Intermediate Have partners respond: *I can say* <u>hello/ my name</u>.

Advanced/Advanced High How can you get along with a new friend? (I can share with a new friend.)

FORMATIVE ASSESSMENT

❯ STUDENT CHECK-IN

Main Selection Have partners retell one thing that friends do.

Paired Selection Have partners share important information they learned from the photograph.

Have children reflect using the Check-in routine.

 Independent Time

Talk About It Have children describe what they read in "What About Bear?" and "How to Be a Friend." Ask: *Are the characters in "What About Bear" friends? What did you learn from "How to be a Friend"?* Have partners describe how the two stories are alike. Help them respond using: *The two stories tell about* ____.

LESSON 3

We can listen actively to learn how a lion and mouse become friends.

OBJECTIVES

Ask and answer questions about unknown words in a text.

With prompting and support, compare and contrast the adventures and experiences of characters in familiar stories.

With prompting and support, describe the relationship between illustrations and the story in which they appear.

Continue a conversation through multiple exchanges.

LANGUAGE OBJECTIVES

Children will discuss the story and the animals using action words and naming words.

ELA ACADEMIC LANGUAGE

• *problem, illustration*

• Cognates: *problema, ilustración*

MATERIALS

Interactive Read Aloud, "The Lion and the Mouse"

Visual Vocabulary Cards

DIGITAL TOOLS

Have children listen to the selection as they follow along to develop comprehension.

Use the vocabulary activity for additional support.

"The Lion and the Mouse"

Prepare to Read

Interactive Read Aloud

Build Background Display illustrations of a lion and a mouse and discuss with children the physical and behavioral characteristics of each animal. Ask questions and discuss to help them compare the animals: *What animal is this? What does a lion/mouse have? What does it do? Where does it live? Is it big or small? Is it strong or weak?* Help children discuss using: *The lion/mouse has/is ___.*

Focus on Vocabulary Use the **Visual Vocabulary Cards** to review the oral vocabulary words: *rescue, grasped,* and *escape.* As you read, use gestures and other visual support to clarify important story words, for example: *promise, trap, solve, plan,* and *different.*

Summarize the Text *This story is about two very different friends: a large lion and a tiny mouse. One day the mouse helps the lion solve a big problem.*

Read the Text

Use the Interactive Question-Response Routine to help children understand the story.

Card 1

Paragraphs 1–4 Read the text. Point to the illustration. *The lion was napping. The mouse wakes up the lion. Who was napping?* (the lion)

Paragraphs 5–7 Read the text. *The lion doesn't believe the mouse. But the lion lets the mouse go. What does the lion do?* (let the mouse go)

 What does the lion do for the mouse? Talk to a partner.

Beginning Help partners point to the illustration and respond using: *The lion does not eat the mouse.*

Intermediate Have partners describe what the lion did using: *The lion does not eat the mouse. The lion let the mouse go.*

Advanced/Advanced High Have partners describe the actions of the lion and mouse: *The lion does not eat the mouse. The mouse promises to help the lion.*

Card 2

Paragraphs 1–2 Read the text. *The mouse hears the lion roar.* Point to the lion. *The lion is caught in a net. The lion wants to break free. What did the mouse hear?* (lion roar) *What is the lion in?* (a net)

Paragraphs 3–5 Read the text. Point to the mouse. *The mouse says that he will rescue, or save, the lion. The mouse will solve the lion's problem. What does the mouse tell the lion?* (The mouse will help the lion.)

 What happened to the lion? Talk to a partner.

Beginning Help partners point to the illustration and respond using: *The lion is in a* net.

Intermediate Have partners describe what the mouse tells the lion using: *The lion is in a* net. *The mouse is going to* help *the lion.*

Advanced/Advanced High Have partners describe what the mouse tells the lion using: *The lion is in a* net. *The mouse is going to* solve *the lion's problem.*

Card 3

Paragraphs 1–3 Read the text. *The lion doesn't believe the mouse can help him. But the mouse has a plan. Does the lion think the mouse can help?* (no)

Paragraphs 4–6 Read the text. *The mouse chews the net and makes a hole. The lion escapes. How does the mouse help the lion?* (The mouse chews the net.)

 How does mouse help the lion? Talk to a partner.

Beginning Help partners point to the illustration and respond using: *The mouse* chews *the net.*

Intermediate Have partners describe what the mouse helps the lion do using: *The mouse* chews *the net. The lion goes through the* hole.

Advanced/Advanced High Have partners describe what the mouse helps the lion do using: *The mouse* chews *the net and* makes *a hole. The lion goes through the* hole.

Card 4

Paragraphs 1–2 Read the text. Point to the lion and the mouse. *The lion is giving the mouse a ride. They are going up the hill to see the sunset. What are they going to do?* (see the sunset) *Are they friends?* (Yes, they are friends.)

Paragraphs 3–4 Read the text. *The mouse likes to watch the sunset on the hill, too. Each day the lion and the mouse watch the sunset together. What do the lion and the mouse like to do together?* (watch the sunset from the hill)

 What do the mouse and the lion do together? Talk to a partner.

Beginning Help partners point to the illustration and respond using: *The lion and the mouse watch the* sunset.

Intermediate Have partners describe what the mouse and the lion do together using: *The mouse and the lion watch the* sunset *together.*

Advanced/Advanced High Have partners describe what the mouse and the lion like to do together using: *The mouse and the lion watch the* sunset *on the* hill *together.*

 Retell Use the illustrations on the **Interactive Read-Aloud Cards** to retell the story with children. Display the cards and model retelling using sequence words, such as *first, next, then,* and *last* as you point to the events and actions in the cards. Then help partners take turns retelling one part using the sequence words.

FORMATIVE ASSESSMENT

❯ STUDENT CHECK-IN

Have partners share what each animal does in the story. Have children reflect using the Check-in routine.

 Independent Time

Draw and Label Have partners select one illustration from the **Interactive Read-Aloud Cards** and describe it. Provide a model and sentence frames for them to use: *I see a lion. I see a ___.* Then have them draw one thing they see and help them label it.

LESSONS
4-5

We can ask and answer questions about the story as we read.

OBJECTIVES

With prompting and support, ask and answer questions about key details in a text.

With prompting and support, identify characters in a story.

With prompting and support, retell familiar stories, including key details.

LANGUAGE OBJECTIVES

Children will inquire, or ask and answer, about characters in a story using naming words and simple sentences.

ELA ACADEMIC LANGUAGE

• *details, ask, answer*

• Cognate: *detalles*

MATERIALS

ELL Leveled Reader:
The Mouse and the Moose

Online Differentiated Texts,
"The Friends"

Online ELL Visual Vocabulary Cards

DIGITAL TOOLS

MULTIMODAL

🎧 Have children listen to the selection as they follow along to develop comprehension.

Use the vocabulary activity for additional support.

The Mouse and the Moose

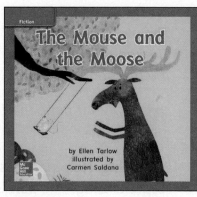

Lexile BR

Prepare to Read

Build Background *We have been reading about friends. Let's think about the Essential Question: How can we get along with new friends?* Have children share ways that friends can get along. Provide a model and sentence frames: *Friends can* share. *Friends can* work/play *together.*

Focus on Vocabulary Use the routine on the **ELL Visual Vocabulary Cards** to preteach *share* and *together.* As you read, use images and any labels to clarify important story words, for example: *mouse, moose, can.*

Read the Text

Use the Interactive Question-Response Routine to help children understand the story.

Pages 2–8

Pages 2–3 Read the text while tracing the words. Have children repeat after you. *The mouse and the moose are playing together. The mouse can swing. The moose can push the swing. What can the mouse do?* (swing) *What can the moose do?* (push)

Main Story Elements: Character Help children identify the characters. Use the illustrations to help them describe: *The mouse and the moose are playing together. I see two characters in the story. Who are the characters?* (the mouse and the moose)

 What can the mouse do? What can the moose do? Talk with a partner.

Beginning Help partners point to the pictures and respond using: *The mouse can* swing. *The moose can* push.

Intermediate Have partners describe what the mouse and moose do together using: *The mouse can* swing. *The moose can* push. *The moose and the mouse are* playing *together.*

Advanced/Advanced High Have partners describe details in the illustrations: *The mouse can* swing. *The moose can* push. *The moose and the mouse are* playing *together. The moose is* helping *the mouse.*

Pages 4–5 Read the text while tracing the words. Help children discuss details. *The mouse can pick an apple. What can mouse do?* (pick an apple) *The moose can help the mouse. What can the moose do?* (help the mouse)

What can the mouse and moose do together? Talk with a partner.

Beginning Help partners point to the pictures and respond using: *The mouse and moose can* <u>pick an apple</u> *together.*

Intermediate Have partners describe what the mouse and moose can share using: *The mouse and moose can* <u>pick an apple</u> *together. The moose and the mouse can* <u>share</u> *the apple.*

Pages 6-8 Read aloud while tracing the words. *The mouse can read. What can the mouse do?* (read) *The moose can help the mouse.*

 What can the mouse and the moose do together? Talk to a partner.

Beginning Help partners point to the pictures and respond using: *The mouse and moose can* <u>read</u> *together.*

Intermediate Have partners describe what the mouse and the moose can share using: *The mouse and moose can* <u>read</u> *together. The mouse and the moose can* <u>share</u> *the story.*

Advanced/Advanced High Have partners describe how the mouse and moose can help each other using: *The mouse and moose can* <u>read</u> *together. The moose can* <u>help</u> *the mouse read. The mouse can* <u>share</u> *the story.*

Ask and Answer Questions Help children ask and answer questions. *What can the mouse do?* (read)

Retell Have partners retell the story. Have them take turns pointing to a picture and describing it each other.

Focus on Fluency

Read pages 2–8 and have children echo read. For additional practice, have children record themselves reading the same text a few times, and then select their favorite recording to play for you.

Build Knowledge: Make Connections

Talk About the Text Have partners discuss how friends get along and work together.

Self-Selected Reading

Help children choose a fiction selection from the online **Leveled Reader Library** or read the **Differentiated Text,** "The Friends."

LITERACY ACTIVITIES

Have children complete the Literacy Activities on the inside back cover of the book.

FORMATIVE ASSESSMENT

❯ STUDENT CHECK-IN

Have partners dicuss how the mouse and the moose help each other and share with each other. Have children reflect using the Check-in routine.

 **LEVEL** UP

IF children can read The *Mouse and the Moose* ELL Level with fluency and correctly answer questions,

THEN tell children that they will read a more detailed version of the story.

HAVE children page through *The Mouse and the Moose* On Level and describe each picture in simple language.

• Have children read the selection, checking their comprehension and providing assistance as necessary.

MODELED WRITING

LESSON 1

LEARNING GOALS

We can learn how to write a sentence.

OBJECTIVES

Use a combination of drawing, dictating, and writing to narrate a single event.

LANGUAGE OBJECTIVES

Children will narrate, or tell, by writing a sentence using the word *share*.

ELA ACADEMIC LANGUAGE

• sentence

Writing Practice Read the sample sentence on p. T18 of the **Teacher's Edition.** Point to each word, and ask children to repeat. Help children analyze the sentence using the Actor/Action routine: *Who is the actor?* (I) *What is the action?* (share books with my friends) Then guide children to answer the prompt using the routine. Write their sentence on the board, and point to each word as children choral read. Then have children draw and write their own sentence in their writer's notebook.

Beginning Help partners think of their sentence. *Who is the actor?* (I) *What do you like to share?* I like to share <u>crayons</u>.

Intermediate Have partners take turns asking and answering *who/what* questions to create their sentence. Provide a sentence frame if needed.

Advanced/Advanced High Challenge children to talk about their sentence using the Actor/Action routine.

FORMATIVE ASSESSMENT ❯ ❯ **STUDENT CHECK-IN** Partners share their sentences. Have children reflect using the Check-in routine.

INTERACTIVE WRITING

LESSON 2

LEARNING GOALS

We can practice writing a sentence.

OBJECTIVES

With guidance and support, respond to questions and suggestions from peers.

LANGUAGE OBJECTIVES

Children will inquire about a character's actions and write a sentence using a describing word.

ELA ACADEMIC LANGUAGE

• text evidence

• Cognates: *evidencia del texto*

Analyze the Prompt Choral read the sample sentence on p. T30 with children as you point to each word. Use the Actor/Action routine to review it. Then review the writing trait: *What does Fox say?* (Bear is too big.) Display the **Big Book,** pp. 14–15. *Let's look for evidence, or clues, in the illustration. What does the illustration show?* (The game is too small for Bear.) Then guide children to point to the side of the paper where they start to write. Help them complete the sentence starters at the bottom of p. T30.

Beginning *What game did Fox pick? Why is this not a good game for Bear?* Fox picks a game that is too <u>small</u> for <u>Bear</u>.

Intermediate Have partners complete both sentence frames. Then have them use the Actor/Action routine for each sentence.

Advanced/Advanced High Challenge children to think of their own sentence about Fox. Encourage them to share it with the group.

FORMATIVE ASSESSMENT ❯ ❯ **STUDENT CHECK-IN** Partners share their responses. Have children reflect using the Check-in routine.

INDEPENDENT WRITING

LEARNING GOALS

We can write about the texts we read.

OBJECTIVES

Use a combination of dictating and writing to narrate several loosely linked events.

LANGUAGE OBJECTIVES

Children will narrate, or retell, by writing a complete sentence using naming words.

ELA ACADEMIC LANGUAGE

• *clues, noun*

Find Text Evidence Use the Independent Writing routine. Help children orally retell the shared read using clues from the text. Ask questions, such as, *What is this?* (a mitt) *What comes next?* (the mop) Next, help children identify the toys. *Is a mop a toy? Why?* (no, you cannot play games with it) Then read the prompt on page T40 of the **Teacher's Edition**: *What toys can the boy see?* Display p. 80 of the **Reading/Writing Companion**: *Let's look for clues. What can you see?* (marbles) *Are marbles toys?* (yes)

Write to the Prompt Display and read the sentence starters on p. T40. Ask a volunteer to retell the prompt in their own words. Model completing the first sentence frame, and have children choral read the response. Repeat the procedure for the remaining sentence frames. Once completed, have children copy the sentences in their writer's notebook.

Beginning Have partners discuss their sentences: I used the noun <u>drum</u>.

Intermediate Have partners tell how they included details from the selection: I wrote about <u>the toys the boy sees</u>.

Advanced/Advanced High Challenge children to come up with their own sentences. Have them identify the nouns they used.

FORMATIVE ASSESSMENT

❯ **STUDENT CHECK-IN** Partners share their sentences. Have children reflect using the Check-in routine.

SELF-SELECTED WRITING

LEARNING GOALS

We can revise our writing.

OBJECTIVES

Use frequently occurring nouns.

LANGUAGE OBJECTIVES

Children will inquire, or ask and answer questions, about their writing by checking their nouns.

ELA ACADEMIC LANGUAGE

• *nouns*

Work with children to revise the group writing activity. Read the sentences, pointing to each word as you read. Model and ask questions as you read. For example, *Is _____ a noun, or naming word?* (Yes/No) *The noun _____ is not spelled correctly. It should be spelled _____. Repeat the spelling with me: _____.* After you have made the necessary corrections, have children copy the sentences in their writer's notebook, or provide them with sentence frames to complete.

For more support with nouns and grammar, use the **Language Transfers Handbook** and **Language Development Card** 1A.

FORMATIVE ASSESSMENT

❯ **STUDENT CHECK-IN** Partners tell what revisions they made. Have children reflect using the Check-in routine.

LESSONS 1-2

LEARNING GOALS

We can understand important ideas and details in a story.

We can use labels to learn new information.

OBJECTIVES

With prompting and support, ask and answer questions about key details in a text.

With prompting and support, identify characters in a story.

With prompting and support, describe the relationship between illustrations and the story in which they appear.

Confirm understanding of a text read aloud or information presented orally or through other media by asking and answering questions about key details and requesting clarification if something is not understood.

LANGUAGE OBJECTIVES

Children will discuss how animals move using key vocabulary and simple sentences.

ELA ACADEMIC LANGUAGE

• events, details, illustrations

• Cognates: *eventos, detalles, ilustraciones*

MATERIALS

Literature Big Book, *Pouch!*

Visual Vocabulary Cards

DIGITAL TOOLS

Have children listen to the selection as they follow along to develop comprehension.

Use the vocabulary activity for additional support.

Pouch!

Literature Big Book

Prepare to Read

Build Background Display the cover and describe kangaroos with children: *These animals are kangaroos. The mother kangaroo carries the baby kangaroo in a pouch.* Point to the pouch and explain that the title of the book is *Pouch! What do you know about kangaroos?* Have children share what they know and help them describe using: *The animal is a ___. Kangaroos have ___. Where do kangaroos live?* Point out Australia on a map. *How do kangaroos move?* Elicit that they hop and have children demonstrate. Help children describe using: *Kangaroos live in ___. Kangaroos can ___.*

Focus on Vocabulary Use the **Visual Vocabulary Cards** to review the oral vocabulary words *movement* and *adventure*. As you read, use gestures and other visual support to clarify important story words: *hop, bee, rabbit, bird,* and *afraid.* Review the words in context as you read, and have children add these words to their personal glossaries.

Summarize the Text Before reading, give a short summary of the story: *This book is about a baby kangaroo that leaves his mother's pouch to see the world.*

Read the Text

Use the Interactive Question-Response Routine to help children understand the story.

Pages 5–13

Pages 5–11 Read the text aloud. Point to the illustrations and describe them. *Joey can see the world from the pouch. Joey wants to hop. He climbed out of the pouch and hopped in the grass. He saw a bee. Then Joey hopped back into the pouch. What can Joey do?* (hop) *What did Joey see?* (bee)

 What can Joey do? What did Joey see? Talk to a partner.

Beginning Have partners point to the illustrations and respond using: *Joey can* hop. *Joey saw a* bee.

Intermediate Have partners describe what Joey did using: *Joey can* hop *to a hill. Joey saw a* bee.

Advanced/Advanced High Have partners describe details about what Joey can do using: *Joey can* hop *to a hill. Joey saw a* bee. *Joey can* climb *out of the* pouch. *Joey can* hop *into the* pouch.

Pages 14–25

Pages 14–18 *Joey hopped out of the pouch. He hopped to the hill. He saw a rabbit and he hopped back to the pouch. What did Joey see?* (a rabbit)

Pages 19–23 *Joey hopped out of the pouch again to the sandy hollow. He saw a bird. Joey wants to go back to the pouch. What did Joey see?* (a bird)

 What did Joey do? What did he see? Talk with a partner.

Beginning Help partners point to the illustrations and respond using: *Joey* <u>hopped</u>. *Joey saw a* <u>rabbit/bird</u>.

Intermediate Have partners describe what Joey wants to do using: *Joey* <u>hopped</u>. *Joey saw a* <u>rabbit/bird</u>. *Joey wants the* <u>pouch</u>.

Advanced/Advanced High Have partners describe details about what Joey did and what he wants to do using: *Joey* <u>hopped</u>. *Joey saw a* <u>rabbit/bird</u>. *Joey wants to* <u>hop</u> *into the* <u>pouch</u>.

Pages 26–34

Pages 26–34 *Joey wants to hop back into the pouch, so he hopped over a fence. He saw another kangaroo. The two kangaroos ran away. They were scared. They both wanted to hop into a pouch. They hopped everywhere together. They are not scared anymore. Who did Joey meet?* (a kangaroo) *What did Joey and the other kangaroo do?* (hopped together)

 What did Joey see? What did Joey and the other kangaroo do? Talk with a partner.

Beginning Help partners point to the illustrations and respond using: *Joey met a* <u>kanagaroo</u>. *Joey and the kangaroo* <u>hopped</u> *together.*

Intermediate Have partners describe what happened when Joey saw a kangaroo using: *Joey* <u>ran</u> *away. Then the two kangaroos* <u>hopped</u> *together.*

Advanced/Advanced High Have partners describe in detail using: *Joey* <u>ran</u> *away. Then the two kangaroos* <u>hopped</u> *together. They were not* <u>scared</u>.

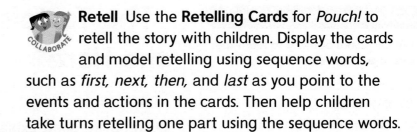 **Retell** Use the **Retelling Cards** for *Pouch!* to retell the story with children. Display the cards and model retelling using sequence words, such as *first, next, then,* and *last* as you point to the events and actions in the cards. Then help children take turns retelling one part using the sequence words.

LESSON 4 **Paired Selection: "Baby Animals on the Move!"**

Pages 35–40 Read the text. *The baby animals can move in different ways.* Point to the animals in the photographs and describe them. *Lions can walk. Fish can swim. Birds can fly. What can baby animals do?* (jump, walk, swim, gallop, crawl, fly)

 How do baby animals move? Talk to a partner.

Beginning Help partners point to a photograph and respond. For example: *Fish can* <u>swim</u>.

Intermediate Have partners respond. For example: *Fish can* <u>swim</u>. *Turtles can* <u>crawl</u>.

Advanced/Advanced High Have partners respond: *Fish can* <u>swim</u>. *Turtles can* <u>crawl</u>. *Birds can* <u>fly</u>.

FORMATIVE ASSESSMENT

❯ STUDENT CHECK-IN

Main Selection Have partners retell two things that that Joey did in the story.

Paired Selection Have partners share important information they learned from the photograph.

Have children reflect using the Check-in routine.

 Independent Time

Talk About It Have children describe what they read in *Pouch!* and "Baby Animals on the Move!" Ask: *What can baby animals do?* Have partners describe how Joey and another baby animal move. Help them respond using: *Kangaroos can ___. [Birds] can ___.*

LESSON 3

LEARNING GOALS

We can listen actively to learn the lesson that the story teaches.

OBJECTIVES

Ask and answer questions about unknown words in a text.

With prompting and support, compare and contrast the adventures and experiences of characters in familiar stories.

With prompting and support, describe the relationship between illustrations and the story in which they appear.

Confirm understanding of a text read aloud or information presented orally or through other media by asking and answering questions about key details and requesting clarification if something is not understood.

LANGUAGE OBJECTIVES

Children will discuss the race using action words and simple sentences.

ELA ACADEMIC LANGUAGE

- *fable, details, illustration*
- Cognates: *fábula, detalles, ilustración*

MATERIALS

Interactive Read Aloud, "The Tortoise and the Hare"

Visual Vocabulary Cards

DIGITAL TOOLS

Have children listen to the selection as they follow along to develop comprehension.

Use the vocabulary activity for additional support.

"The Tortoise and the Hare"

Prepare to Read

Interactive Read Aloud

Build Background Explain to children that they will listen to a story about a tortoise and a hare. *This story is a fable and uses animal characters to teach a lesson.* Display Card 1 and identify the hare and the tortoise. Have children discuss what they know about the animals and how they move. Help them describe using: *A hare can ___. A tortoise can ___.*

Focus on Vocabulary Use the **Visual Vocabulary Cards** to review the oral vocabulary words: *movement, adventure, exhausted, exciting,* and *arrived.* As you read, use gestures and other visual support to teach important story words, for example: *race, fast/faster, crawled, slowly, win,* and *rest.*

Summarize the Text *This story is about two animals, Tommy Tortoise and Henry Hare. They have a race to see who is faster.*

Read the Text

Use the Interactive Question-Response Routine to help children understand the story.

Card 1

Paragraphs 1–2 Read the text. Point to the tortoise and the hare. *Henry can hop and Tommy can crawl. Henry can move fast. Tommy moves slowly. Henry is faster than Tommy. Who is faster?* (Henry)

Paragraphs 3-4 Read the text. *Tommy wants to have a race. Henry tells Tommy that he will win because he is faster than Tommy. What does Tommy want to do?* (have a race)

 How do Henry and Tommy move? Talk to a partner.

Beginning Help partners point to the illustration and respond using: *Henry can hop. Tommy can crawl.*

Intermediate Have partners describe: *Henry can move fast. Tommy can crawl.*

Advanced/Advanced High Have partners describe details about what Tommy wants to do using: *Henry can move fast. Tommy can crawl. Tommy wants to have a race.*

Card 2

Paragraphs 1–5 Read the text. Review the oral vocabulary word *exhausted. Tommy and Henry meet at the starting line. The* starting line *is where a race starts. Henry thinks he will win the race, but Tommy says he will surprise Henry. Tommy thinks Henry is wrong. The race starts and Henry hops past Tommy.*

 Does Henry think he will win the race? Talk with a partner.

Beginning Help partners point to the illustration and respond using: *Henry thinks he will* <u>win</u>.

Intermediate Have partners describe why Henry thinks he will win using: *Henry is* <u>fast</u>.

Advanced/Advanced High Have partners describe details about why Henry thinks he will win using: *Henry thinks he will* <u>win</u>. *Henry is* <u>fast</u>. *Tommy is* <u>slow</u>.

Card 3

Paragraphs 1–2 Read the text. *Henry hopped fast. Soon he was exhausted, or too tired. Henry saw his friend Sam. Henry decided to rest and talk to Sam. Whom did Henry see?* (Sam) *Why did Henry rest?* (to talk to Sam)

Paragraph 3 *Henry stopped to rest, but Tommy crawled slowly. Soon Tommy got to the halfway mark. The* halfway mark *is the middle of the race. Henry did not see Tommy. Henry was busy talking to Sam. Tommy did not see Henry so he continued to crawl.*

 What did Henry do? What did Tommy do? Talk with a partner.

Beginning Help partners point to the illustration and respond using: *Henry stopped to* <u>rest</u>. *Tommy did not* <u>stop</u>.

Intermediate Have partners describe the text: *Henry stopped to* <u>rest</u> *and talk to* <u>Sam</u>. *Tommy did not* <u>stop</u>.

Advanced/Advanced High Have partners describe details about what happened using: *Henry stopped to* <u>rest</u>. *Tommy did not* <u>stop</u>. *Henry did not see* <u>Tommy</u>. *Tommy kept* <u>crawling</u>.

Card 4

Paragraphs 1–4 Read the text. *Henry remembered the race. He did not see Tommy. Henry reached the end of the race. He saw parents and friends cheering, but they were cheering for Tommy. Tommy crossed the line and won the race. Henry was faster than Tommy, but Henry stopped during the race to rest. Tommy did not stop and he won. Henry learned that it is good to be slow and steady. Who won the race?* (Tommy)

 What happened at the end of the race? Talk to a partner.

Beginning Help partners point to the illustration and respond using: *Tommy* <u>won</u> *the race.*

Intermediate Have partners describe what Henry saw using: *Henry reached the* <u>end</u>. *He saw Tommy* <u>win</u>.

Advanced/Advanced High Have partners provide additional details: *He saw parents and friends* <u>cheering</u>. *He saw Tommy* <u>win</u> *the race.*

 Retell Use the illustrations on the **Interactive Read-Aloud Cards** to retell the story with children. Display the cards and model retelling using sequence words, such as *first, next, then,* and *last* as you point to the events and actions in the cards. Then help partners take turns retelling one part using the sequence words.

FORMATIVE ASSESSMENT

> **STUDENT CHECK-IN**

Have partners share why Tommy won the race.

Have children reflect using the Check-in routine.

 Independent Time

Draw and Label Have partners select one illustration from the "The Tortoise and the Hare" and describe it. Provide a model for them to use: *I see a tortoise/hare. The tortoise/hare has a ___.* Then have them draw one thing they see and help them label it.

LESSONS 4-5

We Hop!

Prepare to Read

Build Background Show children a photo of cats and kittens and have children discuss what they know about kittens. Help them describe using: *Cats have ___. Cats can ___.* Explain that *kitten* is the word for a young or baby cat. Discuss with children what kittens do. Help them respond using: *Kittens can ___.*

Focus on Vocabulary Use the routine on the **ELL Visual Vocabulary Cards** to preteach *animals* and *move*. As you read, use images and any labels to clarify important story words, for example: *hop, hat, dress.*

Lexile BR

Read the Text

Use the Interactive Question-Response Routine to help children understand the story.

Pages 2-8

Pages 2–3 Read the text while tracing the words. Have children repeat after you. *These are kittens. The kittens hop. The kittens hop on a chair. The kittens hop on a table. What do kitten do?* (hop) *What is on the table?* (food/milk)

Main Story Elements: Character Help children identify the characters. Use the illustrations to help them describe: *The kittens hop. I see the characters hop. Who are the characters?* (the kittens)

 Where do the kittens hop? Talk to a partner.

Beginning Help children point to the pictures and respond using: *The kittens hop on a* table.

Intermediate Have partners describe what the kittens do using: *The kittens hop on a* table. *The kittens* eat *on a table.*

Advanced/Advanced High Have partners describe details in the pictures: *The kittens hop on a* table. *The kittens* eat *on a table. I see* food *on the table.*

Pages 3–4 Read the text while tracing the words. Have children repeat after you. *The kittens hop on a table. There is a bag of popcorn on the table. The kittens hop on the hat. Where do the kittens hop?* (on the hat)

 Where do kittens hop? Talk to a partner.

Beginning Help children discuss details: *The kittens hop on the* <u>hat</u>.

Intermediate Have partners describe the hat using details: *The kittens hop on the* <u>hat</u>. *The hat is on the* <u>chair</u>.

Advanced/Advanced High Have partners describe details in the pictures: *The kittens hop on the* <u>table</u>. *A bag of popcorn is on the* <u>table</u>. *The kittens hop on the* <u>hat</u>. *The hat is on the* <u>chair</u>.

Pages 6-8 Help children describe where the kittens hop. *The kittens hop on the dog. Where do they hop next?*

 Where do kittens hop? Talk to a partner.

Beginning Help children point to the pictures and respond using: *The kittens hop on the* <u>dress</u>.

Intermediate Have partners describe the dress using: *The kittens hop on the* <u>dress</u>. *The dress is* <u>pink</u>.

Advanced/Advanced High Have partners describe details in the pictures: *The kittens hop on the* <u>dress</u>. *The dress is* <u>pink</u>. *The kittens hop on the* <u>dog</u>. *The dog is on a* <u>pillow</u>.

Ask and Answer Questions Help children ask and answer questions: *Where do the kittens hop? We can look at the picture to find the answer. The kittens hop on the dog.*

Retell Have partners retell the story. Have them take turns pointing to a picture and describing it to each other.

Focus on Fluency

Model reading with accuracy for children. Remind them of the importance of recognizing high-frequency words as well as decoding words in the text correctly. Encourage children to practice reading for accuracy with a partner. Listen in and offer support and corrective feedback as needed.

Build Knowledge: Make Connections

Talk About the Text Have partners discuss how animals move.

Self-Selected Reading

Help children choose a fiction selection from the online **Leveled Reader Library** or read the **Differentiated Text,** "We Move!"

LITERACY ACTIVITIES

Have children complete the Literacy Activities on the inside back cover of the book.

❯ STUDENT CHECK-IN

Have partners retell where the kittens hop in the story. Have children reflect using the Check-in routine.

LEVEL UP

IF children can read *We Hop!* **ELL Level** with fluency and correctly answer the questions,

THEN tell children that they will read a more detailed version of the story.

HAVE children page through *We Can Move!* Beyond Level and describe each picture in simple language.

- Have children read the selection, checking their comprehension and providing assistance as necessary.

ENGLISH LANGUAGE LEARNERS **15**

MODELED WRITING

LESSON 1

LEARNING GOALS

We can learn how to write a sentence.

OBJECTIVES

Use a combination of drawing, dictating, and writing to narrate a single event.

LANGUAGE OBJECTIVES

Children will narrate, or tell, by writing a sentence using the phrase *tried to.*

ELA ACADEMIC LANGUAGE

• *sentence*

Writing Practice Demonstrate a simple tap dance. Read the sample sentence from p. T100 of the **Teacher's Edition.** Have children echo read. Help children analyze the sentence using the Actor/Action routine: *Who is the actor?* (I) *What is the action?* (tried to tap dance) Then guide children to answer the prompt using the routine. Write their sentence on the board, and point to each word as children choral read. Then have children draw and write their own sentence in their writer's notebook.

Beginning Help partners think of their sentence. *Who is the actor?* (I) *What did you try to do?* I tried to <u>fish</u>.

Intermediate Have partners take turns asking and answering *who/what* questions to create their sentence. Provide a sentence frame if needed.

Advanced/Advanced High Challenge children to identify a noun in their sentence. Encourage them to share their sentence with the group.

FORMATIVE ASSESSMENT ❯ **STUDENT CHECK-IN** Partners share their sentences. Have children reflect using the Check-in routine.

INTERACTIVE WRITING

LESSON 2

LEARNING GOALS

We can practice writing a sentence.

OBJECTIVES

Use dictating and writing to narrate and provide a reaction to what happened.

LANGUAGE OBJECTIVES

Children will inquire about a character's actions and write sentences using details.

ELA ACADEMIC LANGUAGE

• *details*
• Cognate: *detalles*

Analyze the Prompt Choral read the sample sentence on p. T112. Use the Actor/Action routine: *Who is the actor?* (Joey) *What is the action?* (wants to see more of the world) Help children think about the writing trait by pointing to an illustration. *Let's look for details about why Joey hops. What does Joey see?* (a bee) Review the writing skill by asking children to point to and name the side of the page the writing starts on. (the left) Then help children complete the sentence starters at the bottom of p. T112.

Beginning Help children complete the sentence starters orally using the illustration on pp. 16-17 of the **Literature Big Book**: Joey hops to <u>the little hill</u>. Joey sees <u>a rabbit</u>.

Intermediate Encourage partners to point to the illustrations that show the actor and action as they complete the sentence frames.

Advanced/Advanced High Challenge partners to think of their own sentences about why Joey hops.

FORMATIVE ASSESSMENT ❯ **STUDENT CHECK-IN** Partners explain how details from the story helped them write a sentence. Have children reflect using the Check-in routine.

INDEPENDENT WRITING

LEARNING GOALS

We can write about the texts we read.

OBJECTIVES

Use a combination of dictating and writing to narrate several loosely linked events.

LANGUAGE OBJECTIVES

Children will narrate by writing a complete sentence using the word *can*.

ELA ACADEMIC LANGUAGE

• *noun*

Find Text Evidence Use the Independent Writing routine. Display the cover of the **Reading/Writing Companion.** *What are these animals?* (pandas) *What can they do?* (climb) Repeat the procedure for the other pages. Then read the prompt on p. T104: *What animals can climb?* Display p. 107 of the **Reading/Writing Companion.** *What are these animals?* (koala bears) *What can they do?* (climb)

Write to the Prompt Display and read the sentence starters on p. T122. Ask a volunteer to retell the prompt in their own words. Model completing the first sentence frame, and have children choral read the response. Repeat the procedure for the remaining sentence frames. Once completed, have children copy the sentences in their writer's notebook.

Beginning Have partners discuss their sentences: I used the noun <u>koalas</u>.

Intermediate Have partners tell how they included ideas from the text: I wrote about <u>animals that can climb</u>.

Advanced/Advanced High Challenge children to come up with their own sentences. Have them identify the nouns they used.

FORMATIVE ASSESSMENT ❯ ❯ **STUDENT CHECK-IN** Partners share their sentences. Have children reflect using the Check-in routine.

SELF-SELECTED WRITING

LEARNING GOALS

We can revise our writing.

OBJECTIVES

Use frequently occurring nouns.

LANGUAGE OBJECTIVES

Children will inquire, or ask and answer questions, about their writing by checking their nouns.

ELA ACADEMIC LANGUAGE

• *nouns*

Work with children to revise the group writing activity. Read the sentence, pointing to each word as you read. Model and ask questions as you read. *Is _____ a noun?* (Yes/No) *The noun _____ is not spelled correctly. It should be spelled _____. Repeat the spelling with me: _____.* After you have made the necessary corrections, have children copy the sentences in their writer's notebook.

For more support with grammar, use the **Language Transfers Handbook** and review nouns with **Language Development Card 1A.**

FORMATIVE ASSESSMENT ❯ ❯ **STUDENT CHECK-IN** Partners tell what revisions they made. Have children reflect using the Check-in routine.

LEARNING GOALS

We can understand important ideas and details in a text.

We can learn new information from sensory words.

OBJECTIVES

With prompting and support, ask and answer questions about key details in a text.

With prompting and support, identify the main topic and retell key details of a text.

With prompting and support, describe the relationship between illustrations and the text in which they appear.

Describe familiar people, places, things, and events and, with prompting and support, provide additional detail.

LANGUAGE OBJECTIVES

Children will inform, or give information, about how we use our senses, using naming words and action words.

ELA ACADEMIC LANGUAGE

• senses, ask, answer, retell

• Cognate: *sentidos*

MATERIALS

Literature Big Book, *Senses at the Shore*

Visual Vocabulary Cards

DIGITAL TOOLS

Have children listen to the selection as they follow along to develop comprehension.

Use the vocabulary activity for additional support.

Senses at the Seashore

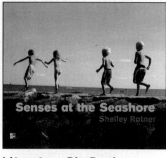

Literature Big Book

Prepare to Read

Build Background Display the cover. *Have you been to the seashore? The seashore is the land near the sea.* Discuss with children what they can do at the seashore, using: *At the seashore, I can ___.*

Focus on Vocabulary Use the **Visual Vocabulary Cards** to review the oral vocabulary words *senses* and *explore*.

As you read, use gestures and visual support to teach important selection words: *see, hear, smell, taste,* and *touch*. Point to the parts of the body to reinforce the meanings of the words. Ask children to share with a partner one or two things they can see, hear, smell, taste, and touch. Have children add these words to their personal glossaries.

Summarize the Text Before reading, give a short summary of the text. *This book is about what we can see, hear, smell, touch, and taste at the seashore.*

Read the Text

Use the Interactive Question-Response Routine to help children understand the text.

Pages 4–11

Pages 4–11 Read the text. Point to the parts of the body as you describe using the senses. *At the seashore, you can see the blue water. You can use your eyes to see. You can hear the waves. You can use your ears to hear. You can smell the lotion. You can use your nose to smell. You can touch the water. You can use your hands and feet to touch. You can also taste the seawater. You can use your mouth to taste. What can you see?* (water) *What can you hear?* (waves) *What can you smell?* (lotion) *What can you touch?* (water) *What can you taste?* (water)

 What can you do at the seashore? Talk with a partner.

Beginning Help partners point to the photographs and respond, using: *I can* see *the water. I can* hear *the waves. I can* smell *the lotion. I can* touch *the water. I can* taste *the water.*

Intermediate Have partners describe a body part they can use, using: *I can use my* ears *to hear. I can use my* nose *to smell. I can use my* hands *to touch. I can use my* mouth *to taste. I can use my* eyes *to see.*

Advanced/Advanced High Have partners discuss what is happening in each photo: *What is the girl doing at the beach? What does she see? The girl sees the* blue water. *What does the boy hear? The boy hears the* waves crash. Continue with the remaining images.

Pages 12–19

Pages 12–19 Read the text. *At the seashore, you can see a fishing boat and smell fresh fish. You can touch the sand and hear the seashell. You can taste food and smell the flowers. You can also hear birds and touch things like feathers. What can you see?* (boat) *What can you hear?* (seashell) *What can you smell?* (fish)

 What can you do at the seashore? Talk with a partner.

Beginning Help partners point and respond, using: *I can* see *a boat. I can* hear *the seashell. I can* smell *fish.*

Intermediate Have partners ask and answer questions about the images: *What can you see? I can* see *a boat. What can you hear? I can* hear *the seashell.* Continue with the remaining images.

Advanced/Advanced High Have partners describe the first photo: *I can see a* boat. *I see two* men *on the boat. They are catching* fish. Then, repeat the routine.

Pages 20–34

Page 20–25 Read the text. *At the seashore, you can see white clouds and taste a fruity pop. You can see a kite flying. You can smell and touch seaweed. You can hear a whistle. You can also taste watermelon. What can you see?* (white clouds) *What can you hear?* (whistle) *What can you taste?* (watermelon)

 What can you do at the seashore? Talk with a partner.

Beginning Help partners point to the photographs and respond by describing a part of the body they use: *I can* see *a cloud. I can use my* eyes *to see.*

Intermediate Have partners talk about the boy in the second photo. *What is he eating? He is eating a* fruity pop. *Do you think it tastes good?* (yes/no) *Have you ever eaten fruit pops or ice cream at the seashore?*

Advanced/Advanced High Challenge partners to tell why eating a fruity pop or flying a kite are fun things to do at the seashore: *Can a fruity pop help keep you cool? A fruity pop can help me stay* cool. *Is there a lot of room to fly a kite? There is room to* fly *a kite.*

 Retell Use the **Retelling Cards** for "Senses at the Seashore" to have children retell what they learned. Have them use sense words *see, hear, smell, taste,* and *touch.* Help children take turns retelling one part using the sequence words.

LESSON 4

Paired Selection: "I Smell Springtime," "Taste of Purple," "Rain"

Pages 36–41 Read the poem on pages 36–37. *The poem tells about the different things we can smell in spring.* Point to the parts of the illustration as you describe: *We can smell grass. We can smell flowers.*

 What can you smell in spring? Talk to a partner.

Beginning Help partners point to the illustration and respond: *I can smell* grass. *I can smell* flowers.

Intermediate Have partners discuss: *What do you like to smell in spring? I like to smell* flowers.

Advanced/Advanced High Have partners describe details in the illustration, using: *I can smell* grass. *I can smell* flowers. *The grass is* green. *The flowers are* pink.

FORMATIVE ASSESSMENT

❯ STUDENT CHECK-IN

Main Selection Have partners retell one thing they can do with each of the five senses.

Paired Selection Have partners share what is in the illustration.

Have children reflect using the Check-in routine.

 Independent Time

Talk About It Have children describe what they read about in *Senses at the Seashore* and "I Smell Springtime." Ask: *What can you smell at the seashore and in spring?* Help them respond, using: *I can smell ___ at the seashore. I can smell ___ in spring.*

LESSON 3

We can listen actively to learn about what our senses tell us when we cook.

OBJECTIVES

Ask and answer questions to help determine or clarify the meaning of words and phrases in a text.

With prompting and support, retell key details of a text.

Actively engage in group reading activities with purpose and understanding.

Confirm understanding of a text read aloud or information presented orally or through other media by asking and answering questions about key details and requesting clarification if something is not understood.

LANGUAGE OBJECTIVES

Children will inform, or give information, about how we use our senses in the kitchen, using key vocabulary and simple sentences.

ELA ACADEMIC LANGUAGE

• *details, photograph*
• Cognate: *detalles, fotografía*

MATERIALS

Interactive Read Aloud, "A Feast of the Senses"

Visual Vocabulary Cards

DIGITAL TOOLS

Have children listen to the selection as they follow along to develop comprehension.

Use the vocabulary activity for additional support.

"A Feast of the Senses"

Prepare to Read

Build Background Show children the first card. *What is this family doing?* Explain that the family is preparing a big meal, called a *feast*. Ask children what they cook at home with their family or what their family members cook for meals. Discuss how the kitchen smells when someone is cooking. Help them respond, using: *My family cooks ____.*

Interactive Read Aloud

Focus on Vocabulary Use the **Visual Vocabulary Cards** to review the oral vocabulary words: *senses, explore, feast, knead,* and *finished.* As you read, use gestures and other visual support to clarify important selection words, for example: *kitchen, cook, fruit, vegetables,* and *bake.*

Summarize the Text This text is about what you can see, smell, hear, touch, and taste when you cook.

Read the Text

Use the Interactive Question-Response Routine to help children understand the text.

Card 1

Paragraphs 1–3 Read the text. Point to the people. *The family is in the kitchen. They are cooking together. Many people learn to cook when they are young. People use the five senses when they cook. The five senses are smell, touch, sight, hearing, and taste. Where is the family?* (in the kitchen) *What are they doing?* (cooking)

 Where is the family? What are they doing? Talk to a partner.

Beginning Help partners point to the photograph and respond, using: *The family is in the* kitchen. *The family is* cooking *together.*

Intermediate Have partners describe one sense people use when they cook, using: *The family is in the* kitchen. *The family is* cooking *together. The family can* smell *the food.*

Advanced/Advanced High Have partners describe the senses people use when they cook, using: *The family is in the* kitchen. *The family is* cooking *together. The family can* smell *the food. The family can also* taste *the food.*

Card 2

Paragraphs 1–3 Read the text aloud. *We use the sense of smell when we cook. Which part of the body do we use to smell?* (nose) *When we shop for fruits and* vegetables, we use the sense of smell and touch. Which part of the body do we use to touch? (hands) Point to the photographs of fruit and vegetables. *The fruits and vegetables are ripe. That means they are ready to eat. Can you eat ripe fruits and vegetables?* (yes) Point to the photographs of bread dough. *When we make bread, we use the sense of touch to make the dough.*

 What sense do you use to make bread? Talk to a partner.

Beginning Help partners point to the photograph and respond, using: *We use the sense of* touch.

Intermediate Have partners describe the part of the body they use for the sense, using: *We use the sense of* touch. *We use our* hands *to touch.*

Advanced/Advanced High Have partners describe other senses people use when they cook, using: *We use the sense of* touch *to make bread. We use our* hands *to touch. We use the sense of* smell *to cook.*

Card 3

Paragraphs 1–7 Read the text aloud. *When we cook, we use our sense of hearing. We can hear when vegetables are frying in a pan because they sizzle. We use our sense of sight to see the food. We can see the bread rise and turn brown. How do we use our sense of hearing?* (to listen) *How do we use our sense of sight?* (to see)

 How do you use your sense of hearing and sight? Talk to a partner.

Beginning Help partners point to the photograph and respond, using: *We use the sense of* hearing *to* hear.

Intermediate Have partners describe, using: *We use the sense of* hearing *to* hear. *We use the sense of* sight *to* see.

Advanced/Advanced High Have partners describe details about using the senses, using: *We use the sense of* hearing *to* hear *vegetables cook. We use the sense of* sight *to* see *bread turn brown.*

Card 4

Paragraphs 1–3 Read the text aloud. Point to the parts of the photograph, and help children confirm their understanding. *The feast is ready. There are many different kinds of food for the feast. The family is ready to eat all the food. They are hungry. What is the family ready to do?* (eat) *What is in the feast?* (different foods)

 What will the family do? Talk to a partner.

Beginning Help partners point to the photograph and respond, using: *The family is ready to* eat.

Intermediate Have partners describe, using: *The family is ready to* eat *the feast.*

Advanced/Advanced High Have partners describe details, using: *The family is ready to* eat *the feast. There are different kinds of* food *in the feast.*

 Retell Use the illustrations on the **Interactive Read-Aloud Cards** to help children retell what they learned from the selection. Model retelling about using the senses to cook, using the images on the cards to confirm understanding. Then help partners take turns describing how people use senses to cook.

FORMATIVE ASSESSMENT

> **STUDENT CHECK-IN**

Have partners retell what they can do with each of the five senses. Have children reflect using the Check-in routine.

 Independent Time

Draw and Label Have partners select one illustration from the Interactive Read-Aloud Cards and describe the senses they can use. Provide a model and sentence frames for them to use: *I see an apple. I can taste an apple.* Then have them draw one thing they see, and help them label it.

LEARNING GOALS

We can ask and answer questions about the text as we read.

OBJECTIVES

Identify the front cover of a book.

With prompting and support, ask and answer questions about key details in a text.

With prompting and support, identify the main topic and retell key details of a text.

Describe familiar people, places, things, and events and, with prompting and support, provide additional detail.

LANGUAGE OBJECTIVES

Children will inquire, or ask and answer questions, about a text using naming words and simple sentences.

ELA ACADEMIC LANGUAGE

• *photo, retelling*

• Cognate: *foto*

MATERIALS

ELL Leveled Reader: *At School*

Online Differentiated Texts, "The Salad"

Online ELL Visual Vocabulary Cards

DIGITAL TOOLS

Have children listen to the selection as they follow along to develop comprehension.

Use the vocabulary activity for additional support.

At School

Prepare to Read

Lexile BR

Build Background Tell children they will read a book about children at a school. Point to the children on the cover. *These children are at school. We are at school too. What do you think the children will do today?* Elicit ideas such as read books, eat lunch, and play games. Point out the front cover of the book. *The front cover shows the name of the book,* At School. *It also shows the name of the author, Lucy Long.* Guide children to look through the book and name any items they know. *Do we see these things in our school?* Help partners name other items they see in the classroom.

Focus on Vocabulary Use the routine on the **ELL Visual Vocabulary Cards** to preteach *education* and *learn*. As you read, use images and labels to clarify important selection words, for example: *school, books, clock, bus.*

Read the Text

Use the Interactive Question-Response Routine to help children understand the text.

Pages 2–8

Pages 2–3 Read the text. Use your finger to track as you read. *We see the school. We see the books. What other things do you see?* (children)

Ask and Answer Questions Help children ask and answer questions about the text: *Where are the children?* (at school)

 What do you see? Talk with a partner.

Beginning Help partners point to the pictures and respond, using: *We see the* school. *We see the* books.

Intermediate Have partners describe other things they see, using: *We see the* school. *We see the* books. *We see the* children.

Advanced/Advanced High Have partners describe where they can see books: *We see the* school. *We see the* books. *We see the* children. *We see books in the* library.

Pages 4–5 Read the text. Use your finger to track as you read. *We see the plants. We see the sandwich. What other things do you see?* (apple)

What do you see? Talk with a partner.

Beginning Help partners point to the pictures and discuss details, using: *We see the* plants. *We see the* sandwich.

Intermediate Have partners describe other details they see, using: *We see the* plants. *We see the* sandwich. *We see the* apple.

Advanced/Advanced High Have partners describe details in the photographs: *We see the* plants. *We see the* sandwich. *We see the* apple. *The apple is* green.

Pages 6-8 Read as you track the test. Help children tell as they point to the photographs: *We can see the drum. What is a drum?*

 What do you see? Talk with a partner.

Beginning Help partners point to the pictures and respond, using: *We see the* drum. *We see the* clock.

Intermediate Have partners describe what they can do with a clock, using: *We see the* drum. *We see the* clock. *We can tell* time *with the clock.*

Advanced/High Advanced Have partners describe what they can do with a drum and a clock, using: *We see the* drum. *We can* play *a drum. We see the* clock. *We can tell* time *with the clock.*

Topic and Details Help children identify topic and details: *What are the things we can see? We can see* many things.

Retell Have partners retell the story. Have them take turns pointing to a picture and describing it each other.

Focus on Fluency

Read pages 2–8 and have children echo-read. For additional practice, have children record themselves reading the same passage a few times, and then select their favorite recording to play for you.

Build Knowledge: Make Connections

Talk About the Text Have partners tell how our senses help us learn.

Self-Selected Reading

Help children choose a nonfiction selection from the online **Leveled Reader Library** or read the **Differentiated Text,** "The Salad."

LITERACY ACTIVITIES

Have children complete the Literacy Activities on the inside back cover of the book.

FORMATIVE ASSESSMENT

❯ STUDENT CHECK-IN

Have partners retell three things they see at the school in the text. Have students reflect using the Check-in routine.

LEVEL UP

IF children can read *At School* ELL Level with fluency and correctly answer questions,

THEN tell children they will read a more detailed version of the story.

HAVE children page through *At School* On Level and describe each picture in simple language.

- Have children read the selection, checking their comprehension and providing assistance as necessary.

MODELED WRITING

LESSON 1

LEARNING GOALS

We can learn how to write a sentence.

OBJECTIVES

Use a combination of drawing, dictating, and writing to narrate a single event.

LANGUAGE OBJECTIVES

Children will narrate using the sense word *see.*

ELA ACADEMIC LANGUAGE

• *senses*

• Cognate: *sentidos*

Writing Practice Point to your eyes as you read the sample sentence from p. T182 of the **Teacher's Edition:** *I see that my sister is tall.* Ask children to repeat the sentence. Remind them that sight is one of their senses. Then use the Actor/Action routine: *Who is the actor?* (I) *What is the action?* (see that my sister is tall) Read the prompt at the bottom of the page, and guide children to answer it as a group. Write their sentence on the board, and point to each word as children chorally read. Then ask children to draw and write their own sentence in their writer's notebooks.

Beginning Help children think of their sentence. What do you see? (mom's hair) *Who is the actor?* (I) *What is the action?* (see my mom's long hair)

Intermediate Have partners take turns asking and answering the prompt. Provide a sentence frame if needed.

Advanced/Advanced High Challenge children to describe their sentences using the Actor/Action routine. Have them share with the group.

FORMATIVE ASSESSMENT ❯ **STUDENT CHECK-IN** Partners share their sentences. Have children reflect using the Check-in routine.

INTERACTIVE WRITING

LESSON 2

LEARNING GOALS

We can practice writing a sentence.

OBJECTIVES

With guidance and support, respond to questions and suggestions from peers.

LANGUAGE OBJECTIVES

Children will inquire, or ask and answer questions, about a story and write a sentence using a sense word.

ELA ACADEMIC LANGUAGE

• *letters*

• Cognate: *letras*

Analyze the Prompt Chorally read the sample sentence on p. T194 with children. Review it using the Actor/Action routine. Address the writing skill by asking: *How many letters are in the word* eyes? (four) Help children complete the sentence frames at the bottom of p. T194. Guide them to use the photos from the **Big Book,** and provide vocabulary as necessary.

Beginning Help children complete the first sentence frame by displaying p. 7 of the Big Book. *What do the children hear?* The children hear the waves crash. Have children identify the actor and action.

Intermediate Have partners use the Actor/Action routine as they complete each sentence frame. Provide vocabulary support as needed.

Advanced/Advanced High Challenge children to think of their own sentence about how they use their senses.

FORMATIVE ASSESSMENT ❯ **STUDENT CHECK-IN** Partners share their sentences. Have children reflect using the Check-in routine.

INDEPENDENT WRITING

LEARNING GOALS

We can write about the texts we read.

OBJECTIVES

Use a combination of drawing, dictating, and writing to narrate several loosely linked events.

LANGUAGE OBJECTIVES

Children will narrate, or tell, by writing a complete sentence using nouns.

ELA ACADEMIC LANGUAGE

• *text, noun*

• Cognate: *texto*

Find Text Evidence Use the Independent Writing routine. Help children orally retell the shared read. *Who is Sam?* (a cat) *What can Sam see?* (the bird) *What can the bird see?* (Sam) Then read the prompt on p. T204: *Why did the bird fly into the tree? Let's look at the text again to find out why.* Display p. 132. *Who can see the bird?* (Sam can see the bird.) Display p. 136 of the **Reading/Writing Companion.** *Where is the bird now?* (in the tree)

Write to the Prompt Display and read the sentence starters on p. T204. Ask a volunteer to retell the prompt in their own words. Model completing the first sentence frame, and have children choral read the response. Repeat the procedure for the remaining sentence frames. Once completed, have children copy the sentences in their writer's notebook.

Beginning Have partners discuss their sentences: The word *bird* is a <u>noun</u>.

Intermediate Have partners tell about the nouns they used in their writing: I used <u>the noun *bird*</u>.

Advanced/Advanced High Challenge children to think of their own sentence. Have them identify the nouns they used.

FORMATIVE ASSESSMENT ❯ **STUDENT CHECK-IN** Partners share their sentences. Have children reflect using the Check-in routine.

SELF-SELECTED WRITING

LEARNING GOALS

We can revise our writing.

OBJECTIVES

Demonstrate command of the conventions of standard English spelling when writing.

LANGUAGE OBJECTIVES

Children will inquire, or ask and answer questions, about their writing by checking their nouns.

ELA ACADEMIC LANGUAGE

• *noun*

Work with children to revise the group writing activity. Read the sentence or label, pointing to each word as you read. Model and ask questions as you read. *Is _____ a noun?* (Yes/No) *The noun _____ is not spelled correctly. It should be spelled _____. Repeat the spelling with me: _____.* After you have made the necessary corrections, have children write their own clean copy of the sentence in their writer's notebook or write and draw for a page in the book.

For more support with grammar, use the **Language Transfers Handbook** and review nouns using **Language Development Card** 1A.

FORMATIVE ASSESSMENT ❯ **STUDENT CHECK-IN** Partners tell what revisions they made. Have children reflect using the Check-in routine.

Summative Assessment
Get Ready for Unit Assessment

Unit 1 Tested Skills

LISTENING AND READING COMPREHENSION	VOCABULARY	GRAMMAR	SPEAKING AND WRITING
• Listening Actively • Details • Text Structure • Sequence	• Words and Categories	• Nouns	• Presenting • Composing/Writing • Supporting Opinions • Retelling/Recounting

Create a Student Profile

Record data from the following resources in the Student Profile charts on pages 136–137 of the Assessment book.

COLLABORATIVE	INTERPRETIVE	PRODUCTIVE

• Collaborative Conversations Rubrics
  • Listening
  • Speaking
	• Leveled Unit Assessment
	  • Listening Comprehension
	  • Reading Comprehension
	  • Vocabulary
	  • Grammar
	• Presentation Rubric
	  • Listening
	• *Wonders* Unit Assessment
		• Weekly Progress Monitoring
		• Leveled Unit Assessment
		  • Speaking
		  • Writing
		• Presentation Rubric
		  • Speaking
		• Write to Sources Rubric
		• *Wonders* Unit Assessment

The Foundational Skills Kit, Language Development Kit, and Adaptive Learning provide additional student data for progress monitoring.

Level Up

Use the following chart, along with your Student Profiles, to guide your Level Up decisions.

LEVEL UP	If **BEGINNING** level students are able to do the following, they may be ready to move to the **INTERMEDIATE** level:	If **INTERMEDIATE** level students are able to do the following, they may be ready to move to the **ADVANCED** level:	If **ADVANCED** level students are able to do the following, they may be ready to move to **ON** level:
COLLABORATIVE	• participate in collaborative conversations using basic vocabulary and grammar and simple phrases or sentences • discuss simple pictorial or text prompts	• participate in collaborative conversations using appropriate words and phrases and complete sentences • use limited academic vocabulary across and within disciplines	• participate in collaborative conversations using more sophisticated vocabulary and correct grammar • communicate effectively across a wide range of language demands in social and academic contexts
INTERPRETIVE	• identify details in simple read alouds • understand common vocabulary and idioms and interpret language related to familiar social, school, and academic topics • make simple inferences and make simple comparisons • exhibit an emerging receptive control of lexical, syntactic, phonological, and discourse features	• identify main ideas and/or make some inferences from simple read alouds • use context clues to identify word meanings and interpret basic vocabulary and idioms • compare, contrast, summarize, and relate text to graphic organizers • exhibit a limited range of receptive control of lexical, syntactic, phonological, and discourse features when addressing new or familiar topics	• determine main ideas in read alouds that have advanced vocabulary • use context clues to determine meaning, understand multiple-meaning words, and recognize synonyms of social and academic vocabulary • analyze information, make sophisticated inferences, and explain their reasoning • command a high degree of receptive control of lexical, syntactic, phonological, and discourse features
PRODUCTIVE	• express ideas and opinions with basic vocabulary and grammar and simple phrases or sentences • restate information or retell a story using basic vocabulary • exhibit an emerging productive control of lexical, syntactic, phonological, and discourse features	• produce coherent language with limited elaboration or detail • restate information or retell a story using mostly accurate, although limited, vocabulary • exhibit a limited range of productive control of lexical, syntactic, phonological, and discourse features when addressing new or familiar topics	• produce sentences with more sophisticated vocabulary and correct grammar • restate information or retell a story using extensive and accurate vocabulary and grammar • tailor language to a particular purpose and audience • command a high degree of productive control of lexical, syntactic, phonological, and discourse features

LESSONS 1-2

LEARNING GOALS

We can understand important ideas and details about a text.

We can use headings to learn new information.

OBJECTIVES

With prompting and support, ask and answer questions about key details in a text.

Ask and answer questions to help determine or clarify the meaning of words and phrases in a text.

With prompting and support, identify basic similarities in and differences between two texts on the same topic.

Continue a conversation through multiple exchanges.

LANGUAGE OBJECTIVES

Children will discuss actions we can do with our hands using key vocabulary and verbs.

ELA ACADEMIC LANGUAGE

• *ask, answer, main topic, retell, heading*

MATERIALS

Literature Big Book, *The Handiest Things in the World*

Visual Vocabulary Cards

DIGITAL TOOLS

Have children listen to the selection as they follow along to develop comprehension.

Use the vocabulary activity for additional support.

The Handiest Things in the World

Prepare to Read

Build Background Point to the hands in the cover photograph and explain that the selection is about ways we use our hands. Show visuals of utensils and demonstrate how we use a knife, fork, and spoon with our hands to eat food. *How do we use a knife? To ____ the food.* Discuss and model other ways we use our hands, such as to write or draw with a pencil.

Focus on Vocabulary Use the **Visual Vocabulary Cards** to review the oral vocabulary words *tools* and *discover*. As you read, use gestures and other visual support to clarify important selection words: *handy, fingers, add, pour, dry, sweep, dig, scoop, dirt,* and *waves*. Review the words in context as you read.

Summarize the Text Before reading, give a short summary of the selection: *The author tells about things you can do with your hands and tools that can help you.*

Read the Text

Use the Interactive Question-Response Routine to help children understand the text.

Pages 4–15

Pages 6–7 Read the text. *The girl eats fruit. She eats with her hands. The boy eats vegetables. He uses chopsticks. What does the boy use to eat?* (chopsticks) *How do the chopsticks help?* They help keep his fingers <u>clean</u>.

Pages 8–9 Read the text. *The boy counts numbers. He counts with his hands. The boy uses a calculator to count. He adds numbers. Show me how you count on your hands. What does a calculator help you do?* (count; add)

Pages 12–13 Read the text. *The children get wet in the rain. The boy holds an umbrella. The umbrella keeps the boy dry.*

 What do the children use with their hands? Talk with a partner.

Beginning Guide children to point to a detail and say it in a sentence after you. For example: *The boy holds an umbrella. The boy is dry.*

Intermediate Help partners use the photos to respond. *He uses <u>chopsticks</u> to eat. The boy uses an <u>umbrella</u> to keep <u>dry</u>.*

Advanced/Advanced High Have children use details from the text and photos. *Raindrops get the children wet. A boy uses an umbrella to keep dry.*

The Handiest Things in the World
by the New York Times bestselling author of Frindle
ANDREW CLEMENTS
Photographs by Raquel Jaramillo

Literature Big Book

Pages 16–25

Pages 18–19 Point to the child's hands. *Hands dig and scoop.* Act out digging and scooping dirt. Point to the tools. *What do the hands move with a tool?* (the dirt)

Pages 24–25 *Show me how to tap a beat. A girl taps the beat on a pot. A girl plays the drums.*

 How can you use your hands to keep the beat? Talk with a partner.

Beginning Help the children point to the photos and describe what they see after you: *The girl taps a pot. The girl plays the drums.*

Intermediate Have children ask and answer: *What does the girl do? The girl taps a* pot *and keeps the beat. The girl keeps the* beat *on the* drums.

Advanced/Advanced High Have partners point as they respond: *You can tap* in rhythm on a pot. *You can keep* the beat on the drums.

Pages 26–35

Pages 30–31 Explain that the child writes "away" in the sand. *What happens to words in the sand?* (They wash away.) Explain that the other child writes "stay" in crayon. *Do these words wash away or stay?* (stay)

 What does the author show about writing? Talk with a partner.

Beginning Help children point and respond: *I can write in* sand. *I can write with a* crayon.

Intermediate Have partners respond: *You can write* in sand. *You can use* crayons *to write on* paper.

Advanced/Advanced High Help partners tell how the writing is different. *You use crayons* to write on paper. *Water will* wash away words *you write* in sand.

 Retell Use the **Retelling Cards** for *The Handiest Thing in the World.* Ask: *What did you learn about using your hands?* Help children take turns describing a tool or instrument we use with our hands.

Paired Selection: "Discover with Tools"

Pages 36–40 Point to each photo or heading as you paraphrase: *The tool is a magnifying glass. It makes things bigger. We can see things close up. This picture is a leaf close up.* Continue with each tool. Then ask guiding questions. *What tool do the children use?* (magnifying glass) *Why do they use it?* (to make things look bigger) *How do the tools help people? The tools help people* discover *and learn new things.*

 How do tools help people discover things? Talk with a partner.

Beginning Guide partners to point to a photograph and respond after you. For example: *The boy sees far away. He sees the Moon.*

Intermediate Help partners respond: *Tools can help people* see *things* far away *or* close up.

Advanced/Advanced High Help partners use complete sentences as they tell what the people discover. *A telescope can help you* see the Moon and stars. *The people find out* about the past.

❯ STUDENT CHECK-IN

Main Selection Have partners retell what we can do with our hands.

Paired Selection Have partners share information they learned about tools from the photographs.

Have children reflect using the Check-in routine.

 ## Independent Time

Oral Language Have children talk about what they read in *The Handiest Thing in the World* and "Discover with Tools." Ask: *What tools help you use your hands? What tools help you see far away or close up?* Have partners discuss what the two texts have in common. Help them respond using: The texts tell about ___.

LEARNING GOALS

We can listen actively to learn how tools helped Timimoto.

OBJECTIVES

Recognize common types of texts (e.g., storybooks, poems).

With prompting and support, describe the relationship between illustrations and the story in which they appear.

Actively engage in group reading activities with purpose and understanding.

Continue a conversation through multiple exchanges.

LANGUAGE OBJECTIVES

Children will narrate, or tell, how the character uses tools throughout the story, using action words.

ELA ACADEMIC LANGUAGE

• *details, illustration*
• Cognates: *detalles, ilustración*

MATERIALS

Interactive Read Aloud, "Timimoto"

Visual Vocabulary Cards

DIGITAL TOOLS

Have children listen to the selection as they follow along to develop comprehension.

Use the vocabulary activity for additional support.

"Timimoto"

Interactive Read Aloud

Prepare to Read

Build Background Tell children that they are going to listen to a story from Japan. Point to Japan on a map and explain that it is a group of islands in the Pacific Ocean. Show pictures of a Japanese rice bowl and chopsticks. *People can use chopsticks to eat.*

Focus on Vocabulary Use the **Visual Vocabulary Cards** to review the oral vocabulary words: *tools, discover, fetch, rumble,* and *defeated.* Then use gestures and other visual support to clarify important story words, for example: *wish, tiny, journey, explore, needle, sword, paddle, giant, discover, tongue,* and *sunset.*

Summarize the Text *The story is about a tiny, or very small, boy. He goes on a journey to see the world. One day the tiny boy meets a big giant.*

Read the Text

Use the Interactive Question-Response Routine to help children understand the story.

Card 1

Paragraphs 1–3 Read the text. Point to the old woman. *An old woman lives in Japan. She is sad. She wants a child. Why is the woman sad?* (She wants a child.)

Paragraphs 4–5 Read the text. Emphasize with your fingers that the baby is one-inch long. *She names him Timimoto. Now she is filled with joy, or happy. How does the woman feel now?* (She feels happy.)

 How do the feelings of the woman change? Talk with a partner.

Beginning Reinforce understanding of the woman's feelings with facial expression and gestures. *First, the old woman feels sad. She wishes, or wants, a child. Next, she finds a tiny* baby; child. *Now she feels* happy.

Intermediate Help children understand how the woman's feelings change because she finds Timimoto. *In the beginning, how does the woman feel?* (sad) *What happens when she finds Timimoto? She feels* happy.

Advanced/Advanced High Help partners explain why her feelings change. Provide additional modeling. *She feels happy because her wish came true.*

Card 2

Paragraphs 1–3 Read the text. *Timimoto wants to go on a journey. Why does Timimoto want to go on a journey? He wants to see the* world.

Paragraphs 4–8 Read the text. Point to details in the illustration and say: *His mother gives him a sewing needle. It is his sword. It will protect him. The rice bowl is his boat. The chopstick is the paddle. Timimoto says good-bye. His parents tell him to watch out for the night giant.*

 Why do Timimoto's parents give him a rice bowl and a chopstick? Discuss with a partner.

Beginning Help children point to details and repeat after you: *Timimoto is so small. The bowl is his boat.*

Intermediate Guide children to describe what they see in the picture: *The bowl is a* boat *for the* journey. *The* chopstick *is the paddle for the boat.*

Advanced/Advanced High Guide children to discuss the gifts. *The gifts are for* the journey. *The bowl and chopstick can be* a boat and paddle *because* Timimoto is tiny.

Card 3

Paragraphs 1–2 Read the text. *A frog tries to eat Timimoto. What tool does he use to make it go away?* (the chopstick)

Paragraphs 3–6 *Timimoto comes to a village.* Point to the people running. *He sees people run. A man tells him about a giant. Timimoto remembers his parents warned him about a giant. He runs to get away.*

 Why does Timimoto run back to his boat? Explain to a partner.

Beginning Help children point to details and repeat after you: *A man says the giant is coming.*

Intermediate Guide children to explain why he runs back to his boat: *There is a* giant. *It is near the* village.

Advanced/Advanced High Help partners respond: *Timimoto's parents warned* him about a night giant.

Card 4

Paragraphs 1–3 Read the text. *It is too late. It is night.* Point to the giant. *He puts Timimoto in his mouth.* Act

out the character of the giant. *What does the night giant do? The giant puts* Timimoto *in his* mouth.

Paragraphs 4–8 Point to the needle in Timimoto's hand. *Timimoto sticks his needle on the giant's tongue. The giant says, "That hurt!" The giant will not come to the village again. Will the giant come back to the village?* (no) *The people say thank you to Timimoto.*

 Why do the people in the village say thank you to Timimoto? Explain to a partner.

Beginning Help children point to details and complete the sentence frame: *Timimoto makes the* giant *go away.*

Intermediate Guide children to explain that the village is safe now: *Timimoto defeats* the giant. *The giant runs back into* the forest.

Advanced/Advanced High Help children explain how Timimoto saves the village from the giant. Timimoto *defeats* the giant. *The people say thank you because* he saved them from the giant.

 Retell Use the illustrations on the **Interactive Read-Aloud Cards** to retell the story with children. Display the cards and model retelling using connecting sequence words, such as *first, next, then,* and *last* as you point to the events and actions in the cards. Then help children take turns retelling one part using the sequence words.

FORMATIVE ASSESSMENT

❯ **STUDENT CHECK-IN**

Have partners retell how the tools help Timimoto.
Have children reflect using the Check-in routine.

 Independent Time

Oral Language Have partners describe the characters Timimoto and the night giant. Have them tell how the characters are different. Encourage them to use the illustrations on the cards to help them.

LEARNING GOALS

We can ask and answer questions about the text as we read.

OBJECTIVES

With prompting and support, ask and answer questions about key details in a text.

With prompting and support, identify the main topic and retell key details of a text.

With prompting and support, describe the relationship between illustrations and the text in which they appear.

Describe familiar people, places, things, and events and, with prompting and support, provide additional detail.

LANGUAGE OBJECTIVES

Children will inquire, or ask and answer questions, about taking a trip, using naming words and key vocabulary.

ELA ACADEMIC LANGUAGE

• *label, collaborate*
• Cognate: *colaborar*

MATERIALS

ELL Leveled Reader: *A Trip*

Online Differentiated Texts, "A Bug!"

Online ELL Visual Vocabulary Cards

DIGITAL TOOLS

Have children listen to the selection as they follow along to develop comprehension.

Use the vocabulary activity for additional support.

A Trip

Prepare to Read

Build Background Prompt discussion about a fishing trip. *People catch fish. People go to rivers and lakes. Where can you go fishing? At rivers and lakes.* Point out the fishing pole. *What do you use to catch a fish?* Provide a sentence frame: *You need a fishing _____.*

Focus on Vocabulary Use the routine on the **ELL Visual Vocabulary Cards** to preteach *investigate* and *outdoors.* As you read, use the images and any labels to clarify important selection words, for example: *trip, pole, pail, paddle, pump.*

Lexile BR

Read the Text

Use the Interactive Question-Response Routine to help children understand the text.

Pages 2–8

Pages 2–3 *What do you see?* I see a <u>backpack</u>. Help children discuss details: *You can use a backpack to carry things on a fishing trip. What does the next photo show?* (a map)

Ask and Answer Questions Help children ask and answer questions about the things they see. *What does a map show?* (places)

 Why do you need a map on a fishing trip? Talk with a partner.

Beginning Use additional visuals to reinforce understanding of important words. Then help children repeat: *A map shows places. You can see water on a map.*

Intermediate Confirm children's understanding that a map shows how to get to places. Then ask: *Where can you go on a fishing trip?* (water; river; lake) *What does a map show? A map shows the <u>water; rivers; lakes</u> to go fishing.*

Advanced/Advanced High Encourage children to discuss how people use a map on a fishing trip. Provide modeling. *A map can help you find rivers or lakes.*

Pages 4-5 Read pages 4–5. Help children discuss by pointing to the picture and label for *pole. What is this? We can look at the label and read that it's a pole.* Remind children that a fishing pole is a tool to catch fish. Point to the picture and label for *pail. What is this called?* (a pail)

 What can you do with a fishing pole and a pail? Talk with a partner.

Beginning Help children point to the picture and say after you: *Fishing pole; you use a fishing pole to catch a fish.*

Intermediate Help children ask and answer questions: *Why do you use a fishing pole? You use a fishing pole to* catch fish.

Advanced/Advanced High Encourage children to use complete sentences as they discuss the purpose of each tool. Provide modeling. *You use a fishing pole to catch fish. You put a fish in a pail of water.*

Pages 6–8 Point to the paddle and act out rowing. *You use paddles to make a boat go.* Point to the pump. *You pump air in the boat.*

 Discuss the reason to have a boat on a fishing trip.

Beginning Help children point to the picture and say after you: *You use a boat to go on water.*

Intermediate Help children ask and answer the question: *Why do you need a boat?* You use a boat to fish on the river; lake; water.

Advanced/Advanced High Challenge partners to explain why people use a boat to fish.

Topic and Details Have partners discuss topic and details of the text. *What things did we see?* (things for a trip) *A trip is the topic. What did we see?* (backpack, map, pole, pail, paddle, pump)

Retell Have partners retell the story. Have them take turns pointing to a picture and describing it to each other. Have children discuss with a partner what they have learned from the text.

Focus on Fluency

Read pages 2–8 and have children echo read. For additional practice, have children record themselves reading the same text a few times, and then select their favorite recording to play for you.

Build Knowledge: Make Connections

Talk About the Text Have partners discuss how tools help us explore.

Self-Selected Reading

Have children choose another informational text from the online **Leveled Reader Library** or read the **Differentiated Text,** "A Bug!"

LITERACY ACTIVITIES

Have children complete the Literacy Activities on the inside back cover of the book.

FORMATIVE ASSESSMENT

❯ STUDENT CHECK-IN

Have partners retell the tools from the text and their uses. Have children reflect using the Check-in routine.

LEVEL UP

IF children can read *A Trip* **ELL Level** with fluency and correctly answer questions,

THEN tell children that they will read a more detailed version of the story.

HAVE children page through *A Trip* On Level and describe each picture in simple language.

• Have children read the selection, checking their comprehension and providing assistance as necessary.

MODELED WRITING

LESSON 1

LEARNING GOALS

We can learn how to write a sentence.

OBJECTIVES

Use a combination of drawing, dictating, and writing to narrate a single event.

LANGUAGE OBJECTIVES

Children will narrate by writing a sentence using the phrase *draw with*.

ELA ACADEMIC LANGUAGE

• *sentence*

Writing Practice Display a pencil, and have children echo read the sample sentence from p. T270 of the **Teacher's Edition.** Guide children to analyze the sentence using the Actor/Action routine: *Who is the actor?* (I) *What is the action?* (like to draw) *How does the actor like to draw?* (with a pencil and pen) Read the prompt. Have children answer the prompt as a group. Write the sentence on the board, and have children choral read. Then have them write their own sentence in their writer's notebook.

Beginning Help children think about their sentence: *Who is the actor?* (I) *What is the action?* (draw) *What tool will you draw with?* (with crayons)

Intermediate Have partners take turns asking and answering *who/what* questions to create their sentences. Provide a sentence frame if needed.

Advanced/Advanced High Challenge children to talk about their sentence using the Actor/Action routine.

FORMATIVE ASSESSMENT ❯ **◗ STUDENT CHECK-IN** Partners share their sentences. Have children reflect using the Check-in routine.

INTERACTIVE WRITING

LESSON 2

LEARNING GOALS

We can practice writing a sentence.

OBJECTIVES

Use dictating and writing to compose informative texts about a topic.

LANGUAGE OBJECTIVES

Children will inquire about the text and write a sentence using the word *handy*.

ELA ACADEMIC LANGUAGE

• *clues*

Analyze the Prompt Have children choral read with you the sample sentence on p. T282. Display a pencil to review the meaning of *handy*: *This pencil is* handy, *or helpful. It helps me write.* Have children say: The pencil is <u>handy</u>. *Let's look for clues about details in the text in the photos of* The Handiest Things in the World (**Big Book**). *What handy tools do you see?* Help children complete the sentence frames on p. T282.

Beginning Help children complete the first sentence frame by displaying p. 23. *What handy tool is the girl using?* (a fan)

Intermediate To complete both sentence frames, have partners use the details in the photos that show handy tools and ways that hands are useful.

Advanced/Advanced High Challenge partners to think of their own sentences. Have them explain what clues about the text they found in the photos.

FORMATIVE ASSESSMENT ❯ **◗ STUDENT CHECK-IN** Partners share their sentences. Have children reflect using the Check-in routine.

INDEPENDENT WRITING

LEARNING GOALS

We can write about the texts we read.

OBJECTIVES

Use a combination of dictating and writing to narrate several loosely linked events.

LANGUAGE OBJECTIVES

Children will narrate the story by writing a complete sentence using verbs, or action words.

ELA ACADEMIC LANGUAGE

• *verb*

• Cognate: *verbo*

 Find Text Evidence Use the Independent Writing routine. Help children orally retell the shared read by asking questions, such as: *Who is this?* (Pam) *What does Pam have?* (a cart) *What can she see first?* (a pot) Then read the prompt on p. T292: *How is the shopping cart a handy tool for Pam and her mother?* Display p. 18 of the **Reading/Writing Companion.** *Do Pam and her mother have a cart?* (yes) *Where did Pam put the pen?* (in the cart)

Write to the Prompt Display and read the sentence frames on p. T292. Ask a volunteer to retell the prompt in their own words. Model completing the first sentence frame, and have children choral read the response. Repeat the procedure for the remaining sentence frames. Once completed, have children copy the sentences in their writer's notebook.

 Beginning Help children talk about their sentences: I used the verb <u>puts</u>.

Intermediate Have partners point to and say the verbs in their writing.

Advanced/Advanced High Challenge partners to come up with their own sentences. Have them identify the verbs they used.

FORMATIVE ASSESSMENT ❯ **STUDENT CHECK-IN** Partners share their sentences. Have children reflect using the Check-in routine.

SELF-SELECTED WRITING

LEARNING GOALS

We can revise our writing.

OBJECTIVES

Use frequently occurring verbs.

LANGUAGE OBJECTIVES

Children will inquire, or ask and answer questions, about their writing by checking their verbs, or action words.

ELA ACADEMIC LANGUAGE

• *verb*

• Cognate: *verbo*

 Work with children to revise the group writing activity. Read the sentences, pointing to each word as you read. Model and ask questions as you read. *Is _____ a verb, or action word?* (Yes/No) *A verb is missing. What verb should we use?* After you have made the necessary corrections, have children copy the sentences in their writer's notebook.

For more support with grammar and verbs, use the **Language Transfers Handbook** and **Language Development Card** 4A.

FORMATIVE ASSESSMENT ❯ **STUDENT CHECK-IN** Partners tell what revisions they made. Have children reflect using the Check-in routine.

LEARNING GOALS

We can understand important ideas and details in story.

We can learn new information from bold print.

OBJECTIVES

With prompting and support, identify the main topic and retell key details of a text.

With prompting and support, describe the relationship between illustrations and the text in which they appear.

With prompting and support, identify basic similarities in and differences between two texts on the same topic.

Continue a conversation through multiple exchanges.

LANGUAGE OBJECTIVES

Children will inform, or give information, about shapes that we can see all around us, using naming words and simple sentences.

ELA ACADEMIC LANGUAGE

• *count, describe, bold print*

• Cognates: *contar, describir*

MATERIALS

Literature Big Book, *Shapes All Around*

Visual Vocabulary Cards

DIGITAL TOOLS

Have children listen to the selection as they follow along to develop comprehension.

Use the vocabulary activity for additional support.

Shapes All Around

Prepare to Read

Build Background Draw four shapes on chart paper: circle, square, rectangle, and triangle. *These are shapes. Let's name each shape.* Guide children to name the shapes. Explain what sides are. Ask: *How many sides does a square/ rectangle/triangle have?* Count aloud with children as you point to each side. Provide a sentence frame: *A triangle has ____ sides.* Work with children to identify different shapes in the classroom. Provide sentence frames: *I see a ____. The paper is a ____.*

Focus on Vocabulary Use the **Visual Vocabulary Cards** to review the oral vocabulary words *materials* and *nature*. As you read, use gestures and other visual support to clarify important selection words: *scrapbook, rings, wheels, parade, umbrella, soccer field, signs, roof,* and *windy*. Review words in context as you read, and have children add words to their personal glossaries.

Summarize the Text Before reading, give a short summary of the text: *This text is about different shapes. Look closely, and you can find shapes all around you.*

Literature Big Book

Read the Text

Use the Interactive Question-Response Routine to help children understand the text.

Pages 4–9

Pages 4–5 Read the text. *The girl is at the playground.* Point to and name the shapes the character has drawn. Then point to each shape again and ask: *What shape is this?* (circle, square, rectangle, and triangle)

Pages 8–9 Read the text. Remind children that a bicycle has two wheels. Point to the colored wheel on page 8. *A wheel is a circle.* Use gestures to show how a wheel turns "round." Then point to and name the umbrellas on page 9. *Umbrellas are circles. Let's count the umbrellas in the picture.*

 What circles do you see? Discuss with a partner.

Beginning Guide children to point to a ball, wheel, and umbrella and name each after you. For example: *A ball is a circle.*

Intermediate Help children name three objects that are circles. *Is a ball a circle? A ball is a circle.*

Advanced/Advanced High Guide partners to describe the circles in complete sentences: *What shape is a wheel?* (A wheel is a circle.)

Pages 10–17

Pages 10–12 Read the text. Identify the square windows in the photo. Then count the sides of a square. Point out that each side is the same length. *How many sides do the squares all have?* (four)

Pages 16–17 Describe one of the rectangles, such as the street sign. *These sides are short. These sides are long. What shape is the sign?* (The sign is a rectangle.)

 What squares and rectangles can you name? Discuss with a partner.

Beginning Help children name the shapes. *It is a square. It is a rectangle.*

Intermediate Guide children to describe the shapes. *The windows are squares. The ruler is a rectangle.*

Advanced/Advanced High Use sentence frames to prompt children to add details. *There are 10 squares in the game. The sandwich is cut into four squares. The soccer net is the shape of a rectangle.*

Pages 18–23

Pages 18–20 Count the sides of each triangle on page 18. Then help children name the triangles. *The house has a roof. What is a triangle?* (the roof)

Pages 22–23 *Shapes are all around us. Sometimes you can see more than one shape in one place.* Guide children to point to each shape they learned about.

 Tell where you see different shapes on pages 22 and 23. Discuss with a partner.

Beginning Have children point to and name each shape. *This shape is a circle.*

Intermediate Ask guiding questions to help children identify the shapes. *How many circles are in the sign?*

Advanced/Advanced High Help partners describe how the shapes are different. (The sign is a triangle. It has three sides. The wheel is a circle. It is round.)

 Retell Use the **Retelling Cards** for *Shapes All Around.* Ask children to describe what they

learned about shapes as you point to details in the cards. Then help them take turns retelling a part of the selection.

Paired Selection: "Find the Shapes"

Pages 24–31 Explain that a riddle tells clues, and you can figure out the answer from the clues. Point to each photo on page 26 as you paraphrase the text. For example: *A pillow is soft. A picture is not soft. The answer to the first riddle is a pillow.* Point to the ball on page 27. *The thing is round and bounces. What is it?* (ball) Repeat with the riddles on pages 28–30.

 On page 31, one picture shows a triangle, square, and rectangle. Discuss with a partner.

Beginning Have partners point to the toy house. Then help them point to and name the shapes.

Intermediate Use sentence frames to help children identify the shapes in the toy house. *The roof is a triangle. The room is a square. I see a rectangle.*

Advanced/Advanced High Provide additional modeling to help children discuss the shapes in the toy house. *The rooms make a rectangle.*

FORMATIVE ASSESSMENT

STUDENT CHECK-IN
Main Selection Have partners retell objects for three kinds of shapes they saw in the text.
Paired Selection Have partners discuss the the riddles.
Have children reflect using the Check-in routine.

Independent Time

Describe a Text Have children describe what they read about in *Shapes All Around* and "Find the Shapes." Ask: *What four shapes do the authors tell about?* (circle, triangle, square, and rectangle) Have partners discuss what the authors show about these shapes. Help them respond using: *You can see ___.*

LESSON 3

LEARNING GOALS

We can listen actively to learn about different kinds of kites.

OBJECTIVES

With prompting and support, ask and answer questions about key details in a text.

Ask and answer questions to help determine or clarify the meaning of words and phrases in a text.

Continue a conversation through multiple exchanges.

Ask and answer questions in order to seek help, get information, or clarify something that is not understood.

LANGUAGE OBJECTIVES

Children will inform, or give information, about different qualities kites can have, using key vocabulary and simple sentences.

ELA ACADEMIC LANGUAGE

• *compare, shapes*

• Cognate: *comparar*

MATERIALS

Interactive Read Aloud, "Kites in Flight"

Visual Vocabulary Cards

DIGITAL TOOLS

MULTIMODAL

🎧 Have children listen to the selection as they follow along to develop comprehension.

Use the vocabulary activity for additional support.

"Kites in Flight"

Prepare to Read

Interactive Read Aloud

Build Background Use visuals to help explain the activity of flying a kite on a windy day. Ask children if they have ever seen a kite fly in the air. *What did the kite look like? Was it a windy day?* Tell children that they are going to read about kites in different places around the world. Show images of Indian, Chinese, and Brazilian kites, or the ones in the photographs. Explain where the kites come from, and use a world map to point out India, China, and Brazil.

Focus on Vocabulary Use the **Visual Vocabulary Cards** to review the oral vocabulary words: *nature, materials, world, games,* and *decoration.* As you read, use gestures and other visual support to teach important selection words, for example: *floating, holidays, festival, simple, wings, floating, light.*

Summarize the Text Before reading, give a short summary of the text: *People all over the world fly kites. Kites can be a little different in different countries.*

Read the Text

Use the Interactive Question-Response Routine to help children understand the text.

Card 1

Paragraphs 1–2 Read the text. Point to the kites and explain that people on the ground are flying, or holding, the kites. *People fly kites for fun. People fly kites on holidays, or special days. Scientists also fly kites to learn about nature and the weather. Why do people fly kites? People fly kites* for fun; to celebrate a holiday; to learn about the weather.

Paragraphs 3–4 Read the text. Review the shapes children have learned. Point to kites in the photo and explain that kites can be different shapes. Point to the kite shaped like a bear. *What animal is this?* (bear) *Kites can be shaped like animals. Many kites have bright colors. What colors do you see?*

 How can kites look different? Talk with a partner.

Beginning *Do all kites look the same?* (no) Have children repeat after you: *Kites can be different. Kites can have different colors. Kites can have different shapes.*

Intermediate Ask children to name colors they see in the kites. *What shapes can kites be? Kites can be shaped like* squares; rectangles; circles; animals.

Advanced/Advanced High Have partners ask and answer: *What can kites look like?* (Kites can have different shapes and colors. Kites can be shaped like animals.)

Card 2

Paragraphs 1–2 Read the text. Point to the photo. *People fly kites in India. Some are shaped like diamonds. The kites are made with light materials. They have bright colors. What do these kites in India look like?* (shaped like diamonds; have bright colors)

Paragraph 3 Read the text. *Children in India play games with kites. The person who keeps the kite in the air the longest time wins the game. What do children do with their kites?* (play games)

 What does the author explain about kites in India? Talk with your partner.

Beginning *Are the shapes of the kites like diamonds?* (yes) *Are the kites light or heavy?* (light) Have children repeat after you: *The children play games with kites.*

Intermediate Create a word bank for children to use to complete sentence frames: *The kites are made from* light *materials. Some are shaped like* diamonds. *They have bright* colors. *Children* play games *with their kites.*

Advanced/Advanced High Guide partners to describe the kites they learned about. Then ask them to explain the game children play with kites.

Card 3

Paragraphs 1–2 Read the text. Show flat materials and explain that Chinese kites may be flat. *On these kites, people show Chinese history, or important events from long ago. The kites have many colors. What do people show on flat kites?* (Chinese history)

Paragraphs 3 Read the text. Explain that other Chinese kites may look like bugs, fish, or birds. Point to the butterfly kite. Point out its wings and colors.

 How do people decorate kites in China? Talk with a partner.

Beginning Help children describe the Chinese kite in the photo: *The kite is a* butterfly. *It has* wings. *It has many colors, such as blue,* green, *and* yellow.

Intermediate Help children describe the different kites: *Flat kites are* colorful *and show* Chinese history. *Other kites look like* bugs, birds, or fish.

Advanced/Advanced High Guide partners to discuss how flat kites have designs that show Chinese history and other kites may show animals from nature.

Card 4

Paragraphs 1–2 Show visuals of a spinning toy top. *People in Brazil fly kites. The kites look like spinning tops. People make kites at home.* Review the meaning of *flag* as you explain that some kites show the flag of Brazil. *Other kites have pictures of soccer teams.*

 How do people make kites in Brazil? Talk with your partner.

Intermediate Use sentence frames: *The kites look like* spinning tops. *People make kites at* home. *Some kites show the flag of* Brazil.

Advanced/Advanced High Guide partners to respond in complete sentences. Provide additional modeling as needed. *People make kites at home. They look like spinning tops. Some kites show the flag of Brazil.*

 Retell Use the photos on the **Interactive Read-Aloud Cards** to retell key details from "Kites in Flight." Guide children to take turns retelling what they learned about kites.

FORMATIVE ASSESSMENT

⊙ STUDENT CHECK-IN
Have partners provide descriptions for two kites from the text. Have children reflect using the Check-in routine.

 Independent Time

Oral Language Have partners discuss the kites in the photos. Ask them to tell about the colors, shapes, or what a kite shows. Encourage them to compare the kites on the cards, and challenge them to discuss how kites are alike and different around the world.

LESSONS 4-5

Play with Shapes!

Prepare to Read

Build Background Draw different shapes on chart paper. Have children name each shape: square, rectangle, circle, and triangle. Then point to things in the classroom and ask, *What shape is this? It's a square; rectangle; circle; triangle.*

Focus on Vocabulary Use the routine on the **ELL Visual Vocabulary Cards** to preteach *fun* and *geometry*. As you read, use images and any labels to clarify important selection words, for example: *blocks, game, train, hoop, tent.*

Lexile BR

Read the Text

Use the Interactive Question-Response Routine to help children understand the text.

Pages 2–8

Pages 2–3 Point to page 2. *What is the girl doing?* (playing with blocks) Point to page 3. *What is this?* (a game) *Trace the yellow square. What is this shape?* (a square) Point to the game pieces. Point to the chess pieces on page 5. *These are called pieces. What shape are the pieces?* (circles)

Topic and Details Help children discuss details in the text. *How are the blocks and game the same?* (They are both square.) *How are the pieces different from the blocks and the game?* (The pieces are circles. They are not square.)

 With a partner, tell what shapes you can see in the blocks and the game.

Beginning Ask children to point to the block and the game. *What shape is the block? It is square. What shape is the game? It is square.*

Intermediate Ask children to name the objects on each page. *What does the game look like? The game is square. The pieces are circles.*

Advanced/Advanced High Guide children to use complete sentences as they talk about the items. (The game is square. It has many squares. The pieces are circles.)

Pages 4–5 Reinforce children's understanding of how the author, or writer, uses the yellow lines to show shapes. Trace the yellow rectangle and circle on pages 4 and 5. *What shape is the train?* (a rectangle) *What shape is the ball?* (a circle)

 How are the train and the ball different? Think about their shapes. Discuss with a partner.

Beginning Have children point to the shapes and repeat after you: *rectangle; circle.*

Intermediate *What shape is the train? The train is a* <u>rectangle</u>. *What shape is the ball? The ball is a* <u>circle</u>.

Advanced/Advanced High *Tell a partner about the shapes you see. The* <u>train/ball</u> *is a* <u>rectangle/circle</u>.

Pages 6-8 Read pages 6–8 as you track the text. *What is the girl holding? The label says, "hoop."* Have children point to the label and repeat the word. *What shape is the hoop?* (a circle) Trace the yellow triangle. *What shape is the slide?* (a triangle)

 What can you do on a slide? Talk with a partner.

Beginning Gesture as you ask: *Do you go down a slide or go round and round? I go* <u>down a slide</u>.

Intermediate Help partners discuss how they play on a slide. *What do you do first? next? I climb the* <u>ladder</u>. *I slide* <u>down</u> *the slide.*

Advanced/Advanced High Help children discuss how they can play on a slide. Provide additional modeling as needed. *You climb up the ladder. You slide down the slide.*

Ask and Answer Questions Read pages 6–8. Help children ask and answer questions about the text. *Which things have a square shape?* (a block, a game)

Retell Have partners retell the shapes they saw in the pictures. Have them take turns pointing to a picture and describing it.

Focus on Fluency

Read pages 2–8 and have children echo read. For additional practice, have children record themselves reading the same passage a few times, and then select their favorite recording to play for you.

Build Knowledge: Make Connections

Talk About the Text Have partners discuss the shapes they see in the classroom.

Self-Selected Reading

Help children choose a nonfiction selection from the online **Leveled Reader Library** or read the **Differentiated Text,** "I Like Shapes."

LITERACY ACTIVITIES

Have children complete the Literacy Activities on the inside back cover of the book.

FORMATIVE ASSESSMENT

❯ STUDENT CHECK-IN

Have partners retell the shapes of three objects from the text. Then, have children reflect using the Check-in routine.

LEVEL UP

IF children can read *Play with Shapes!* **ELL Level** with fluency and correctly answer the questions,

THEN tell children that they will read a more detailed version of the story.

HAVE children page through *Play with Shapes!* On Level and describe each picture in simple language.

- Have children read the selection, checking their comprehension and providing assistance as necessary.

MODELED WRITING

LESSON 1

LEARNING GOALS

We can learn how to write a sentence.

OBJECTIVES

Use dictating and writing to compose informative texts in which they supply some information about the topic.

LANGUAGE OBJECTIVES

Children will inform by writing a sentence using a shape word.

ELA ACADEMIC LANGUAGE

• circle

• Cognate: *círculo*

Writing Practice Display a photo of a drum, and read the sample sentence from page T352 of the **Teacher's Edition.** Guide children to analyze the sentence using the Actor/Action routine: *What is the actor?* (a drum) *What is the action? How can we describe the drum?* (is a circle) Then read the sentence starter at the bottom of the page, and have a volunteer complete it. Provide vocabulary as needed. Write the sentence on the board, and point to each word as children choral read. Then have them write their own sentence in their writer's notebook.

Beginning Help children think about their sentence: *What toy will you write about?* (a ball) *What shape is it?* (It is a circle.)

Intermediate Have partners take turns asking and answering the following: What toy are you writing about? What shape is it? It is a ball/circle.

Advanced/Advanced High Challenge children to talk about their sentence using the Actor/Action routine.

FORMATIVE ASSESSMENT ❯ **STUDENT CHECK-IN** Partners share their sentences. Have children reflect using the Check-in routine.

INTERACTIVE WRITING

LESSON 2

LEARNING GOALS

We can practice writing a sentence.

OBJECTIVES

With guidance and support, add details to strengthen writing as needed.

LANGUAGE OBJECTIVES

Children will inquire about shapes and write a sentence using a shape word.

ELA ACADEMIC LANGUAGE

• *triangle*

• Cognate: *triángulo*

Analyze the Student Model Have children choral read with you the sample sentence on p. T364. Use the Actor/Action routine to discuss the sentence: *What is the actor?* (the wheels) *What is the action? What do the wheels do?* (help the bike move) Remind children about the writing trait: *What are we writing about?* (shapes) *Can I write about colors?* (no) Then help children complete the sentence starters at the bottom of page T364.

Beginning Help partners orally complete the first sentence by providing a visual from the **Big Book**, *Shapes All Around*: The roof is a triangle.

Intermediate Provide sentence frames to help partners ask and answer questions: What shape is the roof? The roof is a triangle. What does the shape do? The shape of the roof keeps the house dry.

Advanced/Advanced High Challenge children to think of their own sentences about shapes. Remind them to stay on the topic of shapes.

FORMATIVE ASSESSMENT ❯ **STUDENT CHECK-IN** Partners share their sentences. Have children reflect using the Check-in routine.

INDEPENDENT WRITING

LEARNING GOALS

We can write about the texts we read.

OBJECTIVES

Use a combination of dictating and writing to narrate several loosely linked events.

LANGUAGE OBJECTIVES

Children will narrate by writing a complete sentence using the verb *give*.

ELA ACADEMIC LANGUAGE

- *details, verb*
- Cognates: *detalles, verbo*

Find Text Evidence Use the Independent Writing routine. Help children orally retell the shared read. *Who is Tam?* (a hamster) *Where is Pam?* (in the classroom) *What can Tam do?* (tap the bell) *Who likes Tam?* (Pam and Sam) Then read the prompt on p. T374: *How does the class take care of Pam?* Display pp. 47-49 of the **Reading/Writing Companion:** *What is Pam doing?* (saying hello to Tam) *What does Sam do?* (give a toy to Tam)

Write a Response Display and read the sentence starters on p. T374. Ask a volunteer to retell the prompt in their own words. Model completing the first sentence frame, and have children choral read the response. Repeat the procedure for the remaining sentence frames. Once completed, have children copy the sentences in their writer's notebook.

Beginning Help children talk about their sentences: I used the verb *gives*.

Intermediate Have children tell how the sentences use details from the story: I wrote about how Sam gives Tam a toy.

Advanced/Advanced High Challenge children to come up with their own sentences. Have them identify the story details they used.

FORMATIVE ASSESSMENT ➤ ❯ **STUDENT CHECK-IN** Partners share their sentences. Have children reflect using the Check-in routine.

SELF-SELECTED WRITING

LEARNING GOAL

We can revise our writing.

OBJECTIVES

Use frequently occurring verbs.

LANGUAGE OBJECTIVES

Children will inquire, or ask and answer questions, about their writing by checking their verbs, or action words.

ELA ACADEMIC LANGUAGE

- *verb*
- Cognate: *verbo*

Work with children to revise the group writing activity. Read the sentences, pointing to each word as you read. Model and ask questions as you read. For example: *Does the sentence begin with a capital letter? Is _____ a verb?* (Yes/No) *A verb is missing. What verb should we use?* After you have made the necessary corrections, have children copy the sentences in their writer's notebook.

For more support with grammar, use the **Language Transfers Handbook** and review verbs using **Language Development Card** 4A.

FORMATIVE ASSESSMENT ➤ ❯ **STUDENT CHECK-IN** Partners tell what revisions they made. Have children reflect using the Check-in routine.

LESSONS 1-2

LEARNING GOALS

We can understand important ideas and details in a poem.

We can use captions to learn new information.

OBJECTIVES

Recognize common types of texts (e.g., storybooks, poems).

With prompting and support, compare and contrast the adventures and experiences of characters in familiar stories.

Actively engage in group reading activities with purpose and understanding.

Speak audibly and express thoughts, feelings, and ideas clearly.

LANGUAGE OBJECTIVES

Children will discuss and provide descriptions for bugs, using key vocabulary and descriptive words.

ELA ACADEMIC LANGUAGE

• *poem, author, captions*

• Cognates: *poema, autor*

MATERIALS

Literature Big Book, *I Love Bugs!*

Visual Vocabulary Cards

DIGITAL TOOLS

Have children listen to the selection as they follow along to develop comprehension.

Use the vocabulary activity for additional support.

I Love Bugs!

Literature Big Book

Prepare to Read

Build Background *We are going to read a story about bugs.* Show images of familiar bugs, such as bees, butterflies, ladybugs, spiders, and grasshoppers. Ask children if they know the names of any of the bugs. Elicit or provide each name. *What kind of bug is this? This is a grasshopper.* Prepare children for the vocabulary in the book by discussing how different bugs look and move. For example: *They have wings and legs. They are striped, colorful, fuzzy, hairy, and slimy. They jump, fly, crawl, sting, and buzz.*

Focus on Vocabulary Use the **Visual Vocabulary Cards** to review the oral vocabulary words *curious* and *observe*. As you read, use gestures and other visual support to clarify important story words: *slimy, fuzzy, honey, creepy, spiky, spiny, wing, sting, curl, crawl,* and *squealing*. Review the words in context as you read. Have children add these words to their personal glossaries.

Summarize the Text Before reading, give a short summary of the story: *This book is about a boy who likes bugs. He likes all kinds of bugs.*

Read the Text

Use the Interactive Question-Response Routine to help children understand the poem.

Pages 4–11

Pages 6–7 Read the text. *The boy is looking in the grass.* Point to the grasshopper. *He loves bugs that jump. This bug jumps. What does this bug do?* (jumps) Point to the insect in front of the boy. *The boy loves slimy bugs.* Help children understand that *slimy* means "wet and slippery." *How does this feel?* (slimy) *The bug crawls. Show me how you can jump and crawl.*

Pages 8–9 Read the text. Point to the spiky parts on the bug's body. *The boy sees a hard, spiny bug.* Point to the ladybugs. *The boy sees a spotty, shiny bug.*

Pages 10–11 Read the text. Point to the bees and say *bees. These bees are fuzzy. They fly with wings. Bees make honey. What do these bugs look like?* (They are fuzzy. They have wings.)

 How do the bugs look? Talk with a partner.

Beginning Have children point to details in pictures on pages 4–11 and describe the bugs after you. *The bug has spots.*

Intermediate Have children point to details as they ask and answer: *What does this bug look like? This bug is* spiky; slimy.

Advanced/Advanced High *How are the bugs different?* (Sample answer: A grasshopper is green and leaps. This bug is slimy.)

Pages 12–21

Pages 12–13 Read the text aloud. Point to the butterflies and "sting bugs". *Butterflies have colorful wings. The bugs like the boy's food. See the stripes. The bugs with stripes can sting.* Act out being stung.

Pages 20–21 Read the text aloud. *The boy loves bugs that hop and fly and crawl.* Point out bugs in the illustration that show each action. *What does the boy love? He loves all* bugs.

 What can the bugs do? Talk with a partner.

Beginning Have partners take turns pointing to the bugs and repeating after you: *The bugs fly. The bug crawls. The bug hops.*

Intermediate Have children ask and answer: *What can the bugs do?* The bugs hop; fly; crawl.

Advanced/Advanced High Guide children to use pages 20–21 to describe all the bugs the boy loves.

Pages 22–27

Pages 22–23 Read the text aloud. *The boy thinks the best bug is hairy and scary.* Point to the details as you say: *The bug has eight legs. I see a dark room. I see a spider web. What kind of bug lives in a web?* (a spider)

Page 26–27 Read the text aloud. *Look at the spider's shadow. Does it look big or small?* (big) *The boy runs away. He is squealing. Let's make a squealing sound.*

 How does the boy feel? Talk with a partner.

Intermediate *Does the boy look scared? The boy looks* scared. *How do you know? He is* squealing *and* runs away *from the spider's shadow.*

Advanced/Advanced High *What does the boy see? What is he doing?* (Sample answer: The boy sees the spider's shadow. He runs because he is scared.)

 Retell Displayy the **Retelling Cards** for *I Love Bugs!* and model retelling as you point to the cards. Then help children take turns retelling the story.

LESSON 4 **Paired Selection: "Bugs All Around"**

Pages 28–32 Point to each photo and paraphrase details: *This is a ladybug. It has six legs. This bug has many legs. Ants work together. They build a nest. They live together in the nest. What do ants do?* (Ants work together and live in a next.) Continue with details about butterflies and grasshoppers.

 What does the author tell about butterflies and grasshoppers? Talk with a partner.

Beginning Have partners point to details and repeat after you: *Butterflies get food from flowers.*

Intermediate Use sentence frames to help children describe each bug. *Butterflies have beautiful* wings.

Advanced/Advanced High Guide children to describe specific text details shown in the photos.

FORMATIVE ASSESSMENT

STUDENT CHECK-IN

Main Selection Have partners describe three bugs from the story.

Paired Selection Have partners discuss important information they learned from the photographs.

Have children reflect using the Check-in routine.

 Independent Time

Oral Language Have children discuss what they learned about bugs from *I Love Bugs!* and "Bugs All Around." Guide them to find details that are similar in both selections. Provide sentence frames, such as: *The authors show butterflies* have colorful wings. *I learned a grasshopper* hops.

LESSON 3

We can listen actively to learn the steps of how a caterpillar becomes a butterfly.

OBJECTIVES

With prompting and support, ask and answer questions about key details in a text.

With prompting and support, describe the connection between two individuals, events, ideas, or pieces of information in a text.

With prompting and support, describe the relationship between illustrations and the text in which they appear.

Ask and answer questions in order to seek help, get information, or clarify something that is not understood.

LANGUAGE OBJECTIVES

Children will inform, or give information, about how a caterpillar changes during its life, using naming words and simple sentences.

ELA ACADEMIC LANGUAGE

• ask, answer

MATERIALS

Interactive Read Aloud, "From Caterpillar to Butterfly"

Visual Vocabulary Cards

DIGITAL TOOLS

Have children listen to the selection as they follow along to develop comprehension.

Use the vocabulary activity for additional support.

"From Caterpillar to Butterfly"

Interactive Read Aloud

Prepare to Read

Build Background Show photos of a caterpillar and a Monarch butterfly. *What kind of bug is this?* This is a caterpillar; butterfly. Discuss what the bugs look like and what they do. Use the photos for support. Provide sentence frames to help children describe the bugs. *What does a caterpillar/ butterfly look like, and what can they do? A caterpillar is small. It has stripes. A butterfly has wings. A caterpillar eats leaves. A butterfly flies. It is colorful.*

Focus on Vocabulary Use the **Visual Vocabulary Cards** to review the oral vocabulary words: *process, observe, slender, attaches,* and *curious.* Then use gestures and other visual support to teach important selection vocabulary, for example: *stages, plants, hatch, jaws, full size, a few weeks, grows,* and *changes.*

Summarize the Text Before reading, give a short summary: *This text is about young butterflies. A caterpillar grows and changes. It becomes a butterfly.*

Read the Text

Use the Interactive Question-Response Routine to help children understand the text.

Card 1

Paragraphs 1–4 Read the text. *Point to the egg. A butterfly has four stages, or steps, when it grows. The first is the egg. The butterfly lays her eggs on plants. A baby hatches, or comes out of the egg. It eats the plant. Where does the butterfly lay her eggs?* (on plants)

 Why does the butterfly lay her eggs on plants? Talk to a partner.

Beginning Help children understand that a baby hatches from the egg. Have them point to the egg and plant and say after you: *The baby eats the plant.*

Intermediate Have children ask and answer: *What hatches from the egg? A baby hatches from the egg. Why is the egg on a plant? The plant is food.*

Advanced/Advanced High With a partner, ask and answer: *Why do caterpillars need plants?* (They need plants for food to grow.)

Card 2

Paragraph 1 Read the text. Point to the caterpillar hatching from the egg. *This is the second stage.* Explain that it looks like a worm and is the size of a child's fingernail. *What does it look like?* (a worm)

Paragraphs 2–3 Read the text. Point to the caterpillar eating. *The caterpillar has strong jaws to eat. First, it eats the egg. Then, it eats the plant. It grows and grows.* Point to the full-size caterpillar. *It is full size. What does the caterpillar use to eat?* (strong jaws)

 What happens to the caterpillar? Talk to a partner.

Beginning Encourage children to point to the photos. *Point to the egg. Is the caterpillar hatching? Yes, the caterpillar hatches from the* egg. *What does the caterpillar eat? The caterpillar eats the* plant.

Intermediate Provide sentence frames to help children reply: *The caterpillar* hatches from the egg. *The caterpillar* eats and grows full size.

Advanced/Advanced High Help partners provide details: *What happens during the second stage of a butterfly's growth?* First, a caterpillar hatches and eats the egg. *Then, it eats* the plant and grows. *Last, it is* full size.

Card 3

Paragraphs 1–2 Read the text. Show three fingers and say: *This is the third stage. It is called the pupa stage.* Point to the chrysalis. *This is a chrysalis, or cocoon. Inside, the caterpillar grows and changes. What is this?* (a chrysalis or cocoon)

 What happens to the caterpillar in the third stage? Talk to a partner.

Beginning Help children point to the chrysalis and say after you: *The caterpillar grows inside.*

Intermediate Provide sentence frames and help children pronounce content words: *The caterpillar* grows *and* changes *inside a* chrysalis, *or cocoon.*

Advanced/Advanced High Point to the chrysalis. *What is inside?* (the caterpillar) *What is it doing?* It is growing *and* changing.

Card 4

Paragraph 1–2 Read the text. Point to the butterfly. *A butterfly comes out of the chrysalis. It rests. It is tired.*

The wings are wet. What happens in this stage? (A butterfly comes out of a chrysalis.)

Paragraphs 2–3 Read the text. *The butterfly's wings dry in the Sun. It flies away. It looks for food. In a few weeks, the butterfly lays eggs. Why does the butterfly fly away?* (It looks for food.)

 What happens in the last stage of a butterfly's life? Talk to a partner.

Beginning Have children point and say *butterfly* after you. Have them repeat: *The butterfly flies away. The butterfly lays more eggs.*

Intermediate Provide sentence frames to help children respond: *The butterfly* flies *away. It looks for* food. *Then it lays* eggs.

Advanced/Advanced High Help children describe the events with additional modeling as needed. (The butterfly's wings dry in the Sun. Then it flies away to look for food. After a few weeks, it lays eggs.)

 Retell Use the photos on the **Interactive Read-Aloud Cards** to retell the stages in the butterfly's life. Display the cards and model retelling using sequence words as you point to the events on the cards. Then help children take turns retelling one stage or part using sequence words.

FORMATIVE ASSESSMENT

❯ STUDENT CHECK-IN

Have partners retell the four stages of a caterpillar's life.

Have children reflect using the Check-in routine.

Independent Time

Draw and Describe Have pairs illustrate one or more stages of a butterfly's life cycle. Provide a template, if needed, with the four stages numbered in a circle. Partners can point to each stage and describe what happens. Use **Oral Language Sentence Frames,** p. 6, to support children as they discuss the stage or stages of the life cycle they have illustrated. Guide them to extend their descriptions using the sentence frames.

LEARNING GOALS

We can ask and answer questions about the story as we read.

OBJECTIVES

With prompting and support, ask and answer questions about key details in a text.

With prompting and support, identify characters and setting in a story.

Recognize common types of texts (e.g., storybooks, poems).

Speak audibly and express thoughts, feelings, and ideas clearly.

LANGUAGE OBJECTIVES

Children will discuss the characters' actions in the story using verbs and key vocabulary.

ELA ACADEMIC LANGUAGE

• *characters, labels, illustrations*
• Cognate: *ilustraciones*

MATERIALS

ELL Leveled Reader: *The Bugs Run*

Online Differentiated Texts, "The Caterpillars"

Online ELL Visual Vocabulary Cards

DIGITAL TOOLS

MULTIMODAL

Have children listen to the selection as they follow along to develop comprehension.

Use the vocabulary activity for additional support.

The Bugs Run

Prepare to Read

Build Background *We have been learning about bugs. Let's think about the bugs we learned about. What do they look like? What can they do?* Provide sentence frames for children to share information about the bugs they know: *A bee is ____. A bee makes ____. It can ____.*

Focus on Vocabulary Use the routine on the **ELL Visual Vocabulary Cards** to preteach *chase* and *insect*. As you read, use images and any labels to clarify important story words, for example: *ant, spider, beetle, ladybug, bee, caterpillar, kitten.*

Fiction

The Bugs Run

by Mary Alice Cooper
illustrated by Janee Trasler

Mc Graw Hill

Lexile BR

Read the Text

Use the Interactive Question-Response Routine to help children understand the story.

Pages 2–8

Pages 2–3 Display page 2 and point to the barn. Help children discuss details in the text. *This is a barn. What kind of place has a barn?* (a farm) *Is the cat inside or outside?* (outside) *The cat is chasing the bugs. What is the cat doing?* (chasing the bugs) Point to the labels. *Let's read the labels: ant, spider. What are the ant and spider doing?* (They run from the cat.)

 Why does the ant run? Why does the spider run? Talk to a partner.

Beginning Have children point to the bugs in the illustrations. *Does the cat run after the [ant]?* Help children reply: *The cat runs after the [ant].*

Intermediate Have partners ask and answer: *What is the cat doing? The cat chases the bugs. What bugs run? The ant and spider run.*

Advanced/Advanced High *What does the cat want? What do the bugs want to do?* (The cat wants to catch the bugs. The bugs want to run/get away.)

Pages 4–5 *What bugs is the cat chasing now?* (a beetle and a ladybug) Point to the labels. *Let's read the labels: beetle, ladybug.*

 What can you see? Talk with a partner.

Beginning Point to the ladybug. Count the ladybug's six legs with children. Ask: *Does a real bug have six legs?* (yes)

Intermediate Provide sentence frames to help children respond: *The ladybug is* black and red. *It has* spots/six legs.

Advanced/Advanced High *What is the ladybug doing that a real bug can't do?* (The ladybug is smiling. The ladybug is running like a person.)

Pages 6-7 Read pages 6–7 as you trace the text. *What bugs do you see in the pictures?* (a bee; caterpillar) Point to the labels. *Let's read the labels: bee, caterpillar.*

 What can the bee do? Talk to a partner.

Beginning Help partners point to the bee as they ask and answer: *What can a bee do? A bee can* fly.

Intermediate Have partners read the text and talk about the illustrations. Then ask: *What can a bee do with its wings? It can* fly.

Advanced/Advanced High *A bee has wings. What can a bee do with its wings?* (The bee can fly away from the cat.)

Ask and Answer Questions Help children ask and answer questions: *How does the cat chase the caterpillar? We can look at the picture. I see that the cat* climbs the tree.

Retell Have partners retell the story. Have them take turns pointing to a picture and describing it to each other.

Focus on Fluency

Read pages 2–8 and have children echo read. For additional practice, have children record themselves reading the same text a few times, and then select their favorite recording to play for you.

Build Knowledge: Make Connections

Talk About the Text Have partners discuss bugs they have seen.

Self-Selected Reading

Have children select another fantasy story from the online **Leveled Reader Library** or read the **Differentiated Text:** "The Caterpillars."

LITERACY ACTIVITIES

Have children complete the Literacy Activities on the inside back cover of the book.

FORMATIVE ASSESSMENT

❯ STUDENT CHECK-IN

Have partners retell the characters' actions using three verbs. Then, have children reflect using the Check-in routine.

LEVEL UP

IF children can read *The Bugs Run* ELL Level with fluency and correctly answer the questions,

THEN tell children that they will read a more detailed version of the story.

HAVE children page through *The Bugs Run* On Level and describe each picture in simple language.

• Have children read the selection, checking their comprehension and providing assistance as necessary.

MODELED WRITING

LEARNING GOALS

We can learn how to write a sentence.

OBJECTIVES

Use dictating and writing to compose informative texts and name the topic.

LANGUAGE OBJECTIVES

Children will inform by writing a sentence using descriptive words.

ELA ACADEMIC LANGUAGE

• *describe*

• Cognates: *describir*

 Writing Practice Display the *ladybug* **Photo Card.** Read the sample sentence from p. T434 of the **Teacher's Edition,** and ask children to repeat. Use the Actor/Action routine to analyze the sentence: *Who is the actor?* (I) *What can we say about the actor?* (likes red ladybugs) Read the sentence starters at the bottom of the page, and have a volunteer complete them. Write the sentences on the board, and have children choral read with you. Then have them write their own sentences in their writer's notebook.

 Beginning *What bug will you write about?* (a beetle) Help children create a word bank they can use to describe their bug.

Intermediate Have partners take turns asking and answering questions about their bugs to create sentences. Provide a sentence starter if needed.

Advanced/Advanced High Challenge partners to talk about their sentence using the Actor/Action routine.

FORMATIVE ASSESSMENT ❯ **STUDENT CHECK-IN** Partners share their sentences. Have children reflect using the Check-in routine.

INTERACTIVE WRITING

LEARNING GOALS

We can practice writing a sentence.

OBJECTIVES

With guidance and support, respond to questions and suggestions from peers.

LANGUAGE OBJECTIVES

Children will inquire about a story and write sentences using text evidence.

ELA ACADEMIC LANGUAGE

• *text*

• Cognate: *texto*

 Analyze the Prompt Have children choral read with you the sample sentence on page T446. Use the Actor/Action routine to review it: *Who is the actor?* (the boy) *What can we say about the actor?* (loves bugs of all sizes) Review the writing trait: *What do we see on the page: words, illustrations, or both?* (both) *Do the words and illustrations help you understand the text, or the story?* (yes) Then help children complete the sentence frames at the bottom of page T446.

 Beginning Display and read p. 22 of the **Literature Big Book.** *What bug does the boy love best?* (spiders) Help the children complete both frames.

Intermediate Have partners work together to complete the sentence frames. Encourage them to point to details in the illustrations.

Advanced/Advanced High Challenge partners to think of their own sentences to tell what bugs the boy loves.

FORMATIVE ASSESSMENT ❯ **STUDENT CHECK-IN** Have partners share their sentences. Have children reflect using the Check-in routine.

INDEPENDENT WRITING

LEARNING GOALS

We can write about the texts we read.

OBJECTIVES

Use dictating and writing to compose an informative texts and supply some information about the topic.

LANGUAGE OBJECTIVES

Children will inquire, or ask and answer questions, about the story by writing a complete sentence using the verb, or action word, *pat.*

ELA ACADEMIC LANGUAGE

• *verb, details*

• Cognate: *verbo, detalles*

Find Text Evidence Use the Independent Writing routine. Help children orally retell the shared read. Ask questions such as: *Who is Pat?* (a frog) *Where is Pat?* (in a pond) *What does Pat sit on?* (a rock) Then read the prompt on p. T456: *Why do you think Pat tapped the plant?* Display pp. 86-87 of the **Reading/Writing Companion:** *What is on the plant?* (a bug) *What does Pat want to eat?* (the bug)

Write to the Prompt Display and read the sentence starters on p. T456. Ask a volunteer to retell the prompt in their own words. Model completing the first sentence frame, and have children choral read the response. Repeat the procedure for the remaining sentence frames. Once completed, have children copy the sentences in their writer's notebook.

Beginning Have partners talk about their sentences: I used the verb *tap*.

Intermediate Have partners tell how they used details from the illustrations.

Advanced/Advanced High Challenge partners to come up with their own sentences. Have them identify the details from the text they included.

FORMATIVE ASSESSMENT ❯ **STUDENT CHECK-IN** Partners share their sentences. Have children reflect using the Check-in routine.

SELF-SELECTED WRITING

LEARNING GOALS

We can revise our writing.

OBJECTIVES

Use frequently occurring verbs.

LANGUAGE OBJECTIVES

Children will revise their writing and check for errors with verbs.

ELA ACADEMIC LANGUAGE

• *verb*

• Cognate: *verbo*

Work with children to revise the group writing activity. Read the sentences, pointing to each word as you read. Model and ask questions as you read. For example: *Does the sentence end with a period? Is ____ a verb?* (Yes/No) *A verb is missing. What verb should we use?* After you have made the necessary corrections, depending on time, have children copy the sentences in their writer's notebook.

For more support with grammar, use the **Language Transfers Handbook,** and review verbs using **Language Development Card** 4A.

FORMATIVE ASSESSMENT ❯ **STUDENT CHECK-IN** Partners tell what revisions they made. Have children reflect using the Check-in routine.

Summative Assessment
Get Ready for Unit Assessment

Unit 2 Tested Skills

LISTENING AND READING COMPREHENSION	VOCABULARY	GRAMMAR	SPEAKING AND WRITING
• Listening Actively • Text Structure • Details	• Words and Categories	• Verbs	• Presenting • Composing/Writing • Supporting Opinions • Retelling/Recounting

Create a Student Profile

Record data from the following resources in the Student Profile charts on pages 136–137 of the Assessment book.

COLLABORATIVE	INTERPRETIVE	PRODUCTIVE
• Collaborative Conversations Rubrics • Listening • Speaking	• Leveled Unit Assessment • Listening Comprehension • Reading Comprehension • Vocabulary • Grammar • Presentation Rubric • Listening • *Wonders* Unit Assessment	• Weekly Progress Monitoring • Leveled Unit Assessment • Speaking • Writing • Presentation Rubric • Speaking • Write to Sources Rubric • *Wonders* Unit Assessment

The Foundational Skills Kit, Language Development Kit, and Adaptive Learning provide additional student data for progress monitoring.

Level Up

Use the following chart, along with your Student Profiles, to guide your Level Up decisions.

LEVEL UP	If **BEGINNING** level students are able to do the following, they may be ready to move to the **INTERMEDIATE** level:	If **INTERMEDIATE** level students are able to do the following, they may be ready to move to the **ADVANCED** level:	If **ADVANCED** level students are able to do the following, they may be ready to move to **ON** level:
COLLABORATIVE	• participate in collaborative conversations using basic vocabulary and grammar and simple phrases or sentences • discuss simple pictorial or text prompts	• participate in collaborative conversations using appropriate words and phrases and complete sentences • use limited academic vocabulary across and within disciplines	• participate in collaborative conversations using more sophisticated vocabulary and correct grammar • communicate effectively across a wide range of language demands in social and academic contexts
INTERPRETIVE	• identify details in simple read alouds • understand common vocabulary and idioms and interpret language related to familiar social, school, and academic topics • make simple inferences and make simple comparisons • exhibit an emerging receptive control of lexical, syntactic, phonological, and discourse features	• identify main ideas and/or make some inferences from simple read alouds • use context clues to identify word meanings and interpret basic vocabulary and idioms • compare, contrast, summarize, and relate text to graphic organizers • exhibit a limited range of receptive control of lexical, syntactic, phonological, and discourse features when addressing new or familiar topics	• determine main ideas in read alouds that have advanced vocabulary • use context clues to determine meaning, understand multiple-meaning words, and recognize synonyms of social and academic vocabulary • analyze information, make sophisticated inferences, and explain their reasoning • command a high degree of receptive control of lexical, syntactic, phonological, and discourse features
PRODUCTIVE	• express ideas and opinions with basic vocabulary and grammar and simple phrases or sentences • restate information or retell a story using basic vocabulary • exhibit an emerging productive control of lexical, syntactic, phonological, and discourse features	• produce coherent language with limited elaboration or detail • restate information or retell a story using mostly accurate, although limited, vocabulary • exhibit a limited range of productive control of lexical, syntactic, phonological, and discourse features when addressing new or familiar topics	• produce sentences with more sophisticated vocabulary and correct grammar • restate information or retell a story using extensive and accurate vocabulary and grammar • tailor language to a particular purpose and audience • command a high degree of productive control of lexical, syntactic, phonological, and discourse features

LESSONS 1-2

OBJECTIVES

Ask and answer questions about unknown words in a text.

With prompting and support, compare and contrast the adventures and experiences of characters in familiar stories.

With prompting and support, identify basic similarities in and differences between two texts on the same topic.

Ask and answer questions in order to seek help, get information, or clarify something that is not understood.

LANGUAGE OBJECTIVES

Children will narrate characters' actions in the story, using verbs.

ELA ACADEMIC LANGUAGE

• *problem*

• Cognate: *problema*

MATERIALS

Literature Big Book, *How Do Dinosaurs Go to School?*, pp. 3–33 and 34–37

Visual Vocabulary Cards

DIGITAL TOOLS

Have children listen to the selection as they follow along to develop comprehension.

Use the vocabulary activity for additional support.

How Do Dinosaurs Go to School?

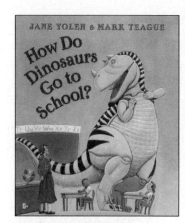

Literature Big Book

Prepare to Read

Build Background *In school, we have to follow rules. What are some school rules?* Model language to talk about rules: *Be quiet in the library. Don't run in the classroom.* Elicit other rules from children that they hear and follow each day at school. Provide sentence frames such as: Raise your _____. Share your _____. _____ nicely on the playground. Don't tease _____. Listen to your _____.

Focus on Vocabulary Use the **Visual Vocabulary Cards** to review the oral vocabulary words *cooperate* and *rules.* As you read, use gestures and other visual support to clarify important story words: *classmate, interrupt, roar.* Review the words in context as you read.

Summarize the Text Before reading, show children the pictures and give a short summary of the story: *This book is called* How Do Dinosaurs Go to School? *Do dinosaurs follow the rules in school? Let's read and find out.*

Read the Text

Use the Interactive Question-Response Routine to help children understand the story.

Pages 4–13

Pages 10–11 Read the text. Point to the bell. *The bell rings when it is time for school to begin.* Make the sound of ringing. Ask a child to point to the stairs. Say, *The dinosaur runs up the stairs. Is it okay to run up stairs at school?* (No) Point to the teacher. *What is the teacher doing?* (looking at her watch) *Why is the dinosaur running? The dinosaur is running because he is* <u>late</u>.

Pages 12–13 Read the text. As you discuss the story, point to the corresponding images. *The girl wants to talk about her bear. But the dinosaur interrupts her. He stops her from talking. What does the dinosaur do?* (He interrupts the girl.) *This makes the girl unhappy. How does the girl feel?* (unhappy) *The dinosaur is not following school rules.*

 The dinosaur does not follow school rules. What does he do that is wrong? Talk with a partner.

Beginning Guide children to point to the dinosaur's action. Tell what is happening, and have children repeat. For example: *The dinosaur runs up the stairs.*

Intermediate Help partners use the illustrations to respond. *The dinosaur does not follow* <u>rules</u>. *He runs* <u>up the stairs</u>. *He interrupts* <u>class/the girl</u>.

Advanced/Advanced High Have children use details from the text and illustrations in their responses. *The dinosaur races* <u>up the stairs</u>. *He interrupts* <u>the girl talking about her bear</u>.

Pages 14–23

Page 18–19 Read the text. *The dinosaur is playing drums. He is making noise. What is the dinosaur doing?* (making noise) *Are the children looking at their work?* (no) *What are they looking at?* (the dinosaur) *The noise makes it hard to learn.*

 Why is it hard for the children to learn? Talk with a partner.

Beginning Have partners point to the illustration as they ask and answer: *What is the dinosaur doing? The dinosaur is making* <u>noise</u>.

Intermediate Have partners ask and answer: *What is the dinosaur doing? The dinosaur is* <u>making noise</u>.

Advanced/Advanced High *What is the problem? The dinosaur is* <u>being loud</u> *so the children* <u>can't learn</u>.

Pages 24–33

Pages 26–27 Read the text. Help children name the images in the illustration and tell what the children are doing. (building with blocks) Point to the dinosaur. *The dinosaur is helping. He is helping his classmate build. Who is the dinosaur helping?* (his classmates)

Pages 30–31 Read the text. Help children name the images. Then say, *The dinosaur tidies his desk. This means he cleans his desk. He cleans his desk before he leaves. What does the dinosaur do before he leaves?* (cleans his desk)

 How are the dinosaurs helping at school? Talk with a partner.

Beginning Help children point to images as they respond. *The dinosaur helps his* <u>classmates</u>.

Intermediate Help partners use illustrations to respond. *The dinosaur helps* <u>his classmates build</u>. *The dinosaur tidies* <u>his desk</u>.

 Retell Use the **Retelling Cards** for *How Do Dinosaurs Go to School?* to retell the story with children. Display the cards. Model telling what the dinosaurs do. Then help children take turns retelling what the dinosaurs are doing and whether or not rules are followed.

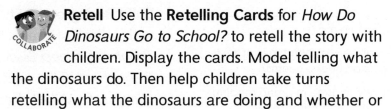

Paired Selection: "Be Safe!"

LESSON 4

Point to each photograph as you talk about rules that help keep you safe. Help children describe what is happening in each photo. If children answer with one word, repeat it back in a complete sentence.

 How can you stay safe when you ride a bike? Discuss with a partner.

Beginning Have children use the pictures as they answer. Example: *What do you see? I see a boy wearing a* <u>helmet</u>.

Intermediate Help children name the two rules discussed on page 36. *First the boy wears a helmet. Then he* <u>stays on the bike path</u>.

Advanced/Advanced High Have children tell why each keeps you safe. *A helmet protects your* <u>head</u>.

FORMATIVE ASSESSMENT

STUDENT CHECK-IN

Main Selection Have partners retell three things that the dinosaur does in the story.

Paired Selection Have partners retell how they can be safe while on the roads.

Then, have children reflect using the Check-in Routine.

 ### Independent Time

Oral Language Have children describe *How Do Dinosaurs Go to School?* and "Be Safe!" Ask: *How are the two texts alike? How are they different?* Use **Oral Language Sentence Frames**, page 1. Guide children to use the sentence frames to talk about the two texts.

LEARNING GOALS

We can actively listen to a fable to learn what it teaches.

OBJECTIVES

Recognize common types of texts (e.g., storybooks, poems).

Actively engage in group reading activities with purpose and understanding.

Ask and answer questions about unknown words in a text.

Speak audibly and express thoughts, feelings, and ideas clearly.

LANGUAGE OBJECTIVES

Children will narrate how the character learns from a poor decision, using verbs and nouns.

ELA ACADEMIC LANGUAGE

• *fable*
• Cognate: *fábula*

MATERIALS

Interactive Read Aloud, "The Boy Who Cried Wolf"

Visual Vocabulary Cards

DIGITAL TOOLS

Have children listen to the selection as they follow along to develop comprehension.

Use the vocabulary activity for additional support.

"The Boy Who Cried Wolf"

Prepare to Read

Interactive Read Aloud

Build Background Show a real photo of a shepherd with a flock of sheep. Point to and name the images *shepherd, sheep.* Discuss what a shepherd does. *This is a shepherd. S/he watches the sheep. S/he keeps the sheep safe. What does a shepherd do? A* shepherd watches the _____. A shepherd keeps the sheep _____. Show an image of a wolf. *A shepherd also looks for wolves. A wolf can hurt or kill the sheep. What does a shepherd look for?* A shepherd looks for _____.

Focus on Vocabulary Use the **Visual Vocabulary Cards** to review the oral vocabulary words *guard, rule, prank, responsible,* and *cooperate.* As you read, use gestures and other visual support to clarify important story words: *village, villagers, counting on, cry out for help, trick, honest.*

Summarize the Text Before reading, show children the pictures and give a short summary of the story: *This story is about a shepherd boy who watches the village sheep. The boy lies about seeing a wolf. He learns it is important to be honest.*

Read the Text

Use the Interactive Question-Response Routine to help children understand the story.

Card 1

Paragraph 1 Read the text. Point to John. *It is John's birthday. He is fifteen years old. He can be a shepherd and guard the sheep.* Point to Uncle Fergus. *Uncle Fergus will teach John how to guard the sheep. What will John do?* (become a shepherd) *Who will teach him?* (Uncle Fergus)

Paragraph 2 Read the text. *Uncle Fergus says that the village is counting on John. This means they need John to do a good job guarding the sheep. What does John need to do?* (guard the sheep)

 How does John feel about becoming a shepherd? Talk to a partner.

Beginning Have children point to John. *Does John look happy?* (yes) *Why is John happy? He can be a* shepherd. *He can guard the* sheep.

Intermediate Point to John. *How does John feel?* (happy) *Why is John happy? He is old enough to be* a shepherd. *Uncle Fergus will teach him to* guard the sheep.

Advanced/Advanced High Have children point to John and Uncle Fergus as they tell how John feels and why: *John feels* happy *because his uncle* will teach him to be a shepherd. *A shepherd's job is to* guard sheep.

Card 2

Paragraphs 1–3 Read the text aloud. *Uncle Fergus tells John two important rules to follow. Rule number one: If you see a wolf, cry out for help. Rule number two: Don't cry wolf unless there is a real wolf. What does Uncle Fergus tell John about?* (two important rules he must follow)

Paragraphs 7–10 Read the text aloud. *The villagers come. But there is no wolf. John laughs about his trick. The villagers don't laugh. Uncle Fergus reminds John about rule number two. Why do the villagers run up the hill?* (Because they think there is a wolf.)

 How does John feel about his trick? Talk to a partner about how he shows his feelings.

Beginning *Does John laugh?* (yes) *Does he think his trick is funny?* (yes)

Intermediate *How does John act when the villagers come? Why? John* <u>laughs</u> *about his trick. John thinks his trick is* <u>funny</u>.

Advanced/Advanced High *How does John act when the villagers come? Why?* (John laughs about his trick because he thinks it is funny.)

Card 3

Paragraph 1 Read the text aloud. *John cries, "Wolf!" again, but there is no wolf. Is there a wolf?* (no)

Paragraphs 6–8 Read the text aloud. *Uncle Fergus is disappointed about what John did. How does Uncle Fergus feel?* (disappointed) *John feels bad. He will not play the prank again. He decides his job is important.*

 Talk to a partner about why John will not play his trick again.

Beginning Have children point to the characters as they answer. *Uncle Fergus is* <u>sad</u>. *This makes John feel* <u>bad</u>. Have children make a sad face.

Intermediate Use the images. *How does Uncle Fergus feel?* (disappointed) *How does this make John feel? John feels* <u>bad</u>. *He will not* <u>play his prank again</u>.

Card 4

Paragraphs 2–5 Read the text aloud. *John sees a wolf. He cries "Wolf" but nobody comes. What does John see?* (a wolf)

Paragraphs 6–7 Read the text aloud. Point to the illustration. *Uncle Fergus sees the wolf. The villagers come and the wolf runs away. The sheep are safe.*

Paragraphs 8–9 Read the text aloud. *John says he has learned he must be honest, or tell the truth. What has John learned? He must* <u>be honest</u>.

 Why didn't the villagers come when John called? Talk to a partner.

Beginning *Did the villagers believe there was a wolf?* (no) *What did John learn? He learned to be* <u>honest</u>.

Intermediate *Did the villagers believe John was telling the truth about the wolf?* (no) *Why not?*

Advanced/Advanced High *Did the villagers believe John was telling the truth about the wolf?* (no) *Why not? He had lied before* <u>about the wolf</u>.

 Retell Use the illustrations on the **Interactive Read-Aloud Cards** to retell the story with children. Display the cards and model retelling using sequence words, such as *first, next, then,* and *last* as you point to the events and actions in the cards. Then help children take turns retelling one part using the sequence words.

FORMATIVE ASSESSMENT

❯ STUDENT CHECK-IN

Have partners retell the lesson that John learned. Then, have children reflect using the Check-in routine.

 ## Independent Time

Role Play Have partners or small groups plan a role play based on one of the cards. Have children practice their role plays before they perform them for the group.

LESSONS 4-5

We can visualize what happens in a fictional story.

OBJECTIVES

With prompting and support, identify characters and events in a story.

Recognize common types of texts (e.g., storybooks, poems).

Describe familiar people, places, things, and events and, with prompting and support, provide additional detail.

Continue a conversation through multiple exchanges.

LANGUAGE OBJECTIVES

Children will discuss how the characters play baseball, using verbs ending in -ing.

ELA ACADEMIC LANGUAGE

• *label, visualize, characters*

• Cognate: *visualizar*

MATERIALS

ELL Leveled Reader: *Go Nat!*

Online Differentiated Text, "We Like Soccer!"

Online ELL Visual Vocabulary Cards

DIGITAL TOOLS

Have children listen to the selection as they follow along to develop comprehension.

Use the vocabulary activity for additional support.

Go, Nat!

Prepare to Read

Build Background Display the cover of *Go, Nat!* and ask children to describe what they see. *Do dogs wear uniforms in real life?* Remind children that this is a *fiction* story. *The events that happen in this story could not happen in real life.* Then discuss the rest of the images with children, helping them name the equipment that you use (ball, bat, glove), where you play (on a field), and what you do (hit the ball, catch the ball, run) in a baseball game. *Have you ever played baseball? _____ , I [have/have not] played baseball.*

Lexile BR

Focus on Vocabulary Use the routine on the **ELL Visual Vocabulary Cards** to preteach *catch* and *tired*. As you read, use images and any labels to clarify important story words.

Read the Text

Use the Interactive Question-Response Routine to help children understand the story.

Pages 2–8

Pages 2–3 Point to the cat. *Who is this?* (a cat) Point to Nat. *Who is this?* (Nat) Guide children to look at the illustrations to find details. *Are they baseball players?* (yes) *Where are they?* (outside) *What is the cat doing?* (hiting a ball) *Nat is trying to catch the ball. What is Nat doing?* (trying to catch the ball)

Main Story Elements: Character Help children identify the characters. Use the illustrations for support: *Nat is one character in this story. Nat is playing baseball with three other characters. Who are the characters?* (mouse, rabbit, cat)

 Tell what is happening. Talk to a partner.

Beginning Have partners point to the images as they repeat details after you: page 2, *This is a bat. This is a ball. The cat is hitting the ball.* Page 3, *This is a glove. Nat wants to catch the ball.*

Intermediate Have partners talk about details as they point to the images: *What is the cat doing? The cat is* hitting the ball. *What is Nat doing? Nat is* catching the ball.

Advanced/Advanced High *What are the players doing? What are they using? The cat is* hitting the ball *with a bat. Nat is* running to catch the ball *with his glove.*

Pages 4–5 Read pages 4-5. Point to Nat. *What is Nat doing?* (trying to catch the ball)

Tell what is happening. Talk to a partner. Have partners describe details that help them **visualize** the story.

Beginning Help partners visualize by providing sentence frames: *The rabbit is hitting* the ball; *Nat wants to catch* the ball.

Intermediate Ask questions to help children visualize. *What is the rabbit doing? The rabbit is* hitting the ball. *What is Nat doing? Nat is trying to* catch the ball. *Does Nat look happy?* (no)

Advanced/Advanced High Encourage children to use complete sentences as they visualize what is happening. Then ask: *Why is Nat worried? Nat thinks he might* not catch the ball.

Pages 6–8 Page 7: *Does Nat catch the ball?* (no) Page 8: *Let's read the sign: "No digging." Nat digs a hole. Is that okay?* (no) *Where does Nat put the ball?* (in the hole)

Point to page 8. Tell what Nat does. Talk to a partner.

Beginning Point to the images. *What does Nat do? Nat digs* a hole. *Nat puts the ball in* the hole.

Intermediate *What does Nat do? Nat digs* a hole. *Nat puts* the ball in the hole. *Why does Nat put the ball in the hole? Model answering. Nat is mad he didn't catch the ball.*

Retell Have partners retell the story. Have them take turns pointing to a picture and describing it to each other.

Focus on Fluency

Read pages 2–8 and have children echo read. For additional practice, have children record themselves reading the same text a few times, and then select their favorite recording to play for you.

Build Knowledge: Make Connections

Talk About the Text Have partners discuss rules they follow while playing.

Write About the Text Have students add their ideas to their Build Knowledge pages of their reader's notebook.

Self-Selected Reading

Help children choose a fiction selection from the online **Leveled Reader Library,** or read the **Differentiated Text,** "We Like Soccer!"

LITERACY ACTIVITIES

Have children complete the Literacy Activities on the inside back cover of the book.

FORMATIVE ASSESSMENT

❯ STUDENT CHECK-IN

Have partners share how the different characters are playing the game. Ask children to visualize the characters hitting and trying to catch the baseball. Then, have children reflect using the Check-in routine.

LEVEL UP

IF children can read *Go, Nat!* **ELL Level** with fluency and correctly answer the questions,

THEN tell children that they will read a more detailed version of the story.

HAVE children page through *Go, Nat!* On Level and describe each picture in simple language.

• Have children read the selection, checking their comprehension and providing assistance as necessary.

MODELED WRITING

LESSON
1

LEARNING GOALS

We can write about how we go to school.

OBJECTIVES

Use dictating and writing to compose informative texts and supply some information about the topic.

LANGUAGE OBJECTIVES

Children will inform by writing a sentence using the phrase *to school.*

ELA ACADEMIC LANGUAGE

• *sentence*

Writing Practice Display the *bus* **Photo Card.** Then read the sample sentence from the **Teacher's Edition,** p. T18. Guide children to analyze the sentence using the Actor/Action routine: *Who is the actor?* (I) *What is the action?* (ride the bus) *Where does the actor ride the bus?* (to school) Next, have children count the words in the sentence. Then read the prompt, and help children respond. Finally, ask children to write their own sentence.

Beginning Provide a sentence frame: I ride in a car to school. *Who is the actor?* (I) *What is the action?* (ride in a car) *Where to?* (school)

Intermediate Have partners ask and answer questions to create their sentences. Provide sentence frames as needed.

Advanced/Advanced High Challenge children to take turns counting the number of words in their sentences.

FORMATIVE ASSESSMENT ❯ ⊗ **STUDENT CHECK-IN** Partners share their sentences. Have children reflect using the Check-in routine.

INTERACTIVE WRITING

LESSON
2

LEARNING GOALS

We can write a new page to a story.

OBJECTIVES

With guidance and support, respond to questions and suggestions from peers.

LANGUAGE OBJECTIVES

Children will narrate by writing a sentence using the word *behaving.*

ELA ACADEMIC LANGUAGE

• *illustration*

• Cognate: *ilustración*

Analyze the Prompt Have children choral read with you the sample sentence on p. T30. *Who is the actor? Who is the sentence about?* (a behaving dinosaur) *What does the actor do?* (likes to take turns) Then guide children in counting the words in the sample sentence. (9) Have children use the illustrations in the **Literature Big Book** to answer the following: *What are we writing about?* (how a behaving dinosaur acts in school) Then help children complete the sentence frames on p. T30.

Beginning Help children generate ideas about how a behaving dinosaur might act in the classroom: *Does a behaving dinosaur raise his hand?* Yes, a behaving dinosaur raises his hand.

Intermediate Have partners take turns asking and answering questions using the sample sentences.

Advanced/Advanced High Have children think of their own sentence about how a dinosaur might behave.

FORMATIVE ASSESSMENT ❯ ⊗ **STUDENT CHECK-IN** Partners share their sentences. Have children reflect using the Check-in routine.

INDEPENDENT WRITING

LEARNING GOALS

We can write about the texts we read.

OBJECTIVES

Use drawing and writing to narrate a single event or several loosely linked events.

LANGUAGE OBJECTIVES

Children will narrate by writing sentences using the verb *play*.

ELA ACADEMIC LANGUAGE

• sentence

Find Text Evidence Use the Independent Writing routine. Help children orally retell the shared read. *What does the girl see?* (a dog, a cat, a fish) *What does she want to do?* (pat the animals) Model patting an animal. *We are going to write a new story using this story as a model.* Read the prompt on p. T40: *Write a new story called "Can I Play With It?"* Point to toys or objects. Each time, ask, *Can I play with it?*

Write to the Prompt Write the sentence starters on the board. Ask a volunteer to retell the prompt in their own words. Model completing the sentence frame, and have children read the response. Repeat with the remaining sentence frames. Once completed, have children copy the sentences into their writer's notebook.

Beginning Have partners create drawings to add details to their stories.

Intermediate Have children tell how they added details: I wrote about <u>how I like to play with a ball</u>.

Advanced/Advanced High Challenge children to come up with their own sentences and talk about ideas and details they used.

FORMATIVE ASSESSMENT ❯ ❯ **STUDENT CHECK-IN** Partners share their sentences. Have children reflect using the Check-in routine.

SELF-SELECTED WRITING

LEARNING GOALS

We can revise our writing.

OBJECTIVES

Capitalize the first word in a sentence and the pronoun *I*.

LANGUAGE OBJECTIVES

Children will inquire about their writing by checking for complete sentences.

ELA ACADEMIC LANGUAGE

• sentence

Work with children to revise the group writing activity. Read the sentences, pointing to each word as you read. Model and ask questions as you read. For example, *What should the sentence begin with? How do you know?* Write an incomplete sentence, and correct the sentence together. Then have children copy the sentences from the group writing activity in their writer's notebook.

For more support with grammar and complete sentences, use the **Language Transfers Handbook** and **Language Development Cards** 21A and 22A.

FORMATIVE ASSESSMENT ❯ ❯ **STUDENT CHECK-IN** Partners tell what revisions they made. Have children reflect using the Check-in routine.

LEARNING GOALS

We can understand important ideas and details in a story.

We can use captions to learn new information.

OBJECTIVES

With prompting and support, describe the relationship between illustrations and the story in which they appear.

With prompting and support, identify basic similarities in and differences between two texts on the same topic.

Actively engage in group reading activities with purpose and understanding.

Speak audibly and express thoughts, feelings, and ideas clearly.

LANGUAGE OBJECTIVES

Children will narrate the happenings in a city, using verbs that end in -ing.

ELA ACADEMIC LANGUAGE

• details, retell
• Cognate: detalles

MATERIALS

Literature Big Book, *Clang! Clang! Beep! Beep! Listen to the City,* pp. 3–32 and 34–39

Visual Vocabulary Cards

DIGITAL TOOLS

Have children listen to the selection as they follow along to develop comprehension.

Use the vocabulary activity for additional support.

Clang! Clang! Beep! Beep! Listen to the City

Literature Big Book

Prepare to Read

Build Background Help children use their prior experiences to understand meanings in English. Display images of a busy city. *You can hear many sounds in a city. What sounds can you hear?* Pointing to an image, model answering the question. *I can hear the bus. I can hear people talking. Tell a partner what you can hear. I can hear _____.* Have partners share ideas.

Focus on Vocabulary Use the **Visual Vocabulary Cards** to review the oral vocabulary words *listen* and *volume.* As you read, use gestures and visual support to clarify important story words: *ringing, ambulance.* Review the words in context as you read.

Summarize the Text Before reading, give a short summary of the story: *A boy lives in the city. It is a noisy place. The boy hears many different sounds.*

Read the Text

Use the Interactive Question-Response Routine to help children understand the story.

Pages 4–15

Pages 6–7 Read the text. Point to images as you talk about them. *It is early in the morning. The boy is still in bed. The alarm clock is ringing. It's very loud. Read the print to make a ringing sound with children. What is ringing?* (the alarm clock) Read the print and make a ringing sound with children.

Pages 10–11 Read the text. Point to the subway. *This is a subway. The boy is riding the subway. It is still early in the morning. Where is the boy?* (on the subway) *The subway makes a roaring noise.* Roar with children. Point to the people. *The riders are making sounds. They are snoring. Some people snore when they sleep. Let's make a snoring sound. What are the riders doing?* (riding the subway; snoring)

 Why are the riders snoring? Talk with a partner.

Beginning Point to the rider in the fifth window from the left. *What is this person doing? She is* <u>sleeping</u>.

Intermediate Have partners ask and answer: *When do people snore? People snore when they are* <u>sleeping</u>.

Advanced/Advanced High *Why are people snoring? They are snoring because* they are sleeping. *Why are people sleeping?* (They are tired.)

Pages 16–25

Page 20–21 Read the text. Point to and say *ambulance. An ambulance drives fast. It takes sick people to the hospital.* Check understanding of *sick* and *hospital. An ambulance has a siren.* Have children point and say *siren. It makes a very loud noise.* Make a siren noise with children. *The noise tells drivers to move out of the way.* Point to and say *driver. What does the siren noise do? It tells drivers to* move.

 Why does a siren make a loud noise? Talk to a partner.

Beginning Have partners act out being the ambulance and a car moving as they say, *The siren tells drivers to move.*

Intermediate *Where is the ambulance going? The ambulance is going to* the hospital. *What does the siren tell drivers to do? The siren tells drivers to* move.

Advanced/Advanced High *Why do other drivers need to hear the siren?* (so they know to move) *Where is the ambulance going?* (The ambulance is going to the hospital.)

Pages 26–33

Pages 28–29 Read the text and point to the illustration. *It is nighttime. The boy is asleep. What is the boy doing?* (sleeping) Point to the moonlight and say, *This is moonlight.* Then point to the alarm clock. *This is the alarm clock. It makes a tick-tock noise. But it is not loud. Is the alarm clock loud now?* (no)

 What is happening on this page? Talk to a partner.

Beginning Help children point to and name images and sounds on the page.

Intermediate Help children answer in complete sentences by providing sentence frames. For example: *The boy* is sleeping. *This is an* alarm clock.

 Retell Use the **Retelling Cards** for *Clang! Clang! Beep! Beep! Listen to the City* to retell the story with children. Display the cards and model retelling using sequence words, such as *first, next, then,* and *last* as you point to the events and actions. Then help children take turns retelling one part using the sequence words.

LESSON 4

Paired Selection: "Sounds are Everywhere"

Pages 34–38 Use a taut string to demonstrate "vibrate." Point to the photos as you read the text. Point to and name the instruments with children repeating after you. Then reread the page and act out with children the actions of playing the instruments.

 Which of the instruments would you like to play? Tell a partner about it.

Beginning *I want to play the _____.* Help point to and name the instrument.

Intermediate Supply sentence frames to help children tell about their instrument. For example: *I want to play the _____. You use _____ to play the _____.*

Advanced/Advanced High Encourage children to speak in complete sentences and point to the images as they tell about their instrument.

FORMATIVE ASSESSMENT

➲ STUDENT CHECK-IN

Main Selection Have partners retell the different kind of city sounds described in the story.

Paired Selection Have partners describe how two instruments from the text are played.

Then, have children reflect using the Check-in routine.

 ### Independent Time

Oral Language *What did you learn about sounds in* Clang! Clang! Beep! Beep! Listen to the City? *How are the sounds different than the sounds in "Sounds are Everywhere"?* Help children answer using images from the two selections.

LEARNING GOALS

We can listen actively to find out how a turtle uses music to escape from a cage.

OBJECTIVES

With prompting and support, retell familiar stories, including key details.

With prompting and support, identify characters and setting in a story.

Ask and answer questions in order to seek help, get information, or clarify something that is not understood.

Describe familiar people, places, things, and events and, with prompting and support, provide additional detail.

LANGUAGE OBJECTIVES

Children will narrate how a character plays a trick on other characters, using key vocabulary.

ELA ACADEMIC LANGUAGE

• folktale

MATERIALS

Interactive Read Aloud,
"The Turtle and the Flute"

Visual Vocabulary Cards

DIGITAL TOOLS

Have children listen to the selection as they follow along to develop comprehension.

Use the vocabulary activity for additional support.

"The Turtle and the Flute"

Prepare to Read

Build Background *We are going to read a folktale from Brazil.* Point to Brazil on a map. *Brazil is a country in South America.* Point out the Amazon River. Show a photo of the jungle. *This is the jungle in Brazil. What kind of animals live in the jungle?* Elicit ideas from children. *What sounds can you hear in the jungle?* Have children share other sounds they hear, using this sentence frame: I hear _____.

Interactive Read Aloud

Focus on Vocabulary Use the **Visual Vocabulary Cards** to review the oral vocabulary words *chat, exclaimed, familiar, listen,* and *volume.* As you read, use gestures and other visual support to clarify important story words: *flute, sway, soup, escape, tricked.*

Summarize the Text *Turtle lives in the jungle. She loves to play the flute and dance. Everyone loves Turtle's music. One day, Turtle's music saves her life.*

Read the Text

Use the Interactive Question-Response Routine to help children understand the story.

Card 1

Paragraphs 2–4 Read the text. Point to and name each animal as you talk about them and model the actions. *Turtle plays the flute. The animals like to listen to Turtle's music. Turtle can dance as she plays. Toad sways to the music. Macaw sings to the music. Tapir whistles to the music.*

 Who likes to listen to Turtle's music? Talk to a partner.

Beginning Help children point to and name the animals on the card.

Intermediate Have partners ask and answer questions about each animal. *What does Macaw/Tapir/Toad like to do? Macaw/Tapir/Toad likes to* listen to Turtle's music.

Advanced/Advanced High *What do the animals do as they listen to Turtle's music?* (Toad sways. Tapir whistles. Macaw sings.)

Card 2

Paragraphs 2–3 Read the text. *Turtle is sleeping with her flute. Where is Turtle's flute?* (with her)

Paragraphs 4–5 Read the text. Point to the illustration. *A man takes Turtle home. He wants to make turtle soup. He puts her in a sturdy, or strong, cage. He doesn't* want Turtle to get out. *Why does the man use a strong cage?* (so Turtle can't get out) Point to the children. *His children see the turtle. The man says, "Don't let the turtle out of the cage." He says he wants to make turtle soup.*

 Why is Turtle in a cage? Talk to a partner.

Beginning *Where is Turtle?* Have children point to and say *The man put Turtle in the cage. He wants to make turtle soup.*

Intermediate *With a partner, ask and answer: Who put Turtle in the cage?* (a man) *Why? The man wants to* make turtle soup.

Advanced/Advanced High *Who put Turtle in the cage?* (the man) *What does he say?* (not to let Turtle out of the cage; they will have turtle soup for dinner)

Card 3

Paragraphs 3–4 Read the text. *Turtle wants to escape, but she can't open the cage. Can Turtle open the cage?* (no) *Turtle has an idea.* Point to Turtle. *She starts playing music. The children listen and sway to the music. What does Turtle do?* (plays music) *What do the children do?* (listen and sway to the music)

Paragraphs 3–4 Read the text. *Turtle tells the children she can dance and play music at the same time. She will show them if they open the cage. The children open the cage.*

 Why do the children open the cage? Talk to a partner.

Beginning Help children answer and point to the open cage: *They want to see Turtle* dance *and* play.

Intermediate *What does Turtle tell the children? If they let her out, she will* dance and play for them.

Advanced/Advanced High Encourage children to use complete sentences as they answer. (She says she will show them how she sings and dances.)

Card 4

Paragraphs 3–4 Read the text. Point to the boy. *The boy plays Turtle's flute.* Point to Turtle. *Turtle crawls away. What does Turtle do as the boy plays?* (crawls away)

Paragraph 5 Read the text. *Turtle crawls around the yard. The children aren't watching Turtle. Turtle crawls into the forest and disappears. Where does Turtle go?* (into the forest)

 How does Turtle escape? Talk to a partner.

Beginning Point to the children. *Do the children see Turtle?* (no) *The children are playing the* flute.

Intermediate *With a partner, ask and answer: What happens first/next/last? First, Turtle* asks *to go for a walk. Then the children* let *Turtle* out *of the cage. Next, the children* play *the flute. They don't* see *Turtle crawling away. Last, Turtle* disappears *into the forest.*

Advanced/Advanced High *Tell a partner how Turtle gets away. Use the words* first, then, *and* next.

 Retell Use the illustrations on the **Interactive Read-Aloud Cards** to retell the story with children. Display the cards and model retelling using sequence words, such as *first, next, then,* and *last* as you point to the events and actions in the cards. Then help children take turns retelling one part using the sequence words.

FORMATIVE ASSESSMENT

❯ STUDENT CHECK-IN

Have partners discuss Turtle's plan for escaping the cage. Then, have children reflect using the Check-in routine.

Independent Time

Oral Language Have partners tell what they see in each picture or ask and answer questions about the pictures. Supply sentence frames as needed.

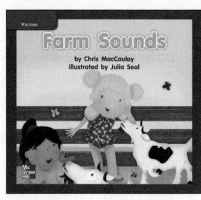

Lexile BR

LEARNING GOALS

We can visualize what happens in a fictional story.

OBJECTIVES

With prompting and support, identify characters and setting in a story.

With prompting and support, retell familiar stories, including key details.

Speak audibly and express thoughts, feelings, and ideas clearly.

Continue a conversation through multiple exchanges.

LANGUAGE OBJECTIVES

Children will discuss the variety of sounds on a farm, using nouns and simple sentences.

ELA ACADEMIC LANGUAGE

• *label, setting*

MATERIALS

ELL Leveled Reader: *Farm Sounds*

Online Differentiated Text, "Zoo Sounds"

Online ELL Visual Vocabulary Cards

DIGITAL TOOLS

Have children listen to the selection as they follow along to develop comprehension.

Use the vocabulary activity for additional support.

Farm Sounds

Prepare to Read

Build Background Show photos of a farm and farm animals, such as cows, pigs, goats, hens, and horses. *This is a farm.* Help children identify each animal. *What are some sounds we can hear on a farm?* Model: *I hear cows. Moo!* As you show each image, make the sound of the animal. Have children repeat.

Focus on Vocabulary Use the routine on the **ELL Visual Vocabulary Cards** to preteach *ear* and *noise.* As you read, use images and any labels to clarify important story words.

Read the Text

Use the Interactive Question-Response Routine to help children understand the story.

Pages 2–8

Pages 2–3 Point to the girls. *Nan and Lin are on a farm. Where are Nan and Lin?* (on a farm) Point to a cow. *What animal is this?* (a cow) *There are two cows. Let's make the sound of a cow: Moo!* Point to the trucks. *What are these?* (trucks) *What sounds do trucks make? Nan and Lin hear the cows. They hear trucks.*

Main Story Elements: Setting Remind children that the setting is where the story takes place. Have children point to the pictures. Ask, *Where are the girls? The girls are on a _____.* (farm)

 What more can you describe about the setting? Talk to a partner.

Beginning Have partners point to the pictures and describe the setting. *There are <u>animals</u> on the farm. People drive <u>trucks</u> on the farm.*

Intermediate Have partners answer questions about the setting: *What time of day is it? It is <u>daytime</u> on the farm.*

Advanced/Advanced High *Describe the details of the setting of this story.* (It is daytime on the farm. There are people, animals, and trucks on the farm.)

Pages 4–5 Point to a hen. *What animal is this?* (a hen) *There are three hens.* Count with children. Read the label: *hens.* Point to a pig. *What animal is this?* (a pig) *There are two pigs. Let's read the label together: pigs. Let's make the sound of a pig: Oink! Oink!*

 What do Nan and Lin hear? Talk to a partner.

Beginning Have partners point to each picture as they tell what the girls hear. *Nan and Lin hear* hens. *Nan and Lin hear* pigs.

Intermediate Have partners ask and answer: *What animals do Lin and Nan hear on pages 4 and 5? They hear* hens *and* pigs.

Advanced/Advanced High *What animals are making noise?* (The hens and the pigs are making noise.)

Pages 6-8 Read pages 6–8. *What do Nan and Lin hear?* (horses, goats, bells) *The woman is ringing the bells. Let's* **visualize***, or picture in our minds, what the bells sound like. Why do you think she is ringing the bell?* (She wants Nan and Lin to hear them.) *What are Nan and Lin doing?* (They are running.) Point to the table. *What is on the table?* (food and drinks)

 What does the sound of the bells mean? Talk to a partner.

Beginning *The bells tell that it is time to eat. What do the bells tell? It is time to* eat. *What is on the table? There is* food *on the table.*

Intermediate Have partners ask and answer: *What do the bells tell Nan and Lin?* (The bells tell Nan and Lin that it is time to eat.)

Advanced/Advanced High Help partners use complete sentences to tell what is happening. Example: *The bells tell that it is time to eat. There is food on the table. The girls come when they hear the bell.*

Retell Have partners retell the story. Have them take turns pointing to a picture and describing it to each other.

Focus on Fluency

Read pages 2–8 and have children echo read. For additional practice, have children record themselves reading the same passage a few times, and then select their favorite recording to play for you.

Build Knowledge: Make Connections

Talk About the Text Have partners discuss sounds they might hear on a farm.

Write About the Text Have students add their ideas to their Build Knowledge pages of their reader's notebooks.

Self-Selected Reading

Have children select another realistic fiction story from the online **Leveled Reader Library,** or read the **Differentiated Text,** "Zoo Sounds."

LITERACY ACTIVITIES

Have children complete the Literacy Activities on the inside back cover of the book.

❯ STUDENT CHECK-IN

Have partners retell the sounds that Nan and Lin hear in the story. Ask children to visualize the sounds. Then, have children reflect using the Check-in routine.

LEVEL UP

IF children can read *Farm Sounds* ELL Level with fluency and correctly answer the questions,

THEN tell children that they will read a more detailed version of the story.

HAVE children page through *Farm Sounds* On Level and describe each picture in simple language.

- Have children read the selection, checking their comprehension and providing assistance as necessary.

MODELED WRITING

LEARNING GOALS

We can write about sounds we hear at school.

OBJECTIVES

Use a combination of dictating and writing to narrate several loosely linked events.

LANGUAGE OBJECTIVES

Children will explain by writing a sentence using the verb *hear*.

ELA ACADEMIC LANGUAGE

• *sentence, capital*

Writing Practice Have children tell what sounds they hear. Then read the sample sentence from the **Teacher's Edition,** p. T100. Have children analyze the sentence using the Actor/Action routine: *Who is the actor?* (I) *What is the action?* (hear children) *What are they doing?* (They are laughing and talking.) Read the prompt, and have children answer. Then have children write their own sentence in their writer's notebook.

Beginning Provide a sentence frame: I will write about <u>the teacher talking at school</u>. *Who is the actor?* (I) *What is the action?* (hear the teacher talking) *Where at?* (school)

Intermediate Have partners create their own sentence. Have them use words from the list in their sentences.

Advanced/Advanced High Have children point out where they capitalized the first word in their sentence.

> FORMATIVE ASSESSMENT

> **STUDENT CHECK-IN** Partners share their sentences. Have children reflect using the Check-in routine.

INTERACTIVE WRITING

LEARNING GOALS

We can write how the words in the art look different from the words in the text.

OBJECTIVES

With guidance and support, add details to strengthen writing as needed.

LANGUAGE OBJECTIVES

Children will explain differences between words by writing complete sentences using the verb *are*.

ELA ACADEMIC LANGUAGE

• *text, sentence, capital*
• Cognate: *texto*

Analyze the Prompt Have children choral read with you the sample sentence on p. T112. *What is this sentence about?* (the words in the art) *What can we say about the words?* (They are different.) Point to the first word in the sample sentence: *What does this sentence start with?* (a capital letter) *What are we writing about?* (the words) *Can I write about the pictures?* (no) Help children complete the sentence frames on p. T112.

Beginning Provide a visual from the **Literature Big Book.** *What color are the words in the text?* The words in the text are <u>black</u>. Ask guiding questions to help partners talk about how the words in the art are different.

Intermediate Have partners complete the sentence frames, pointing to details to show how the words in the art are different from those in the text.

Advanced/Advanced High Have children come up with their own sentences about how the art words are different from the words in the text.

> FORMATIVE ASSESSMENT

> **STUDENT CHECK-IN** Partners explain what sentence they wrote about. Ask children to reflect using the Check-in routine.

INDEPENDENT WRITING

LEARNING GOAL

We can write about the texts we read.

OBJECTIVES

Use a combination of dictating and writing to narrate a single event or several loosely linked events.

LANGUAGE OBJECTIVES

Children will explain by writing sentences using the verb *sounds.*

ELA ACADEMIC LANGUAGE

• *capital letter, period*

Find Text Evidence Use the Independent Writing routine. Ask questions to help children orally retell the shared read. *Who are Nat and Tip?* (a boy and a dog) *Where are Nat and Tip?* (a park) *What do Nat and Tip play with?* (a ball) Then read the prompt on p. T122: *Write about one loud and one soft sound that Nat and Tip hear in the park.* Point to the bird on p. 48 of the **Reading/Writing Companion.** *What sound might Nat and Tip hear?* (a bird chirping) *Do you think that would be a soft sound or a loud sound?* (a soft sound)

Write to the Prompt Write the sentence starters on the board. Model completing the sentence frame, and have children choral read the response. Repeat with the remaining sentence frames. Once completed, ask children to copy the sentences into their writer's notebook.

Beginning Help partners talk about their sentences: My sentence has a capital letter and a period.

Intermediate Help partners tell how they used details from the illustrations: I wrote about the bird in the tree.

Advanced/Advanced High Challenge children to come up with their own sentences.

FORMATIVE ASSESSMENT ❯ ❯ **STUDENT CHECK-IN** Partners share their sentences. Ask children to reflect using the Check-in routine.

SELF-SELECTED WRITING

LEARNING GOALS

We can revise our writing.

OBJECTIVES

Capitalize the first word in a sentence and the pronoun *I.*

LANGUAGE OBJECTIVES

Children will inquire about their writing by checking for complete sentences.

ELA ACADEMIC LANGUAGE

• *sentence*

Work with children to revise the group writing activity. Read the sentences, pointing to each word as you read. Model and ask questions as you read. For example, *What should the sentence begin/end with?* Write an incomplete sentence, and correct it with them. Then have children copy the sentences from the group writing activity in their writer's notebook.

For more support with grammar and sentences, use the **Language Transfers Handbook** and review **Language Development Cards** 21A and 22A.

FORMATIVE ASSESSMENT ❯ ❯ **STUDENT CHECK-IN** Partners tell what revisions they made. Have children reflect using the Check-in routine.

LESSONS
1-2

LEARNING GOALS

LEARNING GOALS

We can understand important ideas and details in a story.

We can use a map to learn new information about the text.

OBJECTIVES

With prompting and support, identify characters, settings, and major events in a story.

With prompting and support, describe the relationship between illustrations and the story in which they appear.

With prompting and support, retell familiar stories, including key details.

Continue a conversation through multiple exchanges.

LANGUAGE OBJECTIVES

Children will narrate the character's thoughts throughout the story, using nouns and verbs.

ELA ACADEMIC LANGUAGE

• *character, details, setting*
• Cognate: *detalles*

MATERIALS

Literature Big Book, *Please Take Me for a Walk*, pp. 2–34 and 36–40
Visual Vocabulary Cards

DIGITAL TOOLS

Have children listen to the selection as they follow along to develop comprehension.

Use the vocabulary activity for additional support.

Please Take Me for a Walk

Prepare to Read

Build Background *We are going to read a story about taking the dog for a walk. Someone who has, or owns, a dog is called the dog's owner. Who usually walks a dog?* Its owner _____ a dog. *What do dogs like to do on a walk?* Have children respond using the sentence frame: Dogs like to _____. *People take their dogs to the park. Where else do people take their dogs?* Show photos of people with their dogs in different places, such as a park, a store, or an outdoor restaurant.

Literature Big Book

Focus on Vocabulary Use the **Visual Vocabulary Cards** to review the oral vocabulary words *neighborhood and routine.* As you read, use gestures and visual support to clarify important story words: *greet, neighbors, pet.* Review the words in context as you read.

Summarize the Text Before reading, give a short summary of the story: *This book is about a dog who wants to go for a walk. He wants to go to different places and meet different people.*

Read the Text

Use the Interactive Question-Response Routine to help children understand the story.

Pages 5–13

Pages 6–7 Read the text. *Who is the main character in this story?* (the dog) Point to page 6. *Where is the dog?* (in the yard) *The dog is chasing the cat. Who is the dog chasing?* (the cat) Point to page 7. *The birds are in their nests. Where are the birds?* (in their nests)

Pages 10–11 Read the text. Point to page 10. *The dog is greeting the postal worker. When you greet, you say hello. The postal worker is waving hello.* Point to page 11. *The neighbor girl is petting the dog. What is the girl doing?* (petting the dog)

  Why does the dog want to go outside? Talk to a partner.

Beginning Guide children to point to an image. Create a sentence frame for the image. For example: *The dog wants to chase* the cat.

Intermediate Have partners use the pictures to respond. *The dog wants to* chase the cat *and* watch the birds. *The dog wants to greet* people on the street.

Advanced/Advanced High Have children ask and answer: *What does the dog want to do on his walk?* (The dog wants to chase the cat and watch the birds.)

Page 14–23

Pages 14–15 Read the text. Point to page 15. Tell or ask what each place is and what it sells. Then say again who works there. Have children repeat after you. Help children tell what each person is giving the dog.

Page 18 Read the text. Tell and point to what the different children are doing and have children repeat.

 What are the children doing in the schoolyard? Talk to a partner.

Beginning Help children point to and name the different objects and activities.

Intermediate Have partners point to details as they respond. *Some children are _____. Other children are _____.* Help with vocabulary as needed.

Advanced/Advanced High Help partners use complete sentences to tell what children are doing.

Pages 24–35

Pages 32–34 Read the text. *Many people are walking their dogs. Who are the dogs looking at?* (the people) *The dog wants everyone to see her and her best friend.*

 Who does the dog want everyone to see? Talk to a partner.

Beginning *The dog is looking at her owner. Her owner is her best <u>friend</u>.*

Intermediate *Who is the dog looking at?* (her owner) *Who is her best friend? The dog's <u>owner</u> is her <u>best</u> <u>friend</u>.*

 Retell Use the **Retelling Cards** for *Please Take Me for a Walk* to retell the story with children. Display the cards and model retelling using sequence words, such as *first, next, then,* and *last* as you point to the events and actions in the cards. Then help children take turns retelling one part using the sequence words.

 Paired Selection: "A Neighborhood"

LESSON 4

Pages 36–40 Point to the map. *This is a map of a neighborhood.* Name the places and have children repeat. Then, point to each photograph as you paraphrase the text. For example. *This is a library. You can listen to stories at a library. You can borrow books from a library. When you borrow something, you must return it.* Ask guiding questions. *Where is this?* (the library) *What are the children doing?* (listening to stories)

 What places are in the neighborhood? Tell your partner about one of the places.

Beginning *What is this place called? This is the _____.* Help children name the details in the photograph.

Intermediate Have partners point to and use details in the photograph as they respond: *I am going to tell about _____. At the _____, you can _____.*

Advanced/Advanced High Guide partners to respond in complete sentences. Provide modeling as needed.

 **FORMATIVE ASSESSMENT**

❯ STUDENT CHECK-IN

Main Selection Have partners retell why the dog wants to go on a walk.

Paired Selection Have partners choose two of the places and describe what you can do at each pleace.

Then, have children reflect using the Check-in Routine.

 Independent Time

Oral Language Have children talk about what they read in *Please Take Me for a Walk* and "A Neighborhood." What places are in Please Take Me for a Walk? *What places are in "A Neighborhood?" What places are in your neighborhood?*

LESSON 3

LEARNING GOALS

We can listen actively to learn about places to visit for field trips.

OBJECTIVES

With prompting and support, ask and answer questions about key details in a text.

With prompting and support, describe the connection between two individuals, events, ideas, or pieces of information in a text.

Ask and answer questions in order to seek help, get information, or clarify something that is not understood.

Speak audibly and express thoughts, feelings, and ideas clearly.

LANGUAGE OBJECTIVES

Children will inquire about different occupations that you might meet on a field trip, using nouns and other key vocabulary.

ELA ACADEMIC LANGUAGE

• *nonfiction, routine*

• Cognates: *no ficción, rutina*

MATERIALS

Interactive Read Aloud, "Field Trips"

Visual Vocabulary Cards

DIGITAL TOOLS

Have children listen to the selection as they follow along to develop comprehension.

Use the vocabulary activity for additional support.

"Field Trips"

Prepare to Read

Build Background *We are going to read a text about field trips. On a field trip, you visit an important place in your community.* Display photos of a state park, an aquarium, a fire station, and a post office. *Here are some places you can visit on a field trip.* Help children name each place. Discuss what you can do and see at each place with the following sentence frame: You can _____ in/at _____. Tell children this is a *nonfiction text. A nonfiction text gives facts, or information, about a topic.*

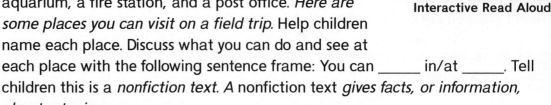

Interactive Read Aloud

Vocabulary Use the **Visual Vocabulary Cards** to review the oral vocabulary words *local, routine, intelligent, volunteer,* and *neighborhood.* As you read, use gestures and other visual support to clarify important selection words: *field trip, community, aquarium, emergency* and *mail.*

Summarize the Text Before reading, give a short summary of the story: *This text is about taking field trips to places in your community.*

Read the Text

Use the Interactive Question-Response Routine to help children understand the text.

Card 1

Paragraph 1 Read the text. *Field trips are fun trips to special places in your community. You take field trips with your class. You can learn about different places on field trips. What is a field trip?* (a trip to a special place in your community)

Paragraph 2 Read the text. Point to the photo. *This is a state park.* Point to the ranger. *This man is a ranger. Rangers work outdoors. This means they work outside. They know a lot about plants and animals. What do rangers know?* (a lot about plants and animals)

 What can you learn on field trips? Talk to a partner.

Beginning *Can you learn about different places on field trips?* (yes) *What is a place you can go on a field trip?* (zoo, state park, museum, etc.)

Intermediate *Name something you can learn on a field trip to a state park. You can learn about* plants and animals.

Advanced/Advanced High Help children respond. *On field trips, you can learn about* different places in your community. *A place you can learn about is _____.*

Card 2

Paragraph 2 Read the text. Point to the photo. *This is a sea otter. Where is the otter?* (in the water) *You can learn about plants and animals that live in the water at an aquarium. What can you learn at an aquarium? You can learn about plants and animals that live in* the water.

Paragraph 4 Read the text. *Aquarium workers work at the aquarium. They can show you how they take care of the animal.*

 What can you learn at an aquarium? Talk to a partner.

Beginning Have children point to the water and repeat after you: *I can learn about plants and animals that live in the water.*

Intermediate Help children respond. *You can learn about* plants and animals that live in the water. *You can also learn how to take care of* the animals.

Advanced/Advanced High Help children respond in complete sentences. Then ask them to tell what animals you might find in an aquarium.

Card 3

Paragraphs 1–3 Read the text. Point to the man in the photo. *This is a firefighter. Firefighters put out fires.* Point to and name the fire hose and fire truck. Have children repeat.

Paragraphs 4 Read the text. *Firefighters can help in an emergency. An emergency is when you need help right away. A fire can be an emergency.*

 How do firefighters keep the community safe? Talk to a partner.

Beginning With a partner, ask and answer: *What do firefighters do? Firefighters put out* fires.

Intermediate With a partner, ask and answer: *What do you know about firefighters? They* fight fires/use hoses.

Advanced/Advanced High With a partner, ask and answer: *How do firefighters keep people safe?* (Firefighters keep people safe by fighting fires.) Encourage children to add details to their answers.

Card 4

Paragraphs 1–2 Read the text. Point to the photo. *This man works at the post office. He is a post office worker. These are letters. This is the mail. On a field trip at the post office you can learn about the mail. You can learn how the mail goes from place to another. There are many things that happen before the mail is delivered, or brought, to your house.*

 What can you learn at a post office? Talk to a partner.

Beginning Have children point the photo. *At a post office you can learn about the* mail.

Intermediate *At a post office you can learn how the mail goes from* one place to another. *You can learn how the mail is delivered to* your house.

Advanced/Advanced High Have children respond in complete sentences. Then have them tell a question they would like to ask a post office worker.

 Retell Use the photos on the **Interactive Read-Aloud Cards** to retell key details from "Field Trips." Guide children to take turns retelling what they learned about field trips.

FORMATIVE ASSESSMENT

> **STUDENT CHECK-IN**

Have partners retell the reponsibilities of different occupations in the text. Then, have children do the Check-In routine.

Independent Time

Plan and Present Have children ask and answer questions: *What places do you go during the week?* Ask children to draw one place. Have partners share and tell about their drawings: I go to the library. I go to _____. I can _____ there.

LESSONS 4-5

We can visualize what happens in a fictional story.

OBJECTIVES

With prompting and support, identify characters and setting in a story.

Recognize common types of texts (e.g., storybooks, poems).

With prompting and support, retell familiar stories, including key details.

LANGUAGE OBJECTIVES

Children will discuss a variety of places where a cab can travel, using place names.

ELA ACADEMIC LANGUAGE

• *realistic fiction, character, setting*
• Cognate: *ficción realista*

MATERIALS

ELL Leveled Reader: *Going by Cab*

Online Differentiated Text, "We Go and Go!"

Online ELL Visual Vocabulary Cards

DIGITAL TOOLS

MULTIMODAL

Have children listen to the selection as they follow along to develop comprehension.

Use the vocabulary activity for additional support.

Going by Cab

Lexile BR

Prepare to Read

Build Background Show photos of taxis. Tell children that the words *taxi* and *cab* mean the same thing. *You pay the driver to take you somewhere.* Point out the sign on the top of the cab. *This sign tells you that the car is a taxi. Have you ever ridden in a cab? Where did you go?*

Focus on Vocabulary Use the routine on the **ELL Visual Vocabulary Cards** to preteach *fare* and *traffic*. As you read, use images and any labels to clarify important story words.

Read the Text

Use the Interactive Question-Response Routine to help children understand the story.

Pages 2–8

Pages 2-3 Read the pages with children. Have them describe the images. Elicit responses as you point to the pictures. *Where is the family going?* (store, beach) *How does the family travel?* (They go by cab.)

Main Story Elements: Characters Have children describe the characters. *This story is mostly about a family. Who are the characters?* (the family members) *What do they do?* (They go to places.)

 Where do the cabs go? Talk to a partner.

Beginning Point to the cab on page 2. *Where is the cab? The cab is at the* store. Repeat routine for page 3.

Intermediate Have partners point to the pages as they ask and answer: *Where do cabs go? They go to* a store. *Where do cabs go? They go to* the beach.

Advanced/Advanced High Have partners tell the places the cab goes and then describe details in the illustrations. Provide modeling. *The cab goes to the store. The woman is carrying a bags.*

Pages 4–5 Read the text with children. *Where is the cab?* (at the zoo) *Where does the cab go?* (to the park) *Read the label* park. Point to the ramp. *This cab is special. It has a ramp. How does the boy get out of the cab? He uses the* ramp.

 Where do the cabs go? Talk to a partner.

Beginning Point to the rebus on page 4. *Where is the cab? The cab is at the* zoo. Repeat routine for page 5.

Intermediate Have partners point to the pages as they answer. *They go to* the zoo. *They go to* the park. *What is in the park?* Help children name what they see.

Advanced/Advanced High Have partners tell the places the cab goes and then describe details in the illustrations. Provide modeling.

Pages 6-8 Read the pages with children. *Where does the family go?* (They go to the vet/see a movie/see a baseball game)

Visualize Help children visualize what is happens at each places. *A vet takes care of sick animals. The family has a sick cat. What can the vet do?* (make the cat well) Repeat the routine with the other pages.

 Where do the cabs go? Talk to a partner.

Beginning *Point to the cab on page 6. Where does this cab go? This cab goes to the* vet. Repeat routine for pages 7 and 8.

Intermediate Have partners point to the pages as they answer. *Cabs take sick animals to* the vet. *Cabs take people to* the movies. *Cabs take people to the* game.

Advanced/Advanced High Have partners tell the places the cab goes and then describe details in the illustrations. Provide modeling.

Retell Have partners retell the story. Have them take turns pointing to a picture and describing it to each other.

Focus on Fluency

Read pages 2–8 and have children echo read. For additional practice, have children record themselves reading the same passage a few times, and then select their favorite recording to play for you.

Build Knowledge: Make Connections

Talk About the Text Have partners discuss the places they go.

Write About the Text Have students add their ideas to their Build Knowledge pages of their reader's notebooks.

Self-Selected Reading

Have children select another realistic fiction story from the online **Leveled Reader Library,** or read the **Differentiated Text,** "We Go and Go!"

FORMATIVE ASSESSMENT

◉ STUDENT CHECK-IN

Have partners retell the places where the cab goes. Ask children to visualize what happens at each place. Then, have children reflect using the Check-in routine.

IF children can read *Going by Cab* **ELL Level** with fluency and correctly answer the questions,

THEN tell children that they will read a more detailed version of the story.

HAVE children page through *Going by Cab* On Level and describe each picture in simple language.

• Have children read the selection, checking their comprehension and providing assistance as necessary.

MODELED WRITING

LEARNING GOALS

We can write about our favorite pet.

OBJECTIVES

Use dictating and writing to compose informative texts and supply some information about the topic.

LANGUAGE OBJECTIVES

Children will inform by writing a sentence using the phrase *like best.*

ELA ACADEMIC LANGUAGE

• *sentence*

Writing Practice Display the *dog, fish,* and *kitten* **Photo Cards.** Then read the sample sentence from the **Teacher's Edition,** p. T182. *What is this sentence about?* (the pet I like best) *What pet does the speaker like best?* (my cat) Then read the prompt at the bottom of the page, and ask a volunteer to answer it. Write the sentence on the board, and point to each word as children choral read. Then ask children to write their own sentence.

Beginning Provide a sentence frame: I will write about a dog. Provide vocabulary support as children think of their sentence.

Intermediate Have partners ask *who/what* questions to create their sentence. Provide a sentence frame to help them talk about why they chose the pet: I will write about a dog because they are fun to play with.

Advanced/Advanced High Have children talk about their sentence using the Actor/Action routine. Encourage them to share it with the group.

FORMATIVE ASSESSMENT ❯ ⊙ **STUDENT CHECK-IN** Partners share their sentence. Ask children to reflect using the Check-in routine.

INTERACTIVE WRITING

LEARNING GOALS

We can write about why the author repeated a phrase.

OBJECTIVES

Use a combination of dictating and writing to narrate several loosely linked events.

LANGUAGE OBJECTIVES

Children will explain by writing a sentence using the verb *wants.*

ELA ACADEMIC LANGUAGE

• *sentence, clues*

Analyze the Prompt Have children choral read with you the sample sentence on p. T194. Use the Actor/Action routine to review it: *Who is the actor?* (the dog) *What is the action?* (wants/likes to go many places) Have children point to and name the end mark on the sentence. (period) *Let's look at the ideas from the story. What do the words say?* (please take me for a walk) *What do the illustrations show?* (all the things the dog wants to do) Help children complete the sentence frames at the bottom of p. T194.

Beginning Help partners orally complete the sentences by providing a visual from the book: The dog wants to go for a walk. *What does the dog like to do? What do you see?* The dog likes to chase the cat.

Intermediate Have partners support their sentences by pointing to details in the illustrations that show what the dog likes to do.

Advanced/Advanced High Challenge children to think of their own sentence to tell why the author repeats the phrase.

FORMATIVE ASSESSMENT ❯ ⊙ **STUDENT CHECK-IN** Partners share their sentences. Ask children to reflect using the Check-in routine.

INDEPENDENT WRITING

LEARNING GOALS

We can write about the texts we read.

OBJECTIVES

Use a combination of dictating and writing to narrate several loosely linked events.

LANGUAGE OBJECTIVES

Children will narrate by writing sentences using clues from the story.

ELA ACADEMIC LANGUAGE

• *clues, punctuation*

• Cognate: *puntuación*

Find Text Evidence Use the Independent Writing routine. Ask questions to help children orally retell the shared read. *Who is in the story?* (Cam and her brother) *Where do they go?* (to a bookstore) *Who do they see?* (Nan and the cat) Then read the prompt on p. T204: *What did Cam and her brother do at the bookshop?* Display pp. 76 and 79 of the **Reading/Writing Companion.** Let's find clues in the story. *What does Cam do?* (pats the cat) *What does her brother do?* (sits with the cat)

Write to the Prompt Write the sentence starters on the board. Model completing the first sentence frame, and have children choral read. Repeat with the remaining sentence frames. Once completed, ask children to copy the sentences into their writer's notebook.

Beginning Have partners identify and name the punctuation, or end marks, in their sentences: I ended my sentence with a period.

Intermediate Have partners tell how they used details from the story to write sentences: I wrote about how Cam and her brother look at the book.

Advanced/Advanced High Challenge children to come up with their own sentences that include details from the text and illustrations.

FORMATIVE ASSESSMENT ❯ **STUDENT CHECK-IN** Partners share their sentences. Ask children to reflect using the Check-in routine.

SELF-SELECTED WRITING

LEARNING GOALS

We can revise our writing.

OBJECTIVES

Recognize and name end punctuation.

LANGUAGE OBJECTIVES

Children will inquire about their writing by checking for complete sentences.

ELA ACADEMIC LANGUAGE

• *sentence*

Work with children to revise the group writing activity. Read the sentences, pointing to each word as you read. Model and ask questions as you read. For example, *What should the sentence begin/end with?* Write a sentence that does not begin with a capital letter or an end mark, and correct it with the children. Then have them copy the sentences from the group writing activity in their writer's notebook.

For more support with grammar and sentences, use the **Language Transfers Handbook** and review **Language Development Cards** 21A and 22A.

FORMATIVE ASSESSMENT ❯ **STUDENT CHECK-IN** Partners tell what revisions they made. Ask children to reflect using the Check-in routine.

Summative Assessment
Get Ready for Unit Assessment

UNIT 3

Unit 3 Tested Skills

LISTENING AND READING COMPREHENSION	VOCABULARY	GRAMMAR	SPEAKING AND WRITING
• Listening Actively • Text Structure • Details	• Words and Categories	• Sentences	• Offering Opinions • Presenting • Composing/Writing • Retelling/Recounting

---

Create a Student Profile

Record data from the following resources in the Student Profile charts on pages 136–137 of the Assessment book.

COLLABORATIVE	INTERPRETIVE	PRODUCTIVE

• Collaborative Conversations Rubrics
  • Listening
  • Speaking
	• Leveled Unit Assessment
	  • Listening Comprehension
	  • Reading Comprehension
	  • Vocabulary
	  • Grammar
	• Presentation Rubric
	  • Listening
	• *Wonders* Unit Assessment
		• Weekly Progress Monitoring
		• Leveled Unit Assessment
		  • Speaking
		  • Writing
		• Presentation Rubric
		  • Speaking
		• Write to Sources Rubric
		• *Wonders* Unit Assessment

The Foundational Skills Kit, Language Development Kit, and Adaptive Learning provide additional student data for progress monitoring.

Level Up

Use the following chart, along with your Student Profiles, to guide your Level Up decisions.

LEVEL UP	If **BEGINNING** level students are able to do the following, they may be ready to move to the **INTERMEDIATE** level:	If **INTERMEDIATE** level students are able to do the following, they may be ready to move to the **ADVANCED** level:	If **ADVANCED** level students are able to do the following, they may be ready to move to **ON** level:
COLLABORATIVE	• participate in collaborative conversations using basic vocabulary and grammar and simple phrases or sentences • discuss simple pictorial or text prompts	• participate in collaborative conversations using appropriate words and phrases and complete sentences • use limited academic vocabulary across and within disciplines	• participate in collaborative conversations using more sophisticated vocabulary and correct grammar • communicate effectively across a wide range of language demands in social and academic contexts
INTERPRETIVE	• identify details in simple read alouds • understand common vocabulary and idioms and interpret language related to familiar social, school, and academic topics • make simple inferences and make simple comparisons • exhibit an emerging receptive control of lexical, syntactic, phonological, and discourse features	• identify main ideas and/or make some inferences from simple read alouds • use context clues to identify word meanings and interpret basic vocabulary and idioms • compare, contrast, summarize, and relate text to graphic organizers • exhibit a limited range of receptive control of lexical, syntactic, phonological, and discourse features when addressing new or familiar topics	• determine main ideas in read alouds that have advanced vocabulary • use context clues to determine meaning, understand multiple-meaning words, and recognize synonyms of social and academic vocabulary • analyze information, make sophisticated inferences, and explain their reasoning • command a high degree of receptive control of lexical, syntactic, phonological, and discourse features
PRODUCTIVE	• express ideas and opinions with basic vocabulary and grammar and simple phrases or sentences • restate information or retell a story using basic vocabulary • exhibit an emerging productive control of lexical, syntactic, phonological, and discourse features	• produce coherent language with limited elaboration or detail • restate information or retell a story using mostly accurate, although limited, vocabulary • exhibit a limited range of productive control of lexical, syntactic, phonological, and discourse features when addressing new or familiar topics	• produce sentences with more sophisticated vocabulary and correct grammar • restate information or retell a story using extensive and accurate vocabulary and grammar • tailor language to a particular purpose and audience • command a high degree of productive control of lexical, syntactic, phonological, and discourse features

OBJECTIVES

With prompting and support, describe the connection between two individuals, events, ideas, or pieces of information in a text.

With prompting and support, identify basic similarities in and differences between two texts on the same topic.

Actively engage in group reading activities with purpose and understanding.

Describe familiar people, places, things, and events and, with prompting and support, provide additional detail.

LANGUAGE OBJECTIVES

Children will inform about how different workers use different shoes and tools, using nouns.

ELA ACADEMIC LANGUAGE

• nonfiction

• Cognate: *no ficción*

MATERIALS

Literature Big Book, *Whose Shoes?*, pp. 3–31 and 32–36

Visual Vocabulary Cards

DIGITAL TOOLS

Have children listen to the selection as they follow along to develop comprehension.

Use the vocabulary activity for additional support.

Whose Shoes?

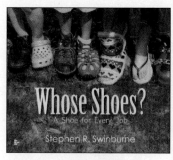

Literature Big Book

Prepare to Read

Build Background *Show me your shoes. What do your shoes help you do?* Elicit responses from children: My shoes help me ____. *We're going to read a book about shoes. It is nonfiction. The author teaches about shoes. We will see shoes and ask, "Whose shoes?" We learn who wears the shoes.*

Focus on Vocabulary Use the **Visual Vocabulary Cards** to review the oral vocabulary words *equipment* and *uniform*. As you read, use gestures and other visual support to clarify important selection words: *whose, favorite, boots, wear, safe, clean,* and *job*. Review the words in context as you read.

Summarize the Text Before reading, give a short summary of the selection: *This book helps you learn about the different shoes people wear for their jobs.*

Read the Text

Use the Interactive Question-Response Routine to help children understand the text.

Pages 5–12

Page 5 Read the text. *The people in the photo wear shoes. The shoes are the same kind. The shoes are not the same color. Are the shoes the same color?* (no)

Pages 6–7 Read the text. Point to the feet. *Do the people in this photo wear shoes?* (no) Point to the shoes on the baby. *What words tell about a baby's shoes?* (soft and small)

Pages 8–9 Read the text. Point to the boots. *Boots keep feet warm in the cold and snow. When do you wear boots?* (when it is cold outside) Have children point to the flip-flops. *When do you wear flip-flops?* (when it is hot outside)

Pages 10–11 Read the text. Point to the boy in the water. *The shoes he likes most are blue. The girl's favorite shoes are silver.*

 Why do children wear boots? When do they wear flip-flops? Discuss with a partner.

Beginning Have children say after you: *Boots keep you warm in snow and cold.*

Intermediate Have partners respond using sentence frames: *Children wear flip-flops* when it is hot. *The boy wears boots to keep his feet* warm in the snow.

Advanced/Advanced High Guide children to describe the photos of children wearing boots or flip-flops. Provide additional modeling as needed.

Pages 13–24

Page 15–16 Read page 15. Help children guess that the picture shows a farm using picture clues. Read page 16. *Who wears the shoes?* (a farmer) *A farmer needs to wear the boots to work outside on a farm. Where does the farmer wear the shoes?* (on a farm)

Page 23–24 Read the text on page 23. Discuss picture clues with children. Read page 24. *Who wears the shoes?* (a construction worker) Help children understand that people wear "work boots" when they work on building sites with heavy materials and powerful equipment.

 Why does a construction worker wear work boots? Talk with a partner.

Beginning Guide children to point to and name the construction worker and the work boots. Have them repeat after you: *The boots keep the man's feet safe.*

Intermediate Guide children to point to details as they respond: *The* construction worker *helps build buildings. The boots keep him* safe and clean.

Pages 25–31

Page 25–26 Read page 25. Discuss picture clues with children, such as the postal bag for mail. Read page 26. *Who wears the shoes?* (a post office worker) Explain how a post office worker helps people send letters and packages.

Page 29–30 Read page 29 and discuss the picture clues. Point out the fun bright colors and funny shoes. Read page 30. *Who wears the shoes?* (a clown) *What do clowns do?* (make people laugh) Confirm understanding of how clowns entertain people.

 How are the shoes of a post office worker and clown different? Talk with a partner.

Intermediate Guide children to tell why a clown's shoes are colorful and a funny shape. Provide sentence frames: *The clown* makes people laugh.

Advanced/Advanced High Guide children to explain how the shoes are worn for different purposes.

(Sample: She is a post office worker. She does not wear a costume to make people laugh.)

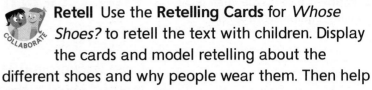 **Retell** Use the **Retelling Cards** for *Whose Shoes?* to retell the text with children. Display the cards and model retelling about the different shoes and why people wear them. Then help children take turns retelling details about what they learned about the jobs.

 LESSON 4 Paired Selection: "Workers and Their Tools"

Pages 32–36 Point to the photos as you paraphrase the text or read the captions. Help children point at the photos as they answer questions. For example: *A chef cooks food. A chef chops with a knife. A chef cooks food in a frying pan. What does a chef do?* (cooks food) *What does a chef use to chop?* (knife)

 What tools do firefighters use? Talk with a partner.

Beginning Help children say the tools after you.

Intermediate Have children respond: *Firefighters use* hoses; boots; an ax; helmets.

Advanced/Advanced High Guide children to explain what tools firefighters wear and what tools they carry on their truck.

FORMATIVE ASSESSMENT

› STUDENT CHECK-IN

Main Selection Have partners retell why certain jobs need special shoes.

Paired Selection Have partners discuss how different workers use different tools.

Then, have children reflect using the Check-in routine.

 Independent Time

Oral Language Have children describe what they learned in *Whose Shoes?* and "Workers and Their Tools." Ask: *What jobs did you learn about* Help them respond using: I learned a _____ uses _____.

LESSON 3

We can listen actively to understand what happens after Little Juan picks up cooking equipment from his grandmother's house.

OBJECTIVES

With prompting and support, ask and answer questions about key details in a text.

With prompting and support, retell familiar stories, including key details.

Confirm understanding of a text read aloud or information presented orally or through other media by asking and answering questions about key details and requesting clarification if something is not understood.

LANGUAGE OBJECTIVES

Children will narrate the character's task and ideas, using key vocabulary and simple sentences.

ELA ACADEMIC LANGUAGE

• *details*
• Cognate: *detalles*

MATERIALS

Interactive Read Aloud,
"Little Juan and the Cooking Pot"

Visual Vocabulary Cards

DIGITAL TOOLS

Have children listen to the selection as they follow along to develop comprehension.

Use the vocabulary activity for additional support.

"Little Juan and the Cooking Pot"

Prepare to Read

Interactive Read Aloud

Build Background Have children discuss what they learned about a chef's job in "Whose Shoes?" and "Workers and Their Tools." Use sentence frames to elicit responses. A chef _____ food. A chef uses a _____ to make food. If possible, show visuals of people cooking with pots, pans, and other cooking utensils. Then help children name meals they eat.

Focus on Vocabulary Use the **Visual Vocabulary Cards** to review the oral vocabulary words *equipment, expect, remained, uniform,* and *utensils* using the **Visual Vocabulary Cards**. As you read, use gestures and other visual support to clarify important story words: *stew, dinner, borrow, sighed, frowned, variety, legs* (of the pot), *burst, beat me home, collected.*

Summarize the Text Give a short summary of the selection: *The story is about a boy named Little Juan. He needs to bring a cooking pot home to his mother. She needs the pot to cook dinner. The pot is very heavy and dinner will be very late.*

Read the Text

Use the Interactive Question-Response Routine to help children understand the story.

Card 1

Paragraphs 1–3 Read the text. *Little Juan likes to play. He does not like to work. Point to Little Juan. What is he doing?* (playing ball) *Mama needs a pot to cook a stew for dinner. She asks him to get a pot from his grandmother. What does Mama need?* (a pot)

Paragraphs 4–6 Read the text. *Little Juan frowns.* Demonstrate frowning. *He does not want to stop playing. He says, "Oh, all right." This means he will go, but he does not want to. What does Little Juan say?* (Oh, all right.)

 What does Mama ask Little Juan to do? How does he feel about it? Discuss with a partner.

Beginning Ask guiding questions to help children respond: *What does Mama need?* (a pot) *Does Little Juan want to go?* (no)

Intermediate Provide sentence frames to help children respond: *Mama asks Little Juan to borrow a* <u>pot</u> *from* <u>his grandmother</u>. *Mama needs the pot to* <u>cook dinner</u>.

Advanced/Advanced High Have partners describe details that show how Little Juan feels. (Little Juan frowns and walks slowly because he wants to play ball.)

Card 2

Paragraphs 1–2 Read the text. *Little Juan loves Abuela Carmen's kitchen. She is wearing her apron and chef's hat. She is cooking. Her house smells like the delicious food that she cooks. How does Abuela Carmen's house smell?* (delicious)

Paragraphs 3–6 Read the text. *Abuela Carmen gives Little Juan the pot. She puts utensils in it.* Have children point to the characters. Name the different utensils. *The pot is very big and heavy. Little Juan says he can carry the pot to his house. What does Little Juan have to carry?* (a heavy pot with utensils)

 Why does Abuela worry about Little Juan carrying the pot? Talk with a partner.

Beginning Act out carrying something heavy and ask children to repeat: *The pot is big and heavy.*

Intermediate Provide sentence frames to help children respond: *The pot is* big and heavy.

Card 3

Paragraphs 1–5 Read the text. *Little Juan gets tired. He puts the pot down.* Show the legs of the pot on Card 4. *Little Juan knows the pot cannot walk. Remember, Little Juan likes to play. Little Juan tells the pot to carry him home on its three legs. What does Little Juan like to do?* (play) *What does he tell the pot?* (He tells the pot to carry him home.)

Paragraphs 6–8 Read the text. *Little Juan gets an idea. He tells the pot to race him home. Little Juan runs fast. What does he tell the pot?* (He tells the pot to race him home.)

 Why does Little Juan say he knows he will win the race? Discuss with a partner.

Intermediate Provide sentence frames to help children make an inference: *Little Juan likes to* play. *He does not like to* work. *He knows* the pot will not race him home.

Advanced/Advanced High Help children infer why Little Juan tells the pot to race him home.

Card 4

Paragraphs 1–5 Read the text. *Little Juan gets home and tells Mama about the race. She says he cannot race a pot like a real boy.*

Paragraphs 6–9 Read the text. *Little Juan says he is sorry. He is also hungry.* Point to Mama. *She holds Little Juan's hand. They go get the pot and bring it home. Dinner will be very late. Who gets the pot?* (Mama and Little Juan)

 Why does Mama say dinner is going to be late? Talk with a partner.

Beginning Help children complete the sentences: *Little Juan and Mama go get* the pot. *Dinner is going to be* late.

Intermediate Provide sentence frames: *Little Juan did not* bring the pot home. *Dinner will be* late *because he and Mama have to* get the pot.

 Retell Use the illustrations on the **Interactive Read-Aloud Cards** to retell the story with children. Display the cards and model retelling using sequence words, such as *first, next, then,* and *last* as you point to the events and actions in the cards. Then help children take turns retelling events using the sequence words.

FORMATIVE ASSESSMENT

⊗ STUDENT CHECK-IN

Have partners retell how Little Juan was confused about the pot's abilities. Then, have children reflect using the Check-in routine.

Independent Time

Picture Glossary Ask children to create a picture glossary of things people use to cook. Remind them to use the illustrations on the cards to help them with ideas of cooking utensils to include.

LESSONS 4-5

We can ask and answer questions about what happens in a nonfiction text.

OBJECTIVES

With prompting and support, identify the main topic and retell key details of a text.

Ask and answer questions to help determine or clarify the meaning of words and phrases in a text.

Speak audibly and express thoughts, feelings, and ideas clearly.

Describe familiar people, places, things, and events and, with prompting and support, provide additional detail.

LANGUAGE OBJECTIVES

Children will inquire about different jobs, using completes sentences.

ELA ACADEMIC LANGUAGE

• *comprehension, respond, topic*
• Cognates: *comprensión, responder*

MATERIALS

ELL Leveled Reader: *On the Job*

Online Differentiated Text, "The Chef"

Online ELL Visual Vocabulary Cards

DIGITAL TOOLS

Have children listen to the selection as they follow along to develop comprehension.

Use the vocabulary activity for additional support.

On the Job

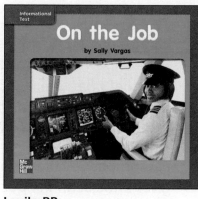

Lexile BR

Prepare to Read

Build Background *You learned about work. You will learn more about what people do at work in this book.* Show **Photo Card** 29 for bus. *What is this? This is a _____. A bus driver works on a bus.* As time allows, use a similar process for *horse, bike,* and *train.* Elicit the name of the Photo Card and model language.

Focus on Vocabulary Use the routine on the **ELL Visual Vocabulary Cards** to preteach *work* and *machine.* As you read, use images and any labels to clarify important selection words, such as *ladder.*

Read the Text

Use the Interactive Question-Response Routine to help children understand the text.

Pages 2-8

Pages 2-3 Read the pages with children. *The author says, "You work on a bus."* Have children point to the horse and cowboy on page 3. *The author says, "You work on a horse."* Where does a cowboy work? (on a horse)

Ask and Answer Questions Have children ask and answer questions about jobs as they read. Model how to ask and answer questions: *Who works on a bus?*

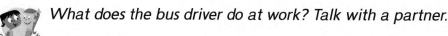 *What does the bus driver do at work? Talk with a partner.*

Beginning Help children ask and answer questions. Ask: *Does the bus driver take the girl to school?* Help children answer: *Yes, the bus driver takes the girl to school.*

Intermediate Have children complete the sentences: *The bus driver works on a bus. The bus driver takes kids home from school.*

Advanced/Advanced High Guide partners to talk about a bus driver's job. Provide additional modeling as needed. (Where does the bus driver drive the kids? She drives the kids to school. After school, she drives kids home.)

Pages 4-5 Point to the man. *The man works on a boat. He catches fish. He is a fisherman. Who works on a boat?* (fisherman) Repeat for page 5.

Topic and Details *The photo gives details about the text.* Point to the man. *The man works on a boat. He catches fish. He is a fisherman.* Have children point to the pilot on page 5. *Where does the pilot work?* (on a plane) *She flies a plane. People travel, or go to places, on planes.*

What does the pilot do at work? Talk with a partner.

Beginning Have children point to the pilot and complete the sentences: *The pilot works on a* plane. *She* flies *the plane.*

Intermediate Have partners ask and answer: *Why does a pilot work on a plane? People* travel *on the plane. What is the topic? The topic is different* jobs *people* have/do.

Pages 6–8 Help children use the photo to find details about the police officer, painter, and train conductor. For example: *I see a police officer. He works on a bike. What does the police officer work on?* (a bike)

Why does the painter need a ladder? Talk with a partner.

Beginning Have children point to the man on the ladder. Help them complete the sentences: *A painter works on a* ladder. *The painter needs to paint the* house.

Intermediate Use sentence frames to help partners respond: *A painter uses a* ladder *to* paint the house.

Advanced/Advanced High Encourage partners to describe in detail where the painter is working. (Sample answer: The painter needs a ladder to paint high up.)

Retell Have partners retell the text. Have them take turns pointing to a picture and describing it to each other.

Focus on Fluency

Read pages 2–5 and have children echo read. For additional practice, have children record themselves reading the same passage a few times, and then select their favorite recording to play for you.

Build Knowledge: Make Connections

Talk About the Text Have partners discuss the tools people use while working.

Write About the Text Have students add their ideas to their Build Knowledge pages of their reader's notebooks.

Self-Selected Reading

Have children choose another fiction selection from the online **Leveled Reader Library,** or read the **Differentiated Text,** "The Chef."

LITERACY ACTIVITIES

Have children complete the Literacy Activities on the inside back cover of the book.

FORMATIVE ASSESSMENT

❯ **STUDENT CHECK-IN**

Have partners ask and answer each other's questions about the topic and details about jobs in the text. Then, have children reflect using the Check-in routine.

LEVEL UP

IF children can read *On the Job* **ELL Level** with fluency and correctly answer the questions,

THEN tell children that they will read a more detailed version of the story.

HAVE children page through *On the Job* On Level and describe each picture in simple language.

• Have children read the selection, checking their comprehension and providing assistance as necessary.

MODELED WRITING

LESSON 1

LEARNING GOALS

We can write about our favorite shoes.

OBJECTIVES

Use dictating and writing to compose informative texts in which they name the topic.

LANGUAGE OBJECTIVES

Children will inform by writing a sentence using a describing word.

ELA ACADEMIC LANGUAGE

• *sentence*

Writing Practice Display the photo of flip-flops on p. 9 of the **Big Book,** and read the sample sentence of the **Teacher's Edition,** p. T270. Guide children to analyze the sentence using the Actor/Action routine: *Who is the actor?* (I) *What is the action?* (like my blue flip-flops) Then read the prompt, and guide the class to answer it. Write the sentence on the board and have children choral read. Then have partners write their own sentences in their writer's notebook.

Beginning Provide a sentence frame: I will write about <u>my sneakers</u>. Help partners think of their sentence: *Who is the actor?* (I) *What is the action?* (like my sneakers) *What can you say about them?* (They are yellow.)

Intermediate Have partners take turns asking and answering *who/what* questions about their shoes to create their sentences.

Advanced/Advanced High Challenge children to include two describing words in their second sentence.

FORMATIVE ASSESSMENT ❯ **❯ STUDENT CHECK-IN** Partners share their sentences. Ask children to reflect using the Check-in routine.

INTERACTIVE WRITING

LESSON 2

LEARNING GOALS

We can write a nonfiction text.

OBJECTIVES

With guidance and support, add details to strengthen writing as needed.

LANGUAGE OBJECTIVES

Children will inform by writing sentences using a period and a question mark.

ELA ACADEMIC LANGUAGE

• *text, sentence, adjective*
• Cognate: *texto*

Analyze the Prompt Choral read the sample question and answer on p. T282 with children. *What is the question?* (Whose coat?) *What is the answer?* (I see a doctor's white coat.) Track the sentence with a finger from one line to the next, and have children repeat the action. *We have to follow the pattern of* Whose Shoes? *by asking and answering* Whose Coat? Then help children complete the sentence frames at the bottom of p. T282.

Beginning Help partners name different types of coats. Start a word bank for children to use as they complete the sentence frames.

Intermediate Ask guiding questions to help partners complete the first sentence: *What kind of coat does the person wear? What color is it?*

Advanced/Advanced High Challenge children to share their first sentence and let a partner guess the answer.

FORMATIVE ASSESSMENT ❯ **❯ STUDENT CHECK-IN** Partners share their sentences. Ask children to reflect using the Check-in routine.

INDEPENDENT WRITING

LEARNING GOALS

We can write about the texts we read.

OBJECTIVES

Use dictating and writing to compose informative texts in which they supply some information about the topic.

LANGUAGE OBJECTIVES

Children will inform by writing sentences using a nonfiction text as a model.

ELA ACADEMIC LANGUAGE

• *pattern*

Find Text Evidence Use the Independent Writing routine. Ask questions to help children orally retell the shared read. *What do you see first?* (a firehouse) *What does the next page show?* (a firetruck) Then read the prompt on p. T292: *Write a new text called "A Nurse's Office." Use "Tom On Top!" as a model.* Display the **Reading/Writing Companion,** p. 18. *What kind of sentence does "Tom On Top!" begin with?* (a question) *We will begin with a question, too. We will follow the same pattern as the text.*

Write to the Prompt Write the sentence starters on the board, and read them. Model completing the first sentence frame, and have children choral read the response. Repeat with the remaining sentence frames. Then ask children to copy the sentences into their writer's notebook.

Beginning Have partners take turns reading their sentences to each other.

Intermediate Have partners talk about how they used "Tom On Top!": I began my draft with a <u>question</u>.

Advanced/Advanced High Challenge children to come up with their own question and answers to tell what they see at a nurse's office.

FORMATIVE ASSESSMENT ❯ **STUDENT CHECK-IN** Partners share their sentences. Ask children to reflect using the Check-in routine.

SELF-SELECTED WRITING

LEARNING GOALS

We can revise our writing.

OBJECTIVES

Capitalize the first word in a sentence and the pronoun *I.*

LANGUAGE OBJECTIVES

Children will inquire about their writing by adding adjectives.

ELA ACADEMIC LANGUAGE

• *adjective*
• Cognate: *adjetivo*

Work with children to revise the group writing activity. Read the sentences, pointing to each word as you read. Model and ask questions as you read. For example, *Is this a common or proper noun? Does it begin with a capital letter?* Then go back and reread the text, and work together to add adjectives. After you have made the necessary revisions, have children copy the sentences from the group writing activity in their writer's notebook.

For more support with grammar and adjectives, use the **Language Transfers Handbook** and **Language Development Cards** 10A, 10B, and 11A.

FORMATIVE ASSESSMENT ❯ **STUDENT CHECK-IN** Partners tell what revisions they made. Ask children to reflect using the Check-in routine.

LEARNING GOALS

We can understand important ideas and details in a story.

We can tell what makes a text a personal narrative.

OBJECTIVES

Recognize common types of texts (e.g., storybooks, poems).

With prompting and support, identify characters, settings, and major events in a story.

Ask and answer questions about unknown words in a text.

Speak audibly and express thoughts, feelings, and ideas clearly.

LANGUAGE OBJECTIVES

Children will discuss the character's neighborhood using describing words.

ELA ACADEMIC LANGUAGE

- *characters, setting, events*
- Cognate: *eventos*

MATERIALS

Literature Big Book, *What Can You Do with a Paleta?*, pp. 3–32 and 33–36

Visual Vocabulary Cards

DIGITAL TOOLS

🎧 Have children listen to the selection as they follow along to develop comprehension.

Use the vocabulary activity for additional support.

What Can You Do with a Paleta?

Prepare to Read

Build Background *We are going to read a story about a girl who likes* paletas. Point to a paleta on the cover. Explain that a paleta is a sweet treat. Act out eating a paleta, describing how it tastes like fruit and is ice-cold like an ice pop.

Literature Big Book

Focus on Vocabulary Use the **Visual Vocabulary Cards** to review the oral vocabulary words *appreciate* and *cultures*. As you read, use gestures and other visual support to clarify important story words: *paint, tongue, scare, juice, decisions, masterpiece,* and *lick.*

Summarize the Text Before reading, give a short summary of the selection: *A girl tells about her barrio, or neighborhood. People can buy paletas there. The girl tells about the fun things you can do with a paleta.*

Read the Text

Use the Interactive Question-Response Routine to help children understand the story.

Pages 4-9

Pages 4–5 Read the text. Point to the girl. *This girl is telling about her neighborhood, or* barrio. Point to the roses. *You can see flowers called roses. What color are the roses?* (red; pink; fuchsia) Point to the man and explain that he plays music. *What can you hear in the barrio?* (music) *The smell of food floats out the window.* Point to the tacos and tortillas. What can you smell? (food)

Pages 6–9 *There is a paleta wagon. What rings?* (its tinkly bell) Guide children to point out the bell in the picture. Then have them say the question the girl asks on page 9: What can you do with a paleta?

 What does the girl tell about her barrio? Talk with a partner.

Beginning Guide children to point to details and complete sentence frames: *You can see* roses. *You can smell* food. *You can hear* music. *You can hear the bell* ring.

Intermediate Provide sentence frames: *You can see* big red roses. *You can smell* the food. *You can hear* music *and* the bell *of a paleta wagon.*

Advanced/Advanced High Encourage partners to tell what you can see, hear, and smell. Provide additional modeling as needed. (You can see roses. You can smell food. You can hear music and the bell on the wagon.)

Pages 10–25

Pages 10–11 Read the text. *The girl's tongue is purple and green. What happens when she paints her tongue these colors?* (She scares her brother.)

Page 16–19 Read the text. *The girl paints with the juice of the paleta. She gives herself a blue moustache. What color is it?* (blue) *She paints a masterpiece.*

 What can the girl do with a paleta? Talk with a partner.

Beginning Help children point to details and respond: *She paints her* <u>tongue</u>. *She can paint a blue* <u>moustache</u>.

Intermediate Provide sentence frames. *You can paint your tongue* <u>purple and green</u> *to scare* <u>your brother</u>. *You can paint a blue* <u>moustache</u> *or a* <u>masterpiece</u>.

Advanced/Advanced High Guide partners to talk about what the girl does with the juice of a paleta. (She paints her tongue and scares your brother. She gives herself a moustache. She creates a masterpiece.)

Pages 26–32

Pages 26–27 Read the text. The girl thinks the very best thing to do with a paleta is to eat it! Point to the girl. *What is the girl doing?* (licking/slurping/sipping/munching the paleta)

Pages 28–31 Read the text. *Where does the girl like to eat a paleta?* (in her barrio/neighborhood) Guide children to point out details in the illustrations that describe the girl's barrio.

 What does the girl say is the best thing to do with a paleta? Talk with a partner.

Beginning Ask children to act out enjoying a paleta with you. Help them respond: *The best thing is to* <u>eat</u> *a* <u>paleta</u>.

Intermediate *The girl likes to* <u>eat a paleta</u> *where roses bloom, music plays, and you can smell food.*

 Retell Use the **Retelling Cards** for *What Can You Do with a Paleta?* to retell the story with children. Display the cards and model retelling

using sequence words as you point to the events and actions in the cards. Then help children take turns retelling parts of the story using the sequence words.

 ## LESSON 4 Paired Selection: "My Great Neighborhood!"

Pages 33–36 Point to each illustration as you paraphrase the text. *This is Caleb. He tells about his neighborhood. It has roads made of dirt. The neighborhood has a creek and trees, too. What does it have?* (dirt roads, a creek, trees) *Look! Caleb went to the creek. Where do kids go to swim and fish?* (lake) *They go to the Grillfest. People bring different foods to eat. They celebrate summer at Grillfest. What do they celebrate?* (summer)

 What makes Caleb's neighborhood great? Talk with a partner.

Beginning Help children point to the illustrations of the creek and lake and retell details after you.

Intermediate Have children respond: *There is a* <u>creek</u>. *Caleb swims and fishes at* <u>the lake</u>. *Neighbors celebrate* <u>summer</u> *at Grillfest.*

Advanced/Advanced High Challenge partners to include words that tell how Caleb feels, such as *excited, like,* and *fun.*

FORMATIVE ASSESSMENT

⟩ STUDENT CHECK-IN

Main Selection Have partners describe the girl's neighborhood using adjectives.

Paired Selection Have partners discuss three things that Caleb likes to do outside.

Then, have children reflect using the Check-in routine.

 ## Independent Time

Draw and Share Help children connect the stories to their own neighborhoods. Help them identify things about their neighborhoods that are like or different from those in the stories. Then ask them to tell about and illustrate something they like about the place where they live.

"Cultural Festivals"

Interactive Read Aloud

Prepare to Read

Build Background Display the cards as you talk about the images. *These people are in a parade. These people are dancing.* Then ask: *What do you see?* I see ____. Repeat what children say to give confirmation and to model proper grammar or pronunciation. Then explain: *These cards show festivals. Festivals celebrate important days. You will learn about these festivals.* If available, use a globe or world map to show the location of each country mentioned as you read the text on the cards.

Focus on Vocabulary Use the **Visual Vocabulary Cards** to review the oral vocabulary words *appreciate, cultures, prefer, proud,* and *tradition.* As you read, use gestures and other visual support to clarify important selection words: *celebrate, holiday, street fair, decorate, good luck, joyful, exchange, new year.* Review the words in context as you read.

Summarize the Text *These cards tell about different cultural festivals. They tell about how different cultures celebrate special days.*

Read the Text

Use the Interactive Question-Response Routine to help children understand the text.

Card 1

Paragraphs 1–3 Read the text. *People have a cultural festival for different reasons. They may celebrate seasons, like fall or spring. People may celebrate being thankful. Or people may celebrate important events or holidays. What do people celebrate?* Have children respond: *People celebrate ____.* Use the photographs to talk about what people do at a cultural festival. *What do people do at a festival?* (eat food, hear music, dance, give gifts)

 What do people do at a cultural celebration? Talk with a partner.

Beginning Use gestures and additional modeling to help children tell about a cultural festival: *People____.* (give gifts, eat, dance)

Intermediate Guide partners to ask and answer: *What do people do at a cultural festival? People like to* give gifts, eat, and dance to music.

Advanced/Advanced High Help partners ask and answer questions about cultural festivals. *What do people enjoy? At a cultural festival, people* give gifts, eat, and dance to music.

Card 2

Paragraphs 1–2 Read the text. *Cinco de Mayo is May 5th. There are parades. People listen to music and dance. What can people do on Cinco De Mayo?* (Listen to music and dance)

Paragraph 4 Read the text. If possible, show photos of the Mexican foods listed. *What can people buy at street fairs?* (traditional foods; tacos, soup, guacamole)

 Help partners respond: Tell a partner about Cinco de Mayo.

Beginning *People can listen to* <u>music</u> *and eat* <u>food</u>.

Intermediate Help children add details to their answers: *There are parades with* <u>music and dancing</u>. *There are traditional* <u>foods</u> *at street fairs.*

Advanced/Advanced High *Ask and answer questions about Cinco de Mayo.* Give examples of questions and provide sentence frames and modeling.

Card 3

Paragraphs 1–2 Read the text. *Diwali is also called the Festival of Lights.* Help children understand how different activities take place each day. Use the photo to describe the lighting of lamps and candles. *What do people light on the third day?* (lamps and candles)

Paragraphs 3–4 Read the text. *People give gifts. Pretend to give a gift to your friend. Tell what the gift is. People also play games during the festival.*

 Tell a partner about Diwali.

Beginning Ask guiding questions and help children complete sentence frames: *How long is the festival? It is* <u>five days</u> *long. What do people give? People give* <u>gifts</u>. *What do people play? People play* <u>games</u>.

Intermediate Have children complete sentence frames related to what people do: *People light* <u>lamps and candles</u> *in their homes. People visit* <u>friends and family</u> *and eat* <u>a feast</u>.

Card 4

Paragraphs 1–2 Read the text. *People in Vietnam celebrate each new year. The celebration is called Tet. People clean and decorate their homes to get ready. Do people clean their homes for Diwali?* (yes)

Paragraphs 4–5 Read the text. Point to the photo. Explain that there are also parades. There are dances. People eat traditional foods from Vietnam. *Each new year is named after an animal. What do people call each year?* (the name of an animal)

 Tell a partner about Tet.

Beginning Point to the image. *This is a holiday parade. What is this? This is a* <u>parade</u> *during Tet.*

Intermediate Help children complete sentence frames: *People celebrate the* <u>new year</u>. *People* <u>clean</u> *and* <u>decorate</u> *their homes for Tet.*

Advanced/Advanced High Guide children to ask and answer questions. Provide additional modeling and sentence frames as needed. For example: *What do families do together? Families eat* <u>foods from Vietnam</u> *together.*

 Retell Use the photographs on the **Interactive Read-Aloud Cards** to retell key details about the celebrations with children. Display the cards and model retelling as you point to the events and actions in the cards. Then help children take turns retelling an activity or detail about a festival.

❯ STUDENT CHECK-IN

Have partners choose one festival and retell three details about it. Then, have children reflect using the Check-in routine.

Independent Time

Draw and Write Have partners talk about their favorite festival from a card. Use **Oral Language Sentence Frames**, page 3, to support children as they give their opinions.

LESSONS 4-5

LEARNING GOALS

We can ask and answer questions about what happens in a fictional story.

OBJECTIVES

With prompting and support, identify characters and setting in a story.

Ask and answer questions about unknown words in a text.

Ask and answer questions in order to seek help, get information, or clarify something that is not understood.

Continue a conversation through multiple exchanges.

LANGUAGE OBJECTIVES

Children will discuss what the characters do at the party, using the verbs *need* and *bring*.

ELA ACADEMIC LANGUAGE

• *label, comprehension, illustrations*

• Cognates: *comprehensión, ilustraciones*

MATERIALS

ELL Leveled Reader: *Neighborhood Party*

Online Differentiated Text, "Neighbors"

Online ELL Visual Vocabulary Cards

DIGITAL TOOLS

Have children listen to the selection as they follow along to develop comprehension.

Use the vocabulary activity for additional support.

Neighborhood Party

Prepare to Read

Build Background *You have learned about neighbors. You can meet your neighbors at a party.* If possible, show a picture of a neighborhood celebration. Help children use prior knowlege to understand meaning. *Have you been to a party?* Elicit responses about what people do at a party. For example, *You eat at a party.* Show the cover of the Leveled Reader and read the title aloud. *What are the people doing at the party? The people are ____. They are having ____.*

Focus on Vocabulary Use the routine on the **ELL Visual Vocabulary Cards** to preteach *celebrate* and *potluck*. As you read, use images and any labels to clarify important story words, such as *tacos, soup, chips,* and *dip,* in context.

Lexile BR

Read the Text

Use the Interactive Question-Response Routine to help children understand the story.

Pages 2–8

Pages 2–3 Read the text and labels on pages 2–3. Point to the soup. *This is* soup. *Say soup. What did the woman bring? She* brought *soup..*

Main Story Elements: Character, Setting Point to the people on page 2 and ask, *Who are the characters? The characters are people of the* neighborhood. *Where are the characters? The people are at a* house *in the* evening.

 What do the characters need for a neighborhood party? What do they do? Talk with a partner.

Beginning Have partners point to the illustrations as they ask and answer: *What do the people need for a party?* (tacos/soup)

Intermediate Help partners ask and answer: *What do we* need *for the* party*? We* need tacos *and* soup.

Advanced/Advanced High Help partners elaborate. (Sample response: We need tacos and soup for the neighborhood party.)

Pages 4–5 Read the text and labels. Demonstrate as you say: *We can eat a chip with dip.* Point to the characters and say: *The neighbor brings chips. The boy brings dip. The neighbors can eat chips and dip. What do we need for the party?* (chips and dip)

What do the neighbors bring to the party? Talk with a partner.

Beginning Have children point to the characters and respond: *The neighbor has* chips. *The boy* has *dip.*

Intermediate Provide sentence frames: *The neighbors bring* chips and dip *to eat at the* party.

Pages 6–8 Have children discuss the foods the neighbors bring to the party. *What did the neighbors bring?* The neighbors bring hotdogs/dumplings/drums. Have children **ask and answer questions** about the setting. *What are the characters?* They are on a rooftop.

 What happens at the neighborhood party? Talk with a partner.

Beginning *What does the woman in the pink hat bring? She brings a plate of* hotdogs *to the* party. *What does he play? He plays* drums.

Intermediate Guide children in describing the activties and things at the party. *The people play* music *and* dance. *The people share* food *and* eat *together. The people* chat *and* laugh.

Advanced/Advanced High Help children explain what the people are doing on page 8. Provide modeling. *Two children eat food. The man plays music on the drums. Neighbors dance to the music.*

Retell Have partners retell the story. Have them take turns pointing to a picture and describing it to each other.

Focus on Fluency

Read pages 2–5 with appropriate tone and expression. Then read the passage aloud and have children echo read. For additional practice, have children record themselves reading the same passage a few times, and then select their favorite recording to play for you.

Build Knowledge: Make Connections

Talk About the Text Have partners discuss people they see in their neighborhood.

Write About the Text Have students add their ideas to their Build Knowledge pages of their reader's notebooks.

Self-Selected Reading

Have children choose another fiction selection from the online **Leveled Reader Library,** or read the **Differentiated Text,** "Neighbors."

LITERACY ACTIVITIES

Have children complete the Literacy Activities on the inside back cover of the book.

FORMATIVE ASSESSMENT

❯ **STUDENT CHECK-IN**

Have students share three things that neighbors brought to the party. Ask children to ask and answer quesitons about the story. Then, have children relfect using the Check-in routine.

 **LEVEL** UP

IF children can read *Neighborhood Party* ELL Level with fluency and correctly answer the questions,

THEN tell children that they will read a more detailed version of the story.

HAVE children page through *Neighborhood Party* On Level and describe each picture in simple language.

- Have children read the selection, checking their comprehension and providing assistance as necessary.

MODELED WRITING

LESSON 1

LEARNING GOALS

We can write about food we like to eat with our neighbors.

OBJECTIVES

Use dictating and writing to compose informative texts in which they name the topic.

LANGUAGE OBJECTIVES

Children will inform by writing a sentence using the verb *like*.

ELA ACADEMIC LANGUAGE

• *sentence*

Writing Practice Read the sample sentence from the **Teacher's Edition,** p. T348. Guide children to analyze the sentence: *Who is the actor?* (I) *What do we learn about the actor?* (like to eat pizza) Then read the prompt, and ask a volunteer to answer it. Write the sentence, and have children choral read it with you. Then ask children to write their own sentence in their writer's notebook. Display food **Photo Cards** to help children write.

Beginning Then help partners think of their sentence. *Who is the actor?* (I) *What do you like to do?* (like to eat oranges)

Intermediate Have partners ask and answer questions: What do you like to eat with friends? I like to eat <u>grapes</u>. Provide a sentence frame as needed.

Advanced/Advanced High Challenge partners to explain who the actor is in their sentence and what the actor likes to eat.

FORMATIVE ASSESSMENT ➤ **STUDENT CHECK-IN** Partners share their sentences. Ask children to reflect using the Check-In routine.

INTERACTIVE WRITING

LESSON 2

LEARNING GOALS

We can write about the neighbors in the barrio.

OBJECTIVES

With guidance and support, respond to questions and suggestions from peers.

LANGUAGE OBJECTIVES

Children will explain by writing sentences using clues from the text and illustrations.

ELA ACADEMIC LANGUAGE

• *text, illustrations*

• Cognates: *texto, ilustraciones*

Analyze the Prompt Choral read with children the sample sentence on p. T360. *Who are the actors?* (neighbors in the barrio) *What can we say about them?* (They are friendly.) Then guide children to stretch the sounds in each word as you point to the letters. Then ask: *How do the illustrations help you know what the neighbors are like?* (They sit together and talk.) Help children complete the sentence frames on p. T360.

Beginning Display the illustration on pp. 30–31 of the **Big Book,** and ask *yes/no* questions: *Are the children happy or sad?* (happy) Create a word bank to help children complete the first sentence frame.

Intermediate Ask guiding questions to help children think of their sentences: *What do all of the children want?* (a paleta) *What do the illustrations show?* (children smiling)

Advanced/Advanced High Challenge children to point to the details in the text and illustrations they used to write their sentences.

FORMATIVE ASSESSMENT ➤ **STUDENT CHECK-IN** Partners share their sentences. Ask children to reflect using the Check-In routine.

INDEPENDENT WRITING

LEARNING GOALS

We can write about the texts we read.

OBJECTIVES

Use a combination of dictating and writing to narrate several loosely linked events.

LANGUAGE OBJECTIVES

Children will inform by writing sentences using adjectives.

ELA ACADEMIC LANGUAGE

• describe, adjective
• Cognates: describir, adjetivo

Find Text Evidence Use the Independent Writing routine. Ask questions to help children orally retell "Sid." For example, *Where are Sid and his mom?* (a new house) *Who taps on the door first?* (Dan) *What does he bring to his new neighbors?* (a plant) Then read the prompt on p. T370: *What can you say about Sid and Mom's new neighbors? We need to think about what the neighbors have done for Sid and his mom so we can write about them.*

Write to the Prompt Write the sentence starters on the board, and read them. Model completing the first sentence frame, and have children choral read the response. Repeat with the remaining sentence frames. Then ask children to copy the sentences into their writer's notebook.

Beginning Provide a sentence frame to help partners talk about their sentences: I used the adjective <u>kind</u>.

Intermediate Provide partners a sentence frame to help them tell what details they used: I wrote about how <u>Dan and Dot</u> bring <u>gifts</u>.

Advanced/Advanced High Challenge children to come up with their own sentences. Have them identify the adjectives they used.

FORMATIVE ASSESSMENT ❯ **STUDENT CHECK-IN** Partners share their sentences. Ask children to reflect using the Check-in routine.

SELF-SELECTED WRITING

LEARNING GOALS

We can revise our writing.

OBJECTIVES

Print many upper- and lowercase letters.

LANGUAGE OBJECTIVE

Children will inquire about their writing by adding adjectives.

ELA ACADEMIC LANGUAGE

• steps, adjective
• Cognate: adjetivo

Work with children to revise the group writing activity. Read the sentences, pointing to each word as you read. Model and ask questions as you read. For example, *Can we add an adjective here?* After you have made the necessary revisions, have children copy the sentences from the group writing activity in their writer's notebook.

For more support with grammar and adjectives, use the **Language Transfers Handbook,** and review **Language Development Cards** 10A, 10B, and 11A.

FORMATIVE ASSESSMENT ❯ **STUDENT CHECK-IN** Partners tell what revisions they made. Ask children to reflect using the Check-in routine.

LESSONS 1-2

We can understand important ideas and details in a text.

We can use captions to learn new information.

OBJECTIVES

With prompting and support, describe the connection between two individuals, events, ideas, or pieces of information in a text.

With prompting and support, identify basic similarities in and differences between two texts on the same topic.

Actively engage in group reading activities with purpose and understanding.

Speak audibly and express thoughts, feelings, and ideas clearly.

LANGUAGE OBJECTIVES

Children will inform about the road building process, using nouns and verbs.

ELA ACADEMIC LANGUAGE

• *sequence, first, next, last*
• Cognate: *secuencia*

MATERIALS

Literature Big Book, *Roadwork,* pp. 3–32 and 33–36

Visual Vocabulary Cards

DIGITAL TOOLS

Have children listen to the selection as they follow along to develop comprehension.

Use the vocabulary activity for additional support.

Roadwork

Prepare to Read

Build Background *People drive cars on a road.* Pretend to drive a car. *We are going to read a book that tells how people build a road. People use a lot of big machines and big trucks to make a road.* Point to the big truck on the cover. *This is a dump truck. What is this?*

Literature Big Book

Focus on Vocabulary Use the **Visual Vocabulary Cards** to review the oral vocabulary words *community* and *improve.*
As you read, use gestures and other visual support to clarify important selection words: *plan, move, load, dump, pack, stop, mark,* and *tidy up.* Review the words in context as you read.

Summarize the Text Before reading, give a short summary of the selection: *First, workers plan the road. Workers and machines make a path. Then they make a road. It is a lot of work. Finally, people drive cars on the road.*

Read the Text

Use the Interactive Question-Response Routine to help children understand the text.

Pages 4–11

Pages 4–5 Read the text. *Is there a road?* (no) *The workers plan the road.* Point to the map. *The map shows where the road will go.* Trace a line between the marking pegs for children to follow. *That is where the road, or path, will go.*

Pages 6–7 Read the text. *These machines are cutting a path for the road. Do you see the marking pegs?* (yes)

Pages 10–11 Read the text. Then point to the details and use gestures to help explain the actions. *This is a dump truck. One end lifts. The stones slide out. This machine spreads the stones.* Point to the sound words. *Is the road finished?* (no)

 What do workers do to start? Talk with a partner.

Beginning Help children respond: *First, workers* <u>plan</u>. *Next, they* <u>move</u> *the earth. Then they* <u>load</u> *the dirt. Last, they* <u>tip</u> *the stones.*

Intermediate Help children complete sentence frames: *First, they* <u>plan the road</u>. *Next, they* <u>move the earth</u>. *Then they* <u>load the dirt</u>. *Last, they* <u>tip the stones</u>.

Advanced/Advanced High Help children add details that tell what the workers do. (Sample response: They tip stones out of the truck.)

Pages 12–19

Pages 12–13 Read the text. *Pack the ground means push it down.* Point to the roller on the machine. *This is a roller. It pushes, or packs, the ground to make it hard. What happens to the ground when the workers pack it?* (It gets hard.)

Pages 16–17 Read the text. *Tar is thick and black. It goes on top. Rollers push it down. Tar gets firm and flat. What is pushed down on top of the road?* (tar)

 What do the workers do next to build the road? Talk with a partner.

Beginning Use illustrations, gestures, and sound words to help children complete sentence frames: *Workers pack the <u>ground</u>. The ground is <u>hard</u>. Workers roll on the <u>tar</u>. The tar is <u>flat</u>.*

Intermediate Have partners ask and answer: *Why do the workers pack the ground? They make it <u>hard</u>. Why do they roll the tar? They make it <u>firm</u> and <u>flat</u>.*

Advanced/Advanced High Guide children to explain in complete sentences why workers *pack* the ground and roll on the tar. (Workers make the ground hard. Workers make tar firm and flat.)

Pages 20–32

Pages 20–23 Read the text. *Workers paint the road. These lines tell drivers where to go. What do the workers paint?* (lines) *They raise, or put up, signs. Signs tell drivers important things. A sign can tell where a road goes.* Elicit what the symbol of a straight arrow pointing to the plane means. (The way to the airport is straight.)

Pages 24–25 Read the text. *Workers put up lights on the road. At night, the lights shine. They light up the road. The lights help drivers at night.*

 Why do workers put up signs and lights? Talk with a partner.

Beginning Help children name the details about the road. *This is a sign. What is this?* (a sign) *What shines at night?* (lights)

Intermediate Provide sentence frames: *A sign can tell drivers <u>where a road goes</u>. At night, <u>lights</u> shine on the road to <u>help drivers</u>.*

 Retell Use the **Retelling Cards** for *Roadwork* to retell the text with children. Display the cards and model retelling using sequence words, such as *first, next, then,* and *last* as you point to events and actions in the cards. Then help children take turns retelling one part using the sequence words.

 LESSON 4 ## Paired Selection: "A Community Garden"

Pages 33–36: *People work together to plant a garden. What do they do?* (plant a garden) *They dig up soil and plant seeds. Then, they water. A garden makes a neighborhood beautiful. People pick the vegetables. People share the vegetables. People share the pretty flowers. What do people share from the garden?*

 Why do people plant a community garden? Talk with a partner.

Beginning Help children point to details and respond: *People grow <u>flowers</u> and vegetables.*

Intermediate Provide sentence frames: *A garden makes a neighborhood <u>beautiful</u>. People share the <u>flowers</u> and <u>vegetables</u> they grow.*

Advanced/Advanced High Help children explain why people enjoy having a community garden. (A garden makes a neighborhood beautiful. People share the flowers and vegetables.)

 FORMATIVE ASSESSMENT

❯ STUDENT CHECK-IN

Main Selection Have partners retell at least three important steps needed to build a road.

Paired Selection Have partners discuss which tools they have seen people use before.

Then, have children reflect using the Check-in routine.

OBJECTIVES

Recognize common types of texts (e.g., storybooks, poems).

With prompting and support, retell familiar stories, including key details.

Ask and answer questions about unknown words in a text.

Ask and answer questions in order to seek help, get information, or clarify something that is not understood.

LANGUAGE OBJECTIVES

Children will narrate how the classmates work together, using key vocabulary and simple sentences.

ELA ACADEMIC LANGUAGE

• *fable, community, events*
• Cognates: *fábula, comunidad, eventos*

MATERIALS

Interactive Read Aloud, "The Bundle of Sticks"

Visual Vocabulary Cards

DIGITAL TOOLS

Have children listen to the selection as they follow along to develop comprehension.

Use the vocabulary activity for additional support.

"The Bundle of Sticks"

Prepare to Read

Interactive Read Aloud

Build Background *We are going to read a story that happens in Japan.* Show Japan on a map. *The teacher is Mrs. Sato. She tells the students about the harvest festival. The students do not agree on what to do for the festival. Mrs. Sato uses a bundle of sticks to teach a lesson. A bundle is a group of things tied together.* Show students one stick on Card 4. Say: *This is one stick.* Show the bundle of sticks on Card 3. Say: *This is a bundle of sticks.* Say bundle of sticks.

Focus on Vocabulary Use the **Visual Vocabulary Cards** to review the oral vocabulary words *community, confused, harvest, improve,* and *quarrel.* As you read, use gestures and other visual support to clarify important story words: *participate, dishes (meals), agree, lanterns, calm down, break, surprising, confused, entire, eager, broken.* Review the words in context as you read.

Summarize the Text Give a short summary of the story: *There is a harvest festival in one week. The children of Mrs. Sato's class argue and cannot agree what to do for it. Mrs. Sato teaches the class a lesson about working together.*

Read the Text

Use the Interactive Question-Response Routine to help children understand the story.

Card 1

Paragraphs 1–3 Read the text. *Mrs. Sato's class makes a project every year for the festival. Last year, the class made masks. They wore the masks in the parade. What did last year's class make?* (masks)

Paragraphs 4–6 Read the text. *Children tell their ideas for the festival. Hiro wants the class to make paper lanterns. Yuki thinks the class should cook foods from the harvest. Can the class agree on what to do?* (no)

 What problem do the children have? Talk with a partner.

Beginning Help partners ask and answer: *What happens in one week?* (the harvest festival) *Does the class agree on what to do?* (no)

Intermediate Provide sentence frames: *The class cannot <u>agree</u> on what to do for the <u>harvest</u> festival. Hiro wants to make paper <u>lanterns</u>. Yuki wants to make special <u>dishes; food</u>.*

Advanced/Advanced High Guide partners to use sequence words to discuss why the children quarrel.

Card 2

Paragraphs 1–2 Read the text. *Mrs. Sato tells the class she wants them to work together. She gets a bundle of sticks. The class does not know what Mrs. Sato will do next. What does Mrs. Sato get?* (a bundle of sticks)

Paragraphs 3–7 Read the text. *Mrs. Sato asks Yuki to break one stick. Yuki breaks the stick in half. It is easy to do. The children do not understand the lesson. What is easy for Yuki to do?* (break a stick)

 Why is the class confused? Talk with a partner.

Beginning Have children point to Yuki and the stick she breaks. *What does Yuki break?* (one stick) Help children repeat after you: *The children do not understand the lesson.*

Intermediate Provide sentence frames: *Mrs. Sato wants the children to work* together. *Mrs. Sato has a bundle of* sticks. *Yuki breaks* one stick. *It is* easy *to break. The children do not* understand *the lesson.*

Card 3

Paragraphs 1–3 Read the text. *Mrs. Sato asks a question: Can a child break a bundle of sticks? Hiro thinks he can. Point to Hiro. Hiro tries hard, but he cannot break the sticks. Can Hiro break the bundle of sticks?* (no)

Paragraphs 4–7 Read the text. *No child can break the bundle. Mrs. Sato tells the lesson: one person is like one stick and not very strong alone. People who work together are strong.*

 What lesson does Mrs. Sato teach with the bundle of sticks? Tell a partner.

Beginning Help partners answer *yes/no* questions. *Is one stick strong?* (no) *Is a bundle of sticks strong and hard to break?* (yes) *Is a group of people strong?* (yes)

Intermediate Provide sentence frames: *A* group *of people is* strong *like a bundle of* sticks.

Advanced/Advanced High Provide additional modeling as needed. (Sample answer: Mrs. Sato teaches the children to work together. A group can do things one person cannot.)

Card 4

Paragraphs 1–2 Read the text. *The children agree to work together in groups. One group makes paper lanterns. One group writes ideas for the food. Do the children work together?* (Yes, they work in groups.)

Paragraphs 3–4 Read the text. *Mrs. Sato is proud of the children. The children work together. How does Mrs. Sato feel?* (proud of the children)

 Why is Mrs. Sato proud of the children? Tell a partner.

Beginning Help children point to the two groups of children and repeat after you: *There are two groups of children. They work together. Mrs. Sato is proud.*

Intermediate Provide sentence frames: *The children* work *together. One group makes* lanterns. *The other* group *writes ideas for* harvest meals. *This makes Mrs. Sato* proud *of* the children.

 Retell Use the illustrations on the **Interactive Read-Aloud Cards** to retell the story with children. Display the cards and model retelling using sequence words as you point to the events. Help children take turns retelling using sequence words.

FORMATIVE ASSESSMENT

❯ STUDENT CHECK-IN

Have partners discuss how the classmates worked together to solve a disagreement. Then, have children reflect using the Check-in routine.

Independent Time

Oral Language Ask groups to help each other ask *what, where, who,* and *when* questions about the story. Have them collaborate to answer their questions.

LEARNING GOALS

We can ask and answer questions about what happens in a text.

OBJECTIVES

With prompting and support, ask and answer questions about key details in a text.

Ask and answer questions to help determine or clarify the meaning of words and phrases in a text.

Continue a conversation through multiple exchanges.

Describe familiar people, places, things, and events and, with prompting and support, provide additional detail.

LANGUAGE OBJECTIVES

Children will discuss how people can fix different things with tools, using key vocabulary and simple sentences.

ELA ACADEMIC LANGUAGE

• order, illustrations

• Cognates: orden, ilustraciones

MATERIALS

ELL Leveled Reader: Can You Fix It?

Online Differentiated Text, "We Can Do It!"

Online ELL Visual Vocabulary Cards

DIGITAL TOOLS

Have children listen to the selection as they follow along to develop comprehension.

Use the vocabulary activity for additional support.

Can You Fix It?

Prepare to Read

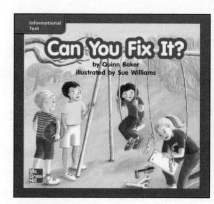

Lexile BR

Build Background Review with children that people can fix things that are broken. *When something breaks, you cannot use it. You need to fix it. Then you can use it again.* Display the cover of the Leveled Reader and read the title aloud. Point out the question mark. *I make my voice go up when I read a question. Read the title like me.* Read the title and have children repeat.

Focus on Vocabulary Use the routine on the **ELL Visual Vocabulary Cards** to preteach *mechanical* and *repair*. As you read, use images and any labels to clarify important selection words, such as *car, sink, swing, bike, door, roof,* and *pool.*

Read the Text

Use the Interactive Question-Response Routine to help children understand the text.

Pages 2–8

Pages 2-3 Read pages with children. Point to the woman. *The story tells the things a woman can fix. What can the woman fix?* (She can fix a car/sink.) *She uses tools to fix the car. She uses tools to fix the sink. How can she use tools? She can use tools to* fix *a car.*

 The woman can fix many things. What can you fix? Tell a partner.

Beginning Help partners point to details in the illustrations as they ask and answer: *What can you fix?* (I can fix the car; sink)

Intermediate Have partners ask and answer questions: *What can you* fix*? I can fix the* car*. I can fix the* sink*.*

Advanced/Advanced High Have partners ask and answer about what they can fix. (What can you fix? I can fix a sink with tools. I can use tools to fix a car.)

Pages 4-5 Read pages with children. Have them **ask and answer questions** about the things the woman can fix. *What can the woman fix?* She can fix the swimg/bike.

Details: Time Order Have children describe in the order of the events on pages 2–5. *What can the woman fix first/next/last?* First, she can fix the car. Next, she can fix the sink. Last, she can fix the bike..

 Tell a partner what the woman can fix in the park.

Beginning Help partners point to details in the illustrations as they answer: *You can fix the* swing.

Intermediate Guide children to ask and answer questions: *Where is she? She is in* the park. *What can she fix? She can* fix the swing.

Pages 6–8 Point to page 6 and say: *The woman makes a little door for the dog. Can she fix the door?* (yes) Have children describe the illustration on page 8. *There is a neighborhood party. Who is at the party? The* neighbors *are at the party. The woman fixes the pool. Who will use the pool? The* children *will use the* pool.

 The woman can fix things in her neighborhood. Tell a partner what she can fix.

Beginning Have partners point to the woman and say after you: *There is a party. She can fix the pool.*

Intermediate Provide sentence frames: *She can fix the* door. *Now a dog can use the little* door. *She* can *fix the* pool *at the party. Now the* children *can use the pool.*

Advanced/Advanced High Have partners ask and answer questions about how the woman helps people in the neighborhood. (She can fix a door for a neighbor. Now the dog can use the door. She can fix the pool at the party. Now the children can use the pool.)

Retell Have partners retell the story. Have them take turns pointing to a picture and describing it each other.

Focus on Fluency

Read pages 2–5 with appropriate expression. Then read the passage aloud and have children echo read. For additional practice, have children record themselves reading the same passage a few times, and then select their favorite recording to play for you.

Build Knowledge: Make Connections

Talk About the Text Have partners discuss ways they can help their community.

Write About the Text Have students add their ideas to their Build Knowledge pages of their reader's notebooks.

Self-Selected Reading

Have children choose another informational text from the online **Leveled Reader Library,** or read the **Differentiated Text,** "We Can Do It!"

LITERACY ACTIVITIES

Have children complete the Literacy Activities on the inside back cover of the book.

FORMATIVE ASSESSMENT

❯ STUDENT CHECK-IN

Have students share things in the text that need to be fixed. Then, have children reflect using the Check-in routine.

IF children can read *Can You Fix It?* ELL Level with fluency and correctly answer the questions,

THEN tell children that they will read a more detailed version of the story.

HAVE children page through *Can You Fix It?* On Level and describe each picture in simple language.

- Have children read the selection, checking their comprehension and providing assistance as necessary.

MODELED WRITING

LEARNING GOALS

We can write about what kind of trucks we see in our neighborhood.

OBJECTIVES

Use dictating and writing to compose informative texts in which they name the topic.

LANGUAGE OBJECTIVES

Children will inform by writing a sentence using the verb *see.*

ELA ACADEMIC LANGUAGE

• *describe*

• Cognate: *describir*

Writing Practice Display photos of different types of trucks. Read the sample sentence from the **Teacher's Edition,** p. T426. Help children analyze the sentence. *Who is the actor?* (I) *What does the actor describe?* (see garbage trucks) Then read the prompt, and ask a volunteer to answer it. Write the sentence, and have children choral read it with you. Then have children write their own sentence in their writer's notebook.

Beginning Provide a sentence frame: I will write about <u>fire trucks</u>. Then help partners think of their sentence: *Who is the actor?* (I) *What is the description?* (see red fire trucks)

Intermediate Have partners take turns asking and answering *who/what* questions to create their sentences. Provide a sentence frame if needed.

Advanced/Advanced High Encourage partners to use the Word Bank to help them spell correctly as they write their sentence.

FORMATIVE ASSESSMENT ❯ ❯ **STUDENT CHECK-IN** Partners share their sentences. Ask children to reflect using the Check-in routine.

INTERACTIVE WRITING

LEARNING GOALS

We can write about why the author added words in big letters.

OBJECTIVES

With guidance and support, respond to questions and suggestions from peers.

LANGUAGE OBJECTIVES

Children will explain by writing a sentence using the verb *tell.*

ELA ACADEMIC LANGUAGE

• *author*

• Cognate: *autor*

Analyze the Prompt Choral read with children the sample sentence on p. T438. *What is this sentence about?* (the big words) *What do the words do?* (show loud sounds) *What idea does the sample sentence focus on?* (the big words) Help children complete the sentence frames on p. T438.

Beginning Read the big words aloud and ask guiding questions: *Are these loud or quiet words?* (loud words) *What do they sound like?* (trucks working) Then help children complete the first sentence frame.

Intermediate Help partners complete the first sentence by providing an example from the book: The words tell about <u>sounds</u>. Ask guiding questions to help partners tell why the author used the words.

Advanced/Advanced High Challenge partners to think of their own sentences to tell why the author added the big words.

FORMATIVE ASSESSMENT ❯ ❯ **STUDENT CHECK-IN** Partners share their sentences. Ask children to reflect using the Check-in routine.

INDEPENDENT WRITING

LEARNING GOALS

We can write about the texts we read.

OBJECTIVES

Use a combination of dictating and writing to narrate several loosely linked events.

LANGUAGE OBJECTIVES

Children will explain by writing a sentence using the verb *can*.

ELA ACADEMIC LANGUAGE

- *adjective*
- Cognate: *adjetivo*

Find Text Evidence Use the Independent Writing routine. Ask questions to help children orally retell the shared read. For example, *Who is the story about?* (a girl and her mom) *Where are the girl and her mom?* (the beach) Then read the prompt on p. T448: *What can the girl and her mom do at the beach?* Display the **Reading/Writing Companion,** pp. 68 and 70. *Let's look for clues. What can the girl do?* (pat the sand) *What can she do?* (tip the bucket)

Write to the Prompt Write the sentence starters on the board, and read them. Model completing the first sentence frame, and have children choral read the response. Repeat with the remaining sentence frames. Then ask children to copy the sentences into their writer's notebook.

Beginning Provide a sentence frame to help partners talk about their sentence: I used the Word Bank to spell <u>can</u>.

Intermediate Encourage parters to use the Word Bank to check their spelling. Have them tell how the sentences focus on one idea at a time.

Advanced/Advanced High Challenge partners to add adjectives to their sentences. Have them use the Word Bank to check their spelling.

FORMATIVE ASSESSMENT ❯ **STUDENT CHECK-IN** Partners share their sentences. Ask children to reflect using the Check-in routine.

SELF-SELECTED WRITING

LEARNING GOALS

We can revise our writing.

OBJECTIVES

Demonstrate command of the conventions of standard English spelling when writing.

LANGUAGE OBJECTIVES

Children will inquire about their writing by adding adjectives.

ELA ACADEMIC LANGUAGE

- *adjective*
- Cognate: *adjetivo*

Work with children to revise the group writing activity. Read the sentences, pointing to each word as you read. Model and ask questions as you read. For example, *Look at the Word Bank. Is ___ spelled correctly?* Then go back and reread the text, and work with children to add adjectives. After you have made the necessary revisions, have children copy the sentences from the group writing activity in their writer's notebook.

For more support with grammar and adjectives, use the **Language Transfers Handbook,** and review **Language Development Cards** 10A, 10B, and 11A.

FORMATIVE ASSESSMENT ❯ **STUDENT CHECK-IN** Partners tell what revisions they made. Ask children to reflect using the Check-in routine.

Summative Assessment
Get Ready for Unit Assessment

Unit 4 Tested Skills

LISTENING AND READING COMPREHENSION	VOCABULARY	GRAMMAR	SPEAKING AND WRITING
• Listening Actively • Text Structure • Details	• Words and Categories	• Adjectives	• Offering Opinions • Presenting • Composing/Writing • Retelling/Recounting

Create a Student Profile

Record data from the following resources in the Student Profile charts on pages 136–137 of the Assessment book.

COLLABORATIVE	INTERPRETIVE	PRODUCTIVE

• Collaborative Conversations Rubrics
  • Listening
  • Speaking
	• Leveled Unit Assessment
	  • Listening Comprehension
	  • Reading Comprehension
	  • Vocabulary
	  • Grammar
	• Presentation Rubric
	  • Listening
	• *Wonders* Unit Assessment
		• Weekly Progress Monitoring
		• Leveled Unit Assessment
		  • Speaking
		  • Writing
		• Presentation Rubric
		  • Speaking
		• Write to Sources Rubric
		• *Wonders* Unit Assessment

The Foundational Skills Kit, Language Development Kit, and Adaptive Learning provide additional student data for progress monitoring.

Level Up

Use the following chart, along with your Student Profiles, to guide your Level Up decisions.

LEVEL UP	If **BEGINNING** level students are able to do the following, they may be ready to move to the **INTERMEDIATE** level:	If **INTERMEDIATE** level students are able to do the following, they may be ready to move to the **ADVANCED** level:	If **ADVANCED** level students are able to do the following, they may be ready to move to **ON** level:
COLLABORATIVE	• participate in collaborative conversations using basic vocabulary and grammar and simple phrases or sentences • discuss simple pictorial or text prompts	• participate in collaborative conversations using appropriate words and phrases and complete sentences • use limited academic vocabulary across and within disciplines	• participate in collaborative conversations using more sophisticated vocabulary and correct grammar • communicate effectively across a wide range of language demands in social and academic contexts
INTERPRETIVE	• identify details in simple read alouds • understand common vocabulary and idioms and interpret language related to familiar social, school, and academic topics • make simple inferences and make simple comparisons • exhibit an emerging receptive control of lexical, syntactic, phonological, and discourse features	• identify main ideas and/or make some inferences from simple read alouds • use context clues to identify word meanings and interpret basic vocabulary and idioms • compare, contrast, summarize, and relate text to graphic organizers • exhibit a limited range of receptive control of lexical, syntactic, phonological, and discourse features when addressing new or familiar topics	• determine main ideas in read alouds that have advanced vocabulary • use context clues to determine meaning, understand multiple-meaning words, and recognize synonyms of social and academic vocabulary • analyze information, make sophisticated inferences, and explain their reasoning • command a high degree of receptive control of lexical, syntactic, phonological, and discourse features
PRODUCTIVE	• express ideas and opinions with basic vocabulary and grammar and simple phrases or sentences • restate information or retell a story using basic vocabulary • exhibit an emerging productive control of lexical, syntactic, phonological, and discourse features	• produce coherent language with limited elaboration or detail • restate information or retell a story using mostly accurate, although limited, vocabulary • exhibit a limited range of productive control of lexical, syntactic, phonological, and discourse features when addressing new or familiar topics	• produce sentences with more sophisticated vocabulary and correct grammar • restate information or retell a story using extensive and accurate vocabulary and grammar • tailor language to a particular purpose and audience • command a high degree of productive control of lexical, syntactic, phonological, and discourse features

LESSONS
1-2

LEARNING GOALS

We can understand important ideas and details in a story.

We can identify rhyme in a poem.

OBJECTIVES

With prompting and support, ask and answer questions about key details in a text.

With prompting and support, retell familiar stories, including key details.

With prompting and support, identify basic similarities in and differences between two texts on the same topic.

Confirm understanding of a text read aloud or information presented orally or through other media by asking and answering questions about key details and requesting clarification if something is not understood.

LANGUAGE OBJECTIVES

Children will narrate what happens in the character's gardens in complete sentences.

ELA ACADEMIC LANGUAGE

• setting

MATERIALS

Literature Big Book, *My Garden*, pp. 3–30 and 32–33
Visual Vocabulary Cards

DIGITAL TOOLS

MULTIMODAL

Have children listen to the selection as they follow along to develop comprehension.

Use the vocabulary activity for additional support.

My Garden

Prepare to Read

Build Background *We are going to read a story about a girl in a garden. The garden is the setting, or where the story happens.* Show pictures of a garden. Model language to talk about the pictures. *Flowers grow in a garden.* Then ask: *What grows in a garden? _____ grow in a garden.* Show a flower seed. Explain that if you plant a seed in the ground, a flower will grow. Help children build vocabulary by providing words for items that children may not know.

Literature Big Book

Focus on Vocabulary Use the **Visual Vocabulary Cards** to review the oral vocabulary words *require* and *plant*. As you read, use gestures and other visual support to clarify important story words: *weed, weeds, bloom, glow, planted.*

Summarize the Text Before reading, give a short summary of the story: *A girl imagines having her own garden. Wonderful things happen in the girl's garden.*

Read the Text

Use the Interactive Question-Response Routine to help children understand the story.

Pages 4–19

Pages 4–5 Read the text. Point to the girl. *Where is the girl?* (in the garden) *The girl helps her mother. She waters. She weeds. This means she pulls the weeds out of the ground. How does the girl help?* (She waters/weeds the garden.) *The girl likes her mother's garden, but her garden would be different.*

Pages 6–9 The girl tells what would be in her garden. Read the text. Point to corresponding images as you discuss the text. *There are no weeds in the garden. The flowers always bloom. This means the flower is always open. The flowers change color.* Point to the flowers on page 9. *Are they the same color?* (no)

Pages 14–15 Read the text. Point to and say *seashells.* Review that when you plant something, you put it in the ground to grow. *If the girl plants seashells, seashells will grow in the garden.*

Pages 16–19 Read the text. Name and point out what grows in the garden. Have children repeat. Ask: *Can these things really grow in a garden?* (no)

 What grows in the girl's garden? Talk to a partner.

Beginning Have children point as they name things. (flowers, seashells)

Intermediate Have children point to the images on each page as they tell what grows in the garden. For example: Seashells *grow in the girl's garden.*

Advanced/Advanced High Have children speak in complete sentences and give details. <u>Flowers</u> *grow in the girl's garden. The flowers can* <u>change colors</u>.

Pages 20–25

Pages 24–25 Read the text and point to the images. *This is the garden at night. The flowers are open and give light.. The strawberries glow, or give light. What gives light in the garden?* (flowers, strawberries) *Do strawberries and flowers give light in real life?* (no)

 What happens at night? Talk to a partner.

Beginning Have children point to the images as they respond. *Flowers* <u>open</u>. *Strawberries* <u>glow</u>.

Intermediate Have children ask and answer: *What do the flowers do? The flowers* <u>open</u>.

Advanced/Advanced High Discuss that the writer compares the flowers to stars. *How are the flowers like stars?* (They shine.) Have children ask and answer: *What do the flowers/strawberries do? The flowers* <u>open</u>. *They* <u>shine</u> *like* <u>stars</u>. *The strawberries* <u>glow</u>.

Pages 26–30

Pages 26–27 Read the text and point to the images. *What is the girl holding?* (a seashell) Then act out the girl's actions with children as you say the actions aloud. *The girl thinks maybe a seashell will grow.*

 What does the girl plant? Talk to a partner.

Beginning Have children point to the illustration on page 26. *What is this? This is a* <u>seashell</u>.

Intermediate Have children ask and answer: *What does the girl have? The girl has* <u>a seashell</u>. *What does the girl want to grow? She wants to* <u>grow seashells</u>.

Advanced/Advanced High Have partners tell each other what the girl does. Provide modeling and sentence frames as needed.

 Retell Use the **Retelling Cards** for "My Garden" to retell the story. Display the cards and model retelling as you point to details in the cards. Then help children take turns retelling one part of the story.

LESSON 4

Paired Selection: "Maytime Magic"

Pages 32–33 Point to images as you discuss the text. Read stanza 1. *When you sow a seed, you plant it.* Read stanza 2. *The seed goes in a hole in the earth, or dirt. Where does the seed go?* (in the earth) Read stanza 3. *The seed needs sun and a shower, or rain. Then it can grow into a flower. What does the seed need to grow?* (sun and rain/water)

 What does a seed need to grow?

Beginning Help children name what they see in the illustration.

Intermediate Supply sentence frames to help children respond, for example: *A seed needs to be planted* <u>in the earth</u>. *Then it needs* <u>sun</u> *and water.*

Advanced/Advanced High Guide partners to respond in complete sentences as they point to the appropriate images in the illustration.

FORMATIVE ASSESSMENT

❯ STUDENT CHECK-IN

Main Selection Have partners retell what can be seen in the girl's garden.

Paired Selection Have partners discuss what a seed needs to grow. Then have children reflect using the Check-In routine.

 ### Independent Time

Oral Language Have children make a text-to-self connection. Ask children to draw a picture of what they would like to grow in a garden. Use Oral Language Sentence Frames, p. 3, to support children as they talk about their picture.

LEARNING GOALS

We can listen actively to a text to learn how plants grow.

OBJECTIVES

With prompting and support, ask and answer questions about key details in a text.

With prompting and support, retell key details of a text.

With prompting and support, describe the connection between pieces of information in a text.

Confirm understanding of a text read aloud or information presented orally or through other media by asking and answering questions about key details and requesting clarification if something is not understood.

LANGUAGE OBJECTIVES

Children will inform about what plants need to grow healthy, using key vocabulary and simple sentences.

ELA ACADEMIC LANGUAGE

• nonfiction

• Cognates: no ficción

MATERIALS

Interactive Read Aloud, "Growing Plants"

Visual Vocabulary Cards

DIGITAL TOOLS

Have children listen to the selection as they follow along to develop comprehension.

Use the vocabulary activity for additional support.

"Growing Plants"

Prepare to Read

Interactive Read Aloud

Build Background Have children share what they've learned about what plants need to grow. Display images of different plants, such as trees, flowers, and vegetables, and the things they need to grow: soil, water, and sunlight. *These are plants. A tree is a plant. What else is a plant? A _____ is a plant.* Use the images to introduce the basic parts of a plant: *roots, stem, leaves.* Finally, use the images to discuss what a plant needs to grow: *sun, water, soil.*

Focus on Vocabulary Use the **Visual Vocabulary Cards** to review the oral vocabulary words *plant, require, soak, harmful,* and *crowd.* As you read, use gestures and other visual support to clarify important selection words: *soil, air, sunlight, space, roots, stem.*

Summarize the Text Before reading, give a short summary of the text: *In this nonfiction text you will learn more about what a plant needs to grow!*

Read the Text

Use the Interactive Question-Response Routine to help children understand the text.

Card 1

Paragraphs 2–3 Read the text. Point to the photo. *There are many different kinds of plants. These are trees. Plants can be trees, or flowers, or vegetables. But all plants need the same things to grow: soil, food, water, air, sunlight, and space.* Use visuals as needed. *What do plants need?* Have children point as they respond.

 What do plants need to grow? Talk to a partner about information you learned about plants.

Beginning Point to the images and have children repeat after you: *soil, food, water, sunlight, air, space.* Then have them take turns telling a partner.

Intermediate With a partner, ask and answer: *What does a plant need? A plant needs* soil/food/water/air/sunlight/space.

Advanced/Advanced High Provide modeling for children to answer in complete sentences. Challenge partners to talk about what they need to grow.

Card 2

Paragraph 1 Read the text. *Plants need food and water.* Point to the roots. *Plants have roots. Their roots soak up, or take in, food and water from the soil, or dirt. Where do plants get food and water?* (the soil)

Paragraphs 3–4 Read the text. *Dead plants and animals leave minerals in the soil, or dirt. The minerals are food for plants. Water moves the food from the roots to the leaves and stems.* Guide children to point to and name the roots, leaves, and stems.

 How does a plant get food?

Beginning Have children point to the soil and repeat after you. *Plants get food from the soil.*

Intermediate Have children respond by completing sentence frames. *A plant gets food from* the soil. *Water moves the food to the* leaves and stems.

Advanced/Advanced High Have partners ask and answer questions. *What do the roots do?* (get food and water from the soil) *What does the water do?* (moves food to leaves and stems)

Card 3

Paragraph 1 Read the text. *Plants can make their own food. Leaves use sunlight, air, and water to make sugar. What can the leaves make?* (sugar)

Paragraph 2 Read the text. *When plants make sugar, they also make oxygen.* Help children say "oxygen." *We need oxygen to breathe.* Demonstrate breathing. *Plants help people have air to breathe. How do plants help people? They help people have air to* breathe.

Paragraph 3 Read the text. *People need plants. Plants keep the air healthy. How do plants help people?* (They keep the air healthy.)

 How do plants help us breathe? Talk to a partner.

Beginning Help children talk about oxygen. *Plants put* oxygen *in the air. Do we need oxygen?* (yes)

Intermediate With a partner, ask and answer: *What do plants put in the air? Plants put* oxygen in the air. *Why do we need it? We need it* to breathe.

Advanced/Advanced High With a partner, talk about where oxygen comes from and why it is important. *Plants make* oxygen. *Oxygen goes* into the air. *People need oxygen* to breathe.

Card 4

Paragraphs 1–2 Read the text. *Plants grow in many different places.* Help children name the places the plants grow. Check understanding of "space" by showing a small and a large space in the classroom.

Paragraph 3 Read the text. *Roots need a lot of soil to get food and water. Trees grow tall to get more sunlight. Plants need space to grow. Why do trees grow tall?* (to get sunlight)

Paragraphs 4–5 Read the text. *People are using a lot of land for buildings and roads. The plants have less space to grow. People need to save land for plants. Plants need space to grow. What do plants need?* (space to grow)

 Why do people need to save land for plants?

Beginning Point to the first picture. *Can a tree grow here?* (no) *A tree needs a* big *space.*

Intermediate Provide a sentence frame to help children respond: *Plants need* space to grow.

 Retell Have children retell using the photos on the **Interactive Read-Aloud Cards.** Help them describe details from "Growing Plants."

FORMATIVE ASSESSMENT

> **STUDENT CHECK-IN**

Have partners retell what a plant needs to grow. Then, have children reflect using the Check-In routine.

 Independent Time

Draw and Label Have children make and label drawings showing what plants need to grow.

OBJECTIVES

With prompting and support, retell familiar stories, including key details.

With prompting and support, identify characters, settings, and major events in a story.

With prompting and support, describe the relationship between illustrations and the story in which they appear.

Describe familiar people, places, things, and events and, with prompting and support, provide additional detail.

LANGUAGE OBJECTIVES

Children will narrate how the character works in her garden, using the words *need* and *have*.

ELA ACADEMIC LANGUAGE

• *problem, solutions*

• Cognates: *problema, soluciones*

MATERIALS

ELL Leveled Reader: *My Garden Grows*

Online Differentiated Text, "My Garden"

Online ELL Visual Vocabulary Cards

DIGITAL TOOLS

MULTIMODAL

Have children listen to the selection as they follow along to develop comprehension.

Use the vocabulary activity for additional support.

My Garden Grows

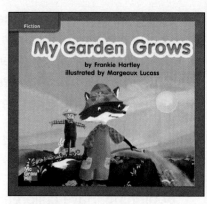

Lexile BR

Prepare to Read

Build Background Use photos of gardens to review what children have learned about gardens. *What does a garden need to grow?* Model responding to the question: *A garden needs water.* Discuss other things that a garden needs. Provide a sentence frame: *A garden needs ____.*

Focus on Vocabulary Use the routine on the **ELL Visual Vocabulary Cards** to preteach *gardener* and *pests*. Use the images and any labels to identify and model the use of key vocabulary in context.

Read the Text

Use the Interactive Question-Response Routine to help children understand the story.

Pages 2–8

Pages 2–3 *Where is Fox?* (in her garden) *What does Fox do in her garden?* (plants seeds) *What do the birds do?* (eat the seeds) Point to Fox's face on page 3. *Is Fox happy?* (no) *How do you know?* (She is frowning.) *Can this story happen in real life?* (no) *Why not?* (Because animals can't have gardens.)

Main Story Elements: Character, Setting, Events Point to Fox. *Who is the character in this story?* (Fox) *Where does the story take place?* (in the garden) *What is happening?* (The birds is eating the seeds.)

 What happens in the garden? Talk to a partner.

Beginning *Have children point to page 2 as they say: Fox plants* seeds.

Intermediate Have partners point to page 2 as they ask and answer: *What events happen? Fox plants* seeds. *The birds* eat the seeds.

Advanced/Advanced High Have partners ask and answer: *What events happen?* (Fox plants seeds. The birds eat the seeds.) *How does Fox feel?* (She is not happy.)

Pages 4–5 Point to the scarecrow. *This is a scarecrow. It scares the birds away. Are there birds in the garden now?* (no) *Does the garden have sun?* (yes) Page 5: *What does Fox do?* (waters the garden)

 Let's reread to help answer this question: What helps the garden grow? Talk to a partner.

Beginning Have children point to the pictures as they respond: *The sun helps the garden grow. The water helps the garden grow.*

Intermediate Have partners point to the words as they ask and answer: *What does the garden need?* (The garden needs sun/water.)

Advanced/Advanced High *Tell what the garden needs.* (sun and water) *How does fox help the garden?* (Fox waters the garden.)

Pages 6–8 *Fox has a problem in the garden.* Point to the rabbits. *There are rabbits in the garden. What do the rabbits do?* (eat the lettuce) Point to the fence. *Fox puts up a fence. What is behind the fence now?* (the rabbits) Point to the weeds. *Fox pulls out the weeds.*

 What are some problems in the garden? Talk to a partner.

Beginning Have children point to the pictures as they respond: *There are rabbits in the garden. The rabbits eat the lettuce.*

Intermediate Supply sentence frames. *One problem is the rabbits. The rabbits eat the lettuce. Another problem is the weeds.*

Advanced/Advanced High Have partners use the images to tell about the problems and the solutions (Rabbits eat the lettuce. They are put behind a fence. There are weeds. Fox pulls out the weeds.)

Retell Have partners retell the story. Have them take turns pointing to a picture and describing it to each other.

Focus on Fluency

Read pages 2–8 with appropriate expression. Then read the text aloud and have children echo read. For additional practice, have children record themselves reading the same text a few times and then select their favorite recording to play for you.

Build Knowledge: Make Connections

Talk About the Text Have partners discuss what plants need to grow.

Write About the Text Then have children add their ideas to their Build Knowledge page of their reader's notebook.

Self-Selected Reading

Have children select another animal fantasy story from the online **Leveled Reader Library,** or read the **Differentiated Text,** "My Garden."

LITERACY ACTIVITIES

Have children complete the Literacy Activities on the inside back cover of the book.

FORMATIVE ASSESSMENT

STUDENT CHECK-IN

Have partners retell how Fox fixes two problems in the garden. Then, have children reflect using the Check-In routine.

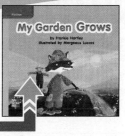

IF children can read *My Garden Grows* **ELL Level** with fluency and correctly answer the Literacy Activity questions,

THEN tell children that they will read a more detailed version of the story.

HAVE children page through *My Garden Grows* On Level and describe each picture in simple language.

- Have children read the selection, checking their comprehension and providing assistance as necessary.

MODELED WRITING

LESSON
1

LEARNING GOALS

We can write about make-believe things we would have in our imaginary garden.

OBJECTIVES

Use a combination of drawing and writing to narrate a single event.

LANGUAGE OBJECTIVES

Children will inform by writing a sentence using the verb phrase *would grow*.

ELA ACADEMIC LANGUAGE

• *period*

Writing Practice Read the sample sentence from the **Teacher's Edition**, p. T18. *When we say something is make-believe, we mean that it doesn't exist in real life. It is something we like to imagine.* Repeat the sample answer. *What does the speaker want in their garden?* (candy bushes) Then read the prompt at the bottom, and ask a volunteer to answer it. Write the sentence, and have children choral read it with you. Then have children write a sentence using the sentence frame at the bottom of the page.

Beginning Provide a sentence frame: I will write about a crayon tree. Encourage children to draw a picture to show what they will write about.

Intermediate Have partners ask and answer questions to create their sentence. Provide a sentence frame if needed.

Advanced/Advanced High Challenge children to point to the period at the end of their sentence. Encourage them to share their sentences.

FORMATIVE ASSESSMENT ❯ ❷ STUDENT CHECK IN Partners share their sentences. Ask children to reflect using the Check-In routine.

INTERACTIVE WRITING

LESSON
2

LEARNING GOALS

We can write about what the girl in the story is good at doing.

OBJECTIVES

With guidance and support, add details to strengthen writing as needed.

LANGUAGE OBJECTIVES

Children will explain by writing sentences using the verbs *can* and *pretend*.

ELA ACADEMIC LANGUAGE

• *idea*
• Cognate: *idea*

Analyze the Prompt Choral read the sample sentence on p. T30. *When we pretend, we make-believe, or imagine, that we are doing something different. Does the girl pretend her garden is different?* (yes) *Does the sample sentence focus on one idea or many ideas?* (one idea) Then help children complete the sentence frames at the bottom of p. T30.

Beginning Display p. 6 of the **Big Book** to help children complete the sentence frame: The girl pretends she has her own garden. Ask guiding questions to help partners think of how to complete the second sentence.

Intermediate Encourage partners to point to details in the story that show what the girl is good at. Then help children complete the second sentence frame: She can describe flowers that change colors.

Advanced/Advanced High Challenge children to think of their own sentences that tell what the girl is good at doing.

FORMATIVE ASSESSMENT ❯ ❷ STUDENT CHECK IN Partners share their sentences. Ask children to reflect using the Check-In routine.

INDEPENDENT WRITING

LEARNING GOALS

We can write about the texts we read.

OBJECTIVES

Use a combination of dictating and writing to narrate a single event or several loosely linked events.

LANGUAGE OBJECTIVES

Children will explain by writing sentences that focus on one idea.

ELA ACADEMIC LANGUAGE

• *idea*

• Cognate: *idea*

Find Text Evidence Use the Independent Writing routine. Ask questions to help children orally retell "Hop Can Hop!" such as: *What does Hop do?* (hop) *What does Dot do with Hop?* (hop) Then, explain that they are going to write about the story. Reread the prompt on page T40: *What do Dot and Hop like to do together?* Review **Reading/Writing Companion**, pp. 23, 25.

Write to the Prompt Write the sentence starters on the board, and read them. Model completing the first sentence frame, and have children choral read the response. Repeat with the remaining sentence frames. Then ask children to copy the sentences into their writer's notebook.

Beginning Have partners circle their end mark and tell about it: I used a period to end my sentence.

Intermediate Have partners tell how the sentences focus on one idea: I wrote about what Dot and Hop do together.

Advanced/Advanced High Challenge children to come up with their own sentences. Have them tell the idea they focused on in each sentence.

FORMATIVE ASSESSMENT ❯ **STUDENT CHECK IN** Partners share their sentences. Ask children to reflect using the Check-In routine.

SELF-SELECTED WRITING

LEARNING GOALS

We can revise our writing.

OBJECTIVES

Demonstrate command of the conventions of standard English grammar and usage when writing.

LANGUAGE OBJECTIVES

Children will inquire about their writing by checking their subjective pronouns.

ELA ACADEMIC LANGUAGE

• *pronoun*

• Cognates: *pronombre*

Work with children to correct the grammatical and spelling errors from their self-selected group writing activity. Read the sentences, pointing to each word as you read. Model and ask questions as you read. For example, *Can this word be replaced with a subjective pronoun? What pronoun should we use?* After you have made the necessary revisions, have children write their own clean copy of the sentences and then publish it.

For more support with grammar and subjective pronouns, use the **Language Transfers Handbook** and **Language Development Card** 16A.

FORMATIVE ASSESSMENT ❯ **STUDENT CHECK IN** Partners tell what revisions they made. Ask children to reflect using the Check-In routine.

LEARNING GOALS

We can understand important ideas and details in a text.

We can use diagrams to learn new information.

OBJECTIVES

With prompting and support, retell familiar stories, including key details.

With prompting and support, describe the relationship between illustrations and the story in which they appear.

With prompting and support, identify basic similarities in and differences between two texts on the same topic.

Continue a conversation through multiple exchanges.

LANGUAGE OBJECTIVE

Students will discuss the life of a tree, using nouns and verbs.

ELA ACADEMIC LANGUAGE

• *illustration*

• Cognates: *ilustración*

MATERIALS

Literature Big Book, *A Grand Old Tree,* pp. 3–32 and 33–36

Visual Vocabulary Cards

DIGITAL TOOLS

Have children listen to the selection as they follow along to develop comprehension.

Use the vocabulary activity for additional support.

A Grand Old Tree

Prepare to Read

Literature Big Book

Build Background *We are going to read a story about a tree.* Show images of different trees, such as a large tree, a flowering tree, and a fruit tree. Use the images to teach the parts of a tree: *roots, trunk, branches, leaves, flowers,* and *fruit.* Say each word and have children repeat after you. Ask: *What does a tree have?* Have children point to the parts as they give answers: *A tree has _____. What animals live in a tree? Birds live in a tree.* Elicit more answers from children: *_____ live in a tree.*

Focus on Vocabulary Use the **Visual Vocabulary Cards** to review the oral vocabulary words *develop* and *amazing.* As you read, use gestures and other visual support to clarify important story words: *creatures, cracked, snapped.* Review the words in context as you read, and have children add these words to their personal glossaries.

Summarize the Text Give a short summary of the selection: *This text is about a big tree that is home to many creatures, or animals.*

Read the Text

Use the Interactive Question-Response Routine to help children understand the text.

Pages 4–17

Pages 6–7 Read the text. Point to the roots. *The tree has roots. The roots are under the ground.* Point to the branches. *The tree has branches. The branches go up into the sky. Where are the roots?* (under the ground)

Pages 8–9 Read the text. Point to the animals. *The tree is a home for many creatures, or animals.* Name the creatures and have children point and repeat. *Where do the animals live?* (in the tree)

Pages 14–15 Read the text and point to the seeds. *These seeds come from the grand tree.* Point to the little trees. *These are the old tree's children. What do the seeds become?* (little trees)

 What lives in the tree? Discuss with a partner.

Beginning Help children respond as they point to creatures in the illustration on pages 8–9. *This is a* bird/squirrel/caterpillar/ladybug.

Intermediate Have children point to the illustration on pages 8–9 as they ask and answer: *What is this? This is a* bird/squirrel/caterpillar/ladybug.

Advanced/Advanced High Challenge partners to name and describe the creatures that live in the tree.

Pages 18–23

Pages 18–19 Read the text. Use gestures to help children understand *basked, bathed, swayed,* and *danced. Show me how you sway.*

Pages 20–21 Read the text. *The tree is very old. Her branches crack and snap in the wind.* Make the sound of wind. Demonstrate *cracked* and *snapped. What happens to the branches?* (crack/snap in the wind)

Pages 22–23 *It is winter. The tree falls. The snow covers her. What does the snow do?* (covers the tree)

 Describe what happens to the old tree. Talk to a partner.

Beginning Have partners point to the illustration as they respond: *The tree <u>falls</u>. Snow covers the <u>tree</u>.*

Intermediate Have partners point to the illustrations: *Branches <u>snap</u>. The old tree <u>falls</u>. Snow <u>covers her</u>.*

Advanced/Advanced High Help partners give details about the tree. Example: *The tree is very old. Her branches crack. She falls. The snow covers her.*

Pages 24–32

Pages 26–27 Read the text. *The tree is different now. There are no leaves or flowers. But creatures still live in her. Name the creatures.* Have children repeat.

Pages 30–31 Read the text. *These trees grew from the old tree's seeds. Many animals live in the new tree.* Help children name the creatures.

 How are the young trees like the old tree? Talk to a partner.

Beginning Have children point to the illustration: *The young trees have <u>creatures/leaves/branches/etc.</u>*

Intermediate *The old tree had <u>creatures/leaves/ branches/etc.</u> The new trees also have <u>(same answers)</u>.*

 Retell Use the **Retelling Cards** for *A Grand Old Tree* to retell the story with children. Display the cards and model retelling using sequence words, such as *first, next, then,* and *last,* as you point to the events and actions in the cards. Then help children take turns retelling one part using the sequence words.

 Paired Selection: "From a Seed to a Tree"

LESSON 4

Pages 33–36 Point to the photos as you paraphrase the text or read the captions. Check understanding of "grow." Help children point to photos as they answer questions. Example: *A seed grows under the ground. It needs water and sun to sprout or grow. What does a seed need to sprout or grow?* (sun and water)

 How does a tree grow? Talk to a partner.

Beginning Guide children to choose a photograph and tell something about it. Example: *A tree starts as a <u>seed</u>.*

Intermediate Have children use the images and captions to help them respond to the question. Example: *A tree starts <u>as a seed</u>. Then the seed grows into <u>a seedling</u>.*

Advanced/Advanced High Have partners tell what is happening on page 34 using *first, then,* and *next.*

FORMATIVE ASSESSMENT

❯ STUDENT CHECK-IN

Main Selection Have partners retell what happens to the tree in the end.

Paired Selection Have partners discuss how a seed grows into a tree.

Then have children reflect using the Check-In routine.

 Independent Time

Oral Language Have children tell what they learned about trees from *A Grand Old Tree* and "From a Seed to a Tree." Supply vocabulary as needed.

LESSON
3

"The Pine Tree"

Prepare to Read

Build Background Discuss how trees are used. Show images of trees, logging, and products made from wood, such as a wood table or house. Show an image of a tree and an image of a piece of lumber. *This is a tree. This is wood. Wood comes from a tree. What can we make with wood? We can make a table.* Elicit other answers. *We can make _____.*

Interactive Read Aloud

Focus on Vocabulary Use the **Visual Vocabulary Cards** to review the oral vocabulary words *enormous, amazing, imagine, develop,* and *content.* As you read, use gestures and other visual support to clarify important story words: *pine tree, logger, wonder, mast.*

Summarize the Text *We will read a fairy tale about a pine tree. The pine tree sees his tree friends cut down. He wants to find out what happened to them.*

Read the Text

Use the Interactive Question-Response Routine to help children understand the story.

Card 1

Paragraph 1 Read the text. Point to the small pine tree. *The young pine tree likes living in the forest. He likes watching the animals and feeling the sun.*

Paragraph 2 Read the text. *One day a truck comes. A logger cuts down several big pine trees.* Point to the tree stumps. *A logger is someone who cuts down trees. The logger takes the trees away on a truck. Who cuts down the trees?* (logger)

Paragraph 3 Read the text. *The pine tree wonders, or wants to know, where his tree friends are going. He asks three sparrows to follow the big trees. What does the pine tree want to know?* (what happens to his tree friends)

 What does the logger do? Talk to a partner.

Beginning With a partner, ask and answer: *What does the logger do? The logger* cuts down *the trees.*

Intermediate With a partner, ask and answer: *What does the logger do? The logger* cuts down *the trees. Then the logger* takes the trees away.

Advanced/Advanced High Guide children to give details about what happens. (The logger cuts down the trees. Then he takes the trees away on his truck.)

Card 2

Paragraphs 1–2 Read the text. Point to the sparrow. *One sparrow follows the big pine tree to the ocean. The sparrow watches workers cut the tree into a mast. They put the mast on the boat. The boat sails away. What does the big tree become?* (a mast)

Paragraphs 3–6 Read the text. *The sparrow tells the little pine tree what she learned. Now the pine tree wants to become part of a boat, too. He wants to have adventures on the ocean. The sparrow thinks the pine tree should be happy in the forest.*

 What does the little pine tree want to be? Talk to a partner.

Beginning Guide children to point to the mast. *The pine tree wants to be a* mast *on a* boat.

Intermediate Have children point to the images. *The little pine tree wants to be a* mast on a boat. *The little pine tree wants to have* adventures on the ocean.

Card 3

Paragraphs 1–2 Read the text. *The second sparrow tells that some trees become a wooden window seat. A family sits on the seat and reads stories. Where does the family sit?* (on the wooden window seat)

Paragraph 4 Read the text. *The little pine tree wants to become a window seat. He wants to hear stories. Why does the little pine tree want to become a window seat?* (to hear stories)

 What does the little pine tree want to be? Talk to a partner.

Beginning Help children complete this sentence. *The little pine tree wants to be a* window seat.

Intermediate Provide a sentence frame to help children add details: *The little pine tree wants to be a* window seat *because he wants* to hear stories.

Advanced/Advanced High Guide partners to talk about what is happening in the picture and why the little pine tree wants to be a window seat.

Card 4

Paragraph 1 Read the text. Point to the pine tree. *For three years, the pine tree grows tall.* Point to the pine cones. *It gets thick cones. How does the pine tree change?* (It gets tall. It gets thick cones.)

Paragraphs 2–4 Read the text. *The pine tree tells the sparrows that he no longer wants to be cut down. He wants to be with the animals. He wants to feel the sun. Where does the pine tree want to live?* (in the forest)

 How has the pine tree changed? Talk to a partner.

Beginning Use Cards 2 and 4: *The pine tree wants to be a* mast. *The pine tree likes the* forest.

Intermediate Provide sentence frames. Example: *The pine tree is* bigger. *It doesn't want* to be cut down.

Advanced/Advanced High Challenge partners to use the images to give details about how the pine tree has changed, including changing what he wants.

 Retell Use the illustrations on the **Interactive Read-Aloud Cards** to retell the story with children. Display the cards and model retelling using sequence words, such as *first, next, then,* and *last* as you point to the events and actions in the cards. Then help partners take turns retelling one part using the sequence words.

FORMATIVE ASSESSMENT

❯ STUDENT CHECK-IN

Have partners retell what the pine tree wants to be. Then, have children reflect using the Check-In routine.

Independent Time

Role Play Have partners or small groups plan a role-play based on one of the cards. Have children practice their role-plays before performing them for the group. Provide modeling and vocabulary as needed.

LESSONS 4-5

LEARNING GOALS

We can reread to better understand the text.

OBJECTIVES

With prompting and support, ask and answer questions about key details in a text.

With prompting and support, identify the main topic and retell key details of a text.

With prompting and support, describe the relationship between illustrations and the text in which they appear.

Describe familiar people, places, things, and events and, with prompting and support, provide additional detail.

LANGUAGE OBJECTIVE

Children will inform about how the trees change, using adjectives, nouns, and simple sentences.

ELA ACADEMIC LANGUAGE

• *illustration*

• Cognates: *ilustración*

MATERIALS

ELL Leveled Reader: *Many Trees*

Online Differentiated Text, "Hens in Nests"

Online ELL Visual Vocabulary Cards

DIGITAL TOOLS

Have children listen to the selection as they follow along to develop comprehension.

Use the vocabulary activity for additional support.

Many Trees

Prepare to Read

Build Background Show a picture of trees. Review tree parts, such as leaves, branches, fruit, or flowers. *What does the picture show? What do trees look like? Trees are ____ and ____. What do trees have? Trees have ____ and ____. How can you have fun with a tree? I can ____.* This text gives us information about trees.

Focus on Vocabulary Use the routine on the **ELL Visual Vocabulary Cards** to preteach *canopy* and *forest.* Use images and labels to identify and model the use of key vocabulary, such as *small, wet,* and *dry.*

Read the Text

Use the Interactive Question-Response Routine to help children understand the text.

Pages 2–8

Pages 2–3 *Where is the girl?* (outside) *What is bigger, the girl or the tree?* (the girl) Point to a label. *This says tree/girl. Repeat the words: tree, girl. What is bigger, the girl or the tree?* (the tree) Read the labels with children. *Why isn't there a swing on the small tree?* (The small tree is not strong enough.)

 How does the tree change? Talk to a partner.

Beginning Have partners point to the illustration on page 2. *Is the tree big or small? The tree is* small. Repeat for page 3. *The tree is* tall/big.

Intermediate Have partners point to the illustrations as they respond. *The tree is* small. *The tree* grows. *Then the tree is* tall/big.

Advanced/Advanced High Provide modeling. *First, the tree is small. Then it grows. It gets bigger. The big tree has long branches. It has more leaves.*

Pages 4–5 Point to and read the word *rain.* Discuss details about the trees: *It is raining. Why are the trees wet?* (It is raining.) Point to page 5. Point to and read *dry. Are the trees wet?* (No, they are dry.) *How do you know?* (Possible response: It is not raining. The sun is shining.) *What does the girl do?* (swing)

 Reread page 5. What is happening? Talk to a partner.

Beginning Have partners point to the illustration as they respond. *The girl is on the* swing. *The trees are* dry. *The sun is* shining.

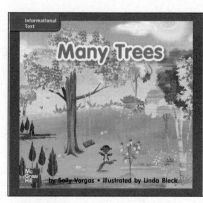

Lexile BR

Intermediate Have partners describe what they see in the illustration. *The girl* is swinging. *The sun* is shining. *The trees* are dry.

Advanced/Advanced High Guide children to use descriptive details. (Example: The girl is swinging on a tree branch.)

Pages 6–8 Page 6: *What color are the leaves?* (green) Page 7: *What color are the leaves now?* (red and yellow) *It is a different time of year. It is fall. What are the leaves doing?* (falling) Explain the two meanings of *fall*. Page 8: *What does the girl see?* (many trees)

Topic and Details Review with children the details they described from the story. *What is the story about?* (Trees grow and change.)

 What is happening on page 7? Talk to a partner.

Beginning Have partners point to the illustration as they respond. *The girl is on the* swing. *The leaves are* red. *The leaves are* falling.

Intermediate Have partners give details about the illustration. *The girl* is swinging. She is wearing a red jacket. *The leaves are* red and yellow. *They are* falling *to the* ground.

Advanced/Advanced High Have partners generate and answer questions. Examples: *What is the girl doing? What colors are the leaves? Where are the leaves?* Help with language as needed.

Retell Have partners retell the story. Have them take turns pointing to a picture and describing it to each other.

Focus on Fluency

Read pages 2–8 with appropriate expression. Then read the text aloud and have children echo read. For practice, have children record themselves reading the text and play their favorite recording for you.

Build Knowledge: Make Connections

Talk About the Text Have partners discuss how plants change as they grow.

Write About the Text Then have children add their ideas to their Build Knowledge page of their reader's notebook.

Self-Selected Reading

Have children select another informational text from the online **Leveled Reader Library,** or read the **Differentiated Text,** "Hens in Nests."

LITERACY ACTIVITIES

Have children complete the Literacy Activities on the inside back cover of the book.

FORMATIVE ASSESSMENT

STUDENT CHECK-IN

Have partners retell descriptive details about the trees and setting. Then have children reflect using the Check-In routine.

LEVEL UP

IF children can read *Many Trees* **ELL Level** with fluency and correctly answer the Literacy Activity questions,

THEN tell children that they will read a more detailed version of the story.

HAVE children page through *Many Trees* On Level and describe each picture in simple language.

• Have children read the selection, checking their comprehension and providing assistance as necessary.

MODELED WRITING

LEARNING GOALS

We can write about how we can play in a tree.

OBJECTIVES

Compose informative texts in which they supply some information about the topic.

LANGUAGE OBJECTIVES

Children will explain by writing a sentence using *can* with an action verb.

ELA ACADEMIC LANGUAGE

• *prompt*

Writing Practice Display the *tree* **Photo Card,** and read the sample sentence from p. T96 of the **Teacher's Edition.** Use the Actor/Action routine: *Who is the actor?* (I) *What is the action?* (can climb a tree and sit) Then read the prompt, and ask a volunteer to answer it. Then have children write a sentence using the sentence frame at the bottom of the page.

Beginning Have partners orally complete this sentence frame before writing: I will write about climbing a tree.

Intermediate Ask partners to ask and answer questions to help them create their sentences: What can you do in a tree? I can climb a tree.

Advanced/Advanced High Challenge children to think of their own sentence and share it with the group.

FORMATIVE ASSESSMENT ❯ ● **STUDENT CHECK IN** Partners share their sentences. Ask children to reflect using the Check-In routine.

INTERACTIVE WRITING

LEARNING GOALS

We can write what we think the tree provided for the animals.

OBJECTIVES

With guidance and support, add details to strengthen writing as needed.

LANGUAGE OBJECTIVES

Children will explain by writing a sentence using the connecting word *and*.

ELA ACADEMIC LANGUAGE

• *idea*

• Cognate: *idea*

Analyze the Prompt Choral read the sample sentence on p. T108. Review the meaning of *provide*: Say, *To* provide *means "to give something that a person or thing needs." Do the birds and squirrels need food to eat?* (yes) Guide children to use their finger to trace how the sample sentence turns a line. *What word in the sentence helps connect two ideas?* (and) Then help children complete the sentence frames at the bottom of p. T108.

Beginning Show children a visual from the book and ask guiding questions: *What animals do you see?* (squirrels, birds) *Where do they live?* (in a tree)

Intermediate Have partners talk about the story and then complete the first sentence frame: The tree gave the animals a place to live.

Advanced/Advanced High Challenge partners to think of their own sentences about what the tree gave the animals.

FORMATIVE ASSESSMENT ❯ ● **STUDENT CHECK IN** Partners share their sentences. Ask children to reflect using the Check-In routine.

INDEPENDENT WRITING

LEARNING GOALS

We can write about the texts we read.

OBJECTIVES

Produce and expand complete sentences in shared language activities.

LANGUAGE OBJECTIVES

Children will explain by writing sentences using connecting words.

ELA ACADEMIC LANGUAGE

• *pronoun*

• *Cognate: pronombre*

Find Text Evidence Use the Independent Writing routine. Ask questions to help children orally retell "Ed and Ned," such as: *Who are Ed and Ned?* (bears) *What do Ed and Ned climb?* Then read the prompt on p. T118: *What do Ed and Ned like to do together?* Display p. 44 of the **Reading/ Writing Companion.** *What do Ed and Ned do?* (climb a tree) Then turn to p. 46. *What do Ed and Ned do together?* (sip water)

Write to the Prompt Write the sentence starters on the board, and read them. Model completing the first sentence frame, and have children choral read the response. Repeat with the remaining sentence frames. Then ask children to copy the sentences into their writer's notebook.

Beginning Provide a sentence frame to help partners talk about their sentences: I used the connecting word *then*.

Intermediate Have children tell the connecting words they used: I used the connecting words *also* and *then*.

Advanced/Advanced High Have partners come up with original sentences. Have them tell what pronouns they used.

FORMATIVE ASSESSMENT ❯ **STUDENT CHECK IN** Partners share their sentences. Ask children to reflect using the Check-In routine.

SELF-SELECTED WRITING

Work with children to correct the grammatical and spelling errors from their self-selected group writing activity. Read the sentences, pointing to each word as you read. Model and ask questions as you read. For example, *What word does this subject pronoun replace?* After you have made the necessary revisions, have children write their own clean copy of the sentences and then publish it.

For more support with grammar, use the **Language Transfers Handbook,** and review **Language Development Card** 16A.

LEARNING GOALS

We can revise our writing.

OBJECTIVES

Demonstrate command of the conventions of standard English grammar and usage when writing.

LANGUAGE OBJECTIVES

Children will inquire about their writing by checking subjective pronouns.

ELA ACADEMIC LANGUAGE

• *pronoun*

• *Cognates: pronombre*

FORMATIVE ASSESSMENT ❯ **STUDENT CHECK IN** Partners tell what revisions they made. Ask children to reflect using the Check-In routine.

Literature Big Book

LEARNING GOALS

We can understand important ideas and details in a text.

We can use lists to learn new information.

OBJECTIVES

With prompting and support, ask and answer questions about key details in a text.

With prompting and support, describe the relationship between illustrations and the text in which they appear.

With prompting and support, identify basic similarities in and differences between two texts on the same topic.

Ask and answer questions in order to seek help, get information, or clarify something that is not understood.

LANGUAGE OBJECTIVES

Children will discuss the journey of an orange from the tree to the market, using sequence words.

ELA ACADEMIC LANGUAGE

• *details, reread*
• Cognates: *detalles*

MATERIALS

Literature Big Book, *An Orange in January,* pp. 3–33 and 34–40
Visual Vocabulary Cards

DIGITAL TOOLS

Have children listen to the selection as they follow along to develop comprehension.

Use the vocabulary activity for additional support.

An Orange in January

Prepare to Read

Build Background Use visuals to review the seasons and that in some places, winter is very cold. Then say, *We are going to read a story about a fruit that grows on a tree. It starts to grow in the spring.* Display an orange. *This is an orange. An orange is a fruit.* Pass the orange around and describe it. *The orange feels/tastes/smells _____. It's round like a ball.*

Focus on Vocabulary Use the **Visual Vocabulary Cards** to review the oral vocabulary words *fresh* and *delicious.* As you read, use gestures and other visual support to clarify important story words: *spring, soil, shared.* Have children add these words to their personal glossaries.

Summarize the Text Before reading, say the summary while pointing to the illustrations. *This book is about how oranges go from the farm to our lunchbox.*

Read the Text

Use the Interactive Question-Response Routine to help children understand the text.

Pages 4–15

Pages 4–5 Read the text. Point to the flowers. *It's spring. These are blossoms or flowers. What season is it?* (spring) *What is on the tree?* (blossoms)

Pages 10–11 Read the text. Point to the trees. *Each tree grows slowly.* Point to the soil. *The soil feeds the trees. The trees grow. What feeds the trees?* (soil)

Pages 12–13 Read the text. Point to the rain. *The rain gives water to the trees.* Point to the sun. *The sun gives sunlight to the trees. Rain and sunlight helps the oranges grow plump, or big. What does the rain give to the trees?* (water) *What does the sun give to the trees?* (sunlight)

 What helps the oranges grow? Talk to a partner.

Beginning Have children point to the images on pages 10–13 and respond with key details. *An orange needs* sunlight/water/soil.

Intermediate Have partners complete the sentence frames with key details. *The* soil/rain/sun *gives* food/water/sunlight *to the trees.*

Advanced/Advanced High Help children answer in complete sentences. (The soil/rain/sun gives food/water/sunlight to the trees. This helps them grow.)

Pages 16–25

Pages 16–21 Point to each location as you read the text. Point to the truck on page 20. *What's inside the truck?* (oranges) *Where does the truck go?* (over mountains, across deserts and plains)

Page 22–23 Read the text. *This is a grocery store.* Help children name what they see in the store. *What is the boy pointing to?* (the orange)

 What happens to the oranges? Talk to a partner.

Beginning Have children point to the images on pages 16–19 as they tell where the oranges are on each page. *The oranges are in a* bag/basket/truck.

Intermediate Have children point to the images as they ask and answer: *Where are the oranges? The oranges are in* a basket/a truck/the grocery store.

Advanced/Advanced High Encourage children to use sequence words, such as *first, then, next,* and *last.*

Pages 26–33

Pages 30–31 Read the text. *It is morning. What's the boy doing?* (He is putting an orange in his lunchbox.)

Pages 32–33 *What season is it?* (winter) *Is it cold outside?* (yes) *The boy is giving some of his orange to his friends. He is sharing his orange.*

 What happens to the orange? Talk to a partner.

Beginning Have partners point to the correct images and respond: *The boy puts the orange in the* lunchbox. *He shares the orange with* his friends.

Intermediate Use sentence frames to help partners respond: *The boy puts* the orange in the lunchbox. *He shares* the orange with his friends.

Advanced/Advanced High Challenge children to give details. Example: *In the morning, the boy puts his orange in his blue lunchbox. Then he shares its segments with his friends.*

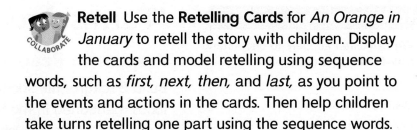 **Retell** Use the **Retelling Cards** for *An Orange in January* to retell the story with children. Display the cards and model retelling using sequence words, such as *first, next, then,* and *last,* as you point to the events and actions in the cards. Then help children take turns retelling one part using the sequence words.

LESSON 4

Paired Selection: "Farmers' Market"

Pages 34–40 Read and then point to the appropriate image as you paraphrase the text. For example, page 34: *This is a farmer's stand. There are fruits and vegetables. What are these called?* (fruits and vegetables) *We will learn who grows the fruits and vegetables. We will learn how the fruits and vegetables get to the stand.*

 What did you learn about fruits and vegetables? Talk to a partner.

Beginning Help partners pick a page and name the fruits and vegetables on the page.

Intermediate Have partners pick a page to talk about. Give them sentence frames as needed to help them tell what they know.

Advanced/Advanced High Have partners tell who grows the food. (farmers) and then point to and tell about the ways the crops get to markets.

FORMATIVE ASSESSMENT

❯ STUDENT CHECK-IN

Main Selection Have partners retell three steps of the journey of an orange.

Paired Selection Have partners discuss two ways farmers might sell their food.

Then have children reflect using the Check-In routine.

 Independent Time

Draw and Share Have children draw a picture of a fruit or vegetable and how it grows. Help them write a caption or label for their picture and read it aloud.

LESSON 3

"Farms Around the World"

Interactive Read Aloud

Prepare to Read

Build Background Show and name images of the foods mentioned in the text: corn, potatoes, rice, and bananas. Discuss with children where each item grows: *Potatoes/Bananas grow under the ground/on a tree. Rice grows in water.* Review that plants grown for food are called crops. Use the images on the card to preteach *field.* Tell that many plants grow in fields. Review what children have learned about how different crops grow and how they get to stores or markets.

Focus on Vocabulary Use the **Visual Vocabulary Cards** to review the oral vocabulary words *raise, fresh, beneath, delicious, special.* As you read, use gestures and other visual support to clarify important selection words: *farm, crops, soil, harvest.*

Summarize the Text Tell children that they will hear a nonfiction text about different crops.

Read the Text

Use the Interactive Question-Response Routine to help children understand the text.

Card 1

Paragraph 1 Read the text. Point to the image. *This is a farm. The farm has a cornfield. What place is this?* (a farm) *What is on the farm?* (a cornfield)

Paragraphs 2–3 Read the text. *Some people raise cows on a farm. Some people grow food, such as corn, on a farm. What do people grow on a farm?* (food, corn) *Plants grown for food are called* crops. *Farmers send their crops to stores. People buy the crops at the store. Some crops are corn, rice, and bananas.*

 What do farmers grow? Talk to a partner.

Beginning Help partners name food that grows on a farm.

Intermediate *With a partner, ask and answer: What food comes from a farm?* Corn *comes from a farm.* Challenge partners to think of four different crops.

Advanced/Advanced High Have partners name and tell about at least three different crops. Guide partners to use complete sentences.

Card 2

Paragraph 1 Read the text. *People all over the world eat potatoes.* Point to the field. *Potatoes grow on farms in fields. Where do potatoes grow?* (farms, fields)

LEARNING GOALS

We can listen actively to understand how food grows on farms.

OBJECTIVES

With prompting and support, ask and answer questions about key details in a text.

With prompting and support, describe the connection between pieces of information in a text.

With prompting and support, describe the relationship between illustrations and the text in which they appear.

Confirm understanding of a text read aloud or information presented orally or through other media by asking and answering questions about key details and requesting clarification if something is not understood.

LANGUAGE OBJECTIVES

Children will explain how farmers grow different crops around the world, using simple sentences.

ELA ACADEMIC LANGUAGE

• *nonfiction*
• Cognates: *no ficción*

MATERIALS

Interactive Read Aloud, "Farms Around the World"

Visual Vocabulary Cards

DIGITAL TOOLS

Have children listen to the selection as they follow along to develop comprehension.

Use the vocabulary activity for additional support.

Paragraph 2 Read the text. Point to the potato plants. *Farmers plant potatoes in the spring. Potatoes grow under the soil, or dirt. Farmers harvest, or get, the potatoes in the fall. Where do potatoes grow?* (under the soil) *When do farmers harvest the potatoes?* (fall)

Paragraphs 3–4 Read the text. *Farmers dig up the potatoes. Farmers send the potatoes to stores. How do farmers get the potatoes?* (They dig up the potatoes.) *Where do the farmers send the potatoes?* (to stores)

 Ask and answer with a partner: Where do potatoes come from?

Beginning Have partners point to the image as they respond. *Potatoes grow in the* <u>soil</u>.

Intermediate Have partners ask and answer: Where do potatoes grow? *Potatoes grow* <u>in the soil</u>.

Advanced/Advanced High *With a partner, ask and answer questions about potatoes.* (Sample questions: Who grows potatoes? Where do potatoes grow?)

Card 3

Paragraphs 1–2 Read the text. Point to the image. *Farmers plant the rice under dirt. Then they cover the dirt with water. The water helps the rice grow. What does rice need to grow?* (water)

Paragraph 4 Read the text. *Farmers ship, or send, the rice to stores in many countries. Where do farmers ship the rice?* (to stores around the world)

 How does rice grow? Talk to a partner.

Beginning Have partners point to the image as they respond. *Rice grows* <u>in water/fields</u>.

Intermediate *With a partner, ask and answer: Does rice grow in water or under the soil? Rice grows* <u>in water</u>.

Advanced/Advanced High *With a partner, ask and answer questions about rice.* (Example: How does rice grow?)

Advanced/Advanced High *With a partner, ask and answer questions about rice. Then tell how potatoes and rice are the same or different.* Provide modeling.

Card 4

Paragraphs 1–2 Read the text. Point to the image. *Bananas grow on tall trees in warm places. Banana plants need wet dirt and warm air to grow. Cold air can hurt the banana plants. What do banana plants need to grow?* (wet dirt, warm air)

Paragraphs 3–5 Read the text. Point to the bag. *Farmers put bags over the bananas to help them grow. The bags protect the bananas from, or keep out, the sun and bugs. What do the bags do?* (protect the bananas) *Farmers ship green bananas to stores. When the bananas turn yellow, they are ripe, or ready to eat. What color is a ripe banana?* (yellow)

 Tell what you know about bananas. Talk to a partner.

Beginning Guide partners to point to details in the image. *The bananas are* <u>green</u>. *They grow on* <u>trees</u>.

Intermediate Have partners use the photograph to respond. *Bananas grow* <u>on trees</u>. *They need* <u>warm air</u>. *The bag protects them from* <u>the sun and bugs</u>.

 Retell Use the **Interactive Read-Aloud Cards** to retell the information with children. Model retelling what crop each card shows. Help partners retell about the crop shown on the card.

FORMATIVE ASSESSMENT

STUDENT CHECK-IN
Have partners retell what crops the farmers grow in the text. Then, have children reflect using the Check-In routine.

 Independent Time

Draw and Share Have children draw one of the plants from the text to show how it grows. Have partners share and tell about their drawings with each other.

LEARNING GOALS

We can reread to better understand the text.

OBJECTIVES

With prompting and support, identify the main topic and retell key details of a text.

Ask and answer questions to help determine or clarify the meaning of words and phrases in a text.

Actively engage in group reading activities with purpose and understanding.

Ask and answer questions in order to seek help, get information, or clarify something that is not understood.

LANGUAGE OBJECTIVES

Children will inform about qualities of fruits and vegetables, using simple sentences.

ELA ACADEMIC LANGUAGE

• *title*
• Cognates: *título*

MATERIALS

ELL Leveled Reader: *Let's Make a Salad!*

Online Differentiated Text, "On a Farm"

Online ELL Visual Vocabulary Cards

DIGITAL TOOLS

MULTIMODAL

Have children listen to the selection as they follow along to develop comprehension.

Use the vocabulary activity for additional support.

Let's Make a Salad!

Prepare to Read

Build Background Show an image of a salad. *What is in a salad?* Model answering the question. *There is lettuce in a salad.* Elicit other answers. *There is/ are _____ in a salad.* Help children with vocabulary as needed. Tell children that they are going to read a nonfiction text. *A nonfiction text gives facts, or information, about a topic. A topic is what a text is about. The title is* Let's Make a Salad! *What do you think the book's topic is? The topic is making a _____.*

Focus on Vocabulary Use the routine on the **ELL Visual Vocabulary Cards** to preteach *healthy* and *teamwork*. Use the images and any labels to identify and model the use of key vocabulary in context.

Lexile BR

Read the Text

Use the Interactive Question-Response Routine to help children understand the text.

Pages 2–8

Pages 2–3 Point to the images. *The farmer is on his farm. What grows on a farm? Let's read the labels together. Repeat the words: lettuce, carrots. These are vegetables. Where do you think the farmer gets them from?* (from his farm)

 Describe, or tell details about, the vegetables. Talk to a partner.

Beginning Have children point to the images as they respond with color words. *The lettuce is* green. *The carrots are* orange.

Intermediate Have partners ask and answer: *What* vegetable *is this? This is* lettuce. *The lettuce is* green. *These are* carrots. *The carrots are* orange.

Advanced/Advanced High Have partners ask and answer questions about the vegetables. (*What vegetable is this? What does it look like? Where does it grow?*)

Pages 4–5 *What does the farmer get?* (tomatoes, peppers) *What else is on the table?* (bowl, spoon) *What do you think will go in the bowl?* (vegetables) *What is the farmer going to make?* (a salad)

Topic and Details Review with children the details they described from Pages 2–5. *What does the farmer do?* (He is making a salad.)

What do you see on the table? Talk to a partner.

Beginning Have children point to the images on both pages as they respond. *I see* tomatoes/peppers/a bowl/ a spoon/lettuce/carrots.

Intermediate Have partners ask a question about one of the vegetables. *What color are tomatoes? The tomatoes* are red.

Advanced/Advanced High Guide partners to give details about what they see. Model details as needed.

Pages 6–8 *Let's read the labels. Repeat after me: radishes, cheese. What does the farmer get?* (radishes, cheese) *Which one is not a vegetable?* (cheese) *Who helps the farmer?* (his family)

Let's go back and **reread** *all the food labels. How does the family help the farmer? Talk to a partner.*

Beginning Have partners point to the family and repeat descriptions after you. *She is cutting the tomato.* Do this for each action. Then ask: *What are they making? They are making a* salad.

Intermediate Have partners point to the different people and ask and answer: *What is she/he doing? She/he is* [action] *the* [vegetable].

Advanced/Advanced High Guide partners to point to images and give details about what they see. Model details as needed.

Retell Have partners retell the story. Have them take turns pointing to a picture and describing it to each other.

Focus on Fluency

Read pages 2-8 with appropriate expression. Then read the text aloud and have children echo read. For additional practice, have children record themselves reading the same text a few times and then select their favorite recording to play for you.

Build Knowledge: Make Connections

Talk About the Text Have partners discuss food that grows on a farm.

Write About the Text Then have children add their ideas to their Build Knowledge page of their reader's notebook.

Self-Selected Reading

Have children select an informational text from the online **Leveled Reader Library,** or read the **Differentiated Text:** "On a Farm."

LITERACY ACTIVITIES

Have children complete the Literacy Activities on the inside back cover of the book.

FORMATIVE ASSESSMENT

◑ STUDENT CHECK-IN

Have partners reread and retell descriptive details about food that comes from a farm. Then have children reflect using the Check-In routine.

LEVEL UP

IF children can read *Let's Make a Salad!* ELL Level with fluency and correctly answer questions,

THEN tell children that they will read a more detailed version of the story.

HAVE children page through *Let's Make a Salad! On Level* and describe each picture in simple language.

• Have children read the selection, checking their comprehension and providing assistance as necessary.

MODELED WRITING

LEARNING GOALS

We can write about our favorite fruit.

OBJECTIVES

Compose informative texts in which they name what they are writing about.

LANGUAGE OBJECTIVES

Children will explain by writing a sentence using the verb *like.*

ELA ACADEMIC LANGUAGE

• *sentence*

Writing Practice Display the *grapes* **Photo Cards.** Then have children echo read the sample sentence from the **Teacher's Edition,** p. T216. Guide children to analyze the sentence: *What is this sentence about? What is the subject?* (grapes) *What can we say about them?* (are my favorite fruit) Read the prompt at the bottom of the page, and ask a volunteer to answer it. Then have children write their own sentence.

Beginning Provide a sentence frame: I will write about <u>apples</u>. Then help partners think of the sentence they will write: *Who is the actor?* (I) *What is the action?* (like apples)

Intermediate Have partners take turns asking and answering *who/what* questions to create their sentence. Provide a sentence frame if needed.

Advanced/Advanced High Encourage children to stretch words to help them write sounds. Have children share their sentence with the group.

FORMATIVE ASSESSMENT ➲ **STUDENT CHECK IN** Partners share their sentences. Ask children to reflect using the Check-In routine.

INTERACTIVE WRITING

LEARNING GOALS

We can write where the orange began and ended its journey.

OBJECTIVES

With guidance and support, add details to strengthen writing as needed.

LANGUAGE OBJECTIVES

Children will inform by writing sentences using order words.

ELA ACADEMIC LANGUAGE

• *sequence*

• Cognate: *secuencia*

Analyze the Prompt Have children echo read the sample sentence on p. T186. *What does* it *refer to in the sentence?* (the orange) Remind children about the writing trait: *We write about events in the order they happen. Should we tell what last happens to the orange first?* (no) Then help children complete the sentence frames at the bottom of the page.

Beginning Display the illustrations at the beginning and end of the **Literature Big Book** story, and have children tell what they see: The orange starts on a <u>tree</u>. The orange ends with a <u>boy</u>.

Intermediate Have partners use the illustrations and sequence words such as *first, next,* and *last* to talk about the orange's journey before completing the sentence frames.

Advanced/Advanced High Challenge children to think of their own sentences to tell about the orange's journey in order.

FORMATIVE ASSESSMENT ➲ **STUDENT CHECK IN** Partners share their sentences. Ask children to reflect using the Check-In routine.

INDEPENDENT WRITING

LEARNING GOALS

We can write about the texts we read.

OBJECTIVES

Use dictating and writing to narrate events in the order in which they occurred.

LANGUAGE OBJECTIVES

Children will inform by writing sentences using order words.

ELA ACADEMIC LANGUAGE

- *event, pronoun*
- Cognates: *evento, pronombre*

Find Text Evidence Use the Independent Writing routine. Ask questions to help children orally retell "Ron with Red," such as: *Who is the story about?* (Ron, Red, Dad, and Mom) *What does Red see?* (a bird) Then read the prompt on p. T196: *What does Ron do at the park?* Display p. 67 of the **Reading/Writing Companion**. *What does Ron do first?* (walk with Red) Then turn to p. 68. *What does Ron do now?* (walk with Red, look for a bird)

Write to the Prompt Write the sentence starters on the board, and read them. Model completing the first sentence frame, and have children choral read the response. Repeat with the remaining sentence frames. Then ask children to copy the sentences into their writer's notebook.

Beginning Have partners take turns reading their sentences to each other. Then help children talk about their sentences: I used the pronoun *he*.

Intermediate Encourage children to point to pronouns in their writing. Then provide a sentence frame to help them talk about the sequence of events they wrote about: I told what <u>Ron did first</u>.

Advanced/Advanced High Challenge children to come up with their own sentences that tell the sequence of events in the story. Have them identify pronouns they used.

FORMATIVE ASSESSMENT ❯ **STUDENT CHECK IN** Partners share their sentences. Ask children to reflect using the Check-In routine.

SELF-SELECTED WRITING

LEARNING GOALS

We can revise our writing.

OBJECTIVES

Demonstrate command of the conventions of standard English grammar and usage when writing.

LANGUAGE OBJECTIVES

Children can inquire about their writing by checking their pronouns.

ELA ACADEMIC LANGUAGE

- *pronoun*
- Cognate: *pronombre*

Work with children to revise group writing activity. Read the sentences, pointing to each word as you read. Model and ask questions as you read. For example, *What pronoun can we replace this word with?* After you have made the necessary revisions, have children write their own clean copy of the sentences and then publish it.

For more support with grammar, use the **Language Transfers Handbook,** and review **Language Development Card** 16A.

FORMATIVE ASSESSMENT ❯ **STUDENT CHECK IN** Partners tell what revisions they made. Ask children to reflect using the Check-In routine.

Summative Assessment
Get Ready for Unit Assessment

Unit 5 Tested Skills

LISTENING AND READING COMPREHENSION	VOCABULARY	GRAMMAR	SPEAKING AND WRITING
• Listening Actively • Text Structure • Sequence	• Words and Categories	• Pronouns	• Offering Opinions • Presenting • Composing/Writing • Retelling/Recounting

Create a Student Profile

Record data from the following resources in the Student Profile charts on pages 136–137 of the Assessment book.

COLLABORATIVE	INTERPRETIVE	PRODUCTIVE

• Collaborative Conversations Rubrics
  • Listening
  • Speaking
	• Leveled Unit Assessment
	  • Listening Comprehension
	  • Reading Comprehension
	  • Vocabulary
	  • Grammar
	• Presentation Rubric
	  • Listening
	• *Wonders* Unit Assessment
		• Weekly Progress Monitoring
		• Leveled Unit Assessment
		  • Speaking
		  • Writing
		• Presentation Rubric
		  • Speaking
		• Write to Sources Rubric
		• *Wonders* Unit Assessment

The Foundational Skills Kit, Language Development Kit, and Adaptive Learning provide additional student data for progress monitoring.

Level Up

Use the following chart, along with your Student Profiles, to guide your Level Up decisions.

LEVEL UP	If **BEGINNING** level students are able to do the following, they may be ready to move to the **INTERMEDIATE** level:	If **INTERMEDIATE** level students are able to do the following, they may be ready to move to the **ADVANCED** level:	If **ADVANCED** level students are able to do the following, they may be ready to move to **ON** level:
COLLABORATIVE	• participate in collaborative conversations using basic vocabulary and grammar and simple phrases or sentences • discuss simple pictorial or text prompts	• participate in collaborative conversations using appropriate words and phrases and complete sentences • use limited academic vocabulary across and within disciplines	• participate in collaborative conversations using more sophisticated vocabulary and correct grammar • communicate effectively across a wide range of language demands in social and academic contexts
INTERPRETIVE	• identify details in simple read alouds • understand common vocabulary and idioms and interpret language related to familiar social, school, and academic topics • make simple inferences and make simple comparisons • exhibit an emerging receptive control of lexical, syntactic, phonological, and discourse features	• identify main ideas and/or make some inferences from simple read alouds • use context clues to identify word meanings and interpret basic vocabulary and idioms • compare, contrast, summarize, and relate text to graphic organizers • exhibit a limited range of receptive control of lexical, syntactic, phonological, and discourse features when addressing new or familiar topics	• determine main ideas in read alouds that have advanced vocabulary • use context clues to determine meaning, understand multiple-meaning words, and recognize synonyms of social and academic vocabulary • analyze information, make sophisticated inferences, and explain their reasoning • command a high degree of receptive control of lexical, syntactic, phonological, and discourse features
PRODUCTIVE	• express ideas and opinions with basic vocabulary and grammar and simple phrases or sentences • restate information or retell a story using basic vocabulary • exhibit an emerging productive control of lexical, syntactic, phonological, and discourse features	• produce coherent language with limited elaboration or detail • restate information or retell a story using mostly accurate, although limited, vocabulary • exhibit a limited range of productive control of lexical, syntactic, phonological, and discourse features when addressing new or familiar topics	• produce sentences with more sophisticated vocabulary and correct grammar • restate information or retell a story using extensive and accurate vocabulary and grammar • tailor language to a particular purpose and audience • command a high degree of productive control of lexical, syntactic, phonological, and discourse features

LESSONS 1-2

We can understand important ideas and details in a story.

We can identify rhyme in a poem.

OBJECTIVES

With prompting and support, identify characters and setting in a story.

Recognize common types of texts (e.g., storybooks, poems).

With prompting and support, describe the relationship between illustrations and the story in which they appear.

Confirm understanding of a text read aloud or information presented orally or through other media by asking and answering questions about key details and requesting clarification if something is not understood.

LANGUAGE OBJECTIVES

Children will narrate the changes in the seasons, using sequence words and key vocabulary.

ELA ACADEMIC LANGUAGE

• *illustration, realistic fiction, sequence*

• Cognates: *illustración, ficción realista, secuencia*

MATERIALS

Literature Big Book, *Mama, Is It Summer Yet?,* pp. 3–33 and 34–39

Visual Vocabulary Cards

DIGITAL TOOLS

Have children listen to the selection as they follow along to develop comprehension.

Use the vocabulary activity for additional support.

Mama, Is It Summer Yet?

Prepare to Read

Build Background Show images of the four seasons and have children name them. *Which season comes after winter? We are going to read about a boy who wants summer to come.* Show images that represent winter, spring, and summer. Talk about what happens in each season. *It is _____ in the _____. I can _____ in the _____.* Tell children they will read a realistic fiction book, a story that could happen in real life.

Literature Big Book

Focus on Vocabulary Use the **Visual Vocabulary Cards** to review the oral vocabulary words *weather* and *seasons.* As you read, use gestures and other visual support to clarify important story words: *yet, little one, buds, swelling, unfold, sprout, swallows, ducklings, bold, honeybees,* and *juicy.* Review the words as you read, and have children add these words to their personal glossaries.

Summarize the Text Before reading, give a summary of the story: *A boy wants summer to come. The boy and his mother do many things before summer comes.*

Read the Text

Use the Interactive Question-Response Routine to help children understand the story.

Pages 4–15

Pages 4–7 Read the text. Point to the trees. *The boy wants summer to come. But The trees have no leaves. The trees have tiny buds. Soon they will have leaves.* Point to the boy on page 6. *The boy wears a big coat, a hat, and a scarf to keep warm. Is it hot or cold outside?* (cold) *How does the illustration help you know?* (The boy is wearing a coat, hat, and scarf.)

Pages 14–15 Read the text. *The boy and Mama plant a garden. The boy waters. Mama plants seeds.* Point to the tree branches. *The buds are growing.* Point to the boy. *The boy wears a jacket. Does the boy still wear his big coat outside?* (no)

 How do you know it is getting warm outside? Talk to a partner.

Beginning Help children point to illustrations and complete sentences: *The boy and Mama plant <u>a garden</u>. The boy does not wear a big <u>coat</u>.*

Intermediate Provide sentence frames: <u>Buds</u> *are growing on the* <u>trees</u>. *The boy and Mama* <u>plant a garden</u> *together. Now the boy wears a* <u>jacket</u>.

Advanced/Advanced High Have partners use illustration details to tell about the change in seasons. (The boy and Mama plant. The boy wears a jacket outside.)

Pages 16–27

Pages 18–23 Read the text. *Mama says the wind will be warm soon.* Point to the swallows on pages 18 and 19. Use context clues to explain the meaning of *swallows are singing.* Point to the ducklings on page 23. *What are these little birds?* (baby ducks; ducklings) *The baby ducks follow their mother.*

Pages 26–27 Point to the characters. *The boy and Mama do not wear jackets. It must be warm now. I see flowers growing on the tree. Apples will grow soon.*

 How do you know summer is coming? Talk with a partner about what happens.

Beginning Have partners point to the illustration as you help them respond: *The birds sing. The air is warm. There are flowers on an apple tree.*

Intermediate Provide sentence frames: *There are birds singing. Baby ducks; ducklings follow their mother. Soon apples will grow on the tree. The boy does not need a jacket.*

Pages 28–33

Pages 30–33 *The sun is warm. The boy and Mama eat berries. They sit in a pool. Now the ducklings are big. The boy feeds the ducks. The boy asks, "Mama, is it summer now?" What is the answer?* (yes)

 What do the boy and Mama do in summer? Talk to a partner.

Beginning Guide children to point to details and say after you: *Mama eats a berry. The boy and Mama sit in a pool. It is summer now.*

Intermediate Help children describe the setting and events: *In summer, the boy and Mama eat berries. They sit in the pool. The boy feeds a berry to a duck.*

Advanced/Advanced High Help children add details from the text and pictures. (They eat berries. The berries are juicy and sweet in summer.)

 Retell Use the **Retelling Cards** for *Mama, Is it Summer Yet?* to retell the story with children.

Display the cards and model retelling using sequence words, such as *first, next,* and *last,* as you point to the events and actions in the cards. Then help children take turns retelling one part using the sequence words.

 4 **Paired Selection: "New Snow," "Rain Song," "Covers," "Honey, I Love"**

Pages 34-40 Read each poem and paraphrase the text. For example: *In "Rain Song," the poet says rain changes colors.* Point out the rain and children in rain jackets holding umbrellas. *In spring, it is pink like a flower. In summer, it is many colors.* Display a visual of a rainbow in summer. *The poet calls it rainbow rain. In fall, it is brown like leaves on the ground. What color is rain in winter?* (White; it becomes snow.)

 What kinds of weather do the poets tell about? Talk to a partner.

Beginning Guide children to point to and name a detail about weather in each poem.

Intermediate Help partners tell how each poet feels about weather. *The poet thinks rain changes colors.*

Advanced/Advanced High Guide children to talk about details in the illustrations. (Example: Two friends walk on green grass in the spring rain.)

FORMATIVE ASSESSMENT

STUDENT CHECK-IN

Main Selection Have partners retell three things that Mama notices outside as the seasons change.

Paired Selection Have partners discuss what the children are doing in each illustration.

Then have children reflect using the Check-In routine.

 Independent Time

Draw and Share Have partners talk about things that happen during each season. Prompt them to draw a picture of a seasonal event or activity.

LESSON 3

LEARNING GOALS

We can listen actively to learn about how the seasons are different.

OBJECTIVES

With prompting and support, ask and answer questions about key details in a text.

With prompting and support, retell key details of a text.

With prompting and support, describe the connection between two individuals, events, ideas, or pieces of information in a text.

Ask and answer questions in order to seek help, get information, or clarify something that is not understood.

LANGUAGE OBJECTIVES

Children will explain how the seasons are different using weather words.

ELA ACADEMIC LANGUAGE

• compare, nonfiction
• Cognates: comparar, no ficción

MATERIALS

Interactive Read Aloud, "A Tour of the Seasons"

Visual Vocabulary Cards

DIGITAL TOOLS

Have children listen to the selection as they follow along to develop comprehension.

Use the vocabulary activity for additional support.

"A Tour of the Seasons"

Interactive Read Aloud

Prepare to Read

Build Background Display visuals of each season and help children name the seasons. Using the images, discuss what happens in each season. Provide sentence frames to show how nature changes in each season.

Focus on Vocabulary Use the **Visual Vocabulary Cards** to review the oral vocabulary words *weather, season, spot, active,* and *migrate.* As you read, use gestures and other visual support to clarify important selection words: *activities, melting, picnics, clouds, thunder,* and *lightning.*

Summarize the Text *We are going to read an about the four seasons.* Remind children that it is a nonfiction text. The topic they will learn about is how seasons change and are all different.

Read the Text

Use the Interactive Question-Response Routine to help children understand the text.

Card 1

Paragraphs 1–2 Read the text. *The weather is cold. It snows.* Point to the trees. *The trees have no leaves. Children can ride sleds down hills when it snows. You can build a snowman like the family in the picture.* Point out that people are wearing warm, winter clothing, such as hats, coats, and gloves. *What season is it?* (winter) *How do we play in winter?* (ride sleds; build a snowman)

Paragraphs 3–4 Read the text. *Each season is different. The weather changes. The weather can be warm or cold. The weather can be rainy or dry. How are the seasons different?* (The weather can be different.)

 What happens in winter? Talk to a partner.

Beginning Have partners point to the photo as they respond. *It is* cold *in winter. The family builds a* snowman *in winter.*

Intermediate Provide sentence frames: *The weather is* cold *in winter. It can* snow. *A family* builds a snowman. *People wear* coats; hats; gloves *to keep* warm.

Advanced/Advanced High Guide children to ask and answer questions about winter. (Sample answer: How do people play in the snow? Children ride sleds. You can build a snowman.)

Card 2

Paragraphs 1–2 *Spring comes after winter. The air is warm. Snow melts. Trees grow leaves. You see animals like squirrels and birds. What color are the leaves?* (green)

Paragraphs 3–5 *The park is green. People play baseball.* Point out the family picnic in the photo. *They have a picnic and eat in the park. Where do people have picnics?* (in a park) *People plant gardens. Farmers also plant crops, or plants like vegetables that we eat. What do people plant?* (gardens; crops)

 Let's compare spring and winter. How are they different? Talk with a partner.

Beginning Help children point to the grass and trees in the park and say after you: *Snow melts in spring. Green grass grows. The trees have green leaves.*

Intermediate Ask guided questions to help children describe spring. *How does the weather change? It gets* warmer *in spring. What does the family do? The family* has a picnic *and plays* in the park.

Advanced/Advanced High Guide children to describe how nature changes and people do springtime activities. (Sample answer: The park is green now. The family can have a picnic together.)

Card 3

Paragraph 1 *In summer, the weather is hot.* Point to the family on the beach. *School ends. Families have fun outside. They go to the beach or a pool. They cook food outside on a grill. What is the weather like?* (hot)

Paragraphs 3–4 *In summer, you can see insects like flies, bees, mosquitoes, crickets, and butterflies. People eat fresh fruits and vegetables. What do people eat in summer?* (vegetables; fruits)

 How do families have fun in summer? Talk to a partner.

Beginning Help children describe details in the photo after you, and help them name summer activities.

Intermediate Provide sentence frames: *A family can go to* the beach *or a pool. Families can cook* on a grill.

Card 4

Paragraphs 1–2 *Autumn, or fall, is the time to pick apples and eat pumpkin pie. Children jump and*

play in piles of leaves on the ground. The weather changes a lot in autumn. Some days you need to wear a sweater or jacket. What is the weather like in autumn? (Some days are hot. Some days are cool.)

Paragraphs 3–5 *In autumn, animals get ready for winter. Plants change. Leaves on trees turn yellow, red, and orange. Then they fall off. Birds migrate, or fly far away to warm places. What happens to tree leaves?* (They change colors and fall off trees.) *What happens at school?* (A new school year begins.)

 What happens in autumn? Talk to a partner.

Beginning Help children form simple sentences: *The leaves* change *colors. School* starts *again.*

Intermediate Provide sentence frames: *Children can play in* (piles of) leaves. *Birds* fly; migrate *to warm places. Leaves turn* red, yellow, and orange. *Children go back to* school.

 Retell Use the illustrations on the **Interactive Read-Aloud Cards** to retell the text with children. Display the cards and model retelling details in the photos and text. Then help partners take turns retelling details about one of the seasons.

❯ **STUDENT CHECK-IN**

Have partners retell how two of the seasons are different. Then, have children reflect using the Check-In routine.

Independent Time

Draw and Share Ask children to fold a piece of paper in half. Have children choose two seasons to compare and draw pictures that show how the two seasons are different. Use **Oral Language Sentence Frames**, p. 1, as they share the differences in the seasons.

LESSONS 4-5

LEARNING GOALS

We can visualize what happens in a story.

OBJECTIVES

With prompting and support, retell familiar stories, including key details.

With prompting and support, identify characters and events in a story.

With prompting and support, describe the relationship between illustrations and the story in which they appear.

Speak audibly and express thoughts, feelings, and ideas clearly.

LANGUAGE OBJECTIVES

Children will narrate how the character spends time in different seasons, using nouns, verbs, and simple sentences.

ELA ACADEMIC LANGUAGE

• *fantasy, comprehension, retelling*
• Cognates: *fantasía, comprensión*

MATERIALS

ELL Leveled Reader: *Little Bear*

Online Differentiated Text, "The Seasons"

Online ELL Visual Vocabulary Cards

DIGITAL TOOLS

Have children listen to the selection as they follow along to develop comprehension.

Use the vocabulary activity for additional support.

Little Bear

Prepare to Read

Build Background Show images of the four seasons. Elicit the names of the seasons: *spring, summer, fall,* and *winter.* Review with children what happens in each season. Ask students to describe the weather and activities people do in each season. Provide modeling. *I like to smell the flowers in spring.* Provide sentence frames: *It is _____ in _____. I like to _____ in ____.*

Focus on Vocabulary Use the routine on the **ELL Visual Vocabulary Cards** to preteach *climate* and *hibernate.* Use the images and any labels to identify and model the use of key vocabulary in context.

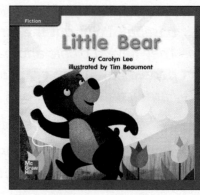

Lexile 300L

Read the Text

Use the Interactive Question-Response Routine to help children understand the story.

Pages 2–8

Pages 2–3 Point to details in the picture on page 2 as you say: *Little Bear walks outside. It looks like spring. It rains. There are flowers. A bird builds its nest. What does Little Bear wear?* (a hat) *Let's read the label together:* hat. *Why is Little Bear wearing a hat?* (It is raining.) Point to picture clues on page 3. *What does Little Bear have?* (a kite) *This story is a fantasy. How do you know? Is Bear real?* (no) *How do you know?* Real bears do not <u>fly kites</u>.

Visualize Discuss the details that help children visualize how Bear feels. *What word tells you that Bear is happy?* (likes)

 What things on these pages help you visualize that it is spring? Talk to a partner.

Beginning Have partners point to details in the pictures as they respond: *I see* <u>flowers; rain; a bird; a kite</u>.

Intermediate Have partners ask and answer: *What do you see? I see* <u>flowers; a bird</u>. *The bird builds a* <u>nest</u>. *It is* <u>raining</u>. *I see a* <u>kite</u> *flying.*

Advanced/Advanced High Guide children to explain why the rain, flowers, and kite are clues that show it is spring. (It rains a lot in spring. Flowers bloom, or grow, in spring. People fly kites in spring.)

Pages 4–5 Point to page 4. *What does Little Bear eat?* (berries) Point to page 5. *What does Little Bear smell?* (flowers) *People can pick juicy berries in summer. What season is it?* (summer)

What does Little Bear like in summer? Talk to a partner.

Beginning Have partners ask and answer: *What does Little Bear like? Little Bear likes* berries; flowers.

Intermediate Help children say descriptive sentences: *Little Bear likes to* eat juicy berries. *He also likes to* smell flowers *in summer.*

Pages 6–8 Point to page 6. *What color are the leaves?* (orange and yellow) *Are the leaves falling from the tree?* (yes) *What does Little Bear catch?* (an orange leaf) *What season is it?* (fall) Point to page 8. *What is falling outside?* (snow) *It must be winter. Bears hibernate, or sleep, in the winter. What does Little Bear like to do?* (take a nap)

Events: Sequence Discuss sequence with children. *What is the order of the seasons in the story?* (spring, summer, fall, winter)

 What does Little Bear like in fall and winter? Talk to a partner.

Beginning Have children point to and describe details after you. For example: *Little Bear likes orange and yellow leaves in fall.*

Intermediate Provide sentence frames: *In fall, Little Bear likes to catch* an orange leaf. *In winter, Bear likes* to take a nap in *his bed.*

Retell Have partners retell the story. Have them take turns pointing to a picture and describing it to each other.

Focus on Fluency

Read pages 2–8 with appropriate expression. Then read the text aloud and have children echo read. For additional practice, have children record themselves reading the same text a few times, and then select their favorite recording to play for you.

Build Knowledge: Make Connections

Talk About the Text Have partners discuss the seasons.

Write About the Text Then have children add their ideas to their Build Knowledge page of their reader's notebook.

Self-Selected Reading

Have children select another story from the online **Leveled Reader Library,** or read the **Differentiated Text,** "The Seasons."

LITERACY ACTIVITIES

Have children complete the Literacy Activities on the inside back cover of the book.

FORMATIVE ASSESSMENT

STUDENT CHECK-IN

Have partners reread and retell one thing that Little Bear does in each season. Then have children reflect using the Check-In Routine.

LEVEL UP

IF children can read *Little Bear* **ELL Level** with fluency and correctly answer the Literacy Activity questions,

THEN tell children that they will read a more detailed version of the story.

HAVE children page through *Little Bear* On Level and describe each picture in simple language.

- Have children read the selection, checking their comprehension and providing assistance as necessary.

WRITING

MODELED WRITING

LEARNING GOALS

We can write about what we like to do in the summer.

OBJECTIVES

Use dictating and writing to compose informative texts in which they name the topic.

LANGUAGE OBJECTIVES

Children will explain by writing a sentence using the verb *like*.

ELA ACADEMIC LANGUAGE

• *season, summer*

Writing Practice Display pp. 32–33 of the **Big Book** and then have children echo read the sample sentence on p. 14 of the **Reading/Writing Companion.** Then have children analyze the sentence using the Actor/ Action routine: *Who is the actor?* (I) *What is the action?* (like to swim) *When?* (in the summer) Read the prompt on p. 15, and ask children to answer it as a group. Write the sentence on the board and point to each word as children choral read. Then ask children to write their own sentence.

Beginning Help partners think of their sentence: *Who is the actor?* (I) *What is the action?* (like going to the beach)

Intermediate Have partners take turns asking and answering *who/what* questions about what they like to do in summer to create their sentences.

Advanced/Advanced High Challenge children to talk about their sentence using the *Actor/Action* routine. Encourage them to share it with the group.

FORMATIVE ASSESSMENT ❱ ➋ **STUDENT CHECK IN** Partners share their sentences. Ask children to reflect using the Check-In routine.

INTERACTIVE WRITING

LEARNING GOALS

We can write what we think about how the author showed that summer is coming.

OBJECTIVES

With guidance and support, respond to questions and suggestions from peers.

LANGUAGE OBJECTIVES

Children will argue by writing sentences using the verbs *think* and *show*.

ELA ACADEMIC LANGUAGE

• *season, summer*

Write a Response: Share the Pen Choral read the sample sentence on p. T270 of the **Teacher's Edition.** Use the Actor/Action routine to review it: *Who is the actor?* (The author) *What is the action* (shows summer is coming) Then ask: *What are we writing about?* (if the author did a good job showing summer is coming) *Can I write about winter?* (no) Help children complete the sentence frames at the bottom of the page.

Beginning Be sure children understand the order of the seasons and what *summer is coming* means. Ask guiding questions to help children recognize the signs that summer is coming in the story.

Intermediate Have partners identify details in the illustrations that show summer is coming: The author shows the flowers blooming.

Advanced/Advanced High Challenge children to think of their own sentence determining if the author does a good job showing summer is coming. Encourage them to share it with the group.

FORMATIVE ASSESSMENT ❱ ➋ **STUDENT CHECK IN** Partners share their sentences. Ask children to reflect using the Check-In routine.

INDEPENDENT WRITING

LEARNING GOALS

We can write about the texts we read.

OBJECTIVES

Use dictating and writing to compose informative texts in which they supply some information about the topic.

LANGUAGE OBJECTIVES

Children will argue by writing sentences using evidence from the text and photos.

ELA ACADEMIC LANGUAGE

• *singular, plural*

• Cognates: *singular, plural*

 Find Text Evidence Use the Independent Writing routine. Ask questions to help children orally retell "Is It Hot?" such as: *What do you see first?* (a cat and flowers) *Is it hot or cold?* (a bit hot) Then read the prompt on p. 29 of the **Reading/Writing Companion:** *Does the author do a good job of showing what spring is like?* Display pp. 20-21 of the text. *What does the author show on this page?* (a kitten and flowers) *The text says it's a bit hot. When does it feel a bit hot? When do flowers grow?* (spring)

 Write a Response Write the sentence starters from the bottom of **Teacher's Edition** p. 280 on the board, and read them. Model completing the first sentence frame, and have children choral read the response. Repeat with the remaining sentence frames. Read the writing checklist, and go through each item on the list. Then have children copy the sentences.

 Beginning Have partners take turns reading their sentences to each other. Then provide a sentence frame to help children talk about their sentences: I started my sentences on the left.

Intermediate Encourage partners to add singular and plural nouns.

Advanced/Advanced High Have partners identify the items on the writing checklist and check off each box.

FORMATIVE ASSESSMENT ❯ **STUDENT CHECK IN** Partners share their sentences. Ask children to reflect using the Check-In routine.

SELF-SELECTED WRITING

LEARNING GOALS

We can revise our writing.

OBJECTIVES

Form regular plural nouns orally by adding /s/ or /es/.

LANGUAGE OBJECTIVES

Children will inquire about their writing by checking singular and plural nouns.

ELA ACADEMIC LANGUAGE

• *plural*

• Cognate: *plural*

 Work with children to correct the grammatical and spelling errors from their self-selected group writing activity. Read the sentences, pointing to each word as you read. Model and ask questions, such as: *Is this word plural? Do we need to add -s or -es at the end?* After you have made necessary revisions, have children write their own clean copy and publish it.

For more support with grammar and plural nouns, use the **Language Transfers Handbook** and **Language Development Cards** 1A, 2A, and 2B.

FORMATIVE ASSESSMENT ❯ **STUDENT CHECK IN** Partners tell what revisions they made. Ask children to reflect using the Check-In routine.

LEARNING GOALS

We can understand important ideas and details in a story.

We can use speech bubbles to learn new information.

OBJECTIVES

With prompting and support, ask and answer questions about key details in a text.

With prompting and support, identify characters, settings, and major events in a story.

Actively engage in group reading activities with purpose and understanding.

Continue a conversation through multiple exchanges.

LANGUAGE OBJECTIVES

Children will narrate how animals react to the rain, using descriptive words.

ELA ACADEMIC LANGUAGE

• fantasy, ask, answer
• Cognates: fantasía

MATERIALS

Literature Big Book, Rain, pp. 4–32 and 33–36
Visual Vocabulary Cards

DIGITAL TOOLS

Have children listen to the selection as they follow along to develop comprehension.

Use the vocabulary activity for additional support.

Rain

Prepare to Read

Build Background Show visuals of rain and a thunderstorm. Help children tell what they can see, hear, and feel when it rains. *I can see _____. What can you hear?* Play the audio of storm sounds. *I can hear _____ and _____. What can you feel? I can feel _____ and _____.*

Focus on Vocabulary Use the **Visual Vocabulary Cards** to review the oral vocabulary words *predict* and *temperature.* As you read, use gestures and other visual support to clarify important story words: *cracked, porcupine, zebras, baboons, boomed, rhino,* and *refreshing.* Review the words in context as you read, and have children add these words to their personal glossaries.

Summarize the Text Before reading, give a short summary of the story: *The animals know that rain is finally coming. Rain brings good things for the animals.* Tell children that this is an animal fantasy story.

Read the Text

Use the Interactive Question-Response Routine to help children understand the story.

Pages 4–15

Pages 4–5 Read the text. *The sun is hot. The grass is dry and yellow. The soil, or earth, is red and cracked. How does the soil look?* (red and cracked)

Pages 6–9 Read the text. *Porcupine can smell that the rain is coming. He tells the zebras. The zebras look up at the sky. They see dark clouds and lightning. They can see rain coming. What do the zebras see?* (clouds, lightning; rain coming)

Pages 12–15 Read the text. Have volunteers name the animals who smell, see, hear, and feel the rain coming. *The lion is sticking out his tongue. He can taste the rain. The lion knows the rain is here. What does the lion do?* (He tastes the rain.)

 How do the animals know the rain is coming? Talk to a partner.

Beginning Review sensory verbs. Then help children point to details and say after you: *Porcupine smells the rain. The zebras see it. The baboons hear it. The rhino feels it. The lion tastes it.*

Intermediate Provide sentence frames: *A porcupine smells the rain. The zebras see clouds and lightning. The baboons hear thunder. The lion tastes the rain.*

Advanced/Advanced High Guide partners to describe specific details animals see and hear. (The zebras see lightning and clouds. Baboons hear thunder boom.)

Literature Big Book

Pages 16–27

Pages 16–20 Read the text. *It rains and rains.* Every river and water hole, or where animals drink, is full of water. The rain causes grasses and leaves to turn green and grow. *What happens to the rivers and water holes?* (They become full.) *Are the grasses dry?* (no) *How do you know?* (They are green, not yellow.)

Pages 24–27 Read the text. Point to the baboons. *The baboons eat fresh, juicy fruit.* Point to the zebras. *The zebras have a refreshing drink. What do the baboons eat?* (fruit) *How does the water taste?* (refreshing)

 How does the rain help the animals? Talk to a partner.

Beginning Have partners point to the pictures as they respond: *The baboons have* fruit *to eat. The zebras have* water *to drink.*

Intermediate Have partners ask and answer: *What do the animals have now? Add details to your answers.* (Sample answer: The baboon has fruit from the trees. The fruit is fresh and juicy.)

Pages 28–32

Pages 28–29 *The porcupine knows the rain will come back. It is important. It gives animals what they need.*

Pages 30–32 *What color is the soil?* (red) *What is happening to the grasses?* (turning yellow and dry) *What is happening to the soil?* (cracking)

 How is the weather different now? Talk to a partner.

Beginning Have partners point to the pictures on pages 30–32 as they respond: *It is* hot. *There is no* rain. *The red soil is* hot. *The red soil is* dry.

Intermediate Provide sentence frames: *The* sun *shines over the land. The soil is drying* out. *The red soil is* hot.

 Retell Use the **Retelling Cards** for *Rain* to retell the story with children. Display the cards and model retelling using sequence words, such as *first, next, then,* and *last* as you point to the

events and actions in the cards. Then help children take turns retelling one part using sequence words.

 ### LESSON 4 Paired Selection: "Cloud Watch"

Pages 33–36 Read the text. Point to each illustration as you paraphrase the text. For example: *The man says these are cirrus clouds. They look like a bird's feathers. He predicts, or makes a guess, that it will stay sunny. Will rain fall from these clouds?* (No, he predicts that it will stay sunny.)

 Talk about each cloud on page 36. What cloud brings rain?

Beginning Help children repeat key details: For example: *The cloud is puffy. The cloud brings rain.*

Intermediate Provide sentence frames: *This cloud* floats *high in the sky. This cloud* changes *into different* shapes. *This cloud brings* rain and storms.

Advanced/Advanced High Have children predict the weather based on the clouds. Provide modeling. *I predict it will rain because dark [cumulonimbus] clouds are in the sky.*

FORMATIVE ASSESSMENT

◆ STUDENT CHECK-IN

Main Selection Have partners retell what the animals did when the rain came.

Paired Selection Have partners describe the three types of clouds in the text.

Then, have children reflect using the Check-In routine.

 ### Independent Time

Draw and Share Have children complete a web with the word *rain* in the center. Have them draw images in the outer circles that show what they learned about rain and clouds. Help children label their drawings.

LEARNING GOALS

We can listen actively to understand the folktale.

OBJECTIVES

Recognize common types of texts (e.g., storybooks, poems).

With prompting and support, compare and contrast the adventures and experiences of characters in familiar stories.

Actively engage in group reading activities with purpose and understanding.

Confirm understanding of a text read aloud or information presented orally or through other media by asking and answering questions about key details and requesting clarification if something is not understood.

LANGUAGE OBJECTIVES

Children will narrate how the two main characters compete in complete sentences.

ELA ACADEMIC LANGUAGE

• *characters, folktale*

MATERIALS

Interactive Read Aloud, "The Battle of Wind and Rain"

Visual Vocabulary Cards

DIGITAL TOOLS

Have children listen to the selection as they follow along to develop comprehension.

Use the vocabulary activity for additional support.

"The Battle of Wind and Rain"

Interactive Read Aloud

Prepare to Read

Build Background Talk with children about what happens during a storm. Point out that sometimes there are strong winds before rain falls in the storm. *We are going to read a folktale called "The Battle of Wind and Rain."* Explain that a folktale is a story that people tell for many years. *In this story, the characters are Wind, Thunder, Lightning, and Rain.*

Focus on Vocabulary Use the **Visual Vocabulary Cards** to review the oral vocabulary words *clever, drought, predict, storm,* and *temperature.* As you read, use gestures and other visual support to clarify important story words: *powerful, bend, admit,* and *embarrassed.*

Summarize the Text Before reading, give a short summary of the selection: *Wind, Thunder, Lightning, and Rain all live in the sky together. Wind wants Rain to play a game to see who is the most powerful.*

Read the Text

Use the Interactive Question-Response Routine to help children understand the story.

Card 1

Paragraphs 1–5 Read the text. *Thunder, Lightning, and Rain are sleeping. Wind is bored. He wants to make a storm. What does Wind want to do?* (make a storm)

Paragraphs 6–9 Read the text. *Wind blows air on Rain, but she does not want to play with him. Wind says he is the most powerful, or strongest, thing in nature. Rain says she wants to sleep. Does Rain want to play with Wind?* (no)

 Why does Wind want Rain to wake up? Talk to a partner.

Beginning Have partners point to the illustration as they tell what each of those characters wants. *Wind wants to make <u>a storm</u>. Rain wants to <u>sleep</u>.*

Intermediate Have partners complete these sentences with details. *Wind wants <u>to make a storm</u>. Wind feels <u>bored</u>. Rain wants <u>to sleep</u>. She feels <u>tired</u>.*

Advanced/Advanced High Guide children to respond in complete sentences. (Wind wants to play and make a storm. He needs Rain to make a storm.)

Card 2

Paragraphs 1–2 *Wind begs Rain to play a game. He wants to find out who is more powerful. He blows air on Rain. What does Wind want to find out?* (who is more powerful)

Paragraphs 3–4 *Rain says she will play. Wind must leave Rain alone* if she wins. Point to Wind. *If Wind wins, Rain cannot go down to Earth unless Wind tells her she can go. What happens if Rain beats Wind?* (Wind has to leave Rain alone.)

Paragraphs 5–6 *Rain worries. Plants, animals, and people need her for water. People and animals need water to drink. Plants need water to grow.*

 How does Rain help the plants, animals, and people on Earth? Talk to a partner.

Beginning Help students complete the sentences. *We need to* drink *water. Plants need water to* grow.

Intermediate Provide sentence frames: *People and animals* need water to drink. *Plants* need water to grow. *People and animals need plants for* food.

Advanced/Advanced High *What will happen if Rain cannot go down to Earth?* (No plants will grow.)

Card 3

Paragraphs 1–3 *Rain tells Wind to make the monkey leave the bamboo tree. Rain knows bamboo will bend, not break.*

Paragraphs 4–6 *Wind blows and blows. The tree sways. But the monkey holds on. Wind gives up. Does Wind beat Rain?* (no)

 What does Wind try to do? Talk to a partner.

Beginning Have children point to details in the picture and say after you: *Wind blows. He wants the monkey to leave. The monkey does not leave the tree.*

Intermediate *Why does Wind want the monkey to leave the tree?* (It is part of the game.) *The tree sways back and forth when Wind blows. What does the monkey do? The monkey holds onto* the tree *and enjoys* the ride.

Card 4

Paragraphs 1–6 *Rain makes a shower fall, but the monkey holds on. Wind laughs at Rain. But Rain is*

patient. Finally, the monkey climbs out of the tree. What does the monkey do? (leaves the tree)

Paragraphs 7–8 *Wind admits, or accepts, that Rain is more powerful. Wind flies off because he is so embarrassed. Now when Wind blows very hard, Rain sometimes stops him. How does Wind feel?* (embarrassed)

 Who wins the game? How? Talk to a partner.

Beginning Help partners respond: *The monkey* leaves *the tree.* Rain wins *the game.*

Intermediate Help children explain how Rain wins. *Rain's drops* keep falling. *At last, the monkey* leaves the tree to find a place to get dry.

 Retell Use the illustrations on the Interactive Read-Aloud Cards to retell the story with children. Display the cards and model retelling using sequence words, as you point to the events and actions in the cards. Then help partners take turns retelling one part using the sequence words.

FORMATIVE ASSESSMENT

⊙ STUDENT CHECK-IN
Have partners retell how Rain wins the game. Then, have children reflect using the Check-In routine.

Independent Time

Asking Questions Have partners talk about a time when they played a game. Have them practice asking questions: *What is the game's name? Who played with you? When did you play it?* Allow children to draw a picture to share.

LEARNING GOALS

We can visualize what happens in a story.

OBJECTIVES

With prompting and support, retell familiar stories, including key details.

With prompting and support, identify characters and events in a story.

With prompting and support, describe the relationship between illustrations and the story in which they appear.

Continue a conversation through multiple exchanges.

LANGUAGE OBJECTIVES

Children will narrate what the characters can do in different weather using key vocabulary.

ELA ACADEMIC LANGUAGE

• *visualize, characters, labels, sequence*

• Cognates: *visualizar, secuencia*

MATERIALS

ELL Leveled Reader: *Weather Is Fun*

Online Differentiated Text, "Lots of Weather"

Online ELL Visual Vocabulary Cards

DIGITAL TOOLS

Have children listen to the selection as they follow along to develop comprehension.

Use the vocabulary activity for additional support.

Weather Is Fun

Prepare to Read

Build Background Ask children about the weather. *What is the weather like outside? It is _____.* Show images of different weather and elicit weather words, such as *cold, warm, hot, sunny, windy, rainy, snowy, cloudy.* Name the four seasons and review the weather in each season. Provide a sentence frame: *It is _____ in _____. What activities can you do?* Model answering the question: *I can go outside on sunny days.* Provide a sentence frame: *I can _____ on _____ days.*

Lexile BR

Focus on Vocabulary Use the routine on the **ELL Visual Vocabulary Cards** to preteach *activity* and *change.* Help children use the words *activity* and *change* in sentences. Reading *is an activity. The weather* changes *in every season.* Use the illustrations and labels to identify and model the use of key vocabulary in context.

Read the Text

Use the Interactive Question-Response Routine to help children understand the story.

Pages 2–8

Pages 2–3 Point to page 2. *Who are the characters?* (the girl; her dog) *What is the weather like?* (snowy) *Let's read the label: snowball. What is the girl throwing?* (a snowball)

Visualize *What do the words help you picture what the girl is doing?* (the girl throwing the snowball) *Is the snowball going fast or slow? Is it cold or hot?*

 What can the girl do on a snowy day? Talk to a partner.

Beginning Have partners point to details in the picture as they respond: *The girl can* throw *a snowball. The girl can play with the* dog.

Intermediate Have partners ask and answer: *What can the girl do with a* snowball; dog? *She can* throw a snowball; play with her dog.

Advanced/Advanced High Help children describe the girl and her dog: *The girl wears a hat and* coat *on a* winter; snowy *day. She and* her dog *play in* the snow.

Pages 4–5 Point to page 4. *It is raining. What does the girl wear?* (raincoat; hat; boots) *She jumps in a puddle of water. The water splashes.* Point to page 5. *It is sunny. What can she do?* (read)

Events: Sequence *What is the sequence, or order, of the seasons on pages 4–5?* (spring, summer)

 How can the girl have fun on a rainy day? Talk with a partner.

Beginning Have partners point to the puddle. Ask: *What can she do? She can* jump. *She can make the water* splash.

Intermediate Provide sentence frames: *She can* jump *in a* puddle *on a rainy day. She can* splash *the water.*

Pages 6–8 Point to page 6. *The leaves are different colors. Leaves fell on the ground. What season is it?* (fall) Point to the label for *swing. What can the girl do?* (swing) Point to the girl on page 7. *What can the girl do in a tent?* (sleep)

 What can the girl do in fall? Talk to a partner.

Beginning Help partners point to the picture and respond: *She can* swing. *She can* sleep *in a tent.*

Intermediate Guide children to add details. *She can* swing *in fall. She can* sleep in a tent. *In the morning, she can* kick leaves.

Retell Have partners retell the story. Have them take turns pointing to a picture and describing it to each other.

Focus on Fluency

Read pages 2–8 with appropriate expression. Then read the text aloud and have children echo read. For additional practice, have children record themselves reading the same text a few times and then select their favorite recording to play for you.

Build Knowledge: Make Connections

Talk About the Text Have partners discuss different kinds of weather.

Write About the Text Then have children add their ideas to their Build Knowledge page of their reader's notebook.

Self-Selected Reading

Have children select another fantasy from the online **Leveled Reader Library,** or read the **Differentiated Text,** "Lots of Weather."

LITERACY ACTIVITIES

Have children complete the Literacy Activities on the inside back cover of the book.

FORMATIVE ASSESSMENT

STUDENT CHECK-IN

Have partners reread and retell how the characters can have fun in different weather. Then have children reflect using the Check-In routine.

 **LEVEL UP**

IF children can read *Weather Is Fun* **ELL Level** with fluency and correctly answer the Literacy Activity questions,

THEN tell children that they will read a more detailed version of the story.

HAVE children page through *Weather Is Fun* On Level and describe each picture in simple language.

- Have children read the selection, checking their comprehension and providing assistance as necessary.

MODELED WRITING

LEARNING GOALS

We can write about what we do when the rain stops.

OBJECTIVES

Use dictating and writing to compose informative texts in which they name the topic.

LANGUAGE OBJECTIVES

Children will explain by writing a sentence using correct spacing between words.

ELA ACADEMIC LANGUAGE

• *sentence*

 Writing Practice Display an image of rain, and have children echo read the sample sentence on p. 44 of the **Reading/Writing Companion.** Guide children to analyze the sentence using the Actor/Action routine: *Who is the actor?* (the worms) *What is the action?* (come out after it rains) Then read the prompt on p. 45, and ask children to answer it as a group. Write the sentence on the board and point to each word as children choral read. Then ask children to write their own sentence.

 Beginning Help partners write their sentences: *Who is the actor?* (I) *What is the action?* (play in puddles)

Intermediate Have partners take turns asking and answering *who/what* questions to create their sentences. Provide a sentence frame if needed.

Advanced/Advanced High Challenge children to point to the spaces between their words as they share their sentences with the group.

FORMATIVE ASSESSMENT ➲ **STUDENT CHECK IN** Partners share their sentences. Ask children to reflect using the Check-In routine.

INTERACTIVE WRITING

LEARNING GOALS

We can write about what the animals enjoy doing after the rain.

OBJECTIVES

With guidance and support, add details to strengthen writing as needed.

LANGUAGE OBJECTIVES

Children will inform by writing about events in sequence, or order.

ELA ACADEMIC LANGUAGE

• *text*

• Cognate: *texto*

 Write a Response: Share the Pen Have children choral read the sample sentence on p. T348 of the **Teacher's Edition.** Use the Actor/Action routine to review it: *Who is the actor?* (the lion) *What is the action?* (enjoyed the shade) *When?* (after the rain) Remind children of the writing trait: *Does the lion enjoy the shade before it rains or after?* (after) Then help children complete the sentence frames at the bottom of the page.

 Beginning Help partners orally complete the first sentence by providing a visual from the book: The baboons ate <u>fruit</u>. Ask children guiding questions to help them think of their sentences.

Intermediate Have partners point to details in the illustrations that show what the animals do after the rain to complete both sentence frames.

Advanced/Advanced High Challenge children to think of their own sentences about what the animals do and share them with the group.

FORMATIVE ASSESSMENT ➲ **STUDENT CHECK IN** Partners share their sentences. Ask children to reflect using the Check-In routine.

INDEPENDENT WRITING

LEARNING GOALS

We can write about the texts we read.

OBJECTIVES

Use drawing and writing to narrate events in the order in which they occurred.

LANGUAGE OBJECTIVES

Children will narrate by writing sentences using words that show order.

ELA ACADEMIC LANGUAGE

• *text, proper noun*

• Cognate: *texto*

 Find Text Evidence Use the Independent Writing routine. Ask questions to help children orally retell "Kim and Nan" such as: *What do Kim and Nan do first?* (*sit on a rock*) *What does Kim do next?* (sip a drink) *Then what does Kim do?* (feed the birds) Then read the prompt on p. 60 of the **Reading/ Writing Companion**: *What might Kim and Nan like to do on another day?* Display pp. 52-53: *Where do Kim and Nan go?* (the beach) *We need to think about another place Kim and Nan might like to go to.*

 Write a Response Write the sentence starters, found at the bottom of the **Teacher's Edition**, p. 358, on the board, and read them. Model completing the first sentence frame, and have children choral read the response. Repeat with the remaining sentence frames. Read the writing checklist, and go through each item on the list. Then have children copy the sentences.

 Beginning Have partners take turns reading their sentences to each other. Then provide a sentence frame to help children: I told the events in order.

Intermediate Encourage children to use proper nouns.

Advanced/Advanced High Have partners identify the items on the writing checklist and check off each box.

FORMATIVE ASSESSMENT ❯ **STUDENT CHECK IN** Partners share their sentences. Ask children to reflect using the Check-In routine.

SELF-SELECTED WRITING

 LESSON 5

LEARNING GOALS

We can revise our writing.

OBJECTIVES

Print many upper- and lowercase letters.

LANGUAGE OBJECTIVES

Children will inquire about their writing by checking proper nouns.

ELA ACADEMIC LANGUAGE

• *proper noun*

 Work with children to correct the grammatical and spelling errors from their self-selected group writing activity. Read the sentences, pointing to each word as you read. Model and ask questions, such as: *Is this a proper noun? Do we need to capitalize it?* After you have made the necessary revisions, have children write their own clean copy and publish it.

For more support with grammar and singular and proper nouns, use the **Language Transfers Handbook** and **Language Development Card** 1B.

FORMATIVE ASSESSMENT ❯ **STUDENT CHECK IN** Partners tell what revisions they made. Ask children to reflect using the Check-In routine.

LEARNING GOALS

We can understand important ideas and details in a story.

We can use directions to learn new information.

OBJECTIVES

With prompting and support, identify characters, settings, and major events in a story.

With prompting and support, compare and contrast the adventures and experiences of characters in familiar stories.

Ask and answer questions about unknown words in a text.

Speak audibly and express thoughts, feelings, and ideas clearly.

LANGUAGE OBJECTIVES

Children will narrate the scenes of a stormy day, using verbs with *-ing*.

ELA ACADEMIC LANGUAGE

• *characters, event, sequence*

• Cognates: *evento, secuencia*

MATERIALS

Literature Big Book, *Waiting Out the Storm,* pp. 4–27 and 28–32

Visual Vocabulary Cards

DIGITAL TOOLS

Have children listen to the selection as they follow along to develop comprehension.

Use the vocabulary activity for additional support.

Waiting Out the Storm

Prepare to Read

Build Background Show images of a storm. *What happens in a storm? There is wind. The wind is strong.* Elicit other answers. Provide sentence frames. For example: *There is _____ and _____. The thunder sounds _____. What do we do in a storm? We stay inside.* Explain that the title, *Waiting Out the Storm,* means to stay inside during a storm.

Literature Big Book

Focus on Vocabulary Use the **Visual Vocabulary Cards** to review the oral vocabulary words *prepare* and *safe.* As you read, use gestures and other visual support to clarify important story words: *treetops, whistle, rumble, flashes, snuggle, burrows, comfy.* Review the words in context as you read.

Summarize the Text Before reading, give a short summary of the story: *A storm is coming. A girl and her mother go inside to stay safe from the weather.* Tell children that this is a realistic fiction story. A realistic fiction story has characters and events that could happen in real life.

Read the Text

Use the Interactive Question-Response Routine to help children understand the story.

Pages 4–15

Pages 6–7 *The wind blows the treetops. It whistles.* Demonstrate a whistling sound. *A storm is coming. Mama says the wind is calling the rain. What is the wind doing?* (blowing, whistling, calling the rain)

Pages 10–11 *Who are the characters?* (the girl and Mama) *It rains. Mama holds an umbrella. What is the weather like?* (It rains.) *How does an umbrella help the girl and Mama?* (It keeps them dry.)

Pages 12–15 Point to pages 12–13. *The storm clouds are dark. The thunder rumbles. What does a rumble sound like?* Help children understand that a rumble is a low sound from far away. *The girl is afraid. Mama says it is only a sound.* Point to pages 14–15. *Lightning flashes. The lightning is bright. What flashes?* (lightning)

 What is the weather like? Talk to a partner.

Beginning Guide partners to point to details on pages 14–15 and respond: *I see lightning; rain; clouds.*

Intermediate Help children add details: *I see clouds; rain; lightning in the sky. The clouds are dark.*

Advanced/Advanced High Guide children to describe the storm. (The clouds are dark. It is raining. There is thunder and lightning. The thunder is loud, and lightning flashes.)

Advanced/Advanced High Ask children to explain why the girl is afraid. (There is a strong wind that blows the treetops. The clouds are dark, and the thunder is loud.)

Pages 16–21

Pages 18–19 Point to the chipmunks' burrow, and explain that the they are safe in their homes. *Where do the chipmunks go in the storm?* (into their burrows) *What do they do?* (snuggle)

Page 20–21 Point to the baby birds. *The baby birds are in their nest. They go beneath, or under, their mama's wings. Who keeps them safe?* (mother bird)

 Where do the animals go in the storm? Talk to a partner.

Beginning Have partners point to the chipmunks' burrow and say after you: *A burrow is their home. The chipmunks go inside. They stay safe.*

Intermediate Guide children to point to and describe what the animals do: *Chipmunks go <u>inside</u> their <u>burrow</u>; <u>home</u>. Baby birds are in their <u>nest</u>. They go <u>beneath</u> their <u>mama's wings</u>.*

Pages 22–27

Pages 22–25 Point to the characters. *The girl and Mama go inside. They will stay inside while the winds blow and rain falls. It is cozy. They are dry and comfortable. Mama says, for now, they will just watch the storm. Where do the girl and Mama go?* (inside)

 What do the girl and Mama do during the storm? Talk to a partner.

Beginning Help children respond: *The girl and Mama are <u>inside</u>; <u>home</u>. The stay <u>safe</u>; <u>warm</u>; <u>dry</u> in a storm.*

Intermediate Help children explain why the characters go inside: *The girl and Mama <u>go inside</u> and <u>watch</u> <u>the storm</u>. They stay <u>warm, dry,</u> and <u>safe</u>.*

 Retell Use the **Retelling Cards** for *Waiting Out the Storm* to retell the story with children. Model retelling using sequence words as you point to the events and actions in the cards.

LESSON 4 Paired Selection: "Be Safe in Bad Weather"

Pages 28–32 Read and then paraphrase the text as you point to photographs. *In winter, there can be snow and wind. Sometimes there is a blizzard. People stay inside to stay safe. In some places, there are also bad storms in spring, summer, and fall.* Review the safety rules in the text that people follow.

 What do you do in a storm? Talk to a partner.

Beginning Have partners point to details that show bad storms. Help them respond: *I listen to a <u>grown-up</u>.*

Intermediate Have partners respond: *During a storm, I <u>listen to a grown-up</u> and <u>stay inside</u>.*

Advanced/Advanced High Ask students to explain why they stay inside during a storm. (I am safe from lightning and wind inside.)

FORMATIVE ASSESSMENT

 STUDENT CHECK-IN

Main Selection Have partners retell how the animals react to the changes in weather.

Paired Selection Have partners describe ways to stay safe in bad weather.

Then have children reflect using the Check-In routine.

 Independent Time

Draw and Share Ask children to talk about how the two selections are alike. *What do the characters do in a storm? What should you do when there is lightning and thunder?* Have children draw a picture showing an activity they do during a storm. Model answering the question: *I play inside at home.* Have them share their pictures with partners.

LESSON 3

OBJECTIVES

With prompting and support, ask and answer questions about key details in a text.

With prompting and support, describe the relationship between illustrations and the story in which they appear.

With prompting and support, compare and contrast the adventures and experiences of characters in familiar stories.

Ask and answer questions in order to seek help, get information, or clarify something that is not understood.

LANGUAGE OBJECTIVES

Children will narrate how the storm changes the characters' day, using singular and plural nouns.

ELA ACADEMIC LANGUAGE

• *character*

MATERIALS

Interactive Read Aloud, "The Storm That Shook the Signs"

Visual Vocabulary Cards

DIGITAL TOOLS

Have children listen to the selection as they follow along to develop comprehension.

Use the vocabulary activity for additional support.

"The Storm That Shook the Signs"

Prepare to Read

Interactive Read Aloud

Build Background Talk with children about what happens in bad weather. Discuss how people prepare for a storm. Use appropriate visuals. *How do people get ready for bad weather? We stay inside. I can close windows. We take things inside so they do not get wet or blow away in wind.*

Focus on Vocabulary Use the **Visual Vocabulary Cards** to review the oral vocabulary words *notice, prepare, safe, enough,* and *celebration.* As you read, use gestures and other visual support to clarify important story words: *market, tailor, fish seller, shoemaker, baker, mix up,* and *racks.*

Summarize the Text Before reading, give a short summary of the selection: *A playful wind plays a trick. First, the wind lets people prepare for her storm. Everyone is happy when the storm is over.*

Read the Text

Use the Interactive Question-Response Routine to help children understand the story.

Card 1

Paragraph 1 Read the text. *People sell things at a market. Who are the characters?* (tailor, fish seller, baker, shoemaker) *Every shop owner has a beautiful sign. The tailor's sign shows a shirt. The fish seller's sign shows a fish. The shoemaker's sign shows a shoe. And the bakers sign shows two cakes. What does a fish seller do?* (sells fish) Ask children what the other shop owners do.

Paragraphs 2–3 *The wind wants to play a trick, or a joke, on the shop owners. She wants to mix up their signs. What does the wind want to do?* (play a trick)

 What do the signs show? Talk to a partner.

Beginning Help partners point to the signs and describe each after you. For example: *The tailor sells shirts. The sign shows a shirt.*

Intermediate Provide sentence frames: *The sign for the tailor shows* <u>a shirt</u>. *The sign for the baker shows* <u>cakes</u>. *The sign for the fish seller is* <u>a fish</u>. *The sign for the shoemaker is a* <u>shoe</u>.

Advanced/Advanced High Ask children to explain the purpose of each sign.

Card 2

Paragraphs 1–5 *The wind blows a small breeze. The sky gets dark. The shop owners prepare for the storm. The tailor closes windows. The shoemaker brings his racks of shoes inside. The fish seller gets candles. Why does the tailor close the windows?* (A storm is coming.)

Paragraphs 6–8 *The wind blows a little harder.* Point to the baker's sign. *The baker's sign starts swinging.* Demonstrate swinging. *All the signs start swaying back and forth.* Show how something sways back and forth.

 How do the shop owners prepare for the storm? Talk to a partner.

Beginning Ask guiding questions: *Does the tailor close the windows?* (yes) *What does the shoemaker bring inside?* (shoes) *Does the baker or the fish seller get candles?* (the fish seller)

Intermediate Have partners ask and answer: *How does the* tailor; shoemaker; fish seller *get ready? The* tailor *closes windows. The shoemaker brings* the racks of shoes inside*. The* fish seller *gets candles.*

Advanced/Advanced High Guide partners to discuss why the shoemaker brings the racks of shoes inside and the fish seller gets candles.

Card 3

Paragraphs 1–2 *The wind blows the leaves off the trees. It blows the signs everywhere. What does the wind do to the signs?* (It blows them everywhere.)

Paragraphs 3–5 *The signs are flying around. The shop owners gasp.* Let's gasp together. *The wind mixes up the signs. Then she stops the storm.*

 What happens to the signs? Talk to a partner.

Beginning Have partners complete the sentences: *The wind* blows *the signs. The signs* fly *around in the air.*

Intermediate Help children explain what the wind does: *The wind* blows *the signs. The chains* break*. The signs fly in the air and get all* mixed up*.*

Card 4

Paragraphs 1–2 *The storm is over. The baker's shop has the shoemaker's sign. The baker goes to buy some new shoes. What does the baker want?* (new shoes)

Paragraphs 3–4 *The shoemaker's shop has the fish seller's sign. The shoemaker is hungry and buys fish. The fish seller's shop has the tailor's sign. The fish seller goes to buy a new shirt. What does the fish seller need?* (a new shirt)

Paragraphs 5–7 *The wind is happy with her trick. Everyone is happy with their new things. They have a celebration. They put their signs back. Why is everyone happy?* (They enjoy their new things.)

 What do the shop owners buy after the storm? Talk to a partner.

Beginning Guide children to say what the shop owner buys. Have them say after you: *The fish seller buys a shirt. The shoe maker buys fish.*

Intermediate Guide children to tell where the signs went and what the shop owners buy. For example: *The fish seller has the* tailor's sign*. She buys a* shirt*.*

 Retell Use the illustrations on the **Interactive Read-Aloud Cards** to retell the story with children. Display the cards and model retelling using sequence words, as you point to events and actions in the cards. Help partners retell one part using sequence words.

FORMATIVE ASSESSMENT

❯ STUDENT CHECK-IN

Have partners retell how the shop owners prepare for the storm. Then, have children reflect using the Check-In routine.

 ## Independent Time

Picture Glossary Have partners create a picture glossary of the shop owners in the story and what they sell. Challenge children to think of shop owners in their town to include in the glossary.

LEARNING GOALS

We can visualize what happens in a story.

OBJECTIVES

With prompting and support, ask and answer questions about key details in a text.

With prompting and support, identify characters and events in a story.

With prompting and support, describe the relationship between illustrations and the story in which they appear.

Describe familiar people, places, things, and events and, with prompting and support, provide additional detail.

LANGUAGE OBJECTIVES

Children will narrate how the character prepares for a storm, using key vocabulary.

ELA ACADEMIC LANGUAGE

• *character, event, visualize*

• Cognates: *evento, visualizar*

MATERIALS

ELL Leveled Reader: *Getting Ready*

Online Differentiated Text, "Safe Inside"

Online ELL Visual Vocabulary Cards

DIGITAL TOOLS

Have children listen to the selection as they follow along to develop comprehension.

Use the vocabulary activity for additional support.

Getting Ready

Prepare to Read

Build Background Show visuals of things people do to prepare for a snowstorm, such as getting food, water, and other supplies. Then talk about how you might get ready for a snowstorm. *Let's pretend a snowstorm is coming. Families have to stay inside for a day. How can we be ready for the snowstorm? I can get water.* Elicit other answers: *I can get _____.*

Lexile BR

Focus on Vocabulary Use the routine on the **ELL Visual Vocabulary Cards** to preteach *hazard* and *security*. Use the images and any labels to identify and model the use of key vocabulary in context.

Read the Text

Use the Interactive Question-Response Routine to help children understand the story.

Pages 2–8

Pages 2–3 *Who is the character?* (a woman) *She is getting ready for a snowstorm. How do you know? Let's read the label:* water. *What does the woman get?* (water) Point to page 3. *What does the woman get?* (food)

 How does the woman get ready for the storm? Talk to a partner.

Beginning Have partners point to the illustration: *She gets* water; food.

Intermediate Guide partners to ask and answer: *What does the woman get? She gets* water; food. Have them point to the text evidence.

Advanced/Advanced High Have partners ask and answer: *What does the woman get?* Help them add details to their responses. (She gets water to drink. She gets food to eat during the storm.)

Pages 4–5 *Let's see what the next event in the story is. Where is the woman?* (outside) *She gets wood. What does she get?* (wood) *She can make a warm fire with the wood.* Point to page 5. *She is back inside her house. She gets* blankets.

 Where does she get wood and blankets? Talk to a partner.

Beginning Have partners point to the illustrations: *The wood is* outside. *She gets* wood. *The blankets are* inside. *She gets* blankets.

Intermediate Have partners point to the illustrations as they ask and answer: *Where is the* <u>wood</u>? *The wood is* <u>outside; in the yard</u>. *Where are the* <u>blankets</u>? *The blankets are* <u>inside; in the closet</u>.

Advanced/Advanced High Help partners explain why she gets wood and blankets. Provide additional modeling as needed. (She can make a warm fire. She can also use the blankets to stay warm.)

Events: Sequence Have children tell the events in sequence. (First, the woman gets water and food. Next, she gets wood. Then, she gets blankets.)

Pages 6–8 *Point to the woman on page 7. She has snacks and games.* Point to the flashlight. *What does she get?* (flashlights) *What do the flashlights help you* **visualize**, *or picture, happening in the storm?* (lights going out) Point out her friends on page 8. *The friends eat snacks and play games. They use flashlights.* Point to the fireplace. *There is a warm fire.*

 What do the friends do during a snowstorm? Talk to a partner.

Beginning Have partners point to details in the pictures and complete sentences: *The friends play* <u>games</u> *during a storm. The friends* <u>eat snacks</u> *and have fun.*

Intermediate Guide children to describe what is happening in the story: *The friends* <u>play a game</u> *during the snowstorm. There is a* <u>warm fire</u> *in the fireplace. They use the* <u>flashlights</u> *to see the game.*

Retell Have partners retell the story. Have them take turns pointing to a picture and describing it to each other.

Focus on Fluency

Read pages 2–8 with appropriate expression. Then read the text aloud and have children echo read. For practice, have children record themselves and play their favorite recording to play for you.

Build Knowledge: Make Connections

Talk About the Text Have partners discuss how to prepare for different kinds of weather.

Write About the Text Then have children add their ideas to their Build Knowledge page of their reader's notebook.

Self-Selected Reading

Have children select another story from the online **Leveled Reader Library,** or read the **Differentiated Text,** "Safe Inside."

ENGLISH LANGUAGE LEARNERS **153**

LITERACY ACTIVITIES

Have children complete the Literacy Activities on the inside back cover of the book.

FORMATIVE ASSESSMENT

> **STUDENT CHECK-IN**

Have partners reread and retell how the woman prepares for the storm. Then have children reflect using the Check-In routine.

LEVEL UP

IF children can read *Getting Ready* **ELL Level** with fluency and correctly answer the Literacy Activity questions.

THEN tell children that they will read a more detailed version of the story.

HAVE children page through *Getting Ready* On Level and describe each picture in simple language.

- Have children read the selection, checking their comprehension and providing assistance as necessary.

MODELED WRITING

LEARNING GOALS

We can write about what we like to do when it rains.

OBJECTIVES

Use dictating and writing to compose informative texts in which they name the topic.

LANGUAGE OBJECTIVES

Children will narrate by writing a sentence using the lines to guide them.

ELA ACADEMIC LANGUAGE

• *lines*

• Cognate: *líneas*

Writing Practice Display the *lightning* **Photo Card,** and have children echo read the sample sentence on p. 74 of the **Reading/Writing Companion.** Guide children to analyze the sentence using the Actor/Action routine: *Who is the actor?* (I) *What is the action?* (see lightning) *Where?* (outside my window) Then read the prompt on p. 75 and ask children to answer it as a group. Review the sentence by writing it on the board and pointing to each word as children choral read. Then ask children to write their own sentence.

Beginning Provide a sentence frame: I will write about watching the sky. Then help partners think of their sentence: *Who is the actor?* (I) *What is the action?* (watch the sky)

Intermediate Have partners take turns asking and answering *who/what* questions to create their sentences. Provide a sentence frame if needed.

Advanced/Advanced High Challenge children to talk about their sentence using the Actor/Action routine. Encourage them to share it with the group.

FORMATIVE ASSESSMENT ➤ ◆ **STUDENT CHECK IN** Partners share their sentences. Ask children to reflect using the Check-In routine.

INTERACTIVE WRITING

LEARNING GOALS

We can write about what the girl and her mother can do when the storm stops.

OBJECTIVES

With guidance and support, respond to questions and suggestions from peers.

LANGUAGE OBJECTIVES

Children will explain by writing questions using the verbs *can* and *love.*

ELA ACADEMIC LANGUAGE

• *describe*

• Cognate: *describir*

Write a Response: Share the Pen Have children choral read the sample sentence on p. T426 of the **Teacher's Edition.** Analyze the sentence: *Who is the actor?* (They) *What can they do?* (go outside to smell pretty flowers) Then say: *When we write, we use words that describe. What word describe the flowers?* (pretty) Help children complete the sentence frames at the bottom of the page.

Beginning Help children complete the first sentence frame by asking questions. *Where might the girl want to go?* Mama, can we go outside?

Intermediate Have partners brainstorm ideas of what the girl and her mother might do after the storm to help them complete the frames.

Advanced/Advanced High Challenge children to think of their own sentences about what the girl and her mother will do. Encourage them to share them with the group.

FORMATIVE ASSESSMENT ➤ ◆ **STUDENT CHECK IN** Partners share their sentences. Ask children to reflect using the Check-In routine.

INDEPENDENT WRITING

LEARNING GOALS

We can write about the texts we read.

OBJECTIVES

Use drawing and writing to narrate events in the order in which they occurred.

LANGUAGE OBJECTIVES

Children will narrate by writing sentences using clues from the text and illustrations.

ELA ACADEMIC LANGUAGE

• *singular, plural*

• Cognates: *singular, plural*

Find Text Evidence Use the Independent Writing routine. Ask questions to help children orally retell "Mack and Ben," such as: *Who are Mack and Ben?* (mice) *Why do Mack and Ben run?* (It starts to rain.) *What do Mack and Ben do when it rains?* (stay inside) Then read the prompt on p. 90 of the **Reading/Writing Companion:** *What might Mack and Ben do if it starts to snow? Write a story.* Display page 84: *What do Mack and Ben do when they stay inside?* (They sit and wait.) Then turn to p. 85. *What does Mack want to do?* (hit and kick the ball)

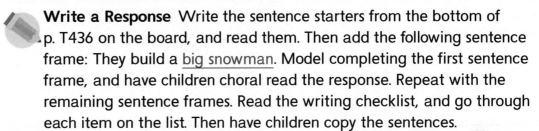

Write a Response Write the sentence starters from the bottom of p. T436 on the board, and read them. Then add the following sentence frame: They build a big snowman. Model completing the first sentence frame, and have children choral read the response. Repeat with the remaining sentence frames. Read the writing checklist, and go through each item on the list. Then have children copy the sentences.

Beginning Have partners take turns reading their sentences to each other. Provide a sentence frame to help them: I used the singular noun snowman.

Intermediate Encourage children to add descriptive words.

Advanced/Advanced High Have partners identify the items on the writing checklist and check off each box.

FORMATIVE ASSESSMENT ❯ **STUDENT CHECK IN** Partners share their sentences. Ask children to reflect using the Check-In routine.

SELF-SELECTED WRITING

LEARNING GOALS

We can revise our writing.

OBJECTIVES

Form regular plural nouns orally by adding /s/ or /es/

LANGUAGE OBJECTIVES

Children will inquire about their writing by checking singular and plural nouns.

ELA ACADEMIC LANGUAGE

• *plural*

• Cognate: *plural*

Work with children to correct the grammatical and spelling errors from their self-selected group writing activity. Read the sentences. Model and ask questions, such as: *Is this word plural? Do we need to add -s or -es at the end?* After you have made necessary revisions, have children write their own clean copy and publish it.

For more support with grammar, use the **Language Transfers Handbook,** and review **Language Development Cards** 1A, 2A, and 2B.

FORMATIVE ASSESSMENT ❯ **STUDENT CHECK IN** Partners tell what revisions they made. Ask children to reflect using the Check-In routine.

UNIT 6

Summative Assessment
Get Ready for Unit Assessment

Unit 6 Tested Skills

LISTENING AND READING COMPREHENSION	VOCABULARY	GRAMMAR	SPEAKING AND WRITING
• Listening Actively • Text Structure • Details	• Words and Categories	• Nouns	• Offering Opinions • Presenting • Composing/Writing • Retelling/Recounting

Create a Student Profile

Record data from the following resources in the Student Profile charts on pages 136–137 of the Assessment book.

COLLABORATIVE	INTERPRETIVE	PRODUCTIVE

• Collaborative Conversations Rubrics
  • Listening
  • Speaking
	• Leveled Unit Assessment
	  • Listening Comprehension
	  • Reading Comprehension
	  • Vocabulary
	  • Grammar
	• Presentation Rubric
	  • Listening
	• *Wonders* Unit Assessment
		• Weekly Progress Monitoring
		• Leveled Unit Assessment
		  • Speaking
		  • Writing
		• Presentation Rubric
		  • Speaking
		• Write to Sources Rubric
		• *Wonders* Unit Assessment

The Foundational Skills Kit, Language Development Kit, and Adaptive Learning provide additional student data for progress monitoring.

Level Up

Use the following chart, along with your Student Profiles, to guide your Level Up decisions.

LEVEL UP	If **BEGINNING** level students are able to do the following, they may be ready to move to the **INTERMEDIATE** level:	If **INTERMEDIATE** level students are able to do the following, they may be ready to move to the **ADVANCED** level:	If **ADVANCED** level students are able to do the following, they may be ready to move to **ON** level:
COLLABORATIVE	• participate in collaborative conversations using basic vocabulary and grammar and simple phrases or sentences • discuss simple pictorial or text prompts	• participate in collaborative conversations using appropriate words and phrases and complete sentences • use limited academic vocabulary across and within disciplines	• participate in collaborative conversations using more sophisticated vocabulary and correct grammar • communicate effectively across a wide range of language demands in social and academic contexts
INTERPRETIVE	• identify details in simple read alouds • understand common vocabulary and idioms and interpret language related to familiar social, school, and academic topics • make simple inferences and make simple comparisons • exhibit an emerging receptive control of lexical, syntactic, phonological, and discourse features	• identify main ideas and/or make some inferences from simple read alouds • use context clues to identify word meanings and interpret basic vocabulary and idioms • compare, contrast, summarize, and relate text to graphic organizers • exhibit a limited range of receptive control of lexical, syntactic, phonological, and discourse features when addressing new or familiar topics	• determine main ideas in read alouds that have advanced vocabulary • use context clues to determine meaning, understand multiple-meaning words, and recognize synonyms of social and academic vocabulary • analyze information, make sophisticated inferences, and explain their reasoning • command a high degree of receptive control of lexical, syntactic, phonological, and discourse features
PRODUCTIVE	• express ideas and opinions with basic vocabulary and grammar and simple phrases or sentences • restate information or retell a story using basic vocabulary • exhibit an emerging productive control of lexical, syntactic, phonological, and discourse features	• produce coherent language with limited elaboration or detail • restate information or retell a story using mostly accurate, although limited, vocabulary • exhibit a limited range of productive control of lexical, syntactic, phonological, and discourse features when addressing new or familiar topics	• produce sentences with more sophisticated vocabulary and correct grammar • restate information or retell a story using extensive and accurate vocabulary and grammar • tailor language to a particular purpose and audience • command a high degree of productive control of lexical, syntactic, phonological, and discourse features

LESSONS 1-2

OBJECTIVES

With prompting and support, ask and answer questions about key details in a text.

With prompting and support, describe the connection between two individuals, events, ideas, or pieces of information in a text.

Actively engage in group reading activities with purpose and understanding.

Continue a conversation through multiple exchanges.

LANGUAGE OBJECTIVES

Children will explain how different types of animals are similar and different, using descriptive details.

ELA ACADEMIC LANGUAGE

• *compare, contrast*

• Cognates: *comparar, contrastar*

MATERIALS

Literature Big Book, *ZooBorns!,* pp. 4–33 and 34–36

Visual Vocabulary Cards

DIGITAL TOOLS

Have children listen to the selection as they follow along to develop comprehension.

Use the vocabulary activity for additional support.

ZooBorns!

Literature Big Book

Prepare to Read

Build Background Show images of different animals, such as an elephant, a fox, a gorilla, a kangaroo, and a hippo at a zoo. Help children name the animals. Then say: *These animals live in a zoo. People called zookeepers take care of them.* If possible, show a picture of a zookeeper taking care of animals. Then elicit students' knowledge of zoos. *What can you see at zoos?* Help children share their experiences of going to or seeing a zoo.

Focus on Vocabulary Use the **Visual Vocabulary Cards** to review the oral vocabulary words *appearance* and *behavior*. As you read, use gestures and other visual support to clarify important selection words: *crawling, insects, stripes.*

Summarize the Text Before reading, show children the pictures and summarize: *This book is called* ZooBorns! *It tells about baby animals in the zoo.*

Read the Text

Use the Interactive Question-Response Routine to help children understand the text

Pages 4–15

Pages 6–7 Read the text. Point to the photo. *Radar Ears is a fox with big ears. He can hear insects, or bugs, crawling.* Gesture to show crawling. *He says they are yummy. What do you think he eats?* (insects) *How do his ears help him?* (He can hear insects crawling.)

Pages 10–11 Read the text. Point to the photo. *Hoover is a tawni frogmouth. Hoover is a bird.* Point to the beak. *Hoover can open his beak really wide, like a frog. Let's open our mouths wide, like a frog. What does Hoover eat?* (bugs)

Pages 14–15 Read the text. Point to the photo. *Amani is an aardvark. Amani has a lot of skin and wrinkles.* Point to the wrinkles and then have children wrinkle their faces. *Does Amani have big ears and a big nose?* (yes)

 Let's compare animals. How are the animals alike, or the same? Talk to a partner.

Beginning Have children look at the fox and the aardvark and tell how they are alike. *The fox has* big ears. *The aardvark has* big ears, *too.*

Intermediate Have partners look at pages 7, 11, 15. *The fox and the* aardvark *both* have big ears. *The* fox *and the bird both* eat bugs.

Pages 16–25

Pages 16–17 *What kind of animal is this?* (a cat; an ocelot) *The ocelot is getting teeth.* Point to the teeth. *What can you see in its mouth?* (teeth) Help children describe the ocelot. (stripes, whiskers, colors, spots)

Pages 20–21 *Read the text. These animals are tigers. Tigers are a kind of big cat.* Help children describe the tigers. (stripes, whiskers, colors, blue eyes)

 Name some ways the tiger and ocelot are the same. Talk to a partner.

Beginning Have children point to the ways the tiger and ocelot are the same. *The tiger has* stripes/whiskers. *The ocelot has* stripes/whiskers.

Intermediate Have partners point to the photos as they respond: *The tiger and the ocelot are both cats. They both have* fur, stripes, and whiskers.

Advanced/Advanced High Have partners add details as they compare. (They both have fur with stripes. They both have sharp teeth. They are both cats.)

Pages 26–33

Pages 26–27 Read the text. Point to the hippo. *This is a pygmy hippo. Pygmy hippos are the smallest hippos. This hippo will always stay small.*

Pages 32–33 *What kind of animal is this?* (a whale) *Bella lives in the water. Bella will turn white when she is older. Where does Bella live?* (in the water)

 Let's contrast the animals. How are the animals different? Talk to a partner.

Beginning Have partners point to the photos as they respond. *The whale is* big. *The hippo is* small.

Intermediate *The whale* is big/lives in the water/will be white. *The hippo* is small/lives on land/is brown.

Advanced/Advanced High Encourage children to speak in complete sentences and point to the images as they tell how the whale and hippo are different.

 Retell Use the **Retelling Cards** for *ZooBorns!* to retell the information with children. Display the cards and model retelling about each animal. Then help partners each choose a card and take turns telling about the animal shown on the card.

LESSON 4 Paired Read: "Kitty Caught a Caterpillar"

Page 36 Say: *Kittens like to catch small animals. Let's read what the kitten caught.* Point to the illustration as you read each line. Ask what the kitten catches. Help children identify the creature and where it is. For lines 5 and 6, explain that a cricket is an insect that hops. After lines 7 and 8, ask: *What do you think the bumblebee does to the kitten?* Guide children to understand the bee might sting the kitten.

 What happens in the poem? Talk to a partner.

Beginning Have partners point to each image as they say what the kitten catches: *The kitten catches a ___.*

Intermediate Have partners use details to describe each image. Example: *The kitten catches a* green caterpillar. *Then she catches a* brown snail.

Advanced/Advanced High Have partners give details, including where the creature is caught and who catches the kitten. Provide modeling as needed.

FORMATIVE ASSESSMENT

STUDENT CHECK-IN

Main Selection Have partners retell how animal pairs from the text are similar or different.

Paired Selection Have partners retell what Kitty caught and what caught Kitty.

Then have children reflect using the Check-In routine.

 Independent Time

Draw and Share Have children draw a picture of their favorite animal from the texts. Provide a sentence frame: *I like the _____.* Have partners share their favorite animals. Encourage children to say why they like that animal the best.

LESSON 3

LEARNING GOALS

We can listen actively to learn about baby farm animals.

OBJECTIVES

With prompting and support, retell key details of a text.

With prompting and support, describe the connection between pieces of information in a text.

With prompting and support, describe the relationship between illustrations and the text in which they appear.

Speak audibly and express thoughts, feelings, and ideas clearly.

LANGUAGE OBJECTIVES

Children will inform about farm animals and their qualites, using nouns, verbs, and key vocabulary.

ELA ACADEMIC LANGUAGE

- *compare, contrast*
- Cognates: *comparar, contrastar*

MATERIALS

Interactive Read Aloud, "Baby Farm Animals"

Visual Vocabulary Cards

DIGITAL TOOLS

Have children listen to the selection as they follow along to develop comprehension.

Use the vocabulary activity for additional practice.

"Baby Farm Animals"

Prepare to Read

Build Background Show images of and name farm animals with their young: hens, horses, cows, ducks, pigs, and sheep. *Where do these animals live?* Help children compare animals. Tell them when you "compare," you look to see how something is the same or different. *A horse has four legs. A cow has four legs.* Provide sentence frames: *A/An _____ is _____.*

Interactive Read Aloud

Focus on Vocabulary Use the **Visual Vocabulary Cards** to review the oral vocabulary words *exercise, wander, plenty, appearance,* and *behavior.* As you read, use gestures and other visual support to clarify important selection words: *fluffy, coat, hatch.*

Summarize the Text Show the children the cards. *The cards tell about different baby farm animals.*

Read the Text

Use the Interactive Question-Response Routine to help children understand the text.

Card 1

Paragraphs 1–2 Read the text. Point to the photo. *Many animals live on a farm together. But these animals look and sound different.* Point to the hen. *This can be called a chicken or a hen. What animal is this?* (a chicken/hen)

Paragraph 3 Read the text. Point to the chicks. *Animals like chicks are born on a farm. Their mothers take care of them. What is a baby chicken called?* (a chick)

 What animals live on a farm? Talk to a partner.

Beginning Have partners point to the hen and chicks in the photo as they say: *This hen lives on a farm. These chicks live on a farm.*

Intermediate Have partners ask and answer: *What animal is this? This is a chicken/chick. Where does a chicken/chick live? A chicken/chick lives on a farm.*

Card 2

Paragraphs 1–2 Read the text. Point to the photo. *A foal is a baby horse. A calf is a baby cow. Point to the hooves and legs. They both have four legs and hooves. How many legs do they both have?* (four)

Paragraph 3 Read the text. Point to the photo. Help children describe the calf and foal. Example: *A foal and calf look different. They make different sounds, too. What sound does a foal/calf make?* (neigh; moo)

Let's compare animals. How are a foal and a calf the same and different? Talk to a partner.

Beginning Have partners point to the photo as they respond. *This is a <u>foal/calf</u>. A <u>foal/calf</u> has <u>four</u> legs. This foal is <u>brown/black</u>. This calf has <u>spots</u>.*

Intermediate Have partners ask and answer: *What does the foal/calf look like?* (A foal/calf has four legs. A foal has a brown/black coat. A calf has spots.)

Advanced/Advanced High Guide partners to give details comparing the animals. (Sample answer: The foal has longer legs than the calf.)

Card 3

Paragraphs 1–2 Read the text. *Chicks are baby chickens. Ducklings are baby ducks. They both have two legs and a soft, fluffy coat. They both hatch, or come from eggs. How are chicks and ducks born?* (They hatch from eggs.)

Paragraph 3 Read the text. Point to the corresponding image as you speak. *Chicks and ducklings are different, too. A chick walks on land. A chick has a beak. A duckling floats in a pond. A duckling has a bill. What does a duckling do?* (floats in a pond)

 Let's compare and contrast a chick and a duckling. Talk to a partner.

Beginning Have children point to the similarities and differences. Use their choices with sentence frames.

Intermediate Have partners point as they respond: *What does a chick look/sound like? A chick/duckling has <u>two legs</u>. A chick has <u>a beak</u>. A duckling has <u>a bill</u>. A chick/duckling goes <u>cheep!/quack</u>!*

Advanced/Advanced High Challenge partners to give details when they compare the animals. Provide sentence frames and modeling as needed.

Card 4

Paragraphs 1–2 Read the text. Point to the photo. *Lambs and piglets are baby sheep and pigs. They both drink their mother's milk after they are born. They stay close to their mothers after they are born. This*

keeps them safe. What do lambs and piglets drink? (They drink their mother's milk.)

Paragraph 3 Read the text. Point to and name the corresponding image as you speak. *A lamb has a fluffy coat. A piglet has smooth skin. Piglets stay in a barn. Lambs stay outside. Where do lambs stay?* (outside)

 How are a lamb and a piglet the same and different? Talk to a partner.

Beginning Have partners point to the photos as they respond: *The lamb and the piglet both have four <u>legs</u>. The piglet has smooth <u>skin</u>. The lamb has a fluffy <u>coat</u>.*

Intermediate Provide sentence frames: *The lamb and the piglet both <u>drink their mother's milk</u>. The piglet lives <u>in the barn</u>. The lamb lives <u>outside</u>.*

Advanced/Advanced High Guide partners to compare the animals. (Sample answer: The lamb has a fluffy white coat. The piglet has pink and black skin.)

 Retell Use the photos on the **Interactive Read-Aloud Cards** to retell the text with children. Display the cards and model retelling details in the photos and text. Then help partners take turns retelling key details about one of the cards.

> STUDENT CHECK-IN

Have partners retell two comparisons of animals from the text. Then, have children reflect using the Check-In routine.

Independent Time

Oral Language Have children share their favorite farm animal and why they like that animal. Provide a sentence frame: *I like _____ because _____.*

We can reread to better understand the text.

OBJECTIVES

With prompting and support, retell key details of a text.

With prompting and support, identify basic similarities in and differences between two texts on the same topic.

Actively engage in group reading activities with purpose and understanding.

Continue a conversation through multiple exchanges.

LANGUAGE OBJECTIVES

Children will inform about how animals are alike and different, using nouns, verbs, and key vocabulary.

ELA ACADEMIC LANGUAGE

• *fact, opinion*
• Cognates: *opinión*

MATERIALS

ELL Leveled Reader: *Animal Bodies*

Online Differentiated Texts, "Kittens"

Online ELL Visual Vocabulary Cards

DIGITAL TOOLS

Have children listen to the selection as they follow along to develop comprehension.

Use the vocabulary activity for additional support.

Animal Bodies

Prepare to Read

Build Background Show images of different animals. Have children name each animal. Talk about the animals' body parts, including the trunk, tail, ears, and feet. *An elephant has a trunk. An elephant has a tail. An elephant has four feet.* Have children take turns describing the animals. Provide a sentence frame: *A/An _____ has _____.*

Lexile 80L

Focus on Vocabulary Use the routine on the **ELL Visual Vocabulary Cards** to preteach *detail* and *feature*. Use the images and labels to identify and model the use of key vocabulary in context.

Read the Text

Use the Interactive Question-Response Routine to help children understand the text.

Pages 2–8

Pages 2–3 *What animals do you see?* Help children name the animals. *Let's read the labels together: foot, worm, snake, fish.* Point to page 2. *What do these animals have?* (feet) *Point to page 3. Do these animals have feet?* (no)

 Let's reread pages 2 and 3. How are the horse and fish different? Talk to a partner.

Beginning Have partners point to the photo that corresponds to each response. Help children form sentences: *The horse has feet. The fish does not have feet.*

Intermediate Have partners point to the photos as they ask and answer: *What does a horse/fish look like? The horse has [example] feet. The fish has [example] no feet. Where is the horse/fish? The horse/fish is in a field/the ocean.*

Advanced *Tell a partner how these animals are different.* (The horse has four legs. The fish has no legs. The horse is on land, but the fish is in water.) *Tell how other animals are different.* (The hippo has four legs. The snake has no legs.)

Fact and Opinion Have children identify if the following statements are fact or opinion: *The animals on page 3 have no feet.* (fact) *The animals with no feet are more interesting.* (opinion) Ask partners to share more facts and opinions about pages 2–3.

Pages 4–5 *What animals do you see?* Help children name the animals. Point to an elephant's trunk. *This is called a trunk.* Have children repeat. *Which animals have trunks?* (elephants)

Pages 6–8 Page 6: *What animals do you see?* Help children name and describe the animals. Read the "tail" label. *Do all these animals have tails?* (yes) Page 7: Read the labels and have children repeat. *Do these animals have tails?* (no) Help children describe the animals. Page 8: *What do you see?* (a boy) Read: *The boy has hands. What does the boy have?* (hands)

 Let's compare and contrast people and animals. Talk to a partner.

Beginning Guide partners to point to the photos and tell how the boy and the horse are alike and different. *The boy and the horse both have [body part]. The horse has a* [body part]. *The boy does not have a* [same body part]. As needed, name body parts children point to.

Intermediate Have partners choose an animal to compare to the boy and use the photos to point to the body parts as they ask and answer: *How is the [animal] like the boy? They both* have [body part]. *How is the [animal] different from the boy? The [animal]* has [body part]. *The boy doesn't* have [body part].

Advanced/Advanced High Have partners choose an animal to describe, giving details. Then have them compare that animal to the boy. Encourage children to ask each other for help with descriptions.

Retell Have partners retell the story. Have them take turns pointing to a picture and describing it to each other.

Focus on Fluency

Read pages 2–8 with appropriate intonation. Then read the text aloud and have children echo read. For additional practice, have children record themselves reading the text a few times, and then select their favorite recording to play for you.

Build Knowledge: Make Connections

Talk About the Text Have partners discuss the similarities and differences between the animals.

Write About the Text Have children add their ideas to their Build Knowledge pages of their reader's notebooks.

Self-Selected Reading

Have children select another story from the online **Leveled Reader Library,** or read the **Differentiated Text,** "Kittens."

LITERACY ACTIVITIES

Have children complete the Literacy Activities on the inside back cover of the book.

FORMATIVE ASSESSMENT

> **STUDENT CHECK-IN**

Have partners retell how people and animals are alike and different. Then, have children reflect using the Check-In routine.

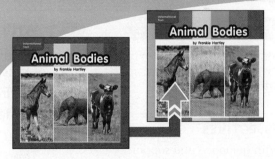

IF children can read *Animal Bodies* ELL Level with fluency and correctly answer the Respond to Reading questions,

THEN tell children that they will read a more detailed version of the story.

HAVE children page through *Animal Bodies* On Level and describe each picture in simple language.

• Have children read the selection, checking their comprehension and providing assistance as necessary.

MODELED WRITING

LESSON
1

We can write about how to take care of a baby animal.

OBJECTIVES

Use dictating and writing to compose informative texts in which they name the topic.

LANGUAGE OBJECTIVES

Children will inform by writing a sentence using an animal name.

ELA ACADEMIC LANGUAGE

• *capital letter*

Writing Practice Display the *dog* **Photo Card** and review the sample sentence on p. 14 of the **Reading/Writing Companion.** Guide children to analyze the sentence using the Actor/Action routine: *What is the object?* (My favorite animal) *What is the description?* (is a puppy) Then read the prompt on p. 15, and ask children to answer it as a group. Review the sentence by writing it on the board and pointing to each word as children choral read. Then ask children to write their own sentence.

Beginning Have children share ideas about baby animals they know with a partner. Then provide a sentence frame: I will write about a kitten.

Intermediate Have partners take turns naming types of baby animals before picking which baby animal they like most.

Advanced/Advanced High Challenge children to identify which capital letter they used to start their sentence as they share it with the group.

FORMATIVE ASSESSMENT ❯ ⊙ STUDENT CHECK IN Partners share their sentences. Have children reflect using the Check-In routine.

INTERACTIVE WRITING

LESSON
2

We can write about how the ocelot and the tiger twins are alike.

OBJECTIVES

With guidance and support, add details to strengthen writing as needed.

LANGUAGE OBJECTIVES

Children will inform by writing sentences that tell how baby animals are the same.

ELA ACADEMIC LANGUAGE

• *capital letter*

Write a Response: Share the Pen Choral read the sample sentence on p. T30 of the **Teacher's Edition.** *Who are the actors?* (the ocelot and tiger twins) *What can we say about them?* (They have long whiskers.) Guide children to think about the writing skill by asking them to identify the capital letter. Remind them of the writing trait: *Descriptive words help tell what something is like. What descriptive word tells about whiskers?* (long) Then help children complete the sentence frames at the bottom of p. T30.

Beginning *How is the ocelot's fur the same as the tiger twins' fur?* The ocelot and tiger twins both have dark spots on their fur.

Intermediate Have partners use the photographs to compare the ocelot and tiger twins. Encourage children to use descriptive words.

Advanced/Advanced High Have partners think of their own sentences about how the animals are the same. Encourage children to share their sentences with the group.

FORMATIVE ASSESSMENT ❯ ⊙ STUDENT CHECK IN Partners share their sentences. Have children reflect using the Check-In routine.

INDEPENDENT WRITING

LEARNING GOALS

We can write about the texts we read.

OBJECTIVES

Use dictating and writing to compose informative texts in which they supply some information about the topic.

LANGUAGE OBJECTIVES

Children will inform by writing sentences using the word *both*.

ELA ACADEMIC LANGUAGE

- *compare, verb*
- Cognates: *comparar, verbo*

Find Text Evidence Use the Independent Writing routine. Ask questions to help children orally retell the shared read, such as: *What is the first animal?* (a wolf pup) *What does the pup do?* (is in a pack, live in a den) Then read the prompt on p. 30 of the **Reading/Writing Companion:** *How are the two lion cubs alike?* Display pp. 24 and 26: *Do the pup and cub both have a mom and a dad?* (yes) *What do the cubs both do?* (sit on a branch)

Write a Response Copy the sentence starters from p. T40 on the board, and read them. Model completing the first sentence starter, and have children choral read the response. Repeat with the second sentence starter. Then have children copy the sentences onto p. 31 of the **Reading/Writing Companion**.

Beginning Encourage partners to identify which capital letters begin their sentences: I started my sentence with a capital *T*.

Intermediate Encourage partners to add descriptive words.

Advanced/Advanced High Have partners identify where they used each checklist item in their writing.

FORMATIVE ASSESSMENT ❯ **STUDENT CHECK IN** Partners share their sentences. Have children reflect using the Check-In routine.

SELF-SELECTED WRITING

LEARNING GOALS

We can revise our writing.

OBJECTIVES

Use frequently occurring nouns and verbs.

ELA LANGUAGE OBJECTIVES

Children will inquire about their writing by verifying that the verb was used correctly.

ELA ACADEMIC LANGUAGE

- *verbs*
- Cognates: *verbos*

Work with children to revise the group writing activity. Point to each word as you read the sentences. Stop to ask questions, such as, *Is the verb correct? Is it spelled correctly?* If needed, write a sentence using a verb incorrectly, and work together to revise the sentence. Then have partners revise each other's sentences before they publish them.

For support with grammar and present-tense verbs, refer to the **Language Transfers Handbook** and **Language Development Card** 4A.

FORMATIVE ASSESSMENT ❯ **STUDENT CHECK IN** Partners tell what revisions they made. Have children reflect using the Check-In routine.

LESSONS
1-2

LEARNING GOALS

We can understand important ideas and details about a story.

We can tell what makes a story a personal narrative.

OBJECTIVES

With prompting and support, ask and answer questions about key details in a text.

With prompting and support, retell familiar stories, including key details.

With prompting and support, describe the relationship between illustrations and the story in which they appear.

Describe familiar people, places, things, and events and, with prompting and support, provide additional detail.

LANGUAGE OBJECTIVES

Children will narrate what the character thinks about different kinds of pets, using verbs and adjectives.

ELA ACADEMIC LANGUAGE

• *illustration*

• Cognates: *ilustración*

MATERIALS

Literature Big Book, *The Birthday Pet,* pp. 4–32 and 33–36

Visual Vocabulary Cards

DIGITAL TOOLS

Have children listen to the selection as they follow along to develop comprehension.

Use the vocabulary activity for additional support.

The Birthday Pet

Prepare to Read

Build Background Show images of different pets, such as a dog, cat, parrot, and turtle. *People like to have these animals as pets.* Discuss the concept of pets, as needed. Have children name the animals and then describe what the animals can do. *What can these animals do?* Model answering the question. *A dog can run. A cat can climb trees.* Provide sentence frames: *A _____ can _____.* Invite children to tell about pets they have or know.

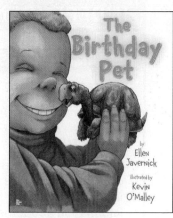

Literature Big Book

Focus on Vocabulary Use the **Visual Vocabulary Cards** to review the oral vocabulary words *responsibility* and *train.* As you read, use gestures and other visual support to clarify important story words: *log, knocks over, cuddly, sneeze.*

Summarize the Text Before reading, show illustrations and give a short summary of the story: *Danny wants a turtle. But his family gives him other animals.*

Read the Text

Use the Interactive Question-Response Routine to help children understand the story.

Pages 4–15

Pages 6–9 Read the text. Point to the corresponding image as you speak. *Danny wants to get a turtle for his birthday. What does Danny want?* (a turtle) *Dad doesn't gets Danny a turtle. He gets him a big dog instead. What does Dad get Danny?* (a dog) *The dog knocks Danny over. He makes Danny fall. The dog runs away. Look at the illustration of Danny. Does he like having a dog?* (no) *How do you know?* (He looks scared.)

Pages 10–14 Read the text. Point to the corresponding image as you speak. *Danny does not want the dog. He still wants a turtle. What does Danny want?* (a turtle) Point to the kitten. *What pet does Mom get Danny?* (a kitten) *The kitten makes Danny sneeze.* Demonstrate sneezing. *The kitten is in the tree. Is the kitten a good pet for Danny?* (no)

 What problems does Danny have with the dog and kitten? Talk to a partner.

Beginning Help children respond. *The dog runs <u>away</u>. The kitten makes Danny <u>sneeze</u>.*

Intermediate Have partners ask and answer: *What does the dog do? The dog <u>runs away</u>. Where is the kitten? The kitten is <u>in the tree</u>.*

Advanced/Advanced High Have partners give details. (*The dog knocks Danny over and runs away. The kitten makes Danny sneeze/gets stuck in the tree.*)

Pages 16–25

Pages 16–17 Read the text and point to the illustration. *How does Danny feel about the rat?* (scared) *How do you know? Look at the illustration.* (His face looks scared.)

Page 20–21 Read the text. The bird squawks. Make a squawking sound. *What is Danny doing?* (covering his ears) *Why?* (The bird is too loud.)

 Does Danny like the rat or the bird? Why? Talk to a partner.

Beginning Have partners point to the illustrations as they respond: *Danny doesn't like the rat or bird. The rat is scary. Danny doesn't like the bird. The bird is loud.*

Intermediate Have partners ask and answer: *How does Danny feel about the rat/bird? He thinks the rat is scary. He thinks the bird is too loud.*

Pages 22–32

Pages 26–29 Read the text. *What does Danny get?* (a turtle) Point to the bugs and lettuce. *Danny takes care of the turtle. He feeds her bugs and lettuce. He plays with her. How does Danny feel?* (happy)

 How does Danny care for the turtle? Talk to a partner.

Beginning Ask children to point to illustrations in the story to tell their answer. Support children in vocalizing their response and ask children to repeat your words.

Intermediate Provide sentence frames. *Danny gives the turtle some lettuce/bugs. Danny plays with the turtle.*

Advanced/Advanced High Have partners give details. (Danny feeds the turtle bugs and green lettuce. Danny makes a gym for the turtle to play.)

Retell Use the **Retelling Cards** to retell *The Birthday Pet* with children. Display the cards and model retelling using sequence words, such as *first, next, then,* and *last,* as you point to the

events and actions on the cards. Then help children take turns retelling one part using the sequence words.

 LESSON 4 Paired Selection: "The Perfect Pet"

Pages 33–36 Read and then paraphrase the text. Point to the corresponding image as you speak. For example, page 33: *Dora and Sofia are at Mr. Gil's pet store. Dora and Sofia want the perfect, or best, pet. Where are Dora and Sofia?* (pet store) *What do they want?* (the perfect pet) Continue the routine to the end of the story. Point out the schedule.

 Tell about the animals at the pet store.

Beginning Have partners choose a pet at the store to describe. For example: *The puppy is brown.*

Intermediate Have partners tell about the animals Sofia and Dora see. For example: *The girls see a puppy. The puppy is brown.*

Advanced/Advanced High Have partners name and describe the animals Sofia and Dora see.

FORMATIVE ASSESSMENT

STUDENT CHECK-IN

Main Selection Have partners retell what Danny likes or doesn't like about each pet.

Paired Selection Have partners retell how Bella and Stella play with their pet.

Then, have children reflect using the Check-In routine.

Independent Time

Oral Language Have partners discuss and give opinions about what animal they think would make a good pet and why. Provide modeling and sentence frames: *I think a cat makes a good pet because you can play with it.* Help children form correct sentences as needed. Then have children share with the group.

LEARNING GOALS

We can listen actively to understand what different pets need.

OBJECTIVES

With prompting and support, retell key details of a text.

With prompting and support, describe the connection between pieces of information in a text.

Ask and answer questions to help determine or clarify the meaning of words and phrases in a text.

Ask and answer questions in order to seek help, get information, or clarify something that is not understood.

LANGUAGE OBJECTIVES

Children will explain how to take care of pets, using pronouns, verbs, and key vocabulary.

ELA ACADEMIC LANGUAGE

• *explain*

MATERIALS

Interactive Read Aloud, "The Family Pet"

Visual Vocabulary Cards

DIGITAL TOOLS

Have children listen to the selection as they follow along to develop comprehension.

Use the vocabulary activity for additional practice.

"The Family Pet"

Prepare to Read

Build Background Show the images on the cards. *What does a pet need? A dog needs walks.* Elicit other answers. Provide a sentence frame: *A _____ needs _____.* Elicit vocabulary, such as *food, water, cage, tank/fishbowl, walks,* etc. Then show images of different types of homes, such as a small apartment in a city, a farmhouse, and a suburban home. Discuss which pet might (or might not) be a good fit for each place and why.

Interactive Read Aloud

Focus on Vocabulary Use the **Visual Vocabulary Cards** to review the oral vocabulary words *depend, compared, social, responsibility,* and *train.* As you read, use gestures and other visual support to clarify important words: *lifestyle, fit.*

Summarize the Text *These cards tell why different people choose different pets.*

Read the Text

Use the Interactive Question-Response Routine to help children understand the text.

Card 1

Paragraphs 1–2 Read the text. Point to the photo. *The girl wants a kitten. Her family must choose a pet carefully. Pets are a big responsibility, or job.*

Paragraph 3 Read the text. Show Cards 2–4. *Three families choose a pet. They each choose a different pet. They think about their lifestyle, or how they live. They know a pet lives with you for a long time. They think about what the pet needs. What do the families think about before they choose a pet?* (lifestyle; what the pet needs)

 What should you think about before you get a pet? Why? Talk to a partner.

Beginning Have partners point to the kitten. Ask the guiding question: *What does a kitten need? A kitten needs* food *and* water.

Intermediate Help partners respond: *You should think about* what a pet needs. *The pet will live with* you for a long time.

Card 2

Paragraphs 1–2 Read the text. Point to the boy. *The Park family lives in a small apartment. They don't have much space.* Check understanding of "space." *They want a pet that can stay inside because they don't have a yard. Why do they want an indoor pet?* (They don't have a yard. They don't have much space.)

Paragraphs 3–4 Read the text. *The family decides to get some fish. The children know how to clean the tank and feed the fish. The fish need very little space. Fish are easy to take care of. How do the children take care of the fish?* (feed the fish; clean the tank)

 Explain, or tell, why the family get fish. Talk to a partner.

Beginning *Are fish easy or hard to take care of? Fish are <u>easy</u> to take care of.*

Intermediate *What is one reason the family gets fish?* (Sample answer: They don't have much space.)

Advanced/Advanced High Have partners give details about why the family gets goldfish. (They need small pets because they live in a small apartment.)

Card 3

Paragraphs 1–2 Read the text. *The Dason family lives in a house. They are busy. They don't have time to walk a dog or play with a cat. But they would like a pet that is fun. The Dason family gets a parakeet. What pet does the family get?* (a parakeet/bird)

Paragraph 3 *Parakeets are fun pets. You can train, or teach, them to talk. Why are parakeets fun?* (You can teach them to talk.)

 Explain, or tell, why the family gets a bird. Talk to a partner.

Beginning Help children respond. *The family wants a pet that is easy and <u>fun</u>.*

Intermediate *The family doesn't have a lot of time to <u>care for a pet</u>. But they still want a pet that <u>is fun</u>.*

Advanced/Advanced High Have partners give details about why the family gets a parakeet.

Card 4

Paragraphs 1–2 *The Johnson family lives in the country. They have a lot of space and time for a pet. They want an animal that likes people. They want to play with their pet. They want to train their pet. What do they want to do with a pet?* (train it, play with it)

Paragraphs 3–4 Read the text. Point to the dog. *The Johnson family gets a puppy. They name the puppy Logan. Everyone helps care for Logan. They help to feed clean, and walk Logan. How do they care for Logan?* (They feed, walk, and clean Logan.)

 Why does the family want to get a dog? Talk to a partner.

Beginning Help children respond. *The family wants a pet that likes <u>people</u>.*

Intermediate *What are two reasons the family gets a dog?* Provide a sentence frame: *They want a pet to play with/cuddle/train.*

Advanced Have partners give details about why the family gets a dog. (Examples: They want to train a dog. They can play with the dog outside.)

Advanced High After partners respond to the Advanced prompt, have them tell which pet they would want and why.

Retell Use the photos on the **Interactive Read-Aloud Cards** to retell the text with children. Display the cards and model retelling details in the photos and text. Then help partners take turns retelling key details about one of the cards.

STUDENT CHECK-IN

Have partners retell how to take care of two of the pets from the text. Then, have children reflect using the Check-In routine.

 Independent Time

What a Pet Needs Have children choose a pet from the cards or their own pet and draw themselves taking care of the pet. Provide a sentence frame and help them fill it in. *A ___ needs ___.* Have children share their drawings and ideas with partners.

Their Pets

Prepare to Read

Build Background Show images of people interacting with their pets: dog, cat, horse, goat, rabbit, bird. Discuss what the pets need. *What does a [pet] need? The rabbit needs a cage. The dog needs to walk.* Elicit other answers. Provide a sentence frame: *The _____ needs _____.*

Lexile BR

Focus on Vocabulary Use the routine on the **ELL Visual Vocabulary Cards** to preteach *affection* and *provide*. Use the images and any labels to identify and model the use of key vocabulary in context.

Read the Text

Use the Interactive Question-Response Routine to help children understand the story.

Pages 2–8

Pages 2–3 *What pets do you see?* (dogs, cats) *How are they alike?* (fur, four legs, tail) *Let's read the labels together:* pets, beds. Point to page 2. *What are the owners doing?* (walking the dogs) Point to page 3. *What are the owners giving their cats?* (a bed)

 What do the pets get? What else do you think the pets will get? Talk to a partner.

Beginning Have partners use the illustrations: *The dogs/cats get* walks/beds. Help them **make a prediction**: *The pets will get* [food].

Intermediate Have partners ask and answer: *What do the* dogs/cats *get? The* dogs/cats *get* walks/beds. *What do you predict? The pets will* get [food].

Advanced/Advanced High Guide children to give details. *The dogs* get walks outside. *The cats* get soft beds. Have children make predictions about the pets.

Pages 4–5 *What pets do you see?* (goats, rabbits) *Let's read the labels:* hay, lettuce. *Pets need food. How do the pet owners* **solve**, *or fix, this* **problem?** (feed their pets) *What do the goats/rabbits eat?* (hay, lettuce)

 What do the owners give their pets? Talk to a partner.

Beginning *Have partners point to the illustrations as they respond. The* goat *gets* hay. *The* rabbit *gets* lettuce.

Intermediate Have partners point to the illustrations as they ask and answer: *What do they give the goats/rabbits? They give the goats hay. They give the rabbits* lettuce/a cage/water.

Advanced/Advanced High Have partners ask and answer: *What do they give the* goats/rabbits*?* Encourage children to add more details to their answers. (They give the goats hay to eat. They give the rabbits lettuce to eat. They give the rabbits a cage and water.)

Pages 6–7 *What pets do you see?* (horses, birds) *Let's read the labels:* water, toys. *What do the horses/birds drink?* (water) *Where are the horses/birds?* (in a field/cage)

Page 8: *What pets do you see?* (dog, cat) *Let's read the label:* friends. *Are the pets and owners happy?* (yes) *How do you know?* (Everyone looks happy.)

 Tell what the horse and bird get. **Confirm your predictions.** *Was your prediction right?*

Beginning Have partners point to the illustrations: *The horse/bird gets* water/toys. Help children recall their predictions.

Intermediate *Have partners ask and answer: What does the* horse/bird *get? The* horse/bird *gets* water/toys. *Did you predict this?*

Advanced/Advanced High Guide children to give details about what the animals get and confirm their predictions.

Retell Have partners retell the story. Have them take turns pointing to a picture and describing it each other.

Focus on Fluency

Read pages 2–8. The reread and have children echo read. For additional practice, have children record themselves reading the same text a few times, and then select their favorite recording to play for you.

Build Knowledge: Make Connections

Talk About the Text Have partners discuss what pets need.

Write About the Text Have children add their ideas to their Build Knowledge pages of their reader's notebooks.

Self-Selected Reading

Have children select another story from the online **Leveled Reader Library,** or read the **Differentiated Text,** "Puppies!"

LITERACY ACTIVITIES

Have children complete the Literacy Activities on the inside back cover of the book.

❯ STUDENT CHECK-IN

Have partners retell what the pet owners give to to their pets. Then, have children reflect using the Check-In routine.

LEVEL UP

IF children can read *Their Pets* **ELL Level** with fluency and correctly answer the Respond to Reading questions,

THEN tell children that they will read a more detailed version of the story.

HAVE children page through *Their Pets* On Level and describe each picture in simple language.

• Have children read the selection, checking their comprehension and providing assistance as necessary.

MODELED WRITING

LEARNING GOALS

We can write about what animal we would choose as a pet.

OBJECTIVES

Use dictating and writing to compose informative texts in which they name the topic.

LANGUAGE OBJECTIVES

Children will inform by writing a sentence using a verb.

ELA ACADEMIC LANGUAGE

• *sentence*

Writing Practice Display a photo of a hamster and review the sample sentence on p. 44 of the **Reading/Writing Companion.** Guide children to analyze the sentence using the Actor/Action Routine: *Who is the actor?* (I) *What is the action?* (feed my pet hamster celery) Then read the prompt on p. 45, and have children answer it as a group. Write the sentence on the board and have children choral read. Ask children to write their own.

Beginning Have children think of things they might do to take care of a pet. Use their responses to create a word bank. Have them use the word bank to complete the sentence frame: I will write about giving <u>my pet exercise</u>.

Intermediate Have partners take turns asking and answering *who/what* questions to create their sentences. Provide a sentence frame if needed.

Advanced/Advanced High Challenge children to talk about their sentence using the Actor/Action routine. Have them point out the verb.

FORMATIVE ASSESSMENT ❯ **STUDENT CHECK IN** Partners share their sentences. Have children reflect using the Check-In routine.

INTERACTIVE WRITING

LEARNING GOALS

We can write a story about choosing a pet.

OBJECTIVES

With guidance and support, respond to questions and suggestions from peers.

LANGUAGE OBJECTIVES

Children will narrate a story by writing a sentence using a descriptive word.

ELA ACADEMIC LANGUAGE

• *descriptive*

• Cognates: *descriptivo*

Write a Response: Share the Pen Choral read the sample sentence on p. T108 of the **Teacher's Edition.** Use the Actor/Action Routine to review it: *Who is the actor?* (I) *What is the action?* (asked my parents) *For what?* (a bright, yellow bird) Remind children of the writing trait: *Which describing words tell you more about the bird?* (bright, yellow) Then help children complete the sentence frames at the bottom of p. T108.

Beginning Be sure children understand they are writing a story. Then ask: *What kind of pet does the character in your story want?*

Intermediate Remind children they are using *The Birthday Pet* as a model. Have partners look through the story to get ideas. Then have them orally complete the sentence frames before writing.

Advanced/Advanced High Challenge children to think of their own sentences to write a story about choosing a pet. Encourage them to share their story with the group.

FORMATIVE ASSESSMENT ❯ **STUDENT CHECK IN** Partners share their sentences. Have children reflect using the Check-In routine.

INDEPENDENT WRITING

LEARNING GOALS

We can write about the texts we read.

OBJECTIVES

Use drawing and writing to narrate events in the order in which they occurred.

LANGUAGE OBJECTIVES

Children will narrate a story by writing a sentence using a verb.

ELA ACADEMIC LANGUAGE

• *prompt*

Find Text Evidence Use the Independent Writing routine. Ask questions to help children orally retell the shared read, such as: *Who is Gus?* (*the boy's new dog*) *What do Gus and the cat do?* (tug and have fun) Then read the prompt on p. 60 of the **Reading/Writing Companion**: *What would your first day with a new pet be like? Write a story about it.* Display pp. 55 and 56. *What do Gus and the boy do?* (play tug) *What does the boy do next?* (gives Gus a bath)

Write a Response Write the sentence starters from p. T118 on the board, and read them. Model completing the first starter, and have children choral read the response. Repeat with the remaining starters. Then have children copy the sentences onto p. 61 of the **Reading/Writing Companion**.

Beginning Provide a sentence frame to help children talk about their sentences: I used the verb <u>play</u>.

Intermediate Encourage children to add descriptive words.

Advanced/Advanced High Have partners identify where they used each checklist item in their writing.

FORMATIVE ASSESSMENT ❯ ⊘ **STUDENT CHECK IN** Partners share their sentences. Have children reflect using the Check-In routine.

SELF-SELECTED WRITING

LEARNING GOALS

We can revise our writing.

OBJECTIVES

Use frequently occurring nouns and verbs.

LANGUAGE OBJECTIVES

Children will inquire about their writing by checking that the verb was used correctly.

ELA ACADEMIC LANGUAGE

• *verb*

• Cognate: *verbo*

Work with children to revise the group writing activity. Point to each word as you read the sentences. Stop to ask questions, such as, *Is the verb used correctly here?* If needed, write a sentence using a verb incorrectly, and work together to revise the sentence. Then have partners revise each other's sentence before publishing it. Provide them with sentence frames on sentence strips as needed.

For support with grammar and to review verbs, refer to the **Language Transfers Handbook** and **Language Development Cards** 4A, 4B.

FORMATIVE ASSESSMENT ❯ ⊘ **STUDENT CHECK IN** Partners tell what revisions they made. Have children reflect using the Check-In routine.

LESSONS 1-2

We can understand important ideas and details about a story.

We can use the glossary to learn new information.

OBJECTIVES

With prompting and support, identify characters and events in a story.

With prompting and support, describe the relationship between illustrations and the story in which they appear.

With prompting and support, compare and contrast the adventures and experiences of characters in familiar stories.

Confirm understanding of a text read aloud or information presented orally or through other media by asking and answering questions about key details and requesting clarification if something is not understood.

LANGUAGE OBJECTIVES

Children will narrate how the characters have fun together, using verbs, adjectives, and nouns.

ELA ACADEMIC LANGUAGE

• discuss, ask, answer

MATERIALS

Literature Big Book, *Bear Snores On*, pp. 5–34 and 35–40

Visual Vocabulary Cards

DIGITAL TOOLS

Have children listen to the selection as they follow along to develop comprehension.

Use the vocabulary activity for additional support.

Bear Snores On

Prepare to Read

Build Background Show an image of a bear hibernating in a den. Explain what a bear does each winter. *Every winter bears go into a den and sleep, or hibernate. A bear's den is a quiet place, like a cave. Bears do not eat or drink during this time. They spend most of their time sleeping.*

Literature Big Book

Focus on Vocabulary Use the **Visual Vocabulary Cards** to review the oral vocabulary words *habitat* and *wild*. As you read, use gestures and other visual support to clarify important story words: *cave, pepper.*

Summarize the Text Before reading, show children the pictures and summarize the book: *It's winter, and the bear is sleeping. His friends come into his cave and have a party. The party wakes the bear up.*

Read the Text

Use the Interactive Question-Response Routine to help children understand the story.

Pages 4–15

Pages 6–7 Read the text. Point to the illustrations. *It is winter. It is snowing. The bear is in his cave. He is snoring.* Demonstrate snoring. *What is the bear doing?* (sleeping, snoring) *What is happening outside?* (It's snowing.)

Pages 10–11 Read the text. Point to the corresponding image as you speak: *Mouse comes into the bear's cave. He builds, or makes, a fire. What does Mouse do?* (He builds a fire.) *Does the bear wake up?* (no)

Pages 12–14 Read the text. Point to the illustrations. *Hare comes into the bear's cave. Mouse and Hare make tea and pop, or make, popcorn. How do Mouse and Hare make noise?* (Mouse slurps. Hare burps.) *Does the bear wake up?* (no)

 What do the animals do in the den? Discuss with a partner.

Beginning Have children use the illustrations on pages 6–7, 9, and 13 to help them respond: *The bear <u>sleeps</u>. Mouse makes a <u>fire</u>. Hare <u>drinks</u> tea.*

Intermediate Have partners *ask and answer questions about what the characters do on pages 8–15. What does <u>the bear/Mouse/Hare</u> do? The bear <u>sleeps</u>. Mouse <u>makes a fire</u>. Hare <u>drinks tea</u>.*

 Advanced/Advanced High Have partners ask and answer: *What does the bear/Mouse/Hare do? What noises do they make?* (The bear sleeps and snores. Mouse builds a fire. Mouse and Hare drink tea and eat corn.)

Pages 16–27

Pages 18–19 Read the text. *Mouse, Hare, and Badger are eating honey-nuts. Eating nuts makes a crunching sound. What else makes this sound? Does the bear wake up?* (no)

Pages 24–27 Point to the corresponding images. *Mouse adds pepper to the stew. The pepper makes the bear sneeze. What makes the bear sneeze?* (the pepper) *Are the animals surprised?* (yes) *Why do you think so?* (Their faces look surprised.)

 What happens to the bear? Talk to a partner.

Beginning Have partners complete sentences: *Mouse adds* pepper *to the stew. The bear* sneezes.

Intermediate Have partners ask and answer: *What does the bear do? The bear* sneezes. *What makes the bear* sneeze*?* Pepper *makes the bear sneeze.*

Pages 28–34

Pages 28–29 Read the text. *The sneeze wakes the bear up!* Act out what the bear does as you read the words. *How does the bear feel now?* (angry) *Why?* (Because they woke him up.) *Are the animals afraid?* (yes) *How do you know?* (They are running.)

Page 34 Read the text. *Is it day or night?* (day) *What are all the animals doing?* (sleeping) *What about the bear?* (He is awake now.)

 The bear looks sad. What is his problem now? Talk to a partner.

Beginning Have partners point to the images. *The bear is* awake. *His friends are* asleep.

Intermediate Have partners discuss what is happening in the illustration on page 34: *Why does the* bear *look sad? The bear* is awake, *but his* friends are asleep.

Retell Use the **Retelling Cards** for *The Bear Snores On* to retell the story with children. Display the cards and model retelling using sequence words as you point to the events and actions

on the cards. Then help children take turns retelling one part using the sequence words.

 Paired Selection: "Animal Homes"

LESSON 4

Pages 35-40 Read and then paraphrase the text. Point to the corresponding illustrations as you speak. For example, on page 36: *This is a prairie dog. What animal is this?* (prairie dog) *It lives underground.* Point to the hole. *It lives in a burrow.* Point to the burrow. *Where does it live?* (in a burrow) *These are the tunnels and the rooms in the burrow.* Continue this routine with the other animals.

What did you learn about the animals' habitats, or homes? Discuss with a partner.

Beginning Help partners pick a page and name what they see. *This is a ___. It lives in a ___.*

Intermediate Have partners pick an animal to talk about. Give them sentence frames as needed to help them tell what they know.

Advanced/Advanced High Guide partners to compare two animals' habitats. (Example: The prairie dog and the snake both have homes underground.)

FORMATIVE ASSESSMENT

> **STUDENT CHECK-IN**

Main Selection Have partners retell things that the animals do in the cave.

Paired Selection Have partners describe the home for two of the animals.

Then, have children reflect using the Check-In routine.

 Independent Time

Oral Language Review the different habitats you've read about in *Bear Snores On* and "Animal Homes." Facilitate a discussion of how the habitats are alike and different than their own homes. For example, the bear's cave and a house keep out the snow.

ENGLISH LANGUAGE LEARNERS **175**

LEARNING GOALS

We can listen actively to understand what we can learn from the folktale.

OBJECTIVES

With prompting and support, ask and answer questions about key details in a text.

Recognize common types of texts (e.g., storybooks, poems).

With prompting and support, compare and contrast the adventures and experiences of characters in familiar stories.

Continue a conversation through multiple exchanges.

LANGUAGE OBJECTIVES

Children will narrate how two characters play a trick on each other, using pronouns and sequence words.

ELA ACADEMIC LANGUAGE

• character, folktale

MATERIALS

Interactive Read Aloud, "Aunt Nancy"

Visual Vocabulary Cards

DIGITAL TOOLS

🎧 Have children listen to the selection as they follow along to develop comprehension.

Use the vocabulary activity for additional practice.

"Aunt Nancy"

Prepare to Read

Interactive Read Aloud

Build Background Show an image of a salt marsh habitat in South Carolina. Point out South Carolina on a map. Explain that a marsh is salty. Show images of the animals (sea turtles, alligators, snakes, minnows, and crawfish) and insects (butterflies, dragonflies, fire ants). Help children name things.

Focus on Vocabulary Use the **Visual Vocabulary Cards** to review the oral vocabulary words *complain, stubborn, join, habitat,* and *wild.* As you read, use gestures and other visual support to clarify important story words: *share, shore.*

Summarize the Text Show children the cards. Tell them that this story is a folktale. A folktale often has characters that are animals. *The story tells about a spider who tries to trick her friend, Sea Turtle.*

Read the Text

Use the Interactive Question-Response Routine to help children understand the story.

Card 1

Paragraphs 1–2 Read the text. Point to the images as you speak. *Aunt Nancy, the spider, lives in the salt marsh. Aunt Nancy is cooking some insects to eat. Where does Aunt Nancy live?* (in the salt marsh) *What is she doing?* (cooking)

Paragraphs 3–5 Read the text. Point to the illustration. *Sea Turtle smells the food. He asks if he can share, or have some, of the food. Aunt Nancy tells Sea Turtle to wash his hands first. What does Sea Turtle want?* (to share the food) *What does Aunt Nancy tell him?* (to wash his hands first)

 What does Sea Turtle have to do before he can eat? Talk to a partner.

Beginning Point to turtle's "hands." Show washing your hands while saying, *Turtle has to wash his hands.* Have children repeat the gesture and sentence.

Intermediate Provide sentence frames. *Turtle wants* to eat. *Aunt Nancy says Turtle* must wash his hands first.

Advanced/Advanced High Guide partners to answer in complete sentences. (Before he can eat, Sea turtle must wash his hands.)

Card 2

Paragraphs 6–10 *Aunt Nancy tells Sea Turtle to wash his hands again. He walks to the shore a second time.* Point to the shore. *When Sea Turtle gets back, all the food is gone! Sea Turtle knows that Aunt Nancy tricked him. Sea Turtle goes home hungry. What did Aunt Nancy do?* (She tricked Sea Turtle.) *Why do you think she tricked him?* (She doesn't want to share.)

 What does Aunt Nancy do to Sea Turtle? Talk to a partner.

Beginning *Is there food for Sea Turtle?* (no) *Why not? Aunt Nancy tricked* Sea Turtle. *She ate the* food.

Intermediate Supply sentence frames. *Aunt Nancy* tricks *Sea Turtle. She tells him to* wash his hands. *While he is gone, Aunt Nancy* eats the food.

Advanced/Advanced High Have partners ask and answer questions about how Aunt Nancy tricks Sea Turtle. Provide modeling as needed.

Card 3

Paragraphs 1–2 Point to Sea Turtle and tell that he is having lunch. *Aunt Nancy wants to join Sea Turtle for lunch. She dives into the water.* Demonstrate diving. *She tries hard to sink, or go under the water. But she is too light. She floats to the top every time.* Demonstrate floating with gestures. *"Why can't Aunt Nancy sink?"* (She is too light. She floats to the top.)

 What problem does Aunt Nancy have? Talk to a partner.

Beginning *What does Aunt Nancy want to do? Eat with* Sea Turtle. *What is the problem? She can't stay under* the water.

Intermediate Give guiding questions. *What does Aunt Nancy want? Aunt Nancy wants to* join *Sea Turtle for* lunch. *What is the problem? Aunt Nancy can't* sink. *She is too* light. *She* floats *to the top.*

Card 4

Paragraph 1 Read the text. Point to the illustration. *Aunt Nancy thinks of a plan. She puts rocks in her pockets.*

The rocks are heavy. They help her sink. How does Aunt Nancy sink? (She puts rocks in her pockets.)

Paragraphs 2–4 Read the text. *Sea Turtle asks Aunt Nancy to take off her jacket. He says it is rude, or not nice, to eat with a jacket on.* Point to her jacket.

Paragraphs 5–7 Read the text. *Aunt Nancy takes off her jacket. She floats to the top. Aunt Nancy knows that Sea Turtle tricked her. Aunt Nancy and Sea Turtle both apologize, or say they are sorry. They promise to share their food from now on.*

 Why do Aunt Nancy and Sea Turtle apologize to each other?

Beginning *What do Aunt Nancy and Sea Turtle both say? They say they are* sorry. *What are they sorry about? They are sorry they did not share their* food.

Intermediate Guide partners to respond: *Aunt Nancy and Sea Turtle apologize because they* tricked each other. *They are sorry they didn't* share their food.

Advanced/Advanced High After partners tell why Aunt Nancy and Sea Turtle apologize, guide them to infer why Turtle tricked Aunt Nancy. Explain and help them use the phrase "to get back at her" if needed.

Retell Use the illustrations on the **Interactive Read-Aloud Cards** to retell the story with children. Display the cards and model retelling using sequence words, as you point to the events on the cards. Help children take turns retelling one part using the sequence words.

FORMATIVE ASSESSMENT

❯ STUDENT CHECK-IN

Have partners retell why Aunt Nancy and Sea Turtle apologized to each other. Then, have children reflect using the Check-In routine.

 Independent Time

Role-play Say: *Have partners plan a role-play based on one of the cards.* Have children practice their role-plays before they perform them for the group.

LEARNING GOALS

We can make and confirm predictions to understand the story.

OBJECTIVES

With prompting and support, identify characters and events in a story.

Recognize common types of texts (e.g., storybooks, poems).

With prompting and support, compare and contrast the adventures and experiences of characters in familiar stories.

Ask and answer questions in order to seek help, get information, or clarify something that is not understood.

LANGUAGE OBJECTIVES

Children will describe where the animals live, using nouns, verbs, and key vocabulary.

ELA ACADEMIC LANGUAGE

• *title, author, illustrator*
• Cognates: *título, autor, ilustrador*

MATERIALS

Leveled Reader: *A New Home*

Online Differentiated Texts, "I Like the Vet"

Online ELL Visual Vocabulary Cards

DIGITAL TOOLS

Have children listen to the selection as they follow along to develop comprehension.

Use the vocabulary activity for additional support.

A New Home

Lexile 300L

Prepare to Read

Build Background Show images of animals from the story (squirrel, bird, mouse, rabbit, beaver, fox) in their real homes. Talk about where the animals live. (in a tree, underground, in the water, etc.) Provide sentence frames: *This is a _____. A _____ lives _____.* Provide content vocabulary, such as *hole, den, lodge,* and *nest.*

Focus on Vocabulary Use the routine on the **ELL Visual Vocabulary Cards** to preteach *nest* and *shelter.* Use the images and any labels to identify and model the use of key vocabulary in context.

Read the Text

Use the Interactive Question-Response Routine to help children understand the story.

Pages 2–8

Pages 2–3 *What animals do you see?* (squirrel, bird) Read the labels. *Squirrel lives in a tree. Squirrel wants Bird's home. What does Squirrel want?* (Bird's home) *Bird lives in a nest in a tree. Where is Bird's home?* (a nest in a tree)

 How are Squirrel's home and Bird's home alike? Talk to a partner.

Beginning Have children point to the tree on each page. *What is this? This is a tree. Squirrel lives in* a tree. *Bird lives in* a tree.

Intermediate Have partners point to the illustrations as they ask and answer: *Where do Squirrel and Bird both live? Squirrel and Bird both* live in a tree.

Advanced/Advanced High Have partners ask and answer: *Where does Squirrel/Bird live? Add details to your answer.* (Squirrel lives in a hole in a tree. Bird lives in a nest.)

Pages 4–5 *What animals do you see?* (squirrel, mouse, rabbit) Point to page 5. *Where is Squirrel putting his head?* (into a hole)

Make Predictions Have children make a prediction about Squirrel. (Squirrel will want more homes.) Ask children why they think that will happen next.

 How are Mouse's and Rabbit's homes alike? Talk to a partner.

Beginning Have partners point to the animal homes in the illustrations as they respond. Mouse/Rabbit *lives in a* hole.

Intermediate Have partners ask and answer: *Where does* Mouse/Rabbit *live?* Mouse/Rabbit *lives* in a hole.

Pages 6–8 Display pages 6–7. *Squirrel wants Beaver's home. Beaver's home is on the water.* Point to the sticks. *It is made of sticks. Where does Beaver live?* (on the water) *Squirrel wants Fox's home. Fox lives on land. He doesn't live on the water.* Point to the rocks. *His home is made of rocks. What is Fox's home made of?* (rocks)

Events: Cause and Effect Display page 8. *Squirrel sees a lot of animal homes. What is the effect?* (Squirrel wants his own home.) *What is the cause?* (Squirrel sees other animals' homes) **Confirm your prediction**. *Was it correct?* (yes/no)

 How are Beaver's home and Fox's home different? Talk to a partner.

Beginning Have partners point and tell about Beaver's home. *This home is made of* sticks. Have them point and tell about Fox's home. *This home is made of* rocks.

Intermediate Have partners point to the illustrations as they ask and answer: *Where does* Beaver/Fox *live?* Beaver/Fox *lives* near the water/on land. *What is this home made of? It is made of* sticks/rocks.

Advanced/Advanced High Have partners ask and answer questions about Beaver's and Fox's homes.

Retell Have partners retell the story. Have them take turns pointing to a picture and describing it to each other.

Focus on Fluency

Read pages 2–8 with appropriate intonation. Then read the text aloud and have children echo read. For additional practice, have children record themselves reading the same text a few times, and then select their favorite recording to play for you.

Build Knowledge: Make Connections

Talk About the Text Have partners discuss where animals live and what they need.

Write About the Text Have children add their ideas to their Build Knowledge pages of their reader's notebooks.

Self-Selected Reading

Have children select another story from the online **Leveled Reader Library,** or read the **Differentiated Text,** "I Like the Vet."

LITERACY ACTIVITIES

Have children complete the Literacy Activities on the inside back cover of the book.

FORMATIVE ASSESSMENT

STUDENT CHECK-IN

Have partners retell descriptions of two of the animal homes. Then, have children reflect using the Check-In routine.

LEVEL UP

IF children can read *A New Home* ELL Level with fluency and correctly answer the Respond to Reading questions,

THEN tell children that they will read a more detailed version of the story.

HAVE children page through *A New Home* On Level and describe each picture in simple language.

- Have children read the selection, checking their comprehension and providing assistance as necessary.

MODELED WRITING

LESSON
1

LEARNING GOALS

We can write about our favorite thing to do in winter.

OBJECTIVES

Use dictating and writing to compose informative texts in which they name the topic.

LANGUAGE OBJECTIVES

Children will inform by writing a sentence using a verb.

ELA ACADEMIC LANGUAGE

• sentence, verb
• Cognates: *verbo*

Writing Practice Display the cover of the **Big Book** *Bear Snores On.* Review the sample sentence on p. 74 of the **Reading/Writing Companion.** Guide children to analyze the sentence using the Actor/Action Routine: *Who are the actors?* (Bears) *What is the action?* (sleep) *When?* (during the winter) Then read the prompt on p. 75, and ask children to answer it as a group. Review the sentence by writing it on the board and pointing to each word as children choral read. Then ask children to write their own sentence.

Beginning Provide a sentence frame: I will write about playing outside. *Who is the actor?* (I) *What is the action?* (playing) *Where?* (outside)

Intermediate Have partners take turns asking and answering *who/what* questions to create their sentences. Provide a sentence frame if needed.

Advanced/Advanced High Encourage children to use the Word Bank to spell words as they write. Have them share their sentences with the group.

FORMATIVE ASSESSMENT ❯ ❯ **STUDENT CHECK IN** Partners share their sentences. Have children reflect using the Check-In routine.

INTERACTIVE WRITING

LESSON
2

LEARNING GOALS

We can write about our favorite character in *Bear Snores On.*

OBJECTIVES

With guidance and support, add details to strengthen writing as needed.

LANGUAGE OBJECTIVES

Children will argue by writing a sentence using the word *because.*

ELA ACADEMIC LANGUAGE

• verb
• Cognates: *verbo*

Write a Response: Share the Pen Choral read the sample sentence on p. T186 of the **Teacher's Edition.** Use the Actor/Description Routine to review the second sentence: *Who is the actor?* (I) *What is the actor describing?* (like his loud sneeze) Have children use the Word Bank to spell *like* and *his.* Remind children of the writing trait: *When we write, we use words that describe. What word described Bear's sneeze?* (loud) Help children complete the sentence frames at the bottom of p. T186.

Beginning Provide a simplified sentence frame: The character I like best is Mouse. Ask children guiding questions to help them tell why.

Intermediate Have partners ask and answer questions about the characters using the illustrations in the book.

Advanced/Advanced High Challenge children to think of their own sentences about their favorite character. Encourage them to share them with the group.

FORMATIVE ASSESSMENT ❯ ❯ **STUDENT CHECK IN** Partners share their sentences. Have children reflect using the Check-In routine.

INDEPENDENT WRITING

 LESSONS 3-4

LEARNING GOALS

We can write about the texts we read.

OBJECTIVES

Use drawing, dictating, and writing to compose opinion pieces that state an opinion about the topic.

LANGUAGE OBJECTIVES

Children will argue by writing a sentence that gives a reason to support their opinion.

ELA ACADEMIC LANGUAGE

• *opinion, verb, future*

• Cognates: *opinión, verbo, futuro*

Find Text Evidence Use the Indendent Writing routine. Ask questions to help children orally retell the shared read, such as: *Who is the woman in the story?* (a vet) *What does she do?* (help animals) Then read the prompt on p. 90 of the **Reading/Writing Companion:** *Will you be a vet when you grow up? Why or why not?* Display pp. 80–81, 86: *What does the vet do?* (see zoo animals) *How does she help the ox?* (She fixes its leg.)

Write a Response Write the sentence starters on the board, and read them. Model completing the first sentence starter, and have children choral read the response. Repeat with the second starter. Then have children copy the sentences onto p. 91 of the **Reading/Writing Companion.**

Beginning Provide a sentence frame to help them talk about their sentences: I used the descriptive word *sick*.

Intermediate Encourage children to add a descriptive word.

Advanced/Advanced High Have partners identify where they used each checklist item in their writing.

FORMATIVE ASSESSMENT

❯ **STUDENT CHECK IN** Partners share their sentences. Have children reflect using the Check-In routine.

SELF-SELECTED WRITING

 LESSON 5

LEARNING GOALS

We can revise our writing.

OBJECTIVES

Use frequently occurring nouns and verbs.

LANGUAGE OBJECTIVES

Children will inquire about their writing by identifying if verb tenses are used correctly.

ELA ACADEMIC LANGUAGE

• *verb, publish*

• Cognates: *verbo, publicar*

Work with children to revise the group writing activity. Point to each word as you read the sentences. Stop to ask questions, such as, *Is the verb used correctly here?* If needed, write a sentence using the verb tense incorrectly, and work together to revise the sentence. Then have partners revise each other's sentences before they publish them. Provide them with sentence frames on sentence strips as needed.

To review verb tenses and for support with grammar, refer to the **Language Transfers Handbook** and **Language Development Cards** 4A and 4B.

FORMATIVE ASSESSMENT

❯ **STUDENT CHECK IN** Partners tell what revisions they made. Have children reflect using the Check-In routine.

Summative Assessment
Get Ready for Unit Assessment

Unit 7 Tested Skills

LISTENING AND READING COMPREHENSION	VOCABULARY	GRAMMAR	SPEAKING AND WRITING
• Listening Actively • Text Structure • Character, Setting, Plot • Details	• Words and Categories	• Verbs	• Offering Opinions • Presenting • Composing/Writing • Retelling/Recounting

Create a Student Profile

Record data from the following resources in the Student Profile charts on pages 136–137 of the Assessment book.

COLLABORATIVE	INTERPRETIVE	PRODUCTIVE

• Collaborative Conversations Rubrics
  • Listening
  • Speaking
	• Leveled Unit Assessment
	  • Listening Comprehension
	  • Reading Comprehension
	  • Vocabulary
	  • Grammar
	• Presentation Rubric
	  • Listening
	• *Wonders* Unit Assessment
		• Weekly Progress Monitoring
		• Leveled Unit Assessment
		  • Speaking
		  • Writing
		• Presentation Rubric
		  • Speaking
		• Write to Sources Rubric
		• *Wonders* Unit Assessment

The Foundational Skills Kit, Language Development Kit, and Adaptive Learning provide additional student data for progress monitoring.

Level Up

Use the following chart, along with your Student Profiles, to guide your Level Up decisions.

LEVEL UP	If **BEGINNING** level students are able to do the following, they may be ready to move to the **INTERMEDIATE** level:	If **INTERMEDIATE** level students are able to do the following, they may be ready to move to the **ADVANCED** level:	If **ADVANCED** level students are able to do the following, they may be ready to move to **ON** level:
COLLABORATIVE	• participate in collaborative conversations using basic vocabulary and grammar and simple phrases or sentences • discuss simple pictorial or text prompts	• participate in collaborative conversations using appropriate words and phrases and complete sentences • use limited academic vocabulary across and within disciplines	• participate in collaborative conversations using more sophisticated vocabulary and correct grammar • communicate effectively across a wide range of language demands in social and academic contexts
INTERPRETIVE	• identify details in simple read alouds • understand common vocabulary and idioms and interpret language related to familiar social, school, and academic topics • make simple inferences and make simple comparisons • exhibit an emerging receptive control of lexical, syntactic, phonological, and discourse features	• identify main ideas and/or make some inferences from simple read alouds • use context clues to identify word meanings and interpret basic vocabulary and idioms • compare, contrast, summarize, and relate text to graphic organizers • exhibit a limited range of receptive control of lexical, syntactic, phonological, and discourse features when addressing new or familiar topics	• determine main ideas in read alouds that have advanced vocabulary • use context clues to determine meaning, understand multiple-meaning words, and recognize synonyms of social and academic vocabulary • analyze information, make sophisticated inferences, and explain their reasoning • command a high degree of receptive control of lexical, syntactic, phonological, and discourse features
PRODUCTIVE	• express ideas and opinions with basic vocabulary and grammar and simple phrases or sentences • restate information or retell a story using basic vocabulary • exhibit an emerging productive control of lexical, syntactic, phonological, and discourse features	• produce coherent language with limited elaboration or detail • restate information or retell a story using mostly accurate, although limited, vocabulary • exhibit a limited range of productive control of lexical, syntactic, phonological, and discourse features when addressing new or familiar topics	• produce sentences with more sophisticated vocabulary and correct grammar • restate information or retell a story using extensive and accurate vocabulary and grammar • tailor language to a particular purpose and audience • command a high degree of productive control of lexical, syntactic, phonological, and discourse features

LESSONS 1-2

We can understand important ideas and details about a story.

We can use headings to learn new information.

OBJECTIVES

Ask and answer questions about unknown words in a text.

With prompting and support, describe the relationship between illustrations and the story in which they appear.

With prompting and support, retell familiar stories, including key details.

Speak audibly and express thoughts, feelings, and ideas clearly.

LANGUAGE OBJECTIVES

Children will explain why the main character's feelings change in the story, using nouns and adjectives.

ELA ACADEMIC LANGUAGE

• character, caption

MATERIALS

Literature Big Book, *When Daddy's Truck Picks Me Up,* pp. 4–32 and 33–36

Visual Vocabulary Cards

DIGITAL TOOLS

Have children listen to the selection as they follow along to develop comprehension.

Use the vocabulary activity for additional support.

When Daddy's Truck Picks Me Up

Prepare to Read

Build Background Show a photo of a tanker truck. *People drive big trucks like this. The trucks take things places. The drivers may drive a long way. A long trip may take a few days. We are going to read a story about a boy. His dad drives a truck like this one. The boy's dad is coming home from a long trip. The boy is excited to see his dad.*

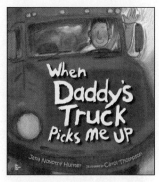

Literature Big Book

Focus on Vocabulary Use the **Visual Vocabulary Cards** to review the oral vocabulary words *transportation* and *vehicle.* As you read, use gestures and other visual support to clarify story words: *tanker truck, engine, waiting, load, stuck.*

Summarize the Text Before reading, give a short summary of the selection: *A boy is excited. His dad is coming home from a long trip. The boy waits for the school day to end. His dad is picking him up in his tanker truck.*

Read the Text

Use the Interactive Question-Response Routine to help children understand the story.

Pages 4–9

Pages 4–5 Read the text. *Look at the pictures on page 4. They show the boy as a baby and Daddy's truck. Today is Daddy's turn to pick him up. Daddy is coming home from a trip. The boy gets up fast today. We can infer, or figure out from the text and illustration, that the boy is excited. Who is picking up the boy from school?* (Daddy)

Pages 6–7 Explain that the boy tells the story. *Sometimes the boy tells about what happens in Daddy's day. The boy also tells about his own day.* Point to page 6. *We see what Daddy is doing. Daddy brushes his teeth. He gets ready to get in his truck.* Point to page 7. *We see what the boy does at home. What are the boy and his dad doing at the same time?* (brushing their teeth)

Pages 8–9 Read the text. *Mom takes the boy to school. The boy says he just can't wait. The boy means it is hard to wait to see his Daddy.*

 How does the boy feel? Talk with a partner.

Beginning Have children point to details and say after you: *The boy feels excited. Daddy is picking him up at school today.*

Intermediate Help children explain how they know the boy is excited. *The boy loves to ride in Daddy's truck. Daddy is picking him up. He says he can't wait.*

Pages 10–21

Pages 14–15 Read the text. *Daddy is driving. The boy waits during lunch. It's hard to wait. The boy thinks of his dad and hums their favorite song. What does the boy do?* (thinks of his dad; hums their favorite song.)

Page 19–21 *School is getting out. The boy's dad is not there to pick him up. The boy looks worried or sad.* Point to the tanker truck on page 21. Explain that the boy's dad is stuck in traffic. *That means he cannot move very fast. How does the boy feel?* (sad)

 How do the boy's feelings change? Discuss with a partner.

Beginning Use the illustrations on pages 15, 17, and 19 to help children understand how the boy's feelings change: *The boy is* excited. *Then the boy is* sad.

Intermediate Have partners ask and answer: *When do the boy's feelings change? At first, the boy is* excited. *Daddy is not at* school. *The boy* becomes sad.

Advanced/Advanced High *Why do the boy's feelings change?* (School gets out, and the boy's dad is not there. Then the boy becomes sad.)

Pages 22–32

Pages 22–23 Read the text. *Daddy looks at his watch. He is late. The boy wants his dad to be there. The teacher says he is coming soon. When is Daddy coming?* (soon)

Pages 30–32 Read the text. *Daddy picks up the boy. He turns in circles. The boy thinks it's fun. What sound does the boy make?* (Whe-eee-eeeee!)

 How do the boy's feelings change again? Talk with a partner.

Beginning Help children describe the boy's feelings. *The boy waits and feels* sad. *Daddy picks up the boy. The boy is* happy.

Intermediate Provide sentence frames: *The boy is* sad *when he* waits. *The boy becomes* happy *when* Daddy picks him up at school.

 Retell Use the **Retelling Cards** for *When Daddy's Truck Picks Me Up* to retell the story. Display the cards and model retelling using sequence words as you point to events on the cards. Then help children take turns retelling one part using the sequence words.

LESSON 4

Paired Selection: "From Here to There"

Pages 33–36 Read the text. Explain that the author tells about how people traveled long ago and today. Paraphrase: *A long time ago, people traveled by stagecoach. Horses pulled the stagecoach. It was slow, or took a long time. It was not comfortable.*

 How is travel different today from long ago? Talk with a partner.

Beginning Help children point to photos and respond: *Long ago, airplanes did not go* far.

Intermediate Provide sentence frames: *Long ago, the roads for cars were* bumpy and full of dust.

Advanced/Advanced High Help children compare specific examples of travel in complete sentences: *Long ago, airplanes were* small and noisy. *Today, jets are* big and quiet.

FORMATIVE ASSESSMENT

❯ STUDENT CHECK-IN

Main Selection Have partners retell how the boy shows his excitement about his day.

Paired Selection Have partners describe three vehicles from the text. Then, have children reflect using the Check-In routine.

 ## Independent Time

Draw and Caption Have children draw a picture of a vehicle they learned about in the selections. Help them say or write a caption that tells how the vehicle goes from here to there.

LEARNING GOALS

We can listen actively to learn how some people traveled long ago.

OBJECTIVES

With prompting and support, ask and answer questions about key details in a text.

With prompting and support, describe the relationship between illustrations and the story in which they appear.

Actively engage in group reading activities with purpose and understanding.

Continue a conversation through multiple exchanges.

LANGUAGE OBJECTIVES

Children will narrate how the characters travel the sea, using sentences with prepositions and key vocabulary.

ELA ACADEMIC LANGUAGE

• *characters*

MATERIALS

Interactive Read Aloud, "The King of the Winds"

Visual Vocabulary Cards

DIGITAL TOOLS

Have children listen to the selection as they follow along to develop comprehension.

Use the vocabulary activity for additional practice.

"The King of the Winds"

Prepare to Read

Build Background *Today you will hear an old story. The story takes place a long time ago. The characters travel in a ship, or a big boat.* Point to the oars and the sails and explain: *People use the oars and sails to make the boat go.*

Interactive Read Aloud

Focus on Vocabulary Use the **Visual Vocabulary Cards** to review the oral vocabulary words *journey, fierce, wide, transportation* and *vehicle.* As you read, use gestures and other visual support to clarify important story words: *gift, stormy, winds, curiously, treasure,* and *sailors.*

Summarize the Text *Odysseus and his men sail to an island. The King of the Winds gives Odysseus a gift to make his trip home easier. The men on the ship open the bag when Odysseus is asleep. Angry winds come out and blow the ship back to the island. This time the King of the Winds will not help Odysseus.*

Read the Text

Use the Interactive Question-Response Routine to help children understand the story.

Card 1

Paragraphs 1–3 *Odysseus travels in a ship. He goes to an island and meets the King of the Winds. Odysseus and his men stay on the island. Who does Odysseus meet?* (The King of the Winds)

Paragraphs 4–6 *After a long time, Odysseus is ready to leave. He misses his family and wants to sail home. The King of the Winds will give Odysseus a gift to help him get home. What will the gift do?* (help Odysseus get home)

 Where are Odysseus and his men? Talk with a partner.

Beginning Help children point to Odysseus and the King of the Winds in the illustration and say after you: *They are on an island.*

Intermediate Help children identify the the ruler of the island. Provide sentence frames: *They are on the <u>island</u>. The <u>King of the Winds</u> lives and rules there.*

Advanced Have answer in complete sentences. Provide additional modeling as needed. (They are on an island that is ruled by the King of the Winds.)

Advanced High Challenge children to explain why Odysseus wants to go home. (He is ready to go home because he misses his family.)

Card 2

Paragraphs 1–2 Read the text. *The king gives Odysseus a bag. The king fills the bag with stormy winds. He ties the bag so the winds cannot get out. What is in the bag?* (stormy winds)

Paragraphs 3–5 Read the text. *Odysseus thanks the king. The King of the Winds says goodbye. Then he uses a good wind to blow Odysseus's ship back to his home. What does the king use?* (a good wind to blow Odysseus's ship home)

 Why is Odysseus happy with the gift? Tell a partner.

Beginning Help children understand the gift. *Stormy winds are bad for a boat. Does the king put the stormy winds in a bag or a good wind in the bag?* (the stormy winds)

Intermediate Provide sentence frames: *Stormy winds* will not bother Odysseus *on his way home. The king uses a good* wind *to* help Odysseus sail home.

Advanced/Advanced High Have partners ask and answer questions about the gift and why it is helpful. (How does Odysseus feel about the gift? He is thankful. Stormy winds will not bother him on his way.)

Card 3

Paragraphs 1–3 Read the text. *Gentle winds push the ship safely across the water. Odysseus sees land. They are almost home! Where is the ship?* (almost home)

Paragraphs 4–6 Read the text. *Odysseus goes to sleep. His men are curious to see what is in the bag. They think it may be treasure. They open it.* Point to the illustration. *Angry winds come out. What do the men do?* (open the bag and let angry winds out)

 Why do the men let the wind out of the bag? Tell a partner.

Beginning Guide children to ask and answer: *What do the men think is in the bag?* (treasure) *What happens when they open it?* (angry winds get out)

Intermediate Provide sentence frames: *The men* do not know what is; stormy winds are *in the bag. They are* curious. *They think* treasure is in the bag.

Card 4

Paragraphs 1–3 *There is a big storm. It pushes the ship away from home. The winds push the ship back to the King of the Winds. What do the winds do?* (push the ship away from home)

Paragraphs 4–6 *Odysseus asks the King of the Winds to help him get home. The king will not help him again. The men are sorry they opened the bag. Odysseus and the men finally get home. How do the men feel about opening the bag?* (sorry)

 How do the men feel? Tell a partner.

Beginning Help children respond: *The men know it was* wrong *to* open *the bag. They feel* sorry.

Intermediate Help children explain how the sailors feel. (Sample answer: The sailors feel sorry. They know what they did was wrong.)

 Retell Use the illustrations on the **Interactive Read-Aloud Cards** to retell the story with children. Model retelling using sequence words as you point to the events on the cards. Then help children take turns retelling one part..

FORMATIVE ASSESSMENT

> STUDENT CHECK-IN

Have partners retell how the men on the ship make a mistake. Then, have children reflect using the Check-In routine.

Independent Time

Oral Language Have partners take turns describing the illustrations on the cards. Ask them to name the characters and tell what is happening in the illustration. Then they can draw their own picture of a part of the story that they enjoyed.

LEARNING GOALS

We can make and confirm predictions to understand the story.

OBJECTIVES

With prompting and support, ask and answer questions about key details in a text.

With prompting and support, identify characters, settings, and major events in a story.

Actively engage in group reading activities with purpose and understanding.

Describe familiar people, places, things, and events and, with prompting and support, provide additional detail.

LANGUAGE OBJECTIVES

Children will narrate how the characters travel, using verbs, prepositions, and key vocabulary.

ELA ACADEMIC LANGUAGE

• identify

• Cognate: identificar

MATERIALS

ELL Leveled Reader: *Run, Quinn!*

Online Differentiated Texts, "Here to There"

Online ELL Visual Vocabulary Cards

DIGITAL TOOLS

Have children listen to the selection as they follow along to develop comprehension.

Use the vocabulary activity for additional support.

Run, Quinn!

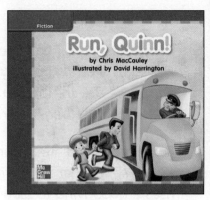

Lexile 70L

Prepare to Read

Build Background *Have you ever been late? If it is time to get on the bus, and you are not close to it. Someone says, "Run!"* Show the cover illustration and read the title aloud. Point out the exclamation point. *I make my voice louder when I read the exclamation point. Quinn is a child. He likes to look at things. It makes him late to get on vehicles.*

Focus on Vocabulary Use the routine on the **ELL Visual Vocabulary Cards** to preteach *excursion* and *transport*. Use images and labels to identify and model the use of key vocabulary, such as *taxi* and *wagon*, in context.

Read the Text

Use the Interactive Question-Response Routine to help children understand the story.

Pages 2–8

Main Story Elements: Characters, Setting, Events Point to the illustrations on pages 2–3. *We can use the illustrations and text to learn about the characters, setting, and events of the story.* Point to the bus. *The bus is here. Quinn needs to get on the bus. His brother says his name loudly. He wants Quinn to run to get on the bus. Let's* **make a prediction** *about the bus. Where will the bus go?* (to school) Point to the van on page 3. *The van is here. Quinn does not get in. He pets a cat. I see soccer balls. Where is the van is taking Quinn?* (to play soccer)

 Tell a partner why the big brother says, "Quinn!"

Beginning Help partners point to details and say the first two events after you: *The bus is here. Quinn needs to go to school. The van is here. Quinn needs to go to a soccer game.*

Intermediate Provide sentence frames: *Quinn needs to* get on the *bus to go to* school. *Quinn needs to get in the van* to go play soccer.

Advanced/Advanced High Guide partners to respond in complete sentences. (Quinn needs to go to school. He needs to get in the van. They go play soccer.)

Pages 4–5 Point to the taxi. *A taxi takes you places. Say* taxi. *The taxi waits for Quinn. It is time to go.* Point to the train. *The train is here. It is time to get on the train. The family does not want to miss the train. Does Quinn run?* (no)

Why does Quinn need to run? Talk with a partner.

Beginning Help partners say: *The taxi is here. It waits for Quinn. He needs to get in. The train is here. It is time to get on.*

Intermediate Guide partners to tell details about Quinn and his family: *A taxi waits* for Quinn. *Quinn's family wants to* get in; take *the taxi. The train is* here. *Quinn needs to* get on the train *with his family.*

Pages 6–8. Point to the boat. *The boat is here. How does a boat travel, or go from here to there?* (on water) *Quinn and his family are on a farm.* Point to the wagon. *This is a wagon. It goes to places on a farm. Does Quinn get in the wagon?* (no) Point to the jet. *This is a jet. How does a jet plane travel?* (in the air) *Is the jet plane here?* (yes)

 Quinn's family travels. They go from here to there. Talk with a partner about the things that take them from here to there.

Beginning Have partners point as they ask and answer: *What is here? The* boat *is here. The* wagon *is here. The* jet plane *is here.*

Intermediate Guide partners to explain how the family travels. *The family takes a* boat on water. *They fly* on a jet plane.

Retell Have partners retell the story. Have them take turns pointing to a picture and describing it to each other.

Focus on Fluency

Read pages 2–5 with appropriate expression. Then read the passage aloud and have children echo read. For additional practice, have children record themselves reading the same passage a few times, and then select their favorite recording to play for you.

Build Knowledge: Make Connections

Talk About the Text Have partners discuss different ways they travel.

Write About the Text Have children add their ideas to their Build Knowledge pages of their reader's notebooks.

Self-Selected Reading

Have children select another story from the online **Leveled Reader Library,** or read the **Differentiated Text,** "Here to There."

LITERACY ACTIVITIES

Have children complete the Literacy Activities on the inside back cover of the book.

FORMATIVE ASSESSMENT

❯ STUDENT CHECK-IN

Have partners retell three of the ways Quinn's family travels. Then, have children reflect using the Check-In routine.

IF children can read *Run, Quinn!* **ELL Level** with fluency and correctly answer the Respond to Reading questions,

THEN tell children that they will read a more detailed version of the story.

HAVE children page through *Run, Quinn!* On Level and describe each picture in simple language.

- Have children read the selection, checking their comprehension and providing assistance as necessary.

MODELED WRITING

LESSON 1

LEARNING GOALS

We can write about who we would like to pick us up from school.

OBJECTIVES

Use dictating and writing to compose opinion pieces about a topic.

LANGUAGE OBJECTIVES

Children will narrate by writing a sentence using an end mark.

ELA ACADEMIC LANGUAGE

• sentence, end mark

Writing Practice Review the sample sentence on p. 14 of the **Reading/Writing Companion**. Guide children to analyze the sentence using the Actor/Action routine. Then read the prompt on p. 15 of the **Reading/Writing Companion** and ask children to answer it as a group. Review the sentence by writing it on the board and pointing to each word as children choral read. Then ask children to write their own sentence. Remind them to check that their sentence ends with an end mark.

Beginning I will write about going to visit <u>my cousins</u>. *Who is the actor?* (I) *What is the action?* (would like to visit) *Who?* (my cousins)

Intermediate Have partners take turns asking and answering *who/what* questions about the trip they would like to take.

Advanced/Advanced High Challenge children to talk about their sentence using the Actor/Action routine.

FORMATIVE ASSESSMENT ❯ **STUDENT CHECK IN** Partners share their sentences. Have children reflect using the Check-In routine.

INTERACTIVE WRITING

LESSON 2

LEARNING GOALS

We can write about what tells us that a character is excited.

OBJECTIVES

With guidance and support, respond to questions and suggestions from peers.

LANGUAGE OBJECTIVES

Children will argue by writing a sentence with a reason for their opinion.

ELA ACADEMIC LANGUAGE

• details
• Cognate: *detalles*

Write a Response: Share the Pen Choral read the sample sentence on p. T270 of the **Teacher's Edition.** Use the Actor/Description routine to review it: *Who is the actor?* (boy) *How can we describe him?* (He is excited.) Remind children of the writing trait: *What thought does the sample sentence tell?* (The boy is excited for his dad to come.) *Is the sentence complete?* (yes) Then help children complete the sentence frames at the bottom of p. T270.

Beginning Display the **Big Book,** p. 15. *What is the boy doing?* (humming) *How does he look?* (happy) *What does he say?* ("Daddy, don't be long.")

Intermediate Have partners talk about their sentences: My sentence tells about how the boy <u>hums to make time go faster</u>.

Advanced/Advanced High Challenge children to think of their own sentence using details from the story and to share them with the group.

FORMATIVE ASSESSMENT ❯ **STUDENT CHECK IN** Partners share their sentences. Have children reflect using the Check-In routine.

INDEPENDENT WRITING

LEARNING GOALS

We can write about the texts we read.

OBJECTIVES

Use drawing and writing to narrate events in the order in which they occurred.

LANGUAGE OBJECTIVES

Children will inform by writing a sentence using the verb *pack*.

ELA ACADEMIC LANGUAGE

- *text, preposition*
- Cognates: *texto, preposición*

Find Text Evidence Use the Independent Writing routine. Ask questions to help children orally retell the shared read, such as: *Why do the girl and her dad have to move?* (Her dad got a job.) *What do they have to do?* (pack) Then read the prompt on p. 30 of the **Reading/Writing Companion**: *How do the girl and her dad get ready to move?* Display p. 22. *What does the author show?* (The girl and her dad pack boxes.) *What do they pack?* (toys, a red hat)

Write a Response Write the following sentences starters on the board, and read them: The girl and her dad ____. They pack ____. Model completing the first starter, and have children choral read the response. Repeat with the remaining second starter. Then have children copy the sentences onto p. 31 of the **Reading/Writing Companion.**

Beginning *What did you use at the end of each sentence?* (a period)

Intermediate Have partners add to a sentence using a preposition.

Advanced/Advanced High Have children identify where they used each checklist item in their writing.

FORMATIVE ASSESSMENT ❯ **STUDENT CHECK IN** Partners share their sentences. Have children reflect using the Check-In routine.

SELF-SELECTED WRITING

LEARNING GOALS

We can revise our writing.

OBJECTIVES

Use the most frequently occurring prepositions.

LANGUAGE OBJECTIVES

Children will inquire about their writing by checking their use of prepositions.

ELA ACADEMIC LANGUAGE

- *preposition*
- Cognate: *preposición*

Work with children to revise the group writing activity. Point to each word as you read the sentences. Stop to ask questions, such as, *Is there a preposition in this sentence? Is it used correctly?* If needed, work together to add a prepositional phrase to one of the sentences. Then have children publish their sentences. Provide them with sentence frames on sentence strips as needed.

For support with grammar and prepositions, refer to the **Language Transfers Handbook** and **Language Development Cards** 18B and 20A.

FORMATIVE ASSESSMENT ❯ **STUDENT CHECK IN** Partners tell what revisions they made. Have children reflect using the Check-In routine.

LESSONS 1-2

OBJECTIVES

With prompting and support, ask and answer questions about key details in a text.

Ask and answer questions to help determine or clarify the meaning of words and phrases in a text.

With prompting and support, identify basic similarities in and differences between two texts on the same topic.

Ask and answer questions in order to seek help, get information, or clarify something that is not understood.

LANGUAGE OBJECTIVES

Children will inform about places in Washington, D.C., using proper nouns.

ELA ACADEMIC LANGUAGE

• *topic, relevant details*
• Cognates: *detalles relevantes*

MATERIALS

Literature Big Book, *Ana Goes to Washington D.C.,* pp. 4–25 and 26–28

Visual Vocabulary Cards

DIGITAL TOOLS

Have children listen to the selection as they follow along to develop comprehension.

Use the vocabulary activity for additional support.

Ana Goes to Washington, D.C.

Literature Big Book

Prepare to Read

Build Background Display the cover. *We are going to read a book about a family that goes to Washington, D.C.* Point out Washington, D.C. on a United States map. Have children point to Washington, D.C. on the map and say the name of the city. *Washington, D.C. is an important place in our country. It is a place where laws are made. It is where the President lives. Have you been to Washington, D.C., or do you know something about it?* Help children share their experiences or what they know: *I know/saw ___. or The city has ___.*

Focus on Vocabulary Use the **Visual Vocabulary Cards** to review the oral vocabulary words *country* and *travel.* As you read, use gestures and other visual support to clarify important selection words: *capital, historic, national, monument, president, statue,* and *court.*

Summarize the Text Before reading, give a short summary of the selection: *Ana, her little sister, and her mom visit her aunt in Washington, D.C.*

Read the Text

Use the Interactive Question-Response Routine to help children understand the text.

Pages 4–9

Pages 4–9 Read the text. *Ana and her family are in Washington, D.C., to see many places. This is the story's main topic.* Point to the map. *These are the places that Ana's family will visit. The places are the details. The first place they visit is the National Mall. A mall can be a big building with a lot of stores. Ana sees a different kind of mall in Washington, D.C. The National Mall has a lot of buildings. The buildings are important to our country's history. In which city are Ana and her family?* (Washington, D.C.) *Where does Ana's family visit?* (the National Mall)

 How is the National Mall different from a mall? Talk to a partner.

Beginning Help partners respond: *The National Mall has many* buildings. *It does not have* stores.

Intermediate Have partners describe: *The National Mall has historic* buildings. *The National Mall has many* buildings, *but it does not have* stores.

Advanced/Advanced High *The National Mall has* historic buildings, *but it does not have* stores. *It also has* trees *and* fields.

Pages 10–19

Pages 10–17 Point to the photographs as you describe: *Ana and her family visit the Washington Monument. We remember George Washington with the* monument, and his face is on the dollar bill and quarter. We remember Abraham Lincoln in the same way. Which presidents are on coins? (George Washington, Abraham Lincoln) Ana visits the Capitol. Our leaders make laws in the Capitol. Laws are like rules. It is important to follow laws and rules. Where do leaders make laws? (the Capitol)

 Where do leaders make laws? Talk to a partner.

Beginning Help partners respond: The leaders make laws in the Capitol.

Intermediate Have partners ask and answer: Where do leaders make laws? The leaders make laws in the Capitol. What are laws? Laws are like rules.

Advanced/Advanced High Have partners describe details about laws: The leaders make laws in the Capitol. Laws are like rules. We need to follow laws.

Pages 20–25

Page 20–25 Point to the photographs: Ana's family visits the Library of Congress. It has almost all the books from the United States. They see the memorial to Dr. Martin Luther King, Jr. He helped all people to be treated fairly. A memorial is like a monument, and it helps to remember important events and people from our history. The cherry trees were a gift from Japan. Where are the cherry trees from? (Japan)

 What places do Ana and her family see? Talk to a partner.

Beginning Help partners respond: Ana and her family see the Library of Congress /Martin Luther King, Jr., statue/cherry trees.

Intermediate Have partners describe: Ana and her family visit the Library of Congress. It has lots of books. Ana's family also see cherry trees.

Advanced/Advanced High Have partners give details: Ana and her family see lots of books at the Library of Congress. Ana's family also sees blossoms on cherry trees. The trees come from Japan.

 Retell Use the **Retelling Cards** for Ana Goes to Washington, D.C. Display the cards and model retelling using sequence words as you point to the events and actions in the cards. Help children take turns retelling one part using the sequence words.

LESSON 4 Paired Selection: "See Our Country"

Pages 26–28 Point to each image as you explain: This is the Statue of Liberty. It is also called Lady Liberty. When people see the statue, they think of our country's freedom. The ancestors of Puebloans lived in Mesa Verde a very long time ago. They built homes into the sides of rock cliffs. These are animals in the Everglades. The Everglades are in Florida. Where can you see these animals? (Everglades)

 What place do you want to visit? Talk to a partner.

Beginning Help partners respond using: I want to visit [Mesa Verde].

Intermediate Have partners respond: I want to visit [Mesa Verde]. I want to see the [homes].

Advanced/Advanced High Have partners respond: (I want to visit Mesa Verde, I want to see the the cliffs.)

FORMATIVE ASSESSMENT

❯ **STUDENT CHECK-IN**

Main Selection Have partners retell three historical buildings or statues from the text and why they are unique.

Paired Selection Have partners briefly describe each place in the text.

Then, have children reflect using the Check-In routine.

Independent Time

Draw and Share Have children draw a picture of the place they would most like to learn more about from Ana Goes to Washington, D.C. or "See Our Country." Children can refer to the text to write the name of the chosen place. Help them describe why they would like to learn more about it.

LESSON **3**

We can listen actively learn about the West.

OBJECTIVES

With prompting and support, ask and answer questions about key details in a text.

With prompting and support, retell key details of a text.

Actively engage in group reading activities with purpose and understanding.

Confirm understanding of a text read aloud or information presented orally or through other media by asking and answering questions about key details and requesting clarification if something is not understood.

LANGUAGE OBJECTIVES

Children will inform about buildings and natural places of the western United States, using proper nouns and key vocabulary.

ELA ACADEMIC LANGUAGE

• *nonfiction*

• Cognate: *no ficción*

MATERIALS

Interactive Read Aloud, "The Best of the West"

Visual Vocabulary Cards

DIGITAL TOOLS

Have children listen to the selection as they follow along to develop comprehension.

Use the vocabulary activity for additional practice.

"The Best of the West"

Interactive Read Aloud

Prepare to Read

Build Background Show a map of the United States. *We will read a nonfiction text about places in the American West.* Point out the West on the map. Point out specific places from the selection: *Grand Canyon in Arizona; Yellowstone National Park in Wyoming, Montana, and Idaho; Seattle, Washington; California; the Pacific Ocean; and San Francisco Bay.* Have children repeat the names. Display images on the cards and describe with children places they have been that are similar to the places on the images. Help them describe: *I visited ____. It has ____.*

Focus on Vocabulary Use the **Visual Vocabulary Cards** to review the oral vocabulary words *connect, careful, purpose, travel,* and *country.* As you read, use gestures and other visual support to clarify important selection words: *cities, mountains, wildlife, canyon, national park, concrete, bridge, incredible.*

Summarize the Text *We will learn about the Grand Canyon, Yellowstone National Park, the Space Needle, and the Golden Gate Bridge.*

Read the Text

Use the Interactive Question-Response Routine to help children understand the text.

Card 1

Paragraphs 1–3 Read the text. Point to the photograph as you describe: *The Grand Canyon is a very large canyon. A canyon is a big crack in the ground. A river is at the bottom of the crack. All of this is the Grand Canyon. These people are viewing, or looking at, it. Some people hike down the canyon. Some people use a raft, a kind of boat, to go on the river. What is this place?* (Grand Canyon)

 What can people do at the Grand Canyon? Discuss with a partner.

Beginning Help partners respond using: *People can look at/hike the canyon.*

Intermediate Have partners complete sentence frames: *People can view/hike the canyon. They can also go on a raft on the river.*

Advanced/Advanced High Have partners respond: *People can hike the canyon and raft on the river.*

Card 2

Paragraphs 1–4 Read the text. *There is a lot to see in Yellowstone National Park. It has hot springs and geysers. Hot springs and geysers have hot water* *underground. One geyser in Yellowstone is called Old Faithful. It sprays water into the air about 20 times a day. You can also see animals in Yellowstone. You can see bison, bears, moose, and elk up close. What is Old Faithful?* (a geyser)

 What can you see at Yellowstone National Park? Talk to a partner.

Beginning Have partners point to the big photo and help them respond: *I can see a* geyser. Repeat for the small photo: *I can see* animals/buffalo.

Intermediate Help partners respond with details: *I can see a* geyser *and* animals. Two animals I can see are bison/bears *and* moose/elk.

Advanced/Advanced High Have partners describe details: *I can see a* geyser *spray water. I can see* bison/bears/moose *up close.*

Card 3

Paragraphs 1–4 Read the text. *A city is a place where a lot of people live. Seattle, Washington is a city. The Space Needle is a very tall building. The Space Needle is made from concrete. A sidewalk is also made of concrete. To make the Space Needle, 467 cement trucks took turns pouring concrete all day. You can ride an elevator to the top of the Space Needle. It has a restaurant. You see the entire city from the top of the Space Needle. Look at the photograph. Is the Space Needle taller than most buildings?* (yes)

 What is the Space Needle? Talk to a partner.

Beginning Help partners respond, using: *The Space Needle is a* very tall *building.*

Intermediate Help partners respond: *The Space Needle is a* very tall *building. What does it have? It has an* elevator/a restaurant.

Advanced High Help partners describe the Space Needle: *The Space Needle is a* very tall building. *It has an* elevator *that goes to the* top of the building.

Card 4

Paragraphs 1–4 Read the text. Point to the photographs as you describe: *The Golden Gate Bridge is about one mile long. The bridge connects the city of San Francisco with other places in California. People ride their bikes, walk, and drive their cars across the bridge. The bridge is orange. It is more than 75 years old. What is this?* (Golden Gate Bridge) *What color is the Golden Gate Bridge?* (orange)

 Tell a partner about the Golden Gate Bridge.

Beginning Help partners respond by asking: *What color is the Golden Gate Bridge? The Golden Gate Bridge is* orange.

Intermediate Help partners give details: *The Golden Gate Bridge is* orange. *It is one* mile *long.*

Advanced/Advanced High Help partners respond using longer sentences, for example: *The Golden Gate Bridge is* orange, *and it is one* mile *long.*

 Retell Use the illustrations on the **Interactive Read-Aloud Cards** to retell with children what they learned about the places. Display the cards and model retelling as you point to the images in the cards. Then help children take turns retelling one part.

FORMATIVE ASSESSMENT

❯ **STUDENT CHECK-IN**

Have partners describe three places from the text. Then, have children reflect using the Check-In routine.

 Independent Time

Draw and Label Have partners select one illustration from the Interactive Read-Aloud Cards and describe it. Provide a model and sentence frames for them to use: *I see a geyser. A geyser is ____.* Then have them draw one thing they see and help them label it.

LEARNING GOALS

We can reread to better understand the text.

OBJECTIVES

With prompting and support, ask and answer questions about key details in a text.

With prompting and support, describe the connection between pieces of information in a text.

With prompting and support, describe the relationship between illustrations and the text in which they appear.

Continue a conversation through multiple exchanges.

LANGUAGE OBJECTIVES

Children will describe places in nature and in the city, using nouns, adjectives, and prepositions.

ELA ACADEMIC LANGUAGE

• details
• Cognates: detalles

MATERIALS

ELL Leveled Reader: *Places to See*

Online Differentiated Texts, "Celebrate!"

Online ELL Visual Vocabulary Cards

DIGITAL TOOLS

MULTIMODAL

Have children listen to the selection as they follow along to develop comprehension.

Use the vocabulary activity for additional support.

Places to See

Prepare to Read

Build Background *You have learned about places to visit in Washington, D.C., and in the West. You read about the city of Seattle, Washington. Now you will read about more locations, or places. What do you know about a city? It has ____ and ____.* Show a photo of a desert, a mountain, and an ocean. Name each and help children tell what they know about each. *This is a desert. A desert ____.*

Focus on Vocabulary Use the routine on the **ELL Visual Vocabulary Cards** to preteach *landscape* and *scene*. Use the images and any labels to identify and model the use of key vocabulary, such as *desert, mountain, city,* and *ocean.*

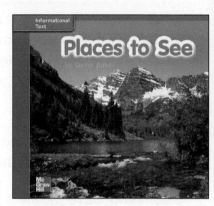

Lexile BR

Read the Text

Use the Interactive Question-Response Routine to help children understand the text.

Pages 2–8

Pages 2–3 *Read the text. Use your finger to track as you read. A desert is a place that is dry. It does not rain much. A plant called a cactus grows in the desert. You can see yellow flowers on the cactus. Where does a cactus grow?* (desert)

 Talk to a partner about a desert.

Beginning Help partners respond, using: *This is a* desert. *The desert has* plants.

Intermediate Have partners point to the photos as they ask and answer: *What is this? This is a* desert/cactus. *The desert has* plants. *The cactus is* yellow.

Pages 4–5 *This mountain has snow on top. The snow is white. Mountain goats live on rocky mountains. Where does a mountain goat live?* (on a mountain)

 Give details about a mountain and a goat. Talk to a partner.

Beginning Help partners **reread** the text, and then point to the photos as they respond: *This is a* mountain. *The mountain has* snow. *This is a* goat. *The goat is on the* mountain.

Intermediate Have partners point to the photos as they ask and answer: *What is this? This is a* mountain/goat. *The mountain has* snow on top. *The goat* lives/is *on the* mountain.

Fact and Opinion Have children identify if the following statements are fact or opinion: *Mountains are tall.* (fact) *The mountains are more beautiful than the desert.* (opinion) *A desert is very dry.* (fact) Ask partners to share more facts and opinions about pages 2–5.

Pages 6–8 *A city is a place where a lot of people live. A city has tall buildings and a lot of cars. Some cars in a city are taxis. A taxi driver stops for people. The taxi driver drives the people to places.* Point to the label on page 8. *This word is* ocean. *Many fish live in the ocean.*

 What can you see in a city? Discuss with a partner.

Beginning Help partners respond, using: *I can see tall* buildings. *I can see yellow* taxis.

Intermediate Have partners point to the photos as they ask and answer: *What is this? This is a* city. *What can you see in a city? I can see* buildings.

Advanced/Advanced High Have partners ask and answer: *What is this? This is a* city. *What can you see in a city? I can see* tall buildings *and lots of* cars. *Some of the cars are yellow* taxis.

Retell Have partners retell the story. Have them take turns pointing to a picture and describing it to each other.

Focus on Fluency

Read pages 2–5 with appropriate tone and expression. Then read the passage aloud and have children echo read. For additional practice, have children record themselves reading the same passage a few times and then select their favorite recording to play for you.

Build Knowledge: Make Connections

Talk About the Text Have partners discuss different places around our country they have seen.

Write About the Text Have children add their ideas to their Build Knowledge pages of their reader's notebooks.

Self-Selected Reading

Have children select another story from the online **Leveled Reader Library,** or read the **Differentiated Text,** "Celebrate!"

LITERACY ACTIVITIES

Have children complete the Literacy Activities on the inside back cover of the book.

FORMATIVE ASSESSMENT

◗ STUDENT CHECK-IN

Have partners retell details about three of the places from the text. Then, have children reflect using the Check-In routine.

LEVEL UP

IF children can read *Places to See* **ELL Level** with fluency and correctly answer the Respond to Reading questions,

THEN tell children that they will read a more detailed version of the story.

HAVE children page through *Places to See* On Level and describe each picture in simple language.

• Have children read the selection, checking their comprehension and providing assistance as necessary.

MODELED WRITING

LEARNING GOALS

We can write about what place in Washington, D.C. we would like to visit.

OBJECTIVES

Understand and use question words (interrogatives).

LANGUAGE OBJECTIVES

Children will inform by writing a sentence in the form of a question.

ELA ACADEMIC LANGUAGE

• *question mark*

 Writing Practice Read the sample sentence on p. 44 of the **Reading/Writing Companion.** Guide children to analyze the sentence: *What is the subject?* (Washington Monument) *What do we want to know about it?* (how tall it is) Then read the prompt on p. 45 and ask children to answer it as a group. Review the sentence by writing it on the board and having children choral read. Then ask children to write their own questions.

 Beginning I will write about the White House. *What do you want to know about the White House? How could we write that as a question?*

Intermediate Have partners use the photographs and illustrations from the **Big Book** to get ideas for their sentences.

Advanced/Advanced High Challenge children to name the type of end punctuation they used as they share their questions with the group.

FORMATIVE ASSESSMENT ➲ **STUDENT CHECK IN** Partners share their sentences. Have children reflect using the Check-In routine.

INTERACTIVE WRITING

LEARNING GOALS

We can write about how the author and illustrator show that Ana had a wonderful trip.

OBJECTIVES

With guidance and support, add details to strengthen writing as needed.

LANGUAGE OBJECTIVES

Children will argue by writing sentences using the text and illustrations to support their opinion.

ELA ACADEMIC LANGUAGE

• *question mark*

 Write a Response: Share the Pen Choral read the sample sentence on p. T348 of the **Teacher's Edition.** Use the Actor/Action routine to review it: *Who is the actor?* (Ana) *What is the action?* (says she had a wonderful day) Remind children of the writing trait: *Sentences can be long or short.* Have children identify the first sentence as long and the second sentence as short. Help children complete the sentence frames at the bottom of p. T348.

 Beginning Help partners orally complete the first sentence by providing a visual from the book: Ana says let's go! Ask children guiding questions to help see how the illustration shows Ana is happy and excited.

Intermediate Have partners point to details in the illustrations that show how Ana feels and then use the details to complete the sentence frames.

Advanced/Advanced High Challenge children to think of their own sentences and to share them with the group.

FORMATIVE ASSESSMENT ➲ **STUDENT CHECK IN** Partners share their sentences. Have children reflect using the Check-In routine.

INDEPENDENT WRITING

LEARNING GOALS

We can write about texts we read.

OBJECTIVES

Use drawing, dictating, and writing to narrate and provide a reaction to what happened.

LANGUAGE OBJECTIVES

Children will inform by writing a sentence using a preposition.

ELA ACADEMIC LANGUAGE

- *preposition*
- Cognate: *preposición*

Find Text Evidence Use the Independent Writing routine. Ask questions to help children orally retell the shared read, such as: *Who is Zeb going to visit?* (Pop) *How does Zeb go to visit Pop?* (on a jet) Then read the prompt on p. 60 of the **Reading/Writing Companion**: *How do you know that Zeb enjoys his trip?* Display p. 54: *How do Pop and Zeb feel?* (happy) *How do you know?* (They look excited.)

Write a Response Write the sentence starters from p. T358 on the board, and read them. Model completing the first starter, and have children choral read the response. Be sure to use a preposition. Repeat with the second starter. Then ask children to copy the sentences on p. 61.

Beginning Provide a sentence frame to help partners talk about their sentences: I used the preposition *with*.

Intermediate Encourage children to use both long and short sentences.

Advanced/Advanced High Have partners identify where they used each item from the checklist in their writing.

FORMATIVE ASSESSMENT ❯ **STUDENT CHECK IN** Partners share their sentences. Have children reflect using the Check-In routine.

SELF-SELECTED WRITING

LEARNING GOALS

We can revise our writing.

OBJECTIVES

Use the most frequently occurring prepositions.

LANGUAGE OBJECTIVES

Children will inquire about their writing by checking their prepositions.

ELA ACADEMIC LANGUAGE

- *preposition*
- Cognate: *preposición*

Work with children to revise the group writing activity. Point to each word as you read the sentences. Stop to ask questions, such as, *What preposition can we use here?* If needed, write a sentence using a preposition incorrectly, and work together to revise the sentence. Then have children publish their sentences. Provide them with sentence frames on sentence strips as needed.

For support with grammar, refer to the **Language Transfers Handbook** and review prepositions using **Language Development Card** 20A.

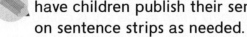

FORMATIVE ASSESSMENT ❯ **STUDENT CHECK IN** Partners tell what revisions they made. Have children reflect using the Check-In routine.

LESSONS
1-2

We can understand important ideas and details about a story.

We can use headings to learn new information.

OBJECTIVES

With prompting and support, ask and answer questions about key details in a text.

Recognize common types of texts (e.g., storybooks, poems).

Actively engage in group reading activities with purpose and understanding.

Speak audibly and express thoughts, feelings, and ideas clearly.

LANGUAGE OBJECTIVES

Children will narrate how the main character tries to reach the moon, using verbs and prepositions.

ELA ACADEMIC LANGUAGE

• *fantasy, events*
• Cognates: *fantasía, eventos*

MATERIALS

Literature Big Book, *Bringing Down the Moon,* pp. 4–28 and 29–32

Visual Vocabulary Cards

DIGITAL TOOLS

Have children listen to the selection as they follow along to develop comprehension.

Use the vocabulary activity for additional support.

Bringing Down the Moon

Prepare to Read

Literature Big Book

Build Background *We are going to read a fantasy about a mole.* Show a photo of a mole. *This is a mole. Some people have not seen a mole before because moles usually live under the ground. What animal is this? It is a mole. Where does a mole spend most of its time?*

Focus on Vocabulary Use the **Visual Vocabulary Cards** to review the oral vocabulary words *distance* and *recognize.* As you read, use gestures and other visual support to clarify important selection words: *burrowed, pull, poked, knock down, slipped, puddle.*

Summarize the Text Before reading, give a short summary of the selection: *Mole sees the moon for the first time. He wants the moon and tries to get it. His friends tell him he cannot get the moon. The moon is not as close as it looks. But Mole keeps trying. When he sees the moon in a puddle, he thinks he has broken the moon. He friends show Mole that he did not.*

Read the Text

Use the Interactive Question-Response Routine to help children understand the story.

Pages 4–15

Pages 4–5 Read the text. Point to Mole. *Mole digs out of the ground. He sees the moon for the first time. He does not know what the moon is. It is bright. He thinks it is the most beautiful thing. What does Mole see for the first time?* (the moon)

Pages 6–9 Read the text. *Mole wants to get the moon. Mole jumps. He wants to grab the moon and pull it down.* Act out jumping to pull something down. *Mole's jumping wakes up Rabbit. How does Mole try to get the moon?* (jumps up) *Rabbit tells Mole the shiny thing in the sky is called the moon. Rabbit tells Mole the moon is far away. It looks close, but the moon is far away. What does Rabbit tell Mole about the moon?* (It is not as close as it looks.)

 What does Mole want? What happens when he tries to get it? Talk with a partner.

Beginning Have children point to the illustrations on pages 4–9 and help them say: *Mole wants the* moon. *Mole* jumps *to get it. Mole wakes up* Rabbit.

Intermediate Help children use the illustrations to complete sentence frames: *Mole* jumps up *and tries to* pull down the moon. *Mole* wakes up *Rabbit. She tells Mole the moon is* not close.

Advanced/Advanced High Help children tell more about the message Rabbit tries to give Mole. (Sample answer: You cannot reach the moon.)

Pages 16–23

Pages 16–17 Read the text. *Mole does not give up, or stop trying. He climbs a tree. He thinks he can carry the moon down from the sky. Why does Mole go up the tree?* (to carry the moon down from the sky)

Pages 18–21 Read the text. *These pages tell several events: Mole falls from the tree. He sees the moon in the puddle. Mole thinks the moon fell down with him. Mole reaches into the water to get the moon. The moon breaks into pieces and disappears. He cannot see it anymore.*

 What happens when Mole tries to get the moon from the tree? Talk with a partner.

Beginning Have children point to details and say after you: *Mole falls. Mole sees the moon in a puddle of water. Mole thinks it is the real moon.*

Intermediate Help partners explain why Mole thinks he breaks the moon: *Mole sees* the moon *in* a puddle. *He touches the water and thinks he has broken* the moon. *The moon is still* in the sky.

Pages 24–29

Pages 24–25 Read the text. *Mole's friends tell him he did not break the moon. They show Mole the moon in the sky. What do Mole's friends show him?* (the moon)

Pages 26–27 Read the text. *The friends all agree. The moon is beautiful, Mole says, but it's not as close as it looks. What do the friends call the moon?* (beautiful)

 How do Mole's friends help him? Talk with a partner.

Beginning Help children say: *The friends show Mole* the moon *in the sky. Now, Mole knows it is not* close.

Intermediate Provide sentence frames: *The friends show Mole* the moon in the sky. *Now he knows it* is not close. *The friends all agree the* moon is beautiful.

 Retell Use the **Retelling Cards** for *Bringing Down the Moon* to retell the story with children. Display the cards and model retelling using sequence words as you point to the events and actions in the cards. Then help children take turns retelling one part using the sequence words.

LESSON 4

Paired Selection: "Day and Night Sky"

Pages 29–32 Paraphrase the text as you point to the photographs. For example: *On page 31, the author shows three photos of the Moon. The Moon looks different as the days in a month go by. It can look full. It can look thin or like a crescent. This picture shows that we can sometimes see the Moon during daytime.*

 What does the author tell about the Moon? Talk with a partner.

Beginning Help children point to the photographs and say: *The Moon looks* round. *The Moon looks* thin.

Intermediate Provide sentence frames: *The Moon can look* full and round. *It can be a* crescent moon.

Advanced/Advanced High Guide children to talk about when the Moon looks different. (The Moon looks different at different times of the month.)

FORMATIVE ASSESSMENT

❯ STUDENT CHECK-IN

Main Selection Have partners retell how Mole tries to get the moon.

Paired Selection Have partners describe how the sky is different during day and night.

Then, have children reflect using the Check-In routine.

Independent Time

Draw and Label Have children talk about the way the moon looks in *Bringing Down the Moon*. Have them draw the full, round moon that Mole sees and help children describe and label their pictures.

LESSON
3

LEARNING GOALS

We can listen actively to learn about the Moon.

OBJECTIVES

With prompting and support, ask and answer questions about key details in a text.

With prompting and support, retell key details of a text.

Ask and answer questions to help determine or clarify the meaning of words and phrases in a text.

Continue a conversation through multiple exchanges.

LANGUAGE OBJECTIVES

Children will inform about the Moon, using nouns, adjectives, and key vocabulary.

ELA ACADEMIC LANGUAGE

• *facts, retell*

MATERIALS

Interactive Read Aloud, "A View from the Moon"

Visual Vocabulary Cards

DIGITAL TOOLS

Have children listen to the selection as they follow along to develop comprehension.

Use the vocabulary activity for additional practice.

"A View from the Moon"

Interactive Read Aloud

Prepare to Read

Build Background *You will hear about the Moon. Remember, in* Bringing Down the Moon, *Mole did not know about the Moon. The author of "A View from the Moon" teaches us about a lot about the Moon.* Show the Photo Card for *astronaut. This is an astronaut. An astronaut travels above the Earth and into space. Astronauts have walked on the Moon.*

Focus on Vocabulary Use the **Visual Vocabulary Cards** to review the oral vocabulary words *space, challenge, surface, distance,* and *recognize.* As you read, use gestures and other visual support to clarify important selection words: *spaceship, mission, spacesuits, mountains,* and *craters.*

Summarize the Text Before reading, give a short summary of the selection: *We will learn facts about the Moon. We will also learn about a mission to the Moon. Astronauts landed on the Moon to learn more about it.*

Read the Text

Use the Interactive Question-Response Routine to help children understand the text.

Card 1

Paragraph 1 Read the text. *In 1969, two astronauts traveled to the Moon. That was about 50 years ago. Where did astronauts go in 1969?* (to the Moon)

Paragraphs 2–3 Read the text. *The Moon looks like it changes shape. It also looks small because it is far away. It is farther away than the clouds. That is why it looks smaller than a cloud. Why does the Moon look small?* (It is far away.)

 Why did we learn a lot about the Moon in 1969? Discuss with a partner.

Beginning Guide children to say: *Astronauts went to the Moon.*

Advanced/Advanced High Help partners ask and answer: *When did astronauts go to* the Moon*? Astronauts went* to the Moon in 1969*.*

Advanced/Advanced High Challenge children to use text evidence to tell why people went to the Moon. (It is far away. People wanted to learn more about it.)

Card 2

Paragraphs 1–2 Read the text. *People wanted to know what the Moon was like, so astronauts went. They flew two spaceships and landed on the Moon. How did the astronauts get to the Moon?* (spaceships)

Paragraphs 3–4 Read the text. *Before the mission, the astronauts had to practice. They wore heavy suits and learned to fly the spaceship. When they left for the Moon, it took four days to get there. How did the astronauts get ready for the trip to the Moon?* (wore spacesuits and learned to fly the spaceship)

 Tell a partner how the astronauts trained, or practiced, before they went to the Moon.

Beginning Guide students to point to the astronauts and identify the spacesuits. Help them complete the sentence: *They learned to* fly *the spaceships.*

Intermediate Provide sentence frames: *They learned about every part of* the spaceships. *They got used to the* heavy spacesuits *they needed to wear in* space. *Living on a spaceship was going to be a* challenge.

Card 3

Paragraphs 1–2 Read the text. Point to the Eagle spaceship in the photo. *The Eagle spaceship landed on the Moon. Then the astronauts walked on the Moon. They got Moon rocks to take back to Earth. They put an American flag on the Moon. They took pictures. What did the astronauts bring back?* (Moon rocks)

Paragraphs 3–4 Read the text. Point out the surface on the Moon on the photo and call attention to the footprints and the lack of color.

 What did the astronauts see on the Moon? Tell a partner.

Beginning Help partners point to details in the text and describe the Moon: *The Moon has* mountains. *You can only see* gray *colors.*

Intermediate Provide sentence frames: *The Moon is covered* in dust. *It has* mountains *and* flat parts. *It has a lot of* gray colors. *There is little* water.

Card 4

Paragraphs 1–4 Read the text. Show the photo to explain what the astronauts saw from the Moon. *Does Earth look big or small from the Moon?* (small)

 How does Earth look when you are on the Moon? Discuss with a partner.

Beginning Have children use the photo to review the words *oceans, land,* and *clouds,* and help them respond: *What color are Earth's oceans?* (blue) *What color is Earth's land?* (brown) *What color are the clouds?* (white)

Intermediate Have partners use the photo to help form sentences: *The Earth looks* small. *You can see white* clouds. *The Earth has the colors* blue *and* brown.

Advanced Ask children to tell about the colors you might see looking down on Earth, such as blue, brown, bright green, white, and yellow. (Sample places to describe: oceans; Earth's lands, rain forests; clouds; deserts)

Advanced High Have children compare the photo of the Earth with the photo of the Moon on Card 1.

Retell Use the illustrations on the **Interactive Read-Aloud Cards** to retell the text with children. Display the cards and model retelling using sequence words, such as *first, next, then,* and *last,* as you point to the events and details on the cards. Then help children take turns retelling one part using the sequence words.

FORMATIVE ASSESSMENT

▶ STUDENT CHECK-IN

Have partners discuss the astronauts' preparation and experience. Then, have children reflect using the Check-In routine.

 Independent Time

Audio Have children listen to the audio recording of their favorite Card in the selection. After they listen multiple times, have them retell the important events to a partner.

LESSONS 4-5

In the Clouds

Prepare to Read

Build Background *You will read a book called* In the Clouds. *Show the Photo Card for* cloud. *This is a cloud. Sometimes people look at a cloud. They think the cloud looks like the shape of something else. Someone may think a cloud looks like a bear. Is the cloud a bear?* (no)

Focus on Vocabulary Use the routine on the **ELL Visual Vocabulary Cards** to preteach *imagination* and *precipitation*. As you read, use the images and any labels to clarify important story words, such as *duck, fox, dog, goat, horse, ship,* and *rain.*

Lexile BR

Read the Text

Use the Interactive Question-Response Routine to help children understand the story.

Pages 2–8

Pages 2–3 *The children are looking at clouds. Point to the cloud. What do the children think it looks like?* (a duck) *Point to the clouds on page 3. The children can see clouds. One cloud looks like a fox.* Point out and read both labels. *Point to the cloud that looks like a fox.*

 What do the children see? Talk with a partner.

Beginning Have partners point to the illustrations as they answer: *What do the children see first?* (a duck) *What do the children see next?* (a fox)

Intermediate Guide children to discuss what the children see. *They see* clouds *in the sky. The clouds look like* a duck *and* a fox.

Advanced/Advanced High Guide partners to ask and answer questions related to the prompt. (Example: What do the children imagine in the clouds? They imagine they see a duck and a fox.)

Pages 4–5 *Then a boy points in the air. He sees a different animal. The children see a dog.* Point to the dog-shaped cloud. *What do the children see in this cloud?* (a dog) Ask children to point to the cloud that looks like a goat.

 Then what do the children see? Talk with a partner.

Beginning Have partners point to the illustrations and name the animal shapes in the clouds. *They see a* dog. *They see a* goat.

Intermediate Guide partners to point to and name the legs and tail in the shape of the dog and the horns in the shape of the goat. Then have them say: *Then they see a* <u>dog</u> *and a* <u>goat</u> *in the clouds.*

Pages 6–8 Display pages 6 and 7. *What do the children see in the clouds?* (a horse and a ship) *The clouds are getting darker.*

Events: Problem and Solution *Do dark clouds tell you there may be a problem?* (yes) *Let's **make a prediction**. What do you think will happen next?* (It will rain.) *Let's **confirm our prediction** on page 8.* Display page 8. *Was your prediction correct?* (yes/no) *How do the children solve their problem?* (They run from the rain.)

 What happens to the clouds at the end of the story? Talk with a partner.

Beginning Help children respond. *The clouds get* <u>dark</u>. *Then it* <u>rains</u>.

Intermediate Have partners ask and answer: *How do the clouds change? In the beginning, the clouds are* <u>white</u>. *The children see shapes in the* <u>white clouds</u>. *The clouds get* <u>dark</u>. *Then it* <u>rains</u>.

Advanced/Advanced High Provide modeling as needed. (The clouds are white and fluffy. The children imagine shapes in the clouds, like animals and a ship. The clouds get dark. Then it rains.)

Retell Have partners retell the story. Have them take turns pointing to a picture and describing it to each other.

Focus on Fluency

Read pages 2–5 with appropriate expression. Then read the passage aloud and have children echo read. For additional practice, have children record themselves reading the same passage a few times and then select their favorite recording to play for you.

Build Knowledge: Make Connections

Talk About the Text Have partners discuss objects in the sky.

Write About the Text Have children add their ideas to their Build Knowledge pages of their reader's notebooks.

Self-Selected Reading

Have children select another story from the online **Leveled Reader Library,** or read the **Differentiated Text,** "Look Up, Up, Up!"

LITERACY ACTIVITIES

Have children complete the Literacy Activities on the inside back cover of the book.

FORMATIVE ASSESSMENT

❯ **STUDENT CHECK-IN**

Have partners retell three things that the children saw in the clouds. Then, have children reflect using the Check-In routine.

IF children can read *In the Clouds* ELL Level with fluency and correctly answer the Respond to Reading questions,

THEN tell children that they will read a more detailed version of the story.

HAVE children page through *In the Clouds* On Level and describe each picture in simple language.

- Have children read the selection, checking their comprehension and providing assistance as necessary.

LESSONS
1-5

MODELED WRITING

LEARNING GOALS

We can write about what we like to see when we look up at the sky.

OBJECTIVES

Use dictating and writing to compose informative texts in which they name what they are writing about.

LANGUAGE OBJECTIVES

Children will inform by writing a sentence using the science word *moon.*

ELA ACADEMIC LANGUAGE

• *sentence*

Writing Practice Display the moon on p. 5 of the **Literature Big Book** and read the sample sentence on p. 74 of the **Reading/Writing Companion.** Guide children to analyze the sentence using the Actor/Description routine: *Who is the actor?* (the moon) *How can we describe it?* (It looks really big.) Read the prompt on p. 75 of the **Reading/Writing Companion** and have children answer it as a group. Write the sentence on the board and have children choral read. Then ask children to write their own sentence.

Beginning Help children list different ways the moon can look and use their responses to create a word bank. Encourage them to use the word bank to complete the sentence frame: I will write about <u>a full moon</u>.

Intermediate Have partners brainstorm words that describe the moon before creating their sentences. Provide a sentence frame if needed.

Advanced/Advanced High Challenge children to talk about where they started and ended their sentences as they share them with the group.

FORMATIVE ASSESSMENT ➲ **STUDENT CHECK IN** Partners share their sentences. Have children reflect using the Check-In routine.

INTERACTIVE WRITING

LEARNING GOALS

We can write about why Mole thinks he broke the moon.

OBJECTIVES

With guidance and support, respond to questions and suggestions from peers.

LANGUAGE OBJECTIVES

Children will argue by writing a sentence using the verb *thinks.*

ELA ACADEMIC LANGUAGE

• *sentence*

Write a Response: Share the Pen Choral read the sample sentence on p. T426 of the **Teacher's Edition.** Use the Actor/Action routine to review it: *Who is the actor?* (Mole) *What is the action?* (thinks he broke the moon) Then ask: *What is a noun in the sentence? (Mole) What is a verb? (thinks)* Help children complete the sentence frames on p. T426.

Beginning Help children think of their sentence by asking guiding questions about p. 23 of the **Big Book:** *Can Mole see the moon?* (no) *What does Mole say?* ("I pulled it down, and I broke it.")

Intermediate Have partners use details from the illustration on pp. 21–23 to help them complete the sentence frames.

Advanced/Advanced High Challenge children to think of their own sentences about why Mole thinks he broke the moon and share them.

FORMATIVE ASSESSMENT ➲ **STUDENT CHECK IN** Partners share their sentences. Have children reflect using the Check-In routine.

INDESTRUCTIBLE INDEPENDENT WRITING

LEARNING GOALS

We can write about the texts we read.

OBJECTIVES

Use drawing and writing to narrate events in the order in which they occurred.

LANGUAGE OBJECTIVES

Children will inform by writing a sentence using a preposition.

ELA ACADEMIC LANGUAGE

- *photos*
- Cognate: *fotos*

Find Text Evidence Use the Independent Writing routine. Ask questions to help children orally retell the shared read, such as: *Who is the man in the story?* (Greg) *What does he tell about?* (his job) *What does he look at for his job?* (things in the sky) Then read the prompt on p. 90 of the **Reading/Writing Companion:** *What does Greg learn while looking at the night sky?* Display pp. 84–86: *Look at the photos. What can Greg see at nighttime?* (stars, the moon) What does he see in the stars? (shapes) What does he see on the moon? (a dot)

Write a Response Write the sentence starters from p. T436 on the board, and read them. Model completing the first starter, and have children choral read the response. Repeat with the second starter. Then ask children to copy the sentences onto p. 91.

Beginning Provide a sentence frame to help children talk about their sentences: I wrote complete sentences.

Intermediate Encourage children to use prepositions in their sentences.

Advanced/Advanced High Have partners identify where they used each item from the checklist in their writing.

FORMATIVE ASSESSMENT ❯ **STUDENT CHECK IN** Partners share their sentences. Have children reflect using the Check-In routine.

SELF-SELECTED WRITING

LEARNING GOALS

We can revise our writing.

OBJECTIVES

Use the most frequently occurring prepositions.

LANGUAGE OBJECTIVES

Children will inquire about their writing by checking their prepositions.

ELA ACADEMIC LANGUAGE

- *title, acrostic poem*
- Cognate: *título*

Work with children to revise the group writing activity. Point to each word as you read the sentences. Stop to ask questions, such as, *Is the preposition used correctly here?* If needed, work together to add a preposition to one of the sentences or lines if you wrote a poem. Then have partners revise each others sentences or poem.

For support with grammar, refer to the **Language Transfers Handbook,** and review **Language Development Card** 20B.

FORMATIVE ASSESSMENT ❯ **STUDENT CHECK IN** Partners tell what revisions they made. Have children reflect using the Check-In routine.

UNIT 8

Summative Assessment
Get Ready for Unit Assessment

Unit 8 Tested Skills

LISTENING AND READING COMPREHENSION	VOCABULARY	GRAMMAR	SPEAKING AND WRITING
• Listening Actively • Details	• Words and Categories	• Prepositions	• Presenting • Composing/Writing • Supporting Opinions • Retelling/Recounting

Create a Student Profile

Record data from the following resources in the Student Profile charts on pages 136–137 of the Assessment book.

COLLABORATIVE	INTERPRETIVE	PRODUCTIVE

• Collaborative Conversations Rubrics
  • Listening
  • Speaking
	• Leveled Unit Assessment
	  • Listening Comprehension
	  • Reading Comprehension
	  • Vocabulary
	  • Grammar
	• Presentation Rubric
	  • Listening
	• *Wonders* Unit Assessment
		• Weekly Progress Monitoring
		• Leveled Unit Assessment
		  • Speaking
		  • Writing
		• Presentation Rubric
		  • Speaking
		• Write to Sources Rubric
		• *Wonders* Unit Assessment

The Foundational Skills Kit, Language Development Kit, and Adaptive Learning provide additional student data for progress monitoring.

Level Up

Use the following chart, along with your Student Profiles, to guide your Level Up decisions.

LEVEL UP	If **BEGINNING** level students are able to do the following, they may be ready to move to the **INTERMEDIATE** level:	If **INTERMEDIATE** level students are able to do the following, they may be ready to move to the **ADVANCED** level:	If **ADVANCED** level students are able to do the following, they may be ready to move to **ON** level:
COLLABORATIVE	• participate in collaborative conversations using basic vocabulary and grammar and simple phrases or sentences • discuss simple pictorial or text prompts	• participate in collaborative conversations using appropriate words and phrases and complete sentences • use limited academic vocabulary across and within disciplines	• participate in collaborative conversations using more sophisticated vocabulary and correct grammar • communicate effectively across a wide range of language demands in social and academic contexts
INTERPRETIVE	• identify details in simple read alouds • understand common vocabulary and idioms and interpret language related to familiar social, school, and academic topics • make simple inferences and make simple comparisons • exhibit an emerging receptive control of lexical, syntactic, phonological, and discourse features	• identify main ideas and/or make some inferences from simple read alouds • use context clues to identify word meanings and interpret basic vocabulary and idioms • compare, contrast, summarize, and relate text to graphic organizers • exhibit a limited range of receptive control of lexical, syntactic, phonological, and discourse features when addressing new or familiar topics	• determine main ideas in read alouds that have advanced vocabulary • use context clues to determine meaning, understand multiple-meaning words, and recognize synonyms of social and academic vocabulary • analyze information, make sophisticated inferences, and explain their reasoning • command a high degree of receptive control of lexical, syntactic, phonological, and discourse features
PRODUCTIVE	• express ideas and opinions with basic vocabulary and grammar and simple phrases or sentences • restate information or retell a story using basic vocabulary • exhibit an emerging productive control of lexical, syntactic, phonological, and discourse features	• produce coherent language with limited elaboration or detail • restate information or retell a story using mostly accurate, although limited, vocabulary • exhibit a limited range of productive control of lexical, syntactic, phonological, and discourse features when addressing new or familiar topics	• produce sentences with more sophisticated vocabulary and correct grammar • restate information or retell a story using extensive and accurate vocabulary and grammar • tailor language to a particular purpose and audience • command a high degree of productive control of lexical, syntactic, phonological, and discourse features

LEARNING GOALS

We can understand important ideas and details in a story.

We can use the format of a play to learn new information.

OBJECTIVES

With prompting and support, ask and answer questions about key details in a text.

With prompting and support, compare and contrast the adventures and experiences of characters in familiar stories.

Actively engage in group reading activities with purpose and understanding.

Describe familiar people, places, things, and events and, with prompting and support, provide additional detail.

LANGUAGE OBJECTIVES

Children will narrate the character's problem, using verbs that end in *-ing* and key vocabulary.

ELA ACADEMIC LANGUAGE

• *character, problem*
• Cognate: *problema*

MATERIALS

Literature Big Book, *Peter's Chair,* pp. 4–31 and 32–36
Visual Vocabulary Cards

DIGITAL TOOLS

🎧 Have children listen to the selection as they follow along to develop comprehension.

Use the vocabulary activity for additional support.

Peter's Chair

Literature Big Book

Prepare to Read

Build Background Show the cover of the book. *The title of this book is* Peter's Chair. Point to the boy. *Who do you think this is?* This is _____. *Peter is the main character of this story. What things does Peter have with him?* Peter has a _____. *Do you think Peter can sit in his chair?* No, it is too _____. *Can someone else use it?* Yes, a _____ can use it.

Focus on Vocabulary Use the **Visual Vocabulary Cards** to review the oral vocabulary words *chores* and *contribute*. As you read, use gestures and other visual support to clarify important story words, such as *high chair, run away, fit,* and *grown-up*. Review the words in context as you read, and have children add these words to their personal glossaries.

Summarize the Text. *Peter has a new baby sister called Susie. Peter's parents are giving Susie Peter's old things. Peter is upset, or not happy, about this. Then he discovers he is too big for his old chair and makes an important decision about helping his family.*

Read the Text

Use the Interactive Question-Response Routine to help children understand the story.

Pages 4–15

Pages 6–7 Point to the dog and the falling building. Read the text. *CRASH! Peter's mother tells Peter to play quietly because there is a new baby in the house. Why does Peter need to play quietly?* (because they have a new baby) *How does Peter look?* (He looks sad.)

Pages 10–11 Read the text. Point to the high chair. *A high chair is a chair for a baby. Peter's dad is painting the high chair. He will give the chair to Peter's new baby sister. Peter says it is his chair. Who will use the high chair?* (the baby)

Pages 12–15 Read the text. *Peter doesn't want his chair painted pink.* Point to Peter and the dog. *Peter takes the chair to his room. Why does he take the chair to his room?* (He doesn't want it painted pink/his sister to have it.)

 What does Peter do with his chair? Why? Talk to a partner.

Beginning Have children point to the illustrations on pages 12–15 and help them say: *Peter takes his* chair. *He doesn't want* his sister *to have the* chair.

Intermediate Help children use the illustrations to complete sentence frames: *Peter is taking the* chair to his room. *He doesn't want his sister* to have the chair.

Advanced/Advanced High Have children tell more about why Peter takes the chair and how he feels. (He is mad his parents are giving the baby his things.)

Pages 16–23

Pages 16–17 Read the text. *Peter looks sad. He wants to run away with his dog, Willie, and his things. When you run away, you leave your home for a long time. What does Peter want to do?* (run away with his dog)

Pages 20–21 Read the text. *Peter tries to sit in his chair. He doesn't fit! He is too big. Why can't Peter sit in his chair?* (He isn't a baby anymore.)

 What is Peter's problem? Talk to a partner.

Beginning *Does Peter want to sit in his chair?* (yes) *Does he fit?* (no) *Why not? Peter is* <u>too big</u>.

Intermediate Have partners ask and answer: *Why doesn't Peter fit into* <u>his chair</u>? *He is* <u>too big</u>.

Pages 24–31

Pages 28–31 Peter goes back inside. Page 28: *Peter sits in a grown-up chair. A grown-up is an older person. Peter now wants to paint his chair for Susie.* Page 31: *What is Peter doing?* (painting) *Is Peter feeling better?* (yes) *How do you know?* (He is smiling.)

 What does Peter want to do at the end of the story? Talk to a partner.

Beginning *What is Peter doing? Peter is* <u>painting</u> *the chair. Who will get the chair?* (Susie)

Intermediate Have partners ask and answer: *What is Peter doing? Peter is* <u>painting the chair</u>. *Why? Peter wants to* <u>give it to Susie</u>.

Advanced/Advanced High Have partners ask and answer: *Why is Peter* <u>painting the chair</u>? (because he wants to give it to Susie)

Retell Use the Retelling Cards for *Peter's Chair* to retell the story with children. Display the cards and model retelling using sequence words, such as *first,*

next, then, and *last,* as you point to the events and actions on the cards. Then help children take turns retelling one part using the sequence words.

 ### LESSON 4 Paired Selection: "Mom's Helpers"

Pages 32–36 Read the text, have children describe the illustrations, and then paraphrase the text as you point to the corresponding images; for example, page 34: *The children are helping mom. They fold the clothes. They bring her a blanket. They help dad make soup.*

How does the family help mom? Talk to a partner.

Beginning Guide partners to choose a page to describe. Have them point to actions. Create sentence frames about their choices for children to complete.

Intermediate For each page, help children use the illustrations to complete sentence frames. For example: Page 34: *Ana folds* <u>the clothes</u>. *Juan brings Mom* <u>a blanket</u>.

Advanced/Advanced High Have partners tell what the problem is (Mom is sick) and give descriptive details telling how everyone helps. Provide modeling and sentence frames as needed.

FORMATIVE ASSESSMENT

❯ STUDENT CHECK-IN

Main Selection Have partners retell how Peter feels at different parts of the story.

Paired Selection Have partners describe how the family helps mom.

Then have children reflect using the Check-In routine.

 ### Independent Time

Oral Language Have children discuss how *Peter's Chair* and "Mom's Helpers" are alike. Ask: *What do the characters do in both stories? In both stories, the characters* <u>help people in their families</u>. Help children give text evidence to support their responses.

We can listen actively to learn about how family members help each other.

OBJECTIVES

With prompting and support, ask and answer questions about key details in a text.

With prompting and support, retell key details of a text.

With prompting and support, describe the relationship between illustrations and the text in which they appear.

Confirm understanding of a text read aloud or information presented orally or through other media by asking and answering questions about key details and requesting clarification if something is not understood.

LANGUAGE OBJECTIVES

Children will use verbs, nouns, and key vocabulary to discuss ways to help out at home.

ELA ACADEMIC LANGUAGE

• *nonfiction, facts, topic*

• Cognate: *no ficción*

MATERIALS

Interactive Read Aloud, "Helping Out at Home"

Visual Vocabulary Cards

DIGITAL TOOLS

Have children listen to the selection as they follow along to develop comprehension.

Use the vocabulary activity for additional support.

"Helping Out at Home"

Interactive Read Aloud

Prepare to Read

Build Background Review what children learned about helping out in *Peter's Chair* and "The Clean Up!" *The jobs we do at home are called chores.* Show images of people doing the chores mentioned in the cards. Help children tell what the people are doing. Provide vocabulary and modeling as needed.

Focus on Vocabulary Use the **Visual Vocabulary Cards** to review the oral vocabulary words: *member, chores, contribute, organize,* and *accomplish.* As you read, use gestures and other visual support to clarify important selection words, for example: *laundry, babysitting, meals,* and *set the table.*

Summarize the Text *All family members do chores. They work together. Let's learn how family members help out. This is a nonfiction text about doing chores. A nonfiction text gives facts, or information, about a topic.*

Read the Text

Use the Interactive Question-Response Routine to help children understand the text.

Card 1

Paragraphs 2–3 Read the text. Point to the photo. *The whole family does chores. Some chores are cleaning your room and feeding the pet. What are some chores?* (Answers will vary.) *Chores can happen inside or outside the house. This family is outside. They are washing the car together. Everyone is helping.*

 How do the family members in the photo help? Talk to a partner.

Beginning Have partners point to the photo as they respond: *The family members all* <u>wash</u> *the car.*

Intermediate Have partners complete sentence frames: *The family members* <u>wash the car</u> *together. Everyone* <u>helps/washes</u>.

Advanced/Advanced High Challenge partners to add details to their responses such as telling where the car is washed and what the family uses to wash the car. (Example: The family washes the car with soap.)

Card 2

Paragraph 1–2 Read the text. Point to the photo. *Helping out means the same as helping. Sometimes older family members need help. Older family members might be a grandmother or grandfather. You can bring them food, walk with* *them, or help them do things in the house.* Point to the images as you refer to them. *This girl is helping her grandfather. She is helping with his tie. How can you help older family members?* (bring them food; walk with them)

 Who are the people? How is the girl helping? Talk to a partner.

Beginning Have partners point to the photo as they respond: *This is <u>a girl/her grandfather</u>. The girl is helping <u>her grandfather</u> with his tie.*

Intermediate Have partners tell what is happening in the photo. *The <u>girl</u> is helping her <u>grandfather</u>. She is <u>helping him with his tie</u>.*

Advanced/Advanced High After partners tell what the girl is doing, have them tell ways to help older family members.

Card 3

Paragraphs 1–2 Read the text. Point to the photo. *The family members help make a meal. The mother is mixing the salad. The father is cutting a cabbage. A meal is breakfast, lunch, or dinner. What do family members help make?* (meals)

Paragraphs 3–4 Read the text. *Children can help make meals. They can wash vegetables and stir ingredients. Ingredients are the food you use to make something.* Give examples and then act out stirring ingredients. *How can children help prepare, or make meals?* (wash vegetables, stir ingredients) *Children can help set, or put things on, the table. They can help clean up. They can wash dishes and put them away. How can you help?* (make food; set table; wash dishes)

 How can people help with meals? Talk to a partner.

Beginning Have partners point to the photo and help them say: *The mother can make the <u>salad</u>. The daughter can hold the <u>bowl</u>.*

Intermediate Guide partners to tell how children can help with meals: *Children can help make <u>the meal</u>. After the meal, they can help <u>wash the dishes</u>.*

Advanced Have partners ask and answer: *How can children help prepare meals? How can they help clean up afterwards?*

Advanced High Partners can extend "Advanced" by telling their own experiences helping with meals.

Card 4

Paragraph 1 Read the text. *Family members do chores outdoors. This family is raking the leaves.* Act out the chores as you name them. *In the winter, some families shovel snow. In the spring and summer, they take care of gardens. What chores do families do outside?* (rake leaves in fall; shovel snow; care for gardens)

Paragraph 3 Read the text. *We can stay healthy doing chores outdoors. We can move our bodies and breathe the fresh air. How can chores help us stay healthy?* (We move our bodies and breathe fresh air.)

 What chores can you do outdoors? Talk to a partner.

Beginning Have partners point to the photo as they respond: *I can <u>rake leaves</u>.*

Intermediate Have partners tell about an outside chore. Provide sentence frames: *I can _____.*

Retell Have partners take turns pointing to a photo and describing what they learned about helping and doing chores. Provide questions for partners to answer as they describe: *Who helps? How do they help?*

FORMATIVE ASSESSMENT

❯ STUDENT CHECK-IN

Have partners retell how children can help out at home.

Then have children reflect using the Check-In routine.

 ## Independent Time

Draw and Write Have children draw and tell about a picture showing a chore they do at home. Help them write a sentence about it.

LEARNING GOALS

We can ask and answer questions to understand the story.

OBJECTIVES

With prompting and support, ask and answer questions about key details in a text.

With prompting and support, identify characters and major events in a story.

Actively engage in group reading activities with purpose and understanding.

Describe familiar people, places, things, and events and, with prompting and support, provide additional detail.

LANGUAGE OBJECTIVES

Children will narrate how the main character helps, using pronouns and key vocabulary.

ELA ACADEMIC LANGUAGE

• *events*

• Cognate: *eventos*

MATERIALS

ELL Leveled Reader: *How Can Jane Help?*

Online Differentiated Texts, "Helping Out"

Online ELL Visual Vocabulary Cards

DIGITAL TOOLS

Have children listen to the selection as they follow along to develop comprehension.

Use the vocabulary activity for additional support.

How Can Jane Help?

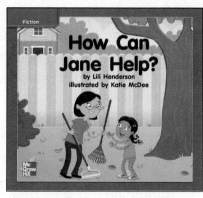

Lexile 140L

Prepare to Read

Build Background *You will read a book called* How Can Jane Help? *The story tells about different chores that Jane does.* Show the illustrations. Then review the chores children have learned about in the other texts. Write their ideas. Help children tell a chore. Example: *Children can help* _____ .

Focus on Vocabulary Use the routine on the **ELL Visual Vocabulary Cards** to preteach *assist* and *reliable*. Use the images and any labels to identify and model the use of key vocabulary in context.

Read the Text

Use the Interactive Question-Response Routine to help children understand the story.

Pages 2–8

Pages 2–3 Point to page 2. Point to the corresponding images as you discuss the page. *Jane helps her brother. She holds their pet. He cleans the cage.* Point to page 3. *Jane helps her sister wash the car. Let's read the labels:* cage, car.

 How does Jane help? Talk to a partner.

Beginning Have partners point to the illustrations as they respond: *Jane helps her brother clean* the cage. *Jane helps her sister wash* the car.

Intermediate Have partners **ask and answer questions** about the text: *What does Jane do? Jane helps her* brother/sister. *How does Jane help? She* holds/washes *the* pet/car.

Advanced/Advanced High Have partners give more details. (Jane helps her brother clean the cage. She holds the pets. She helps her sister wash the car.)

Pages 4–5 Point to page 4. *Jane helps her mother make lunch. It looks like they are making sandwiches.* Help children name images. Point to page 5. *Jane helps her dad carry the bags. Let's read the label:* bag. *What characters, or people in the story, do you see?* (Jane, her mother, her father) *What do Jane and her mother do?* (make lunch) *What is Jane holding?* (a bag)

 How does Jane help? Talk to a partner.

Beginning Have children point to the illustrations as they respond: *Jane helps* make lunch/carry the bags.

Intermediate Have children ask and answer: *What does Jane do? Jane helps her* mother/father make lunch/carry the bags.

Advanced/Advanced High Challenge partners to be descriptive as they ask and answer questions about how Jane is helping.

Events: Sequence Have children discuss the order of events on pages 2–5. (First, Jane helps helps her brother clean the cage. Then, she helps her sister wash the car. Next, she helps make lunch.)

Pages 6–8 Point to page 6. *This is Jane's neighbor. Jane can help rake. Let's read the label:* rake. Point to the question marks on page 7. *What are these?* (question marks) Jane has a question in her mind. *What is the question?* (How can I help?)

 Point to page 8. *How does Jane help the dog?* Talk to a partner.

Beginning Have partners point to the illustration and help them to respond: *Jane* feeds/gives food *to the dog.*

Intermediate Have partners ask and answer: *What does Jane do? Jane* feeds *the* dog.

Advanced/Advanced High Help partners describe in detail what Jane does and what they see in the illustration. (Jane feeds the dog. She pours food into bowl. The dog is waiting for its food.)

Retell Have partners retell the story. Have them take turns pointing to a picture and describing it to each other.

Focus on Fluency

Read pages 2–8 with appropriate intonation. Then read the text aloud and have children echo read. For additional practice, have children record themselves reading the same text a few times, and then select their favorite recording to play for you.

Build Knowledge: Make Connections

Talk About the Text Have partners discuss ways they can help others.

Write About the Text Have children add their ideas to their Build Knowledge page of their reader's notebook.

Self-Selected Reading

Have children select another realistic fiction story from the online **Leveled Reader Library,** or read the **Differentiated Text,** "Helping Out."

LITERACY ACTIVITIES

Have children complete the Literacy Activities on the inside back cover of the book.

FORMATIVE ASSESSMENT

◉ STUDENT CHECK-IN

Have partners retell how Jane helps her family and pets. Then have children reflect using the Check-In routine.

LEVEL UP

IF children can read *How Can Jane Help?* ELL Level with fluency and correctly answer the Literacy Activity questions,

THEN tell children that they will read a more detailed version of the story.

HAVE children page through *How Can Jane Help?* On Level and describe each picture in simple language.

- Have children read the selection, checking their comprehension and providing assistance as necessary.

LESSONS 1-5

MODELED WRITING

LESSON 1

LEARNING GOALS

We can write about what makes us mad.

OBJECTIVES

Use a combination of dictating and writing to narrate a single event.

LANGUAGE OBJECTIVES

Children will narrate by writing sentences using the adjective *mad*.

ELA ACADEMIC LANGUAGE

• *adjective*

• Cognate: *adjetivo*

Writing Practice Act mad as you read the sample sentence on p. 14 of the **Reading/Writing Companion.** Guide children to analyze the sentence using the Actor/Action Routine: *Who is the actor?* (I) *What is the action?* (felt mad) *Why?* (because my sister broke my toy) Then read the prompt on p. 15, and ask children to answer it as a group. Write it on the board and for children to choral read. Then have children write their own sentences.

Beginning Provide a sentence frame: I will write about when I couldn't go to the park. Then help partners think of their sentences: *Who is the actor?* (I) *What is the action?* (couldn't go) *Where?* (to the park) *How did this make you feel?* I felt <u>mad</u>.

Intermediate Have partners take turns asking and answering *who/what* questions about a time they felt mad. Provide sentence frames if needed.

Advanced/Advanced High Challenge children to talk about their sentences using the Actor/Action routine. Encourage them to share their sentences with the group.

FORMATIVE ASSESSMENT ❯ ⊘ STUDENT CHECK IN Partners share their sentences. Ask children to reflect using the Check-In routine.

INTERACTIVE WRITING

LESSON 2

LEARNING GOALS

We can write about how Peter shows that he is mad.

OBJECTIVES

With guidance and support, respond to questions and suggestions from peers.

LANGUAGE OBJECTIVES

Children will argue by writing a sentence using the verb *decides*.

ELA ACADEMIC LANGUAGE

• *events*

• Cognate: *eventos*

Write a Response: Share the Pen Choral read the sample sentences on p. T30 of the **Teacher's Edition.** Use the Actor/Action routine to analyze the sentences: *Who is the actor?* (Peter) *What is the action?* (shows he's mad) *How?* (when he shouts) Then guide children to think about the writing trait by identifying the word that connects events. *(also)* Then help children complete the sentence frames at the bottom of p. T30.

Beginning Help children complete the first sentence frame. Point to Peter on p. 11 of the **Big Book:** *Does Peter look happy or mad?* Peter looks <u>mad</u>.

Intermediate Have partners ask and answer questions about p. 11 to complete the second sentence frame. What does Peter decide to do because he is mad? Peter decides to <u>run away</u>.

Advanced/Advanced High Challenge children to think of their own sentences about how Peter shows he is mad.

FORMATIVE ASSESSMENT ❯ ⊘ STUDENT CHECK IN Partners share their sentences. Ask children to reflect using the Check-In routine.

INDEPENDENT WRITING

LEARNING GOALS

We can write about the texts we read.

OBJECTIVES

Use a combination of drawing, dictating, and writing to narrate several loosely linked events.

LANGUAGE OBJECTIVES

Children will narrate by writing sentences using details.

ELA ACADEMIC LANGUAGE

- *describe*
- Cognate: *describir*

Find Text Evidence Use the Independent Writing routine. Ask questions to help children orally retell the shared read, such as: *Who are Jake and Dale?* (boys) *What do they do first?* (wake up) Then read the prompt on p. 30 of the **Reading/Writing Companion:** *How does Dale help out at home? We need to describe what Dale does.* Display p. 21. *What does Dale do?* (make a bed) Then display p. 22. *What does Dale do?* (gets a tan cup)

Write a Response Write the following sentence starters on the board, and read them: Dale helps by _____. He also _____. Model completing the first starter, and have children choral read the response. Repeat with the remaining starters. Then ask children to copy the sentences onto p. 31.

Beginning Provide a sentence frame to help children talk about their sentences: I used the connecting word *also.*

Intermediate Encourage children to use words that connect the different ways Dale helps. Help them check this item off the writing checklist.

Advanced/Advanced High Read the writing checklist with children, and have them identify where they used each item in their writing.

FORMATIVE ASSESSMENT ❯ **STUDENT CHECK IN** Partners share their sentences. Ask children to reflect using the Check-In routine.

SELF-SELECTED WRITING

LEARNING GOALS

We can revise our writing.

OBJECTIVES

Demonstrate command of the conventions of standard English grammar and usage when writing.

LANGUAGE OBJECTIVES

Children will inquire about their writing by adding an adjective.

ELA ACADEMIC LANGUAGE

- *adjective*
- Cognate: *adjetivo*

Work with children to revise the group writing activity. Point to each word as you read the sentences. Stop to ask questions, such as, *Can we add an adjective here?* Then, if children are ready, have them work with a partner to revise their own sentences before they publish them.

For support with and grammar and adjectives, refer to the **Language Transfers Handbook** and **Language Development Cards** 10A and 10B.

FORMATIVE ASSESSMENT ❯ **STUDENT CHECK IN** Partners tell what revisions they made. Ask children to reflect using the Check-In routine.

LESSONS 1-2

LEARNING GOALS

We can understand important ideas and details in a story.

We can use captions to learn new information.

OBJECTIVES

With prompting and support, ask and answer questions about key details in a text.

With prompting and support, retell familiar stories, including key details.

Continue a conversation through multiple exchanges.

Describe familiar people, places, things, and events and, with prompting and support, provide additional detail.

LANGUAGE OBJECTIVES

Children will narrate the characters' problems using verbs and key vocabulary.

ELA ACADEMIC LANGUAGE

• *problem*

• Cognate: *problema*

MATERIALS

Literature Big Book, *Hen Hears Gossip,* pp. 4–32 and 33–36

Visual Vocabulary Cards

DIGITAL TOOLS

Have children listen to the selection as they follow along to develop comprehension.

Use the vocabulary activity for additional support.

Hen Hears Gossip

Prepare to Read

Build Background Show the cover of the book. Point to Hen. *This is a hen. What animal is this?* This is a _____. *A hen lives on a farm. What other animals live on a farm?* _____ and _____ live on a farm. *The title is* Hen Hears Gossip. Explain that *gossip* is talk about someone's private life. Often, gossip is not true.

Focus on Vocabulary Use the **Visual Vocabulary Cards** to review the oral vocabulary words *citizen* and *respect.* As you read, use gestures and other visual support to clarify important story words, such as *thorn, horn,* and *calf.*

Summarize the Text Preview the illustrations as you summarize the story: *Hen hears Cow and Pig whispering. Hen wants to tell what she thinks they said. She runs to share the gossip with her friends.*

Literature Big Book

Read the Text

Use the Interactive Question-Response Routine to help children understand the story.

Pages 4–15

Pages 6–7 Read the text. *Hen listens to Cow and Pig whispering. Hen loves gossip. Hen can't wait to tell everyone. What will Hen do?* (tell everyone the gossip)

Pages 8–9 Read the text. *Hen tells Duck the gossip. Sadie the dog has a thorn!* Point to the thorn. *A thorn is the sharp part of a plant. What do you think Duck will do?* (tell someone else the gossip)

Pages 10–11 Read the text. *Duck tells Goose the gossip. Daisy the cat grew a horn!* Point to the horn. Look at pages 8–9. *What did Hen tell Duck?* (The dog has a thorn.) *Then what did Duck tell Goose?* (The cat grew a horn.) *Is this information the same?* (no) *The gossip is different every time.*

Pages 14–15 Read the text. *Turkey tells Hen, "You're lazy, fat, and ate all the corn!" Who is the gossip about now?* (Hen) *Is Hen surprised?* (yes) *What does Hen say?* ("I did NOT eat all the corn!") *What happens to the gossip each time?* (It changes.) *This could be a problem.*

 What do the animals do? Tell what happens in order. Talk to a partner.

Beginning Have children use the illustrations to retell what happens: *Hen tells Duck. Hen says the dog has a thorn.* Repeat this routine for the other examples.

Intermediate Model an example and provide sentence frames for children to continue. Hen *tells* Duck. Hen *says* the dog has a thorn.

Advanced/Advanced High Have partners use the illustrations to retell what happens. Then ask: *What happens to the gossip each time?* (It changes.)

Pages 16–25

Pages 16–17 Read the text. *Turkey and Hen find corn in the barn. Turkey and Hen ask Goose, "Why did you say Hen ate all the corn?" Goose answers, "I didn't say THAT!"* Did Goose say Hen ate the corn? (no)

Pages 20–24 Read the text. Point to the images on each page as appropriate. Explain that on each page, the animals mishear what is said. On page 24, tell children that the animals learn the truth. *Cow says a baby calf was born. A calf is a baby cow. What really happened?* (A calf was born.)

 Hen learns what really happened, or the truth. What does Hen learn? Talk to a partner.

Beginning Provide a sentence frame: *Hen learns that a baby calf was born.*

Intermediate Have partners ask and answer: *What did Cow really say?* (She said her baby calf was born.)

Pages 26–32

Pages 26–27 Read the text. *Hen tells everyone the truth. A baby calf was born. Each animal hears something different. What does Goose hear?* (A lazy rat was born.)

Pages 28–29 Read the text. *Hen tells the animals again. A baby calf was born. She wants to makes sure they understand what was really said.*

 What does Hen tell everyone? What problem happens? Talk to a partner.

Beginning Help children respond: *Hen tells that the baby calf was born. The animals hear different things.*

Intermediate Have partners ask and answer: *What does Hen say? Hen says that a baby calf was born.*

What do the other animals hear? The other animals hear different information/things.

Advanced/Advanced High Have partners ask and answer: *What does Hen do? What problem does Hen have? How does she fix it?*

Retell Use the **Retelling Cards** for *Hen Hears Gossip.* Help children retell the story as you display the cards. Model using sequence words for additional support.

 LESSON 4 **Paired Selection: "Team Up to Clean Up"**

Pages 33–36 Read and then paraphrase the text/captions as you point to the corresponding images, for example: *On page 33, the playground is messy. The class makes plans for a Clean-Up Day. What do the children want to do?* (clean up the playground)

 How do the children make the playground a better place? Talk to a partner.

Beginning Have partners use a photo to tell one way the children help. *The children plant a tree.*

Intermediate Have partners use the photos to tell how the children help, using complete sentences.

Advanced/Advanced High Have partners use the photographs to retell what happens in the text.

FORMATIVE ASSESSMENT

STUDENT CHECK-IN

Main Selection Have partners retell how the gossip changes in the story.

Paired Selection Have partners describe how the children clean up the playground.

Then have children reflect using the Check-In routine.

 Independent Time

Oral Language Have children discuss what happens in *Hen Hears Gossip* and "Team Up to Clean Up" *What did you learn about being a good citizen?* Model responses and supply sentence frames.

LESSON 3

LEARNING GOALS

We can listen actively to find out who is and who isn't a good citizen.

OBJECTIVES

With prompting and support, compare and contrast the adventures and experiences of characters in familiar stories.

Actively engage in group reading activities with purpose and understanding.

Confirm understanding of a text read aloud or information presented orally or through other media by asking and answering questions about key details and requesting clarification if something is not understood.

Speak audibly and express thoughts, feelings, and ideas clearly.

LANGUAGE OBJECTIVES

Children will discuss how the main character works hard, using nouns, verbs, and key vocabulary.

ELA ACADEMIC LANGUAGE

• *fable, characters*
• Cognate: *fábula*

MATERIALS

Interactive Read Aloud, "The Little Red Hen"

Visual Vocabulary Cards

DIGITAL TOOLS

Have children listen to the selection as they follow along to develop comprehension.

Use the vocabulary activity for additional support.

"The Little Red Hen"

Prepare to Read

Interactive Read Aloud

Build Background Tell children that "The Little Red Hen" is a very old story. The Little Red Hen wants to make bread. Show a picture of wheat and flour. Explain that flour comes from wheat. Flour is needed to make bread. Tell children that this story is a fable. Fables often have characters that are animals. The animal characters do things that real animals can't do.

Focus on Vocabulary Use the **Visual Vocabulary Cards** to review the oral vocabulary words: *tidy, citizen, necessary, hauled,* and *respect.* As you read, use gestures and other visual support to clarify important story words, for example: *lazy, grain of wheat, stalks, flour,* and *mill.*

Summarize the Text Show the cards as you summarize the story: *This story is about a Little Red Hen. She wants to make bread. She asks for help, but nobody wants to help her do the work. However, they do all want to help her eat it.*

Read the Text

Use the Interactive Question-Response Routine to help children understand the story.

Card 1

Paragraph 1 Read the text. Point to the illustration. *Little Red Hen lives on a farm with her friends. She works hard. She does chores. Her friends are very lazy. They don't like to work. What does Little Red Hen do on the farm?* (She does chores, works hard.) *Do her friends like to work?* (no)

Paragraphs 2–7 Read the text and point to the corresponding images. *Little Red Hen finds a grain of wheat. She wants to plant the grain. "Who will help me plant this grain of wheat?" she asks. No one wants to help Little Red Hen. So, Little Red Hen plants the grain herself. What does Little Red Hen do with the grain of wheat?* (She plants it.) *Does anyone help?* (no)

 How is Little Red Hen different from her friends? Talk to a partner.

Beginning Provide sentence frames: *Little Red Hen <u>works</u> hard. Her friends are <u>lazy</u>.*

Intermediate *With a partner, ask and answer: What does Little Red Hen do? Little Red Hen <u>works hard/cleans/does chores</u>. What do her friends do? Her friends <u>rest and play</u>.*

Advanced/Advanced High *With a partner, ask and answer these questions: What does Little Red Hen do? What do her friends do?* (She works hard and does chores. Her friends rest because they are lazy.)

Card 2

Paragraph 1 Read the text. Point to the wheat. *The wheat grows tall.* Point to the watering can. *Little Red Hen waters the stalks. Soon, Little Red Hen needs to cut down the stalks. She will take the wheat to the mill. The miller will make flour from the grain. A miller works in a mill. What does Little Red Hen need to do?* (cut the stalks; take them to the miller)

Paragraphs 2–8 Read the text. Point to the illustration. *Little Red Hen asks her friends, "Who will help me cut the wheat and take it to the mill?" None of the animals want to help. She does the work by herself.*

 What chores does Little Red Hen do with the wheat? Who helps? Talk to a partner.

Beginning Provide sentence frames: *Little Red Hen waters the stalks. She cuts the stalks. She takes the stalks to the miller. Does anyone help her?* (no)

Intermediate Help partners respond. *Little Red Hen waters the wheat/stalks and cuts the stalks. She carries the stalks to the miller. Who helps?* (no one)

Advanced/Advanced High Guide partners to discuss what Little Red Hen and the other animals do.

Card 3

Paragraphs 3–9 Read the text. Point to the illustration. *No one wants to help Little Red Hen make the bread. She will make the bread herself. Who will help Little Red Hen make bread?* (no one)

 What will Little Red Hen do with the flour? Who will help her? Talk to a partner.

Beginning Review the words *flour* and *bread.* Help children say: *Hen will use the flour to make bread.*

Intermediate Help partners respond: *Little Red Hen will use the flour to make bread. Nobody will help her.*

Card 4

Paragraphs 3–8 Read the text. Point to the illustration. *Little Red Hen made the bread. Little Red Hen asks, "Who will help me eat this bread?" "I will!" says everyone. Who wants to help eat the bread?* (the other animals) *But Little Red Hen shakes her head. She did all the work, so she will eat the bread herself.*

 What do the animals want? What does Little Red Hen do? Why? Talk to a partner.

Beginning Help children use the illustration to respond. *The animals want to help eat the bread. Little Red Hen eats all the bread herself.*

Intermediate Supply sentence frames: *The animals want to help eat the bread. Little Red Hen doesn't share the bread because the animals didn't help.*

Advanced Guide partners to use the illustration to discuss both what the other animals do and what Little Red Hen does on this card. Supply modeling and sentence frames as needed.

Advanced High Extend Advanced by asking partners to explain whether or not they think Little Red Hen was right to not share the bread.

Retell Use the illustrations on the Interactive Read-Aloud Cards to retell the story with children. Display the cards and model retelling using sequence words, as you point to the events and actions in the cards. Then help children take turns retelling one part using the sequence words.

FORMATIVE ASSESSMENT

❯ STUDENT CHECK-IN

Have partners retell how someone can be a good citizen.

Then have children using the Check-in routine.

 Independent Time

Role-play Have small groups plan a role-play based on one of the cards. Have children practice their role-plays before performing them for the other groups.

LESSONS 4-5

Clive and His Friend

Prepare to Read

Build Background Have children review what they've learned about how good citizens behave. Tell children that this is a story about Clive and his friend. The story tells about what they do on a school day. It tells how they follow school rules and are good citizens. Elicit examples of school rules. Tell children that this story is a fantasy. The animal characters do things that real animals cannot do.

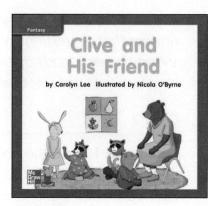

Fantasy

Clive and His Friend

by Carolyn Lee illustrated by Nicola O'Byrne

McGraw Hill

Lexile 110L

Focus on Vocabulary Use the routine on the **ELL Visual Vocabulary Cards** to preteach *obey* and *sensible*. Use the images and any labels to identify and model the use of key vocabulary in context.

Read the Text

Use the Interactive Question-Response Routine to help children understand the story.

Pages 2–8

Pages 2–3 Point to the images as you discuss what is happening. Page 2: *Clive and his friend stop by the street. They look for cars. They make sure it is safe to cross the street.* Page 3: *Clive and his friend walk down the hallway.*

What rules are Clive and his friend following? Talk to a partner.

Beginning Have children point to the illustration as they respond. *They look for* cars *before crossing the* street. *They walk in the* hallway.

Intermediate Help partners respond: *Clive and his friend are looking both ways before* crossing the street. *They walk* quietly in the hallway.

Advanced/Advanced High Have partners describe what is happening on the pages and discuss who is and who is not following the rules. (Example: Bear, Mouse, and Rabbit are running in the hallway. They are not following the rules.)

Events: Cause and Effect Have children discuss a cause-and-effect relationship on pages 2–3. *Clive's friend stops to look before* crossing *the street. Clive* stops *too.*

Pages 4–5 Point to the images as you discuss what is happening. Page 4: *Clive and his friend help put the books on the shelf. Let's read the label:* books. *Where are Clive and his friend?* (the library; the classroom) Page 5: *Clive and his friend smile. They listen to the teacher. Let's read the label:* teacher. *What causes them to smile?* (They are happy/having fun.)

Look at page 4. Describe, or tell, how Clive and his friend help. Talk to a partner.

Beginning Have partners point to the illustration as they respond. *They put the* <u>books</u> *on the* <u>shelf</u>.

Intermediate Have partners point to the images: *They put* <u>the books</u> *on* <u>the shelf</u>. *Why is this helpful?* (Answers will vary. Use children's answers to create sentence frames as needed.)

Advanced/Advanced High Have partners use details to describe what is happening in the illustration. Then ask: *Why is this helpful?*

Pages 6–8 Point to the images as you discuss what is happening. Page 6: *Clive and his friend wash their hands in the sink. What do they do?* (wash their hands) Page 7: *Clive and his friend sit at the table. They get milk. They say, "Thank you." What will they drink?* (milk) Page 8: *Clive and his friend play on the playground. Clive is on the slide. Where is Clive?* (on the slide)

 Tell how Clive is being a good citizen. Talk to a partner.

Beginning Help children choose a page to *reread*, and then talk about, for example: *Clive gets* <u>milk</u>. *Clive says* <u>thank you</u>.

Intermediate Have partners choose a page. Help them respond to the prompt, for example: *Clive waits his turn to* <u>wash his hands</u>.

Retell Have partners retell the story. Have them take turns pointing to a picture and describing it to each other.

Focus on Fluency

Read pages 2–8 with appropriate intonation. Then read the text aloud and have children echo read. For additional practice, have children record themselves reading the same text a few times and then select their favorite recording to play for you.

Build Knowledge: Make Connections

Talk About the Text Have partners discuss how they can be good citizens.

Write About the Text Have children add their ideas to their Build Knowledge page of their reader's notebook.

Self-Selected Reading

Help children choose a fantasy story from the online **Leveled Reader Library,** or read the **Differentiated Text,** "Dale's Kite."

LITERACY ACTIVITIES

Have children complete the Literacy Activities on the inside back cover of the book.

FORMATIVE ASSESSMENT

❯ **STUDENT CHECK-IN**

Have partners retell how the characters follow the rules. Then have children reflect using the Check-In routine.

 **LEVEL** UP

IF children can read *Clive and His Friend* **ELL Level** with fluency and correctly answer the Literacy Activity questions,

THEN tell children that they will read a more detailed version of the story.

HAVE children page through *Clive and His Friend* On Level and describe each picture in simple language.

- Have children read the selection, checking their comprehension and providing assistance as necessary.

MODELED WRITING

LESSON 1

LEARNING GOALS

We can write about whom we like to share secrets with.

OBJECTIVES

Use a combination of dictating and writing to narrate several loosely linked events.

LANGUAGE OBJECTIVES

Children will narrate by writing a sentence using an adjective.

ELA ACADEMIC LANGUAGE

• *adjective*

• Cognate: *adjetivo*

Writing Practice Have children echo read the sample sentences on p. 44 of the **Reading/Writing Companion.** Guide them to analyze the second sentence using the Actor/Description routine: *What is the subject?* (a sad berry) *What can we say about it?* (It's a blueberry.) Explain that *blue* can be used to mean "sad." Then read the prompt on p. 45, and have children answer it as a group. Write it on the board and point to each word as children choral read. Then ask children to write their own sentences.

Beginning Provide sentence frames and model completing them: I put my clothes on <u>backward</u>. My friends think I am walking the <u>wrong</u> way!

Intermediate Have partners take turns asking and answering *who/what* questions to create their sentences. Provide a sentence frame if needed.

Advanced/Advanced High Challenge children to stay between the lines as they write their sentences. Encourage children to share out their sentences.

FORMATIVE ASSESSMENT ❯ ⊙ **STUDENT CHECK IN** Partners share their sentences. Ask children to reflect using the Check-In routine.

INTERACTIVE WRITING

LESSON 2

LEARNING GOALS

We can write about how the message changes as it is retold in the story.

OBJECTIVES

With guidance and support, add details to strengthen writing as needed.

LANGUAGE OBJECTIVES

Children will inform by writing a sentence using the verb *tells*.

ELA ACADEMIC LANGUAGE

• *evidence*

• Cognate: *evidencia*

Write a Response: Share the Pen Choral read the first sample sentence on p. T108 of the **Teacher's Edition.** Use the Actor/Action routine to review it: *Who is the actor?* (Hen) *What is the action?* (tells Duck the dog has a thorn) Then guide children to think about the writing skill by having them point to the capital letter at the beginning of the sentence. Remind children of the writing trait: *Special words can help us tell the order of events. What time-order words do you see?* (first, then) Help them complete the sentence frames on p. T108.

Beginning For the first sentence, provide a visual from p. 13 of the **Big Book:** *What does Goose tell Turkey?* Goose tells Turkey that the bat <u>raced a storm</u>.

Intermediate Encourage children to look for evidence on each page that tells what the animals said to complete the sentence frames.

Advanced/Advanced High Challenge children to think of their own sentences about what the animals say and share them with the group.

FORMATIVE ASSESSMENT ❯ ⊙ **STUDENT CHECK IN** Partners share their sentences. Ask children to reflect using the Check-In routine.

INDEPENDENT WRITING

 LESSONS 3-4

LEARNING GOALS

We can write about the texts we read.

OBJECTIVES

Use drawing, dictating, and writing to compose opinion pieces that state an opinion about the topic.

LANGUAGE OBJECTIVES

Children will argue by writing a sentence using a time-order word.

ELA ACADEMIC LANGUAGE

• *illustrations*

• Cognate: *ilustraciones*

 Find Text Evidence Use the Independent Writing routine. Ask questions to help children orally retell the shared read, such as: *Who rides bikes?* (Mike and Kate) *Where is Mike?* (in a line) Then read the prompt on p. 60 of the **Reading/Writing Companion:** *How are Kate, Pam, and Mike alike? Let's look at illustrations.* Display p. 52: *What does Mike do?* (lets Pam in line) Then turn to p. 54. *What does Mike let Pam do?* (ride his bike)

 Write a Response Write the sentence frames from p. T118 on the board, and read them. Model completing the first sentence frame, and have children choral read the response. Repeat with the remaining sentence frames. Then ask children to copy the sentences onto p. 61.

Beginning Provide a sentence frame to help partners talk about their sentences: I told the events in order.

Intermediate Remind children to begin each sentence with a capital letter and then help them check this item off the writing checklist.

Advanced/Advanced High Read the checklist with children, and have partners identify where they used each item in their writing.

FORMATIVE ASSESSMENT > **STUDENT CHECK IN** Partners share their sentences. Ask children to reflect using the Check-In routine.

SELF-SELECTED WRITING

 LESSON 5

LEARNING GOALS

We can revise our writing.

OBJECTIVES

Demonstrate command of the conventions of standard English grammar and usage when writing.

LANGUAGE OBJECTIVES

Children will inquire about their writing by checking articles.

ELA ACADEMIC LANGUAGE

• *article*

• Cognate: *artículo*

 Work with children to revise the group writing activity. Point to each word as you read the sentences. Stop to ask questions, such as, *Is a/the used correctly here?* If needed, write a sentence using *a* or *the* incorrectly, and work together to revise the sentence. Then, if children are ready, have them work with a partner to revise their own sentences before they publish them.

For support with grammar and articles, refer to the **Language Transfers Handbook** and **Language Development Card** 14A.

FORMATIVE ASSESSMENT > **STUDENT CHECK IN** Partners tell what revisions they made. Ask children to reflect using the Check-In routine.

LESSONS 1-2

LEARNING GOALS

We can understand important ideas and details in a text.

We can use photographs to learn new information.

OBJECTIVES

With prompting and support, describe the connection between pieces of information in a text.

With prompting and support, identify basic similarities in and differences between two texts on the same topic.

Actively engage in group reading activities with purpose and understanding.

Continue a conversation through multiple exchanges.

LANGUAGE OBJECTIVES

Children will inform about different kinds of bread, using nouns and adjectives.

ELA ACADEMIC LANGUAGE

• *nonfiction, facts*

• Cognate: *no ficción*

MATERIALS

Literature Big Book, *Bread Comes to Life,* pp. 4–31 and 32–36
Visual Vocabulary Cards

DIGITAL TOOLS

Have children listen to the selection as they follow along to develop comprehension.

Use the vocabulary activity for additional support.

Bread Comes to Life

Prepare to Read

Build Background Show photos of different bread products, ideally from different parts of the world. *What do you call this food?* This food is ____. Elicit specific names, such as *rolls, toast, bagels,* or *tortillas.* Ask students to turn to a partner and say: *I like to eat _____. I eat _____ every day. All of these foods are made from wheat.* Show a photo of a wheat stalk. *The grains are ground to make flour.* Show a photo of flour. *Flour is used to make bread.*

Literature Big Book

Focus on Vocabulary Use the **Visual Vocabulary Cards** to review the oral vocabulary words *natural resources* and *create.* As you read, use gestures and other visual support to clarify important selection words, such as *baker, sowing, sprout, grind,* and *dough.*

Summarize the Text *There are many different kinds of bread. We use wheat to make flour. We use flour to make bread. Let's read about how bread is made.* Tell students this is a nonfiction text that gives facts about a topic.

Read the Text

Use the Interactive Question-Response Routine to help children understand the text.

Pages 4–13

Pages 6–7 Read the text. Point to the images. *There are many different kinds of bread: white bread, black bread, rolls, and bread with holes.* Reread the kinds of bread and have children point to the corresponding photos.

Pages 10–13 Read the text. Point to the corresponding images. Pages 10–11: *The baker sows, or plants, wheat seeds in his yard. The seeds sprout into grass. Sprout means "to grow a small stem from a seed." What do the seeds do?* (sprout/grow into grass) Pages 12–13: *The grass grows tall. What does the grass do?* (grows tall)

 How does the baker grow wheat? Talk to a partner.

Beginning Have partners point to the photos that correspond to their responses: *The baker* sows *seeds. The seeds* sprout *into grass. The grass grows* tall.

Intermediate Have partners ask and answer: *What does the baker do? The baker* sows *the* seeds. *What do the seeds do? The seeds* sprout *into* grass. *What does the grass do? The* grass *grows* tall.

Advanced/Advanced High Challenge partners to use what they've learned to ask and answer questions about how wheat grows. (Modeling questions: What does the baker do? What happens to the seeds? What color is the wheat?)

Pages 14–21

Pages 14–15 Read the text. *When the crop is ripe, or ready to pick, it is gold.* Point to the grains. *Each stalk has many grains. What color is the ripe wheat?* (gold)

Pages 20–21 Read the text. Point to the images. *The baker grinds the grains. He makes flour. It is called whole wheat flour. He will use the flour to make bread. What will the baker make?* (bread)

 Look at page 20. How does the baker make flour? Talk to a partner.

Beginning Have partners point to the photo as they respond: *The baker* grinds *the grains.*

Intermediate Have partners ask and answer: *What does the baker do? The baker* grinds the grains *into* flour. *What kind of flour is it? It is* whole wheat flour.

Pages 22–31

Pages 22–23 Read the text. *The baker makes dough. He puts flour, yeast, honey, water, salt, and oil in a bowl. He stirs it. What does the baker make?* (dough)

Pages 24–27 Read the text. *Gesture for each photo and name the actions. Show me one thing the baker does with the dough.*

 Look at pages 22–27. How does the baker make bread? Talk to a partner.

Beginning Have partners use the photos to help them act out making bread as they respond: *The baker makes* dough. *He* (actions from page 24) *the dough. The dough* rises. *He puts the dough in the* oven.

Intermediate Have partners take turns telling the steps: *The baker makes* dough. *He* (action words) *the dough. The dough* rises. *He shapes the* dough. *He puts the* dough *in the* oven.

Advanced/Advanced High Have partners use the images as they explain the steps in the process.

Retell Use the **Retelling Cards** for *Bread Comes to Life*. Help children retell the story as you display the cards. Model using sequence words, such as *first, next, then,* and *last,* for children to use in retelling.

LESSON 4

Paired Selection: "Nature Artists"

Pages 32–36 Read and then paraphrase the text/captions as you point to the corresponding images, for example, page 33: Point to the actions and designs as you read about them. Then say: *This artist is weaving, or making, a basket.*

 Tell about what an artist is making. Talk to a partner.

Beginning Help partners choose an artist and identify items and actions they see on the page.

Intermediate Have partners use the images to describe what the artist is doing. Supply sentence frames and vocabulary appropriate to the page.

Advanced/Advanced High Have partners tell something about what each artist is making. Model examples and supply vocabulary as needed.

FORMATIVE ASSESSMENT

⊘ STUDENT CHECK-IN

Main Selection Have partners retell the process for making bread.

Paired Selection Have partners describe what the artists make. Then have children reflect using the Check-In routine.

Independent Time

Draw and Write Have children talk about what was made in *Bread Comes to Life* and "Nature Artists." Then have them draw and write a label or a caption for something they would like to make from nature. Have them use a word from the text. *I want to make _____.* Have children share their ideas and provide more sentence frames as needed. Help children complete the frames. Challenge children to write a longer caption telling why they want to make the item.

LESSON 3

LEARNING GOALS

We can listen actively to learn about why natural resources are important.

OBJECTIVES

With prompting and support, ask and answer questions about key details in a text.

Recognize common types of texts (e.g., storybooks, poems).

With prompting and support, describe the relationship between illustrations and the story in which they appear.

Confirm understanding of a text read aloud or information presented orally or through other media by asking and answering questions about key details and requesting clarification if something is not understood.

LANGUAGE OBJECTIVES

Children will discuss how an art fair works, using verbs that end with -ing and key vocabulary

ELA ACADEMIC LANGUAGE

• play, characters, narrator
• Cognate: narrador

MATERIALS

Interactive Read Aloud, "Nature's Art Fair"

Visual Vocabulary Cards

DIGITAL TOOLS

Have children listen to the selection as they follow along to develop comprehension.

Use the vocabulary activity for additional support.

"Nature's Art Fair"

Prepare to Read

Build Background Show a photo of actors on stage in a play. Tell children that "Nature's Art Fair" is a play. Remind children of plays they have read or have seen. Like a story, plays have different characters, or people in the story. Actors play the parts of the characters. Some plays have narrators. The narrator helps tell what is happening. Show Card 1. *This is a nature art fair. Have you ever been to an art fair? What do you think you can buy there?*

Focus on Vocabulary Use the **Visual Vocabulary Cards** to review the oral vocabulary words: *designs, weave, knowledge, create,* and *natural resources.* As you read, use gestures and other visual support to clarify important story words, for example: *wool, gourd,* and *paperweight.*

Summarize the Text Show the cards and as you summarize the play: *This play is about a family that goes to a nature art fair. At a nature art fair, the art is made from things in nature. The family learns how this art is made.*

Read the Text

Use the Interactive Question-Response Routine to help children understand the story.

Card 1

Paragraphs 1–5 Read the text. Point to the family. *The characters are Mom, Jen, and Zac.* Point to the booth. *The setting is an art fair.* Point to Zac. *Zac wants to watch an artist painting rocks.* Point to the rock designs. *Jen loves the designs. Mom wants to buy three. What does Zac want to watch?* (an artist painting rocks)

 What does the artist do? Talk to a partner.

Beginning Have partners point to the illustration: *The artist <u>paints</u> rocks.*

Intermediate Have partners ask and answer: *What is the artist painting? The artist is <u>painting rocks</u>. What does the artist paint on the rocks? The artist paints <u>designs</u> on the rocks.*

Advanced/Advanced High Have partners ask and answer: *What is the artist painting? What makes each rock special? Tell about the designs.* (The artist is painting rocks. Each rock has a different design.)

Card 2

Paragraphs 1–3 Read the text. Point to the corresponding images. *Zac sees another booth with two sheep inside a pen. The artist is using wool from one*

Interactive Read Aloud

sheep to weave a rug. The artist weaves on a loom, or a weaving machine. Where does wool come from? (sheep)

Paragraphs 4–5 Read the text. *The artist explains that her mother taught her how to weave. She says that one day, or in the future, she will teach her child to weave.* Who will the artist teach one day? (her child)

 How does the artist use the wool? Talk to a partner.

Beginning Help children point to the images and say: *The artist weaves the wool. She is weaving a rug.*

Intermediate Have partners use the images to answer the prompt. Encourage them to use complete sentences. *The artist uses wool from sheep. She uses the wool to weave a rug on a loom.*

Advanced/Advanced High Use guiding questions to help partners give details. Example: *What natural resource does the artist use?* (wool) *Where does it come from? What does she do with it?* (The artist uses wool to weave a rug on a loom.)

Card 3

Paragraphs 1–3 Read the text. Point to the corresponding images. *The family watches a man playing an instrument with strings made from a gourd. Mom says that gourds are fruits, like squash. Pumpkins are squash.* Guide children to point to and name the gourds. *The gourds are dried and used to make things.*

Paragraphs 4–7 Read the text. *Jen and Zac see other things made from gourds. They see bowls, birdhouses, and drums. Jen wants to make a drum from a gourd.* What does Jen want to make? (a drum)

 What can you do with a gourd?

Beginning Have partners point to and name the items made from gourds in the illustration. (instruments, bowls, drums)

Intermediate Have partners ask and answer: *What can you make from a gourd? You can make instruments/bowls/drums from a gourd.*

Card 4

Paragraphs 3–6 Read the text. Point to the corresponding images. *Zac wants to learn how to paint rocks. He wants to make a paperweight for his teacher. A paperweight holds down papers. Jen wants to learn how to make a drum from a gourd. Mom is going to take pictures of the children making things.* What will Mom do? (take pictures)

 What do Zac and Jen want to do? Talk to a partner.

Beginning Help children say: *Zac wants to paint a rock. Jen wants to make a drum/instrument.*

Intermediate Provide sentence frames: *Zac wants to paint a rock to make a paperweight. Jen wants to make a drum from a gourd.*

Advanced/Advanced High Challenge partners to add details as they answer the prompt. Model as needed.

Retell Use the illustrations on the **Interactive Read-Aloud Cards** to retell the story with children. Display the cards and model retelling, using sequence words, as you point to the events and actions on the cards. Then help children take turns retelling one part using the sequence words.

FORMATIVE ASSESSMENT

❯ STUDENT CHECK-IN

Have partners retell how people use different natural resources.

Then have children reflect using the Check-In routine.

 ## Independent Time

Audio Have children listen to the audio recording of their favorite Card in the selection. After they listen multiple times, have them retell the important events to a partner.

OBJECTIVES

With prompting and support, retell key details of a text.

With prompting and support, describe the connection between pieces of information in a text.

Actively engage in group reading activities with purpose and understanding.

Speak audibly and express thoughts, feelings, and ideas clearly.

LANGUAGE OBJECTIVES

Children will inform about breakfast foods, using singular nouns, plural nouns, and key vocabulary.

ELA ACADEMIC LANGUAGE

• *sequence, comprehension*

• Cognates: *secuencia, comprensión*

MATERIALS

ELL Leveled Reader: *What's for Breakfast?*

Online Differentiated Texts, "Seed to Tree"

Online ELL Visual Vocabulary Cards

DIGITAL TOOLS

Have children listen to the selection as they follow along to develop comprehension.

Use the vocabulary activity for additional support.

What's for Breakfast?

Lexile 30L

Prepare to Read

Build Background Show photos of different breakfast foods, including eggs. Help children name the food items. Point to the eggs. *Where do eggs come from? Which animal lays eggs?* Ask about the other foods. Tell children that the foods we eat for breakfast come from plants and animals. Invite children to share what they like to eat for breakfast. Tell children that this book they will read is a nonfiction text about breakfast foods. A nonfiction text gives facts, or information, about a topic.

Focus on Vocabulary Use the routine on the **ELL Visual Vocabulary Cards** to preteach *goods* and *produce*. Use the images and any labels to identify and model the use of key vocabulary in context.

Read the Text

Use the Interactive Question-Response Routine to help children understand the text.

Pages 2–8

Pages 2–3 Point to the images as you discuss them. *Bread is made from wheat. Wheat is a plant. Let's read the labels:* bread, wheat. Point to page 3. *Jam is made from fruit, like strawberries. These are strawberry plants. Where does bread come from?* (wheat) *What is wheat?* (a plant)

 Where do bread and jam come from? Talk to a partner.

Beginning Have children point to the photo: Jam/Bread *is from* fruit/wheat.

Intermediate Have partners **reread** pages 2–3 before responding: *Bread comes from* wheat. *You can use* strawberries/fruit *to make jam.*

Advanced/Advanced High Point to the wheat. *What is this?* (wheat) *What can you make from wheat?* (bread) Page 3: *What are these plants? What can you make from fruit?* (These plants are strawberries. You can make jam from fruit.)

Pages 4–5 Point to the images as you discuss them. Page 4: *Milk comes from cows. Raise your hand if you like milk. Where does milk come from?* (cows) Page 5: *Butter is made from milk. Let's read the labels:* milk, cow, butter. *What can you do with milk?* (make butter)

 Tell what you learned on these two pages. Talk to a partner.

Beginning Have partners point to the appropriate images as they respond. <u>Milk</u> *comes from cows.* <u>Butter</u> *comes from milk.*

Intermediate Provide a sentence frame: <u>Milk/Butter</u> *comes from* <u>cows/milk.</u>

Advanced/Advanced High Encourage partners to also talk about what you do with these foods. (*Milk comes from cows. You drink milk. Butter comes from milk. You put butter on bread.*)

Pages 6–8 Point to page 6. *Oranges grow in an orange* <u>grove</u>. Page 7: *Hens lay* <u>eggs</u>. *Let's read the labels: hens, eggs.* Page 8: *Look at the breakfast foods. Which do you prefer to eat in the morning?*

 Where does all food come from? Give some examples. Talk to a partner.

Beginning Have children point to the photos: *All food comes from plants and* <u>animals</u>. <u>Bread/Eggs</u> *come(s) from* <u>wheat/hens</u>.

Intermediate Have partners ask and answer: *Where does/do* <u>orange juice/eggs</u> *come from?* <u>Orange juice/Eggs</u> *come(s) from* <u>oranges/hens</u>.

Details: Time and Order Have children discuss the sequence to make orange juice. *First, you plant orange* <u>trees</u> *and let them* <u>grow</u>. *Next, you can* <u>pick</u> *the oranges. Finally, you can make orange* <u>juice</u>.

Retell Have partners retell the story. Have them take turns pointing to a picture and describing it to each other.

Focus on Fluency

Read pages 2–8 with appropriate tone and expression Then read the passage aloud and have children echo read. For additional practice, have children record themselves reading the same passage a few times, and then select their favorite recording to play for you.

Build Knowledge: Make Connections

Talk About the Text Have partners discuss things that come from nature.

Write About the Text Have children add their ideas to their Build Knowledge page of their reader's notebook.

Self-Selected Reading

Help children choose an informational text from the online **Leveled Reader Library,** or read the **Differentiated Text,** "Seed to Tree."

LITERACY ACTIVITIES

Have children complete the Literacy Activities on the inside back cover of the book.

FORMATIVE ASSESSMENT

❯ STUDENT CHECK-IN

Have partners retell where different breakfast foods come from. Then have children reflect using the Check-In routine.

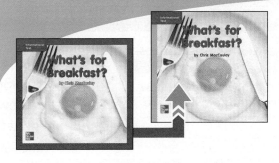

IF children can read *What's for Breakfast?* **ELL Level** with fluency and correctly answer the Literacy Activity questions,

THEN tell children that they will read a more detailed version of the story.

HAVE children page through *What's for Breakfast?* On Level and describe each picture in simple language.

• Have children read the selection, checking their comprehension and providing assistance as necessary.

MODELED WRITING

LEARNING GOALS

We can write about what we enjoy eating on bread.

OBJECTIVES

Use dictating and writing to compose informative texts in which they supply some information about the topic.

LANGUAGE OBJECTIVES

Children will inform by writing a sentence using the verb *bake.*

ELA ACADEMIC LANGUAGE

• *sentence*

 Writing Practice Display the bread on pp. 4-5 of the **Literature Big Book,** and choral read the sample sentence on p. 74 of the **Reading/Writing Companion.** Guide children to analyze the sentence using the Actor/Action routine: *Who is the actor?* (I) *What is the action?* (mix flour, eggs, and milk together) Then read the prompt on p. 75, and have children answer it as a group. Write the sentences on the board and have children choral read. Then ask children to write their own sentences.

 Beginning Provide a sentence frame: I will write about baking a cake. Then help partners think of their sentence using the Actor/Action routine. Encourage children to add details to their sentences.

Intermediate Have partners take turns asking and answering *who/what* questions to create their sentences. Provide a sentence frame if needed.

Advanced/Advanced High Challenge children to talk about their sentences using the Actor/Action routine and share them with the group.

FORMATIVE ASSESSMENT ❯ **STUDENT CHECK IN** Partners share their sentences. Ask children to reflect using the Check-In routine.

INTERACTIVE WRITING

LEARNING GOALS

We can write about how the blades of wheat are different.

OBJECTIVES

With guidance and support, respond to questions and suggestions from peers.

LANGUAGE OBJECTIVES

Children will inform by writing sentences using the words *this* and *that.*

ELA ACADEMIC LANGUAGE

• *text, photograph*
• Cognates: *texto, fotografía*

 Write a Response: Share the Pen Choral read the sample sentences on p. T186 of the **Teacher's Edition.** Use the Actor/Description routine to review the first sentence: *What is the subject?* (the first blade of wheat) *What can we say about it?* (It is green and growing.) Remind children of the writing trait: *When we write, we focus on one topic. What topic are these sentences about?* The topic is how the wheat is different. Then help children complete the sentence frames at the bottom of p. T186.

 Beginning Help children generate ideas for how the wheat looks and create a word bank. Encourage children to use the word bank to complete the sentence frames: This blade of wheat is green. That blade of wheat is gold.

Intermediate Have partners ask and answer questions about the wheat in the photographs before completing the sentence frames.

Advanced/Advanced High Challenge children to think of their own sentences about the blades of wheat, adding details from the photographs.

FORMATIVE ASSESSMENT ❯ **STUDENT CHECK IN** Partners share their sentences. Ask children to reflect using the Check-In routine.

INDEShortPENDENT WRITING

INDEPENDENT WRITING

LESSONS 3-4

LEARNING GOALS

We can write about the texts we read.

OBJECTIVES

Use drawing and writing to compose informative texts in which they supply some information about the topic.

LANGUAGE OBJECTIVES

Children will retell a selection and then write to contrast two houses.

ELA ACADEMIC LANGUAGE

- *compare, photographs*
- Cognates: *comparar, fotografías*

Find Text Evidence Use the Independent Writing routine. Ask questions to help children orally retell the shared read, such as: *Whom is the first home for?* (people) *Can pets have special homes?* (yes) Then read the prompt on p. 90 of the **Reading/Writing Companion:** *How is the house on page 82 different from the house on page 86?* Display p. 82 of the text. *What animal is this home for?* (a dog) Then display p. 86. *Whom is this home for?* (people)

Write a Response Write the sentence starters at the bottom of p. 196 of the **Teacher's Edition** on the board, and read them. Model completing the first sentence frame, and have children choral read the response. Repeat with the second frames. Then ask children to copy the sentences into p. 91 of the Reading/Writing Companion.

Beginning Provide a sentence frame to help children talk about how each sentence focuses on one topic: I wrote about the houses.

Intermediate Encourage children to use adjectives to describe the different homes and then help them check this item off the writing checklist.

Advanced/Advanced High Read the writing checklist with children and have them identify where they used each item in their writing.

FORMATIVE ASSESSMENT ❯ **STUDENT CHECK IN** Partners share their sentences. Ask children to reflect using the Check-In routine.

SELF-SELECTED WRITING

LESSON 5

LEARNING GOALS

We can revise our writing.

OBJECTIVES

Demonstrate command of the conventions of standard English grammar and usage when writing.

LANGUAGE OBJECTIVES

Children will inquire about their writing by checking for adjectives.

ELA ACADEMIC LANGUAGE

- *adjective*
- Cognate: *adjetivo*

Work with children to revise the group writing activity. Point to each word as you read the sentences. Stop to ask questions, such as, *Can we add an adjective to this sentences?* Then have partners work to revise their own sentences before they publish them.

For support with grammar and adjectives, refer to the **Language Transfers Handbook** and **Language Development Cards** 10A–11B.

FORMATIVE ASSESSMENT ❯ **STUDENT CHECK IN** Partners tell what revisions they made. Ask children to reflect using the Check-In routine.

Summative Assessment
Get Ready for Unit Assessment

Unit 9 Tested Skills

LISTENING AND READING COMPREHENSION	VOCABULARY	GRAMMAR	SPEAKING AND WRITING
• Listening Actively • Details • Character, Setting, Plot	• Words and Categories	• Adjectives	• Offering Opinions • Presenting • Composing/Writing • Retelling/Recounting

Create a Student Profile

Record data from the following resources in the Student Profile charts on pages 136–137 of the Assessment book.

COLLABORATIVE	INTERPRETIVE	PRODUCTIVE

• Collaborative Conversations Rubrics
  • Listening
  • Speaking
	• Leveled Unit Assessment
	  • Listening Comprehension
	  • Reading Comprehension
	  • Vocabulary
	  • Grammar
	• Presentation Rubric
	  • Listening
	• *Wonders* Unit Assessment
		• Weekly Progress Monitoring
		• Leveled Unit Assessment
		  • Speaking
		  • Writing
		• Presentation Rubric
		  • Speaking
		• Write to Sources Rubric
		• *Wonders* Unit Assessment

The Foundational Skills Kit, Language Development Kit, and Adaptive Learning provide additional student data for progress monitoring.

Level Up

Use the following chart, along with your Student Profiles, to guide your Level Up decisions.

LEVEL UP	If **BEGINNING** level students are able to do the following, they may be ready to move to the **INTERMEDIATE** level:	If **INTERMEDIATE** level students are able to do the following, they may be ready to move to the **ADVANCED** level:	If **ADVANCED** level students are able to do the following, they may be ready to move to **ON** level:
COLLABORATIVE	• participate in collaborative conversations using basic vocabulary and grammar and simple phrases or sentences • discuss simple pictorial or text prompts	• participate in collaborative conversations using appropriate words and phrases and complete sentences • use limited academic vocabulary across and within disciplines	• participate in collaborative conversations using more sophisticated vocabulary and correct grammar • communicate effectively across a wide range of language demands in social and academic contexts
INTERPRETIVE	• identify details in simple read alouds • understand common vocabulary and idioms and interpret language related to familiar social, school, and academic topics • make simple inferences and make simple comparisons • exhibit an emerging receptive control of lexical, syntactic, phonological, and discourse features	• identify main ideas and/or make some inferences from simple read alouds • use context clues to identify word meanings and interpret basic vocabulary and idioms • compare, contrast, summarize, and relate text to graphic organizers • exhibit a limited range of receptive control of lexical, syntactic, phonological, and discourse features when addressing new or familiar topics	• determine main ideas in read alouds that have advanced vocabulary • use context clues to determine meaning, understand multiple-meaning words, and recognize synonyms of social and academic vocabulary • analyze information, make sophisticated inferences, and explain their reasoning • command a high degree of receptive control of lexical, syntactic, phonological, and discourse features
PRODUCTIVE	• express ideas and opinions with basic vocabulary and grammar and simple phrases or sentences • restate information or retell a story using basic vocabulary • exhibit an emerging productive control of lexical, syntactic, phonological, and discourse features	• produce coherent language with limited elaboration or detail • restate information or retell a story using mostly accurate, although limited, vocabulary • exhibit a limited range of productive control of lexical, syntactic, phonological, and discourse features when addressing new or familiar topics	• produce sentences with more sophisticated vocabulary and correct grammar • restate information or retell a story using extensive and accurate vocabulary and grammar • tailor language to a particular purpose and audience • command a high degree of productive control of lexical, syntactic, phonological, and discourse features

LEARNING GOALS

We can understand important ideas and details in a story.

We can tell what makes an opinion text.

OBJECTIVES

With prompting and support, retell familiar stories, including key details.

With prompting and support, compare and contrast the adventures and experiences of characters in familiar stories.

With prompting and support, identify basic similarities in and differences between two texts on the same topic.

Continue a conversation through multiple exchanges.

LANGUAGE OBJECTIVES

Children will discuss how the characters solve a problem, using verbs, nouns, and key vocabulary.

ELA ACADEMIC LANGUAGE

• *fantasy, problem, solve*

• Cognates: *fantasía, problema*

MATERIALS

Literature Big Book, *What's the Big Idea, Molly?*, pp. 4–40 and 41–44

Visual Vocabulary Cards

DIGITAL TOOLS

Have children listen to the selection as they follow along to develop comprehension.

Use the vocabulary activity for additional support.

What's the Big Idea, Molly?

Prepare to Read

Build Background Show the cover and read the title. *An idea is a thought. We have ideas or thoughts all the time.* Provide examples, such as: *When we make a plan, we use ideas.* Describe with children what the mouse on the cover is doing. Help them respond using: *The mouse is ___.* Elicit that the mouse is looking for ideas. *We are going to read a fantasy story about animals with different ideas.* Provide an example of how people get ideas: *I get ideas when I take a walk.* Have children describe what they do to get ideas, using: *I get ideas when I ___.*

Focus on Vocabulary Use the **Visual Vocabulary Cards** to review the oral vocabulary words *decide* and *opinion.* As you read, use visual support to clarify story words, such as *idea, gift, draw, working together, season,* and *love.*

Summarize the Text Before reading, give a short summary of the story. *Molly and her friends need ideas for a birthday gift for their friend, Turtle.*

Read the Text

Use the Interactive Question-Response Routine to help children understand the story.

Pages 4–19

Pages 6–9 Read the text. *Tomorrow is Turtle's birthday. Molly and her friends need to come up with, or think of, an idea for a gift., but all the friends have the same idea. This is a problem. They all want to draw a picture of a flower. What is the problem?* (All the friends want to draw a flower.)

Pages 12–19 Read the text. *Molly and her friends think of a new idea. Molly sat down to think of an idea. Rabbit ran to think of an idea. Frog swam, Goose fished, and Pig slept to think of an idea. What did the friends do to think of an idea?* (Molly sat, Rabbit ran, Frog swam, Goose fished, Pig slept)

 What problem do Molly and her friends have? Talk to a partner.

Beginning Display pages 8-9 and help children respond: *The friends have a* problem. *All the friends want to draw a* flower.

Intermediate Have partners respond, using: *The friends have a* problem. *They have the* same *idea. All the friends want to* draw *a* flower.

Advanced/Advanced High Have partners add details of what one friend did: *The friends have a* problem. *They have the* same *idea to* draw *a* flower. *Frog* swam *to think up a* new *idea.*

Literature Big Book

Pages 20–29

Pages 20–26 Read the text. *Everyone had the same idea again! They all drew a picture of a tree. They still have a problem. Then Molly gets a new idea and all her friends love Molly's new idea. At first, did the friends solve the problem?* (no) *Why?* (The friends all had the same idea.)

 At first, did Molly and her friends solve the problem? Talk to a partner.

Beginning Display the illustration on page 24, and help children respond: *At first, the friends did <u>not</u> solve the problem. All the friends had the <u>same</u> idea again.*

Intermediate Have partners respond, using: *At first, the friends <u>did not solve</u> the problem. All the friends had <u>the same</u> idea again. All the friends drew <u>a tree</u>.*

Advanced/Advanced High Help partners respond: *At first, the friends <u>did not solve the problem</u>. All the friends had <u>the same idea again</u>. They <u>drew</u> <u>a tree</u>.*

Pages 30–40

Pages 32–37 Read the text. *The friends made a book for Turtle. Rabbit, Goose, Frog, and Pig drew a tree in the summer, autumn, winter, and spring. Molly wrote a poem for each season. Turtle loved the book. Molly and her friends solved their problem. What did Turtle say about his gift?* (He loves the book.)

 Was the book a good idea for a gift? Did the friends solve their problem? Talk to a partner.

Beginning Help partners answer these questions: *Does Turtle love the book? <u>Yes</u>, Turtle <u>loves</u> the book. Did the friends solve the problem? <u>Yes</u>, the friends solved the <u>problem</u>.*

Intermediate Have partners respond, using: *The book was a <u>good</u> idea because Turtle <u>loves</u> it. The friends <u>solved</u> the <u>problem</u>.*

Advanced/Advanced High Have partners describe details about the gift: *The book was a <u>good</u> idea because the friends <u>solved</u> the <u>problem</u>. Rabbit, Goose, Frog, and Pig <u>drew</u> trees, and Molly <u>wrote</u> poems.*

Retell Use the **Retelling Cards** for *What's the Big Idea, Molly?* to retell the story with children. Display the cards and model retelling, using sequence words. Then help children take turns retelling.

LESSON 4 **Paired Selection: "Better Together"**

Pages 41–44 Read the text. *The people work together to build a house for other people who don't have a home. These are players on a soccer team. They work together to win. The children work together to solve problems. The swimmers are performing in the Olympics. How can they perform well?*

 Why do the groups of people work together? Talk to a partner.

Beginning Help children point to the corresponding photo as they respond about one group, for example: *The children solve a <u>problem</u> together.*

Intermediate Help partners use photos to respond, for example: *These people <u>build a house</u> together. These swimmers <u>work</u> together to perform <u>well</u>.*

Advanced/Advanced High Have partners retell what each group does: *The [players/students/swimmers] work together to <u>[win/solve a problem/perform well]</u>.*

FORMATIVE ASSESSMENT

▶ STUDENT CHECK-IN

Main Selection Have partners retell how the characters worked together.

Paired Selection Have partners describe how the different teams can work together.

Then have children reflect using the Check-In routine.

Independent Time

Oral Language Have children compare *What's the Big Idea, Molly?* and "Better Together." Ask: *How do the characters and groups of people solve problems?* Help children respond, using: *They all ____ to solve problems.*

LEARNING GOALS

We can listen actively to learn about working together.

OBJECTIVES

Recognize common types of texts (e.g., storybooks, poems).

With prompting and support, describe the relationship between illustrations and the story in which they appear.

Actively engage in group reading activities with purpose and understanding.

Confirm understanding of a text read aloud or information presented orally or through other media by asking and answering questions about key details and requesting clarification if something is not understood.

LANGUAGE OBJECTIVES

Children will discuss how the characters help each other, using key vocabulary and complete sentences.

ELA ACADEMIC LANGUAGE

• *fairy tale, characters*

MATERIALS

Interactive Read Aloud, "The Elves and the Shoemakers"

Visual Vocabulary Cards

DIGITAL TOOLS

Have children listen to the selection as they follow along to develop comprehension.

Use the vocabulary activity for additional support.

"The Elves and the Shoemakers"

Prepare to Read

Interactive Read Aloud

Build Background Display Cards 1 and 3. Read the title. Tell children that the story "The Elves and the Shoemakers" is a fairy tale that has been told for a very long time. Point to the shoemakers on Card 1. *A shoemaker is someone who makes shoes.* Point to the elves on Card 3. Explain that elves are not real but made-up and that fairy tales have characters that are not real. Describe with children characters from other fairy tales that they know that are not real, such as Pinocchio or Tom Thumb. Help them describe, using: *The character has ___. The character can ___.*

Focus on Vocabulary Use the **Visual Vocabulary Cards** to review the oral vocabulary words: *decide, marvel, opinion, grateful,* and *ragged.* As you read, use gestures and other visual support to clarify important story words, for example: *poor, buy, leather, shoes, neighbors, elves,* and *clothes.*

Summarize the Text *This story is about two shoemakers who get help from elves who make shoes.*

Read the Text

Use the Interactive Question-Response Routine to help children understand the story.

Card 1

Paragraphs 1–5 Read the text. Point to the illustration as you describe. *The man and his wife were shoemakers. They made and repaired shoes. They were honest, hardworking, but poor. One day, the shoemakers only had a few pieces of leather. They did not have money to buy food or supplies. The shoemakers left the leather pieces on the table and went to bed hungry. What did the shoemakers do?* (made and repaired shoes) *Did they have money to buy supplies or food?* (no)

 What is the shoemakers' problem? Talk to a partner.

Beginning Have partners point to the illustration and help them complete this sentence: *The shoemakers cannot* <u>buy</u> *supplies or* <u>food</u>.

Intermediate Have partners respond, using: *The problem is the shoemakers do not have* <u>money</u> *to buy supplies or food.*

Advanced/Advanced High Help partners explain the problem: *The shoemakers' problem is that they* <u>have no money</u> *to buy* <u>supplies</u> *or food.*

Card 2

Paragraphs 1–6 Read the text. Point to the illustration as you describe: *The next morning, the shoemakers found a perfect pair of shoes. They did not know who had made the shoes. A king's man bought the shoes. Then the shoemakers bought food and leather. They left pieces of leather and went to sleep. What did the shoemakers find in the morning?* (a pair of shoes) *Who bought the shoes?* (the king's man) *What did the shoemakers buy?* (food and more leather)

 What happened to the pair of shoes? Talk to a partner.

Beginning Help partners point to the illustration and respond, using: *A man bought the shoes.*

Intermediate Guide children to answer and tell how it affected the shoemakers: *A man bought the shoes. The shoemakers had money to buy supplies and food.*

Advanced/Advanced High Help partners respond: *A man bought the shoes. The shoemakers had money to have a celebration and buy supplies and food.*

Card 3

Paragraphs 1–9 Read the text. Point to the illustration as you describe: *While the shoemakers slept, two elves made shoes and left. Two ladies saw the shoes and bought them. The shoemakers wondered, or wanted to know, who was making the shoes. That night, they stayed up and watched their shop. Who made the shoes?* (two elves) *What happened to the shoes?* (Two ladies bought them.) *What did the shoemakers want to do?* (find out who was making the shoes)

 How did the elves help the shoemakers? Talk to a partner

Beginning Help partners complete sentences: *The elves made shoes. Two ladies bought the shoes. The shoemakers had money.*

Intermediate Have partners respond: *The elves made two pairs of shoes. People bought the shoes. Then the shoemakers had money to buy many things.*

Advanced/Advanced High Have partners include time words: *At night, the elves made the shoes. The next morning, two ladies bought the shoes. Then the shoemakers used money to buy supplies and food.*

Card 4

Paragraphs 1–5 Point to the images as you describe the events on the page. *What did the shoemakers do for the elves?* (made clothes and left a note)

 What do the shoemakers do for the elves? Talk to a partner.

Beginning Help partners point and respond: *The wife made clothes. The shoemakers wrote a note.*

Intermediate Help partners respond with one long sentence: *The wife made new clothes, and the shoemakers wrote a thank-you note.*

Advanced/Advanced High Have partners respond in their own words. (Example: The wife saw their raggedy clothes and made new clothes.)

Retell Use the illustrations on the **Interactive Read-Aloud Cards** to retell the story with children. Display the cards and model retelling using sequence words, as you point to the events and actions on the cards. Then help children take turns retelling one part, using the sequence words.

FORMATIVE ASSESSMENT

❯ **STUDENT CHECK-IN**

Have partners retell how the characters help each other.

Then have children reflect using the Check-In routine.

 Independent Time

Ask Questions Have partners practice asking *wh*-questions using the illustrations on the **Interactive Read-Aloud Cards**. Have partners take turns asking and answering questions. Provide examples and sentence frames to help them: *Who do you see? Where are they? What are they doing? I see _____.*

We can make and confirm predictions to understand the story.

OBJECTIVES

With prompting and support, retell familiar stories, including key details.

With prompting and support, identify characters, settings, and major events in a story.

Recognize common types of texts (e.g., storybooks, poems).

Continue a conversation through multiple exchanges.

LANGUAGE OBJECTIVES

Children will narrate the characters' plans, using verbs, nouns, and key vocabulary.

ELA ACADEMIC LANGUAGE

• *characters, confirm*

• Cognates: *confirmar*

MATERIALS

ELL Leveled Reader: *We Want Honey*

Online Differentiated Texts, "Good Work!"

Online ELL Visual Vocabulary Cards

DIGITAL TOOLS

Have children listen to the selection as they follow along to develop comprehension.

Use the vocabulary activity for additional support.

We Want Honey

Prepare to Read

Build Background Display the cover and use the image to help children discuss what they know about bears and honey. *The title of this book is We Want Honey. Who wants honey? Who makes honey?* Help them describe, using: *I know that bears/bees ___.* Tell children that this story is a fantasy with animal characters. *In some fantasies, the characters do things that they cannot do in real life. What are bears doing in the picture that they cannot do in real life?* Help children respond.

Lexile 90L

Focus on Vocabulary Use the routine on the **ELL Visual Vocabulary Cards** to preteach *plot* and *polite*. Use the images and any labels to identify and model the use of key vocabulary in context.

Read the Text

Use the Interactive Question-Response Routine to help children understand the story.

Pages 2–8

Pages 2–3 Read the text and labels. *The bears want honey. The bears watch the beehive. Bears have a plan, or an idea, to get the honey. Where do bees live?* (in a beehive) *What do the bees do?* (chase away the bears)

 What do the bears do? Talk to a partner.

Beginning Have children point to the illustrations as they respond. *The bears want honey. The bears have a plan. It is not a good plan.*

Intermediate Help partners describe what happens: *The bears surprise the bees. It is not a good plan. The bees chase the bears.*

Events: Sequence Have partners discuss the sequence on pages 2–3. First, the bears watch the bees. Then, they make a plan. Next, they try to get the honey. Finally, the bees chase away the bears.

Pages 4–5 Read the text and the labels. *June Bear has a plan. The bears wear bee costumes. They surprise the bees. But it is not a good plan. The bees chase the bears away. What do the bears wear?* (They wear bee costumes.)

 What is the bears' new plan? Is it a good plan? Talk to a partner.

Beginning Have partners point to the illustration. *The bears wear bee* costumes. *It is* not *a good* plan. *The bees* chase away *the bears.*

Intermediate Have partners respond: *The bears wear bee* costumes. *It is* not *a good* plan. *The bees* chase away the bears. *The bears* do not *get* honey.

Pages 6–8 Read pages 6–7. *Baby Bear has a plan! Let's **make a prediction**. Will this be a good plan?* Read page 8. *The bears ask bees nicely for honey. The bees give the bears honey. The bears say, "Thank you!" It is a good plan. What do the bears do?* (ask bees for honey) *What do the bees do?* (give honey to the bears)

 ***Confirm your prediction**. Was it correct? What is a good plan?*

Beginning Have children point to the illustrations as they respond. *The bears* ask *the bees for honey. The bees* give *the bears* honey.

Intermediate Have partners tell the events in sequence: *The bears* ask *the bees for honey. The bees* give *the bears* honey. *The bears say,* "Thank you!"

Advanced/Advanced High Guide partners to elaborate: *The bears* ask nicely *for some* honey. *The* bees *give the bears* some honey. *The bears are* happy *and say,* "Thank you!"

Retell Have partners retell the story. Have them take turns pointing to a picture and describing it to each other.

Focus on Fluency

Read pages 2–8 with appropriate expression. Then read the text aloud and have children echo read. For additional practice, have children record themselves reading the same text a few times and then select their favorite recording to play for you.

Build Knowledge: Make Connections

Talk About the Text Have partners discuss a time when they worked together.

Write About the Text Have children add their ideas to their Build Knowledge page of their reader's notebook.

Self-Selected Reading

Help children choose an animal fantasy story from the online **Leveled Reader Library,** or read the **Differentiated Text,** "Good Work!"

LITERACY ACTIVITIES

Have children complete the Literacy Activities on the inside back cover of the book.

FORMATIVE ASSESSMENT

❯ STUDENT CHECK-IN

Have partners retell the characters' different plans. Then have children reflect using the Check-In routine.

LEVEL UP

IF children can read *We Want Honey* ELL Level with fluency and correctly answer the Literacy Activity questions,

THEN tell children that they will read a more detailed version of the story.

HAVE children page through *We Want Honey* On Level and describe each picture in simple language.

• Have children read the selection, checking their comprehension and providing assistance as necessary.

MODELED WRITING

LEARNING GOALS

We can write about the best present we ever received.

OBJECTIVES

Use a combination of drawing, dictating, and writing to narrate several loosely linked events.

LANGUAGE OBJECTIVES

Children will narrate by writing a sentence going from left to right on the page.

ELA ACADEMIC LANGUAGE

• *sentence*

 Writing Practice Display pp. 28–29 of the **Big Book** and then read the sample sentences on p. 14 of the **Reading/Writing Companion.** Guide children to analyze the first sentence using the Actor/Action routine: *Who is the actor?* (My uncle) *What is the action?* (helped) *Who?* (me) *To do what?* (work on a puzzle) Then read the prompt on p. 15, and have a volunteer answer it. Write the sentences on the board and have children choral read them. Then ask children to write their own sentences.

 Beginning Provide a sentence frame: I will write about <u>building a tower.</u> *Who is the actor?* (My friend and I) *What is the action?* (built a tower) *What can you say about it?* (It was tall.)

Intermediate Have partners take turns asking and answering *who/what* questions about a time they worked with a friend.

Advanced/Advanced High Challenge partners to add descriptive words to make their writing interesting.

FORMATIVE ASSESSMENT ❯ ➊ **STUDENT CHECK IN** Partners share their sentences. Ask children to reflect using the Check-In routine.

INTERACTIVE WRITING

LEARNING GOALS

We can write about what we think is a good birthday gift for Turtle.

OBJECTIVES

With guidance and support, respond to questions and suggestions from peers.

LANGUAGE OBJECTIVES

Children will argue by writing a sentence using the verb *would.*

ELA ACADEMIC LANGUAGE

• *text, detail*

• Cognates: *texto, detalle*

 Write a Response: Share the Pen Choral read the first sample sentence on p. T272 of the **Teacher's Edition.** Analyze the sentence using the Actor/Action routine: *Who is the actor?* (I) *What is the action?* (would get Turtle a red hat) Remind children of the writing trait: *We use descriptive words to make our writing more interesting. What word describes the hat?* (red) Then help children complete the sentence frames at the bottom of p. T272.

 Beginning Show a visual of Turtle from p. 31 of the **Big Book.** Ask guiding questions to help children think of ideas of good gifts for Turtle.

Intermediate Have partners ask and answer questions about gift ideas for Turtle using the illustrations in the book.

Advanced/Advanced High Challenge children to think of their own sentences to tell what they would get Turtle. Encourage them to include describing words.

FORMATIVE ASSESSMENT ❯ ➊ **STUDENT CHECK IN** Partners share their sentences. Ask children to reflect using the Check-In routine.

INDEPENDENT WRITING

LEARNING GOALS

We can write about the texts we read.

OBJECTIVES

Use a combination of drawing and writing to compose informative texts in which they supply some information about the topic.

LANGUAGE OBJECTIVES

Children will inform by writing a sentence using a pronoun.

ELA ACADEMIC LANGUAGE

- *pronoun*
- Cognate: *pronombre*

Find Text Evidence Use the Independent Writing routine. Ask questions to help children orally retell the shared read, such as: *What do the children do for Luke?* (set up a date for a party) *What do the children do to get ready?* (decorate, bake a cake) Then read the prompt on p. 30 of the **Reading/Writing Companion:** *What kind of party would you like to go to? What type of party do they have for Luke?* (a birthday party) *Let's think about what type of party we could go to.*

Write a Response Write the sentence frames from p. T282 on the board, and read them. Model completing the first frame, and have children choral read the response. Repeat with the second frame. Then ask children to copy the sentences into p. 31 of the Reading/Writing Companion.

Beginning Have partners take turns reading their sentences to each other. Provide a sentence frame: I turned <u>lines</u> when I wrote.

Intermediate Encourage children to use pronouns and then help them check this item off the writing checklist.

Advanced/Advanced High Read the writing checklist with children and have them identify where they used each item in their writing.

FORMATIVE ASSESSMENT ❯ **STUDENT CHECK IN** Partners share their sentences. Ask children to reflect using the Check-In routine.

SELF-SELECTED WRITING

LEARNING GOALS

We can revise our writing.

OBJECTIVES

Demonstrate command of the conventions of standard English grammar and usage when writing.

LANGUAGE OBJECTIVES

Children will inquire about their writing by their pronouns.

ELA ACADEMIC LANGUAGE

- *pronoun*
- Cognate: *pronombre*

Work with children to revise the group writing activity. Point to each word as you read the sentences. Stop to ask questions, such as, *Is this pronoun used correctly?* If needed, write a sentence using a pronoun incorrectly, and work together to revise the sentence. Then, have partners work to revise their own sentences before they publish them.

For support with grammar and subjective pronouns, refer to the **Language Transfers Handbook** and **Language Development Card** 16B.

FORMATIVE ASSESSMENT ❯ **STUDENT CHECK IN** Partners tell what revisions they made. Ask children to reflect using the Check-In Routine.

LESSONS 1-2

LEARNING GOALS

We can understand important ideas and details in a poem.

We can tell what makes an opinion text.

OBJECTIVES

With prompting and support, retell familiar stories, including key details.

Recognize common types of texts (e.g., storybooks, poems).

Actively engage in group reading activities with purpose and understanding.

Describe familiar people, places, things, and events and, with prompting and support, provide additional detail.

LANGUAGE OBJECTIVES

Children will discuss different kinds of family groups, using words for comparing, such as *all, similar,* and *same.*

ELA ACADEMIC LANGUAGE

• *poem, rhyme*

• Cognates: *poema, rima*

MATERIALS

Literature Big Book, *All Kinds of Families!,* pp. 4–33 and 34–36

Visual Vocabulary Cards

DIGITAL TOOLS

Have children listen to the selection as they follow along to develop comprehension.

Use the vocabulary activity for additional support.

All Kinds of Families!

Prepare to Read

Build Background Show the cover and read the title. Explain that it is about different kinds of families. Discuss what families are made of and have volunteers describe their own family. Help them describe, using: *In my family, I have ___.* Discuss with children the image on the cover to elicit words, such as *mother, father, daughter,* and *son.* Point out the groups of objects on the cover. *Families can also be groups of things that are alike, or similar. What similar things do you see?* Help children discuss, using: *I see ___. They are alike/different.*

Literature Big Book

Focus on Vocabulary Use the **Visual Vocabulary Cards** to review the oral vocabulary words *sort* and *similar.* As you read, use visual support to clarify important story words, such as *born, snowmen, appear, arrive,* and *grow.*

Summarize the Text *Families come in all shapes and sizes. Let's read this poem about different kinds of families.*

Read the Text

Use the Interactive Question-Response Routine to help children understand the story.

Pages 4–15

Pages 8–11 Read the text. Point to page 8. *When you are born, you are part of a family. Your family gets bigger.* Point out the words *son* and *one. Poems can have words that rhyme, or have the same ending sounds. The shoes make a family because they are similar. The ribbons make a family, too, because they are also similar. What other things can make a family?* (rulers, rocks, pencils)

 Have children look at pages 8–11. *What can be a family? Talk to a partner.*

Beginning Help children identify the items in the illustrations. Then have them respond, for example: *The* rocks *can be a family. The* pencils *can be a family, too.*

Intermediate Have partners explain why the groups of things can be a family: *The* marbles *can be a family. All the* marbles *have the same size and* shape.

Advanced/Advanced High Have partners describe why the things can be a family: *The* leaves *can be a family because they* all come from trees.

Pages 16–25

Pages 16–17 Read the text. Point to each family as you describe: *Your hand has a family of fingers. Your foot has a family of toes. What do you have on your hand and foot?* (families of fingers and toes)

Pages 24–25 Read the text. Point to each family as you describe: *You can make a family of numbers because 9, 6, and 2 are kinds of numbers. You can make a family of letters because Y, O, and S are kinds of letters. What are 9, 6, and 2?* (They are similar. They are kinds of numbers.)

 Revisit pages 24–25 with children. *What families do you see? What makes a family?*

Beginning Help children use the illustrations to respond: *I see a family of* numbers/letters. Have partners identify the numbers and the letters.

Intermediate Have partners respond: *I see a family of* numbers. *Nine, six, and* [two] *are* numbers. *I see a family of* letters, *too. Y,* [C], *and* [D] *are* letters.

Advanced/Advanced High Have partners identify what they see in the illustrations and then respond: *The nine,* [seven], *and* [three] *are in a family of* numbers. *The Y,* [C], *and* [E] *are in a family of* letters.

Pages 26–33

Pages 30–33 Read the text. *Everyone in a family comes from other families in the past. You come from a family, and your parents also come from a family. People from families make new families. When you grow up, you will have a new family. Where do people come from?* (families)

 What will happen when you grow up? Talk to a partner.

Beginning Have partners respond, using: *You will have a new* family.

Intermediate Have partners add details: *When I grow up, I will have a* [big] family.

Advanced/Advanced High Have partners describe: *When I* grow *up, I will have a big* family. *We will* have fun.

Retell Use the **Retelling Cards** for *All Kinds of Families* to retell the story with children. Help children retell the story as you display the cards. Model using sequence words for children to use in retelling.

LESSON 4 **Paired Selection: "Good for You"**

Pages 34–36 Read the text. *These food groups are part of a good diet. Fruits and vegetables have vitamins and give you energy. Grains are good for you, too. Bread, cereal, and rice are grains. Eggs, meat, beans, and fish are all protein. They help you build bones and muscles. Milk and yogurt are dairy foods. They have calcium in them. Calcium is good for your bones. What groups of foods did we read about?* (fruits, vegetables, grains, proteins, dairy foods)

 Describe a group of food. Talk to a partner.

Beginning Help partners point to the photos and respond: *One group of food has* fruits *and* vegetables.

Intermediate Have partners describe details: *One group of food has* fruits *and* vegetables. *An* apple *is a kind of fruit. A* carrot *is a kind of* vegetable.

Advanced/Advanced High Have partners describe details: *One group of food has* fruits *and* vegetables. *An* apple *is a* kind *of fruit. A* carrot *is a* kind *of* vegetable.

FORMATIVE ASSESSMENT

STUDENT CHECK-IN

Main Selection Have partners retell different kinds of families from the story.

Paired Selection Have partners describe the different food groups and give examples of each.

Then have children reflect using the Check-In routine.

 Independent Time

Oral Language Have children describe what they read about in *All Kinds of Families!* and "Good for You." Ask: *What families did you learn about in each text?* Have partners discuss what the two stories have in common. Help them respond, using: _____ *can be a family.*

LESSON 3

LEARNING GOALS

We can listen actively to learn about how artists make different paint colors.

OBJECTIVES

With prompting and support, ask and answer questions about key details in a text.

Ask and answer questions to help determine or clarify the meaning of words and phrases in a text.

Ask and answer questions in order to seek help, get information, or clarify something that is not understood.

Actively engage in group reading activities with purpose and understanding.

LANGUAGE OBJECTIVES

Children will inform about what painters do, using verbs and complete sentences.

ELA ACADEMIC LANGUAGE

• *nonfiction, ask, answer*

• Cognate: *no ficción*

MATERIALS

Interactive Read Aloud, "The Perfect Color"

Visual Vocabulary Cards

DIGITAL TOOLS

Have children listen to the selection as they follow along to develop comprehension.

Use the vocabulary activity for additional support.

"The Perfect Color"

Prepare to Read

Build Background Display the photograph on Card 1 to build vocabulary around the topic of painting. *The person is a painter. She paints a picture. It is a painting. She uses a brush. She uses paints.* Ask children to point to and describe details in the photograph, using: *She is ___. She paints a ___. She uses ___.*

Interactive Read Aloud

Focus on Vocabulary Use the **Visual Vocabulary Cards** to review the oral vocabulary words: *perfect, endless, similar, sort,* and *experiment.* As you read, use gestures and other visual support to clarify important selection words, for example: *sunset, invent, mix, primary and secondary colors, shades,* and *creative.*

Summarize the Text Give a brief summary of the selection: *The author teaches us about what painters do with colors. Painters are artists. In this nonfiction text, we learn how a painter can create colors and art that no one has seen before.*

Read the Text

Use the Interactive Question-Response Routine to help children understand the text.

Card 1

Paragraphs 1–3 Read the text. Point to the canvas in the photo. *See the different colors of paint. I see blues and greens. Sometimes painters see or imagine a new color for a picture. They can invent, or create, the color and then use the new color in a painting. Why do painters invent new colors?* (to paint the colors they imagine)

 What can painters invent for a painting? Talk with a partner.

Beginning Help children respond: *Painters can invent* <u>new colors</u>.

Intermediate Provide a sentence frame: *Painters can imagine and* <u>invent new colors</u> *for a painting.*

Advanced/Advanced High Challenge children to talk about why a painter creates new colors. (Painters match the colors they see or imagine. They want to use the colors in a painting.)

Card 2

Paragraphs 1–3 Read the text. Point to the palette, paints, and brush in the photo and review the terms as needed. Explain that you can mix the primary colors and black and white to make other colors. If possible, demonstrate with the following:

Mix yellow and blue paints to make green. Mix yellow and red paints to make orange. *What three colors are the primary colors?* (yellow, blue, red)

Paragraphs 4–5 Read the text. Review the colors of paints in the photo. Display darker and lighter shades of colors. *Do you want to make a color lighter? Add white. Do you want to make a color darker? Add black. How can we make a light blue and dark blue paints?* (Mix blue and white; mix blue and black paints.)

 What happens when you mix two primary colors? Talk with a partner.

Beginning Guide children to respond: *I mix yellow and blue to make* green *paint. I mix yellow and red to make* orange *paint.*

Intermediate Provide sentence frames: *To make green paint, we mix* blue *and* yellow. *To make orange paint, we mix* red *and* yellow.

Advanced/Advanced High Ask partners to describe how to make green, orange, and purple. (Mixing blue and red makes purple.)

Card 3

Paragraph 1 Read the text. Confirm children's understanding that colors have shades. *Artists can sort colors. They may put all the shades of one color, such as red, into a group. How can artists sort their colors?* (They can put the shades of a color in a group.)

Paragraph 2 Read the text. Point to details in the photo as your review the words *easel, canvas, brush,* and *palette. What do artists paint on?* (paper; canvas)

 What tools do artists use? Talk to a partner.

Beginning Have partners point to the photo: *What tool is this? This is a* brush; palette; canvas.

Intermediate Have partners ask and answer: *What tool does the girl use? The girl uses a* brush; paint; a palette; an easel; a canvas.

Advanced/Advanced High Help children explain how the tools are used. (Sample response: She uses her brush to paint the picture on the canvas.)

Card 4

Paragraphs 1–4 Read the text. Point to the photo. *How can you experiment with colors? Try putting different colors together. See what happens. What do you do when you experiment with colors?* (You put different colors together to see what you get.) *You can experiment with tools, too. There are big and small brushes. Use your fingers and hands. What tools can you use to paint?* (brushes, fingers, hands)

 How can you experiment with colors and tools? Talk to a partner.

Beginning Help children complete sentences: *I can mix different* colors. *I can paint with* my brushes.

Intermediate Provide sentence frames: *I can* mix together different colors to invent *new colors. I can use* brushes or my fingers and hands.

Advanced/Advanced High Challenge children to elaborate on how to experiment with colors. (I can use more or less of a paint color. I can use white or black to make a color light or dark.)

Retell Use the illustrations on the **Interactive Read-Aloud Cards** to retell the text with children. Display the cards and model retelling details in the photos and text. Then help partners take turns retelling key details.

FORMATIVE ASSESSMENT

❯ STUDENT CHECK-IN
Have partners discuss tools that artists can use to make paint colors. Then have children reflect using the Check-In routine.

 Independent Time

Oral Language Have children use descriptive words to talk about the photos on the cards. Provide questions and sentence frames: *What do you see? Who do you see? I see _____. He/She/It is _____. They are _____.*

LESSONS
4-5

LEARNING GOALS

We can ask and answer questions
to understand the story.

OBJECTIVES

With prompting and support, ask and
answer questions about key details in
a text.

With prompting and support, identify
characters, settings, and major events
in a story.

Actively engage in group reading
activities with purpose and
understanding.

Describe familiar people, places,
things, and events and, with
prompting and support, provide
additional detail.

LANGUAGE OBJECTIVES

Children will narrate how the
characters play music, using objective
pronouns and key vocabulary.

ELA ACADEMIC LANGUAGE

• *purpose, comprehension*
• Cognate: *comprensión*

MATERIALS

ELL Leveled Reader: *Let's Make
a Band*

Online Differentiated Texts,
"Come and Sort"

Online ELL Visual Vocabulary Cards

DIGITAL TOOLS

Have children listen to
the selection as they follow
along to develop comprehension.

Use the vocabulary activity for
additional support.

Let's Make a Band

Prepare to Read

Build Background Read the title. *A band is a group
of people. A band makes music together.* Display a
visual of one or more music bands and name musical
instruments with children. Show the cover illustration.
*These children make a band. First, they make
instruments.* Point out some items used as instruments,
such as a water bottle, pot, box, and pencils. If
possible, demonstrate how the items can be used to
make sounds. Tell children that the story is a realistic fiction story. *In this story, the
characters do things that people can do in real life.*

Focus on Vocabulary Use the routine on the **ELL Visual Vocabulary Cards** to
preteach *musician* and *participate*. Use the images and any labels to identify and
model the use of key vocabulary in context.

Lexile 30L

Read the Text

Use the Interactive Question-Response Routine to help children understand
the story.

Pages 2–8

Pages 2–3 *The children are at school. The children want to make a band. What
do the children want to do?* (make a band) Point to and read aloud the labels with
children. *The children need plates and beans. They need a box and rubber bands.
They make musical instruments. Then they make music.*

 *What do the children need to make a band? Talk to a partner about
the details.*

Beginning Help children point to details and say: *The children need plates. The
children need beans. The children need a box and rubber bands.*

Intermediate Guide children to complete sentences: *The children need musical
instruments. They need plates and beans. They need a box and rubber bands.*

Advanced/Advanced High Guide children to describe what the items are or their
typical purpose. (The beans are food. We eat food on the plates.)

Pages 4–5 Point to page 4. *The girl needs a tube and rice. She puts the rice in
the tube.* Act out shaking a tube. *It makes sounds.* Point to page 5. *The boy brings
a bottle. He puts water in the bottle.* Act out blowing air into a bottle to make
sounds. *He blows into the bottle. It makes sounds.*

 *What do children need to make sounds, or music, in the band? Talk with a
partner.*

Beginning Help children describe the illustrations: *There is a* tube *and* rice. *There is a* bottle of water.

Intermediate Provide sentence frames: *They need* a tube and rice *to make sounds. They also need a* bottle of water.

Pages 6–8 Ask children to read the labels on pages 6–7. On page 8, point out and demonstrate how the children use their instruments. *The children play music with their instruments.*

 What do the children do on page 8? **Ask and answer questions** *with a partner.*

Beginning Help children point to and name the items. Then help them respond: *The children make a* band. *They play* music *together.*

Intermediate Provide sentence frames: *The children make a* band. *What do they use to make* music*? He/she plays music with* a spoon and pot; cans and pencils. *They boy hits the* pot *with* a spoon.

Main Story Elements: Character, Setting, Events Have children discuss the main story elements. The characters are the students and teacher. The setting is the classroom. The events are collecting items and making instruments.

Retell Have partners retell the story. Have them take turns pointing to a picture and describing it to each other.

Focus on Fluency

Read pages 2–8 with appropriate expression. Then read the text aloud and have children echo read. For additional practice, have children record themselves reading the same text a few times and then select their favorite recording to play for you.

Build Knowledge: Make Connections

Talk About the Text Have partners discuss a time when they used an everyday object in a creative way.

Write About the Text Have children add their ideas to their Build Knowledge page of their reader's notebook.

Self-Selected Reading

Have children select another realistic fiction story from the online **Leveled Reader Library,** or read the **Differentiated Text,** "Come and Sort."

LITERACY ACTIVITIES

Have children complete the Literacy Activities on the inside back cover of the book.

FORMATIVE ASSESSMENT

⊘ STUDENT CHECK-IN

Have partners retell how the children make and play instruments. Then have children reflect using the Check-In routine.

 **LEVEL UP**

IF children can read *Let's Make a Band* **ELL Level** with fluency and correctly answer the Literacy Activity questions,

THEN tell children that they will read a more detailed version of the story.

HAVE children page through *Let's Make a Band* On Level and describe each picture in simple language.

• Have children read the selection, checking their comprehension and providing assistance as necessary.

MODELED WRITING

LESSON 1

LEARNING GOALS

We can write about what we like to do with our families.

OBJECTIVES

Use a combination of dictating and writing to compose informative texts in which they supply some information about the topic.

LANGUAGE OBJECTIVES

Children will inform by writing a sentence using the noun *family*.

ELA ACADEMIC LANGUAGE

• *sounds, noun*
• Cognate: *sonidos*

Writing Practice Display p. 5 of the **Literature Big Book** and read the sample sentence on p. 44 of the **Reading/Writing Companion.** Guide children to analyze the first sentence using the Actor/Description routine: *What is the sentence about?* (eggs in a carton) *How can we describe them?* (are a food family) Then read the prompt on p. 45, and ask a volunteer to answer it. Write the sentences on the board and point to each word as children choral read. Then have children write their own sentences.

Beginning Provide a sentence frame: I will write about <u>buttons</u> and <u>blocks</u>. Then help children think of their sentences. *What can be a family?* <u>Buttons</u> can be a family. <u>Blocks</u> can be a family, too.

Intermediate Have partners use the illustrations from the Big Book to get ideas of kinds of families to write about. Provide a sentence frame if needed.

Advanced/Advanced High Encourage children to say each sound in the words slowly to help them spell correctly. Then challenge them to share their sentences.

FORMATIVE ASSESSMENT ❯ **STUDENT CHECK IN** Partners share their sentences. Ask children to reflect using the Check-In routine.

INTERACTIVE WRITING

LESSON 2

LEARNING GOALS

We can write about what families the author shows outside.

OBJECTIVES

With guidance and support, add details to strengthen writing as needed.

LANGUAGE OBJECTIVES

Children will inform by writing a sentence using the verb *shows*.

ELA ACADEMIC LANGUAGE

• *sentence*

Write a Response: Share the Pen Choral read the sample sentences on p. T350 of the **Teacher's Edition.** Have children analyze the first sentence using the Actor/Action routine: *Who is the actor in the first sentence?* (The author) *What is the action?* (shows a lamb family outside) Point to the first sentence: *Is the sentence long or short?* The sentence is <u>long</u>. Then help children complete the sentence frames at the bottom of p. T350.

Beginning Help partners orally complete the first sentence by providing a visual from the book: The author shows <u>the stars, sun, and moon</u> outside.

Intermediate Challenge children to add details to create longer sentences. Encourage them to talk about the details they added.

Advanced/Advanced High Challenge children to think of their own sentence about the families the author shows outside.

FORMATIVE ASSESSMENT ❯ **STUDENT CHECK IN** Partners share their sentences. Ask children to reflect using the Check-In routine.

INDEParticleENT WRITING

LEARNING GOALS

We can write about the texts we read.

OBJECTIVES

Use a combination of drawing and writing to compose informative texts in which they supply some information about the topic.

LANGUAGE OBJECTIVES

Children will inform by writing sentences of different lengths.

ELA ACADEMIC LANGUAGE

- *pronoun*
- Cognate: *pronombre*

Find Text Evidence Use the Independent Writing routine. Ask questions to help children orally retell the shared read, such as: *Where are the children going?* (to school) *How do Jan and Pete go to school?* (on a bus) Then read the prompt on p. 60 of the **Reading/Writing Companion**: *Which children get exercise on their way to school? Explain how.* Display p. 52: *Do Jan and Pete get exercise?* (no) Then display p. 53: *Does Tom get exercise?* (yes)

Write a Response Write the sentence starters on p. T360 on the board, and read them. Model completing the first sentence frame, and have children choral read the response. Repeat with the second sentence frame. Then ask children to copy the sentences into p. 61 of the Reading/Writing Companion.

Beginning Encourage children to say the sounds in the words slowly to help them spell correctly. Then have partners take turns reading their sentences to each other.

Intermediate Encourage children to use both long and short sentences and then help them check this item off the writing checklist.

Advanced/Advanced High Read the writing checklist with children and have them identify where they used each item in their writing.

FORMATIVE ASSESSMENT ❯ **STUDENT CHECK IN** Partners share their sentences. Ask children to reflect using the Check-In routine.

SELF-SELECTED WRITING

LEARNING GOALS

We can revise our writing.

OBJECTIVES

Demonstrate command of the conventions of standard English grammar and usage when writing.

LANGUAGE OBJECTIVES

Children will inquire about their writing by checking their pronouns.

ELA ACADEMIC LANGUAGE

- *pronoun*
- Cognate: *pronombre*

Work with children to revise the group writing activity. Point to each word as you read the sentences. Stop to ask questions, such as, *Is this pronoun used correctly?* If needed, write a sentence using an object pronoun incorrectly, and work together to revise the sentence. Then, partners work together to revise their sentences before they publish them.

For support with grammar and object pronouns, refer to the **Language Transfers Handbook** and **Language Development Card** 16B.

FORMATIVE ASSESSMENT ❯ **STUDENT CHECK IN** Partners tell what revisions they made. Ask children to reflect using the Check-In routine.

LEARNING GOALS

We can understand important ideas and details in a text.

We can use captions to learn new information.

OBJECTIVES

With prompting and support, retell key details of a text.

With prompting and support, describe the connection between pieces of information in a text.

With prompting and support, identify basic similarities in and differences between two texts on the same topic.

Speak audibly and express thoughts, feelings, and ideas clearly.

LANGUAGE OBJECTIVES

Children will inform about how panda bears grow, using pronouns and key vocabulary.

ELA ACADEMIC LANGUAGE

• *nonfiction, facts*
• Cognate: *no ficción*

MATERIALS

Literature Big Book, *Panda Kindergarten,* pp. 4–33 and 34–36

Visual Vocabulary Cards

DIGITAL TOOLS

Have children listen to the selection as they follow along to develop comprehension.

Use the vocabulary activity for additional support.

Panda Kindergarten

Prepare to Read

Build Background Show photos of pandas and panda cubs. *What animal is this?* This is a ____. *A baby panda bear is called a cub. Let's describe what a panda bear looks like.* A panda bear is ____. *Panda bears live in China. China is a country in Asia.* Point to China on a map or globe. *There is a special place in China called the Wolong Nature Reserve. Pandas are born in this place. They are protected there. People take care of baby pandas and keep them safe.*

Literature Big Book

Focus on Vocabulary Use the **Visual Vocabulary Cards** to review the oral vocabulary words *environment* and *protect.* As you read, use gestures and other visual support to clarify important selection words, such as *nursery, bamboo forests,* and *mountains.*

Summarize the Text Before reading, give a brief summary of the text: *In the Wolong Nature Reserve, panda bears are protected and loved. Panda cubs are born here. The cubs spend time with their mother. Then they go to kindergarten.* Tell children that this is a nonfiction text about a topic. The author tells facts, or things that are true, about people taking care of baby panda bears.

Read the Text

Use the Interactive Question-Response Routine to help children understand the text.

Pages 4–15

Pages 8–9 Read the text. *The mother carries her baby panda. The baby cannot see. The baby drinks the mother's milk for food. How does the mother panda care for the baby?* (She holds her baby panda. She feeds, or gives, milk to her baby.)

Pages 12–15 Read the text. *When two babies are born, the mother takes care of one panda.* Point to the photos on pages 12–13. *The other baby goes to a nursery. People feed and keep the baby healthy. What happens in the nursery?* (People feed the cub.) *The two babies take turns with their mother. The pandas grow and grow. Then their eyes open, and they can see. What happens when the eyes of the babies open?* (The baby pandas can see.)

 How does a mother take care of her panda cubs? Talk to a partner.

Beginning Have partners point to the photos on pages 8–9 and help them respond: *The mother panda* holds *her cub. The mother* gives *the baby milk.*

Intermediate Have partners ask and answer: *What does the mother panda do? She* cares for; holds; feeds milk to *the cub.*

Pages 16–27

Pages 18–19 Read the text. *In panda kindergarten, pandas have a playground. They swing, climb, and play together. How do young pandas have fun with new friends?* (They swing, climb, and play together.)

Page 24–27 Read the text. *Pandas try new things. They climb high. They learn. The pandas get tired and sleepy. They take a nap. Look at the pandas sleep. Why do the pandas take a nap?* (They are tired.)

 What do the pandas do in panda kindergarten? Talk to a partner.

Beginning Have partners point to the photos as they respond: *The pandas play with new friends.*

Intermediate Provide sentence frames to help partners describe what the pandas do: *The pandas play with new friends. They climb and swing and learn new things in their outdoor playground.*

Advanced/Advanced High Help partners work together to describe how the pandas learn on the playground. (The pandas discover new things with new friends. They play in the snow. They touch their toes. They swing and climb.)

Pages 28–33

Pages 28–29 Read the text. *The young pandas stay in kindergarten for about one year. Some pandas stay at their home. They will have their own cubs. How long do pandas stay in kindergarten?* (one year)

Pages 30–31 Read the text. *Other pandas leave the nature preserve. They will live in bamboo forests. The forests are in nearby mountains. The pandas will use everything they learned in panda kindergarten. Where do some pandas live?* (in the bamboo forests; outside the reserve in mountains)

 What do pandas do after panda kindergarten? Talk to a partner.

Beginning Guide children to repeat after you: *Some pandas stay. The pandas may have babies. Some pandas leave. They live in forests.*

Intermediate Provide sentence frames: *Some pandas stay at their home. The pandas may have cubs. Some pandas live in bamboo forests in the mountains.*

Retell Use the **Retelling Cards** for *Panda Kindergarten* to retell the text with children. Display the cards and model retelling, using sequence words as you point to details. Help children take turns retelling text sections.

LESSON 4 **Paired Selection: "Save Big Blue"**

Pages 34–36 Point to photos and paraphrase the text. *The blue whale is the largest animal on Earth. Blue whales need our help. Hunters caught too many whales. Dirty water hurts the whales. We can protect them. We can help keep ocean waters clean. How can we protect the blue whale?* (keep oceans clean)

 How can we help protect blue whales? Talk to a partner.

Beginning Help children repeat: *We can help keep beaches clean. This helps keep blue whales safe.*

Intermediate Have partners respond: *We need to help keep ocean water clean for blue whales.*

Advanced/Advanced High Have partners talk about why we need to protect blue whales. (Hunters caught too many whales. Dirty water hurts whales.)

FORMATIVE ASSESSMENT

❯ STUDENT CHECK-IN

Main Selection Have partners retell how the pandas learn and grow in panda kindergarten.

Paired Selection Have partners describe how we can help protect blue whales and the ocean waters.

Have children reflect using the Check-In routine.

 Independent Time

Oral Language Guide children to describe what they read about in *Panda Kindergarten* and "Save Big Blue!" Ask: *How do people protect baby pandas and blue whales?* Help children discuss what the selections have in common.

LEARNING GOALS

We can listen actively to learn about why it is important to protect the environment.

OBJECTIVES

With prompting and support, ask and answer questions about key details in a text.

With prompting and support, retell key details of a text.

Actively engage in group reading activities with purpose and understanding.

Confirm understanding of a text read aloud or information presented orally or through other media by asking and answering questions about key details and requesting clarification if something is not understood.

LANGUAGE OBJECTIVES

Children will inform about ways to protect the environment, using verbs that end with -ing and key vocabulary.

ELA ACADEMIC LANGUAGE

- *nonfiction, details*
- Cognates: *no ficción, detalles*

MATERIALS

Interactive Read Aloud, "Protect the Environment"

Visual Vocabulary Cards

DIGITAL TOOLS

Have children listen to the selection as they follow along to develop comprehension.

Use the vocabulary activity for additional support.

"Protect the Environment!"

Interactive Read Aloud

Prepare to Read

Build Background Show visuals of clean environments as well as polluted ones. Use the images to elicit ideas of what we can do to protect the environment and keep it clean.

Focus on Vocabulary Use the **Visual Vocabulary Cards** to review the oral vocabulary words: *environment, protect, recycle, wisely,* and *encourage.* As you read, use gestures and other visual support to clarify important selection words, for example: *clean, plant, recycle, energy, dryer, compost pile, wildlife.*

Summarize the Text Before reading, provide a summary of the selection: *This nonfiction text teaches us about protecting the environment. It is important that we keep the air, water, and land clean and protect the homes of animals.*

Read the Text

Use the Interactive Question-Response Routine to help children understand the text.

Card 1

Paragraphs 1–2 Read the text. Point to the photo and use gestures as you tell why we need a healthy environment. *We need clean air to breathe and fresh water to drink. What do we need?* (clean air and water; a healthy environment)

Paragraph 3 Read the text. Help children understand the meaning of saving water. *Take short showers. Turn off the faucet when you brush your teeth. How can you save water?* (Take shorter showers. Turn off the faucet.)

Paragraph 4 Read the text. *People can help keep the air clean. Cars make the air dirty, or cause pollution. People can use cars less. They can ride bikes, walk, or take the bus more. Trees keep the air clean. We can plant more trees. How can people help keep the air clean?* (walk; ride a bike; take buses; plant trees)

What are the children in the photograph doing? How does this protect the environment? Talk to a partner.

Beginning Have children point to the photo as they respond: *The children <u>are planting</u> a tree. Trees make the air <u>clean</u>.*

Intermediate Provide sentence frames: *They <u>are planting a tree</u>. Trees help keep <u>the air clean</u>.*

Advanced/Advanced High Provide additional modeling as needed. (The children are planting a tree. Trees take in some dirty air. Trees make clean air.)

Advanced High Challenge children to add details in complete sentences. (Planting a tree protects the environment because a tree helps keep our air clean.)

Card 2

Paragraphs 1–2 Read the text. *We need to reduce, or make less, garbage. We make less trash when we buy fewer things.* Explain that children can share or use things again to create less garbage.

Paragraphs 3–4 Read the text. Reuse *means "to use something many times." We reuse things to make less trash.* Point to and describe details in the photo of boys carrying a recycling bin. Explain that cardboard and paper can be recycled as well. *What can we recycle?* (cans, plastic, glass, paper, grass, leaves)

 What are the children in the photograph doing? Talk to a partner.

Beginning Help partners respond: *The boys have a recycling* bin. *There are* plastic bottles *in the bin.*

Intermediate Help partners ask and answer questions: *What are the boys carrying? They are carrying* a recycling bin. *What is inside the* bin*? There are* plastic bottles and metal cans *in the bin.*

Advanced/Advanced High Ask children to explain how the children protect the environment.

Card 3

Paragraphs 1–2 Read the text. Demonstrate turning off the lights as you leave a room. *Using too much energy can hurt the environment.* Point to the photo. *Hang clothes to dry. This also saves energy.*

Paragraph 3 Read the text. *Heating and air conditioning use energy. When it's cold, you use the heat. Close doors and windows to save energy. How can you save energy?* (close doors and windows)

 Why do people turn off the lights when they leave a room? Talk to a partner.

Beginning Help children say after you: *People turn off the lights to save energy.*

Intermediate Provide sentence frames: *People* turn off *the lights to save* energy; electricity. *Using too much energy can* hurt the environment.

Card 4

Paragraph 1 Read the text. Point to the photo. *People may build homes and roads where animals live. People put trash in rivers. This hurts fish and other animals.*

Paragraphs 2–4 Read the text. Then explain how people and children can protect nature. *People recycle food waste, or compost. They plant trees or a garden. This helps keep the land healthy. You can learn about animals and how to keep land safe for animals.*

 How can you help wildlife? Talk to a partner.

Beginning Help children say: *I can learn about* animals. *I can help keep* the land *safe and clean.*

Intermediate Guide children to respond: *I can learn about* wildlife *at a* park. *I can learn more about how* animals live. *I can help* keep the land safe and clean.

 Retell Use illustrations on the **Interactive Read-Aloud Cards** to retell the text with children. Display the cards and model retelling details in the photos and text. Then help partners take turns retelling details that they learned on a card.

FORMATIVE ASSESSMENT

❯ STUDENT CHECK-IN

Have partners retell ways to protect the environment.

Then, have children reflect using the Check-In routine.

Independent Time

Asking and Answering Questions Have children practice asking and answering questions about the photographs on the cards. Provide sentence frames and modeling to help them use question words, such as *what, where,* and *why.* For example: *What are _____? Where are _____? Why do _____?*

LESSONS 4-5

LEARNING GOALS

We can reread to understand the text.

OBJECTIVES

With prompting and support, identify the main topic and retell key details of a text.

With prompting and support, describe the connection between pieces of information in a text.

Actively engage in group reading activities with purpose and understanding.

Speak audibly and express thoughts, feelings, and ideas clearly.

LANGUAGE OBJECTIVES

Children will inform about how to keep Earth clean, using object pronouns and key vocabulary.

ELA ACADEMIC LANGUAGE

• details

• Cognates: *detalles*

MATERIALS

ELL Leveled Reader: *Let's Save Earth*

Online Differentiated Texts, "At the Lake"

Online ELL Visual Vocabulary Cards

DIGITAL TOOLS

Have children listen to the selection as they follow along to develop comprehension.

Use the vocabulary activity for additional support.

Let's Save Earth

Prepare to Read

Build Background Read the title. Say: *Let's save Earth means "let's keep Earth clean and healthy." One way to keep Earth clean is to make less trash. We make less trash when we use things again, or recycle. We can use less energy to help keep Earth healthy.* Tell children that this nonfiction text tells about ways we can help save, or protect, Earth.

Lexile 110L

Focus on Vocabulary Use the routine on the **ELL Visual Vocabulary Cards** to preteach *planet* and *waste*. Use the images and any labels to identify and model the use of key vocabulary in context.

Read the Text

Use the Interactive Question-Response Routine to help children understand the text.

Pages 2–8

Pages 2–3 Point to page 2. *The family shops. The family brings the bag to the store.* Point to the bag. *They will use the bag again. They use it each time they go to the store.* Point to page 3. Demonstrate sorting paper and plastic into groups. *How do we sort trash?* (Each kind of trash goes in a bin.) Explain that the trash in each bin in the photo can be recycled, or turned into new things.

 How does the family help save Earth? Talk to a partner.

Beginning Provide a sentence frame: *They can use the bag <u>again</u> at the store.*

Intermediate Have partners point to the photo as they ask and answer: *What is the family doing? The family <u>is shopping</u> at the store. What do they bring to the store? The family brings <u>a bag</u>. They can use it <u>again the next time they shop</u>.*

Advanced/Advanced High Ask children to explain why using a bag again helps save Earth. Provide additional modeling as needed. (The family makes less trash when they use the bag again. This helps keep Earth clean.)

Pages 4–5 Point to page 4. *The girl turns off the lights to save energy.* Point to page 5. *The girl turns off the water when she brushes her teeth. She saves water. How can you save water?* (turn off the water while brushing your teeth)

 How do the girls help save Earth? Talk to a partner.

Beginning Help children point and respond: *The girl turns off the <u>lights; water</u>.*

Intermediate Have partners ask and answer: *What does the girl do? The girl turns off the* lights; water. *She saves* energy; water.

Advanced/Advanced High Have partners ask and answer: *What do the girls do? Why?* (The girls turn off the lights and water. They want to save energy and water.)

Pages 6–8 Point to page 6. *The boy and his father take the bus.* Point to page 7. *These people do not drive their cars. They save energy.* Point to page 8. *These people pick up litter, or trash. Litter needs to be cleaned up. They keep the beach clean and safe.*

 How do the people in the photos save energy and help keep the air clean? Talk to a partner.

Beginning Have children *reread* and respond: *The people take the* bus. *The people* walk. *The people ride* bikes. *They do not* drive *cars.*

Intermediate Have children give details: *The people* take the bus, walk, and ride their bikes. *They do not* drive cars.

Topic and Details Help children identify the topic of the text. *Each page tells something people can do to help* save Earth. *This is the* topic. *What are some details about the topic?* People can use bags again. *People can sort their* trash. *People can take the* bus.

Retell Have partners retell the text. Have them take turns pointing to a picture and describing it to each other.

Focus on Fluency

Read pages 2–8 with appropriate expression. Then read the text aloud and have children echo read. For additional practice, have children record themselves reading the same text a few times, and then select their favorite recording to play for you.

Build Knowledge: Make Connections

Talk About the Text Have partners discuss ways they can help the environment.

Write About the Text Have children add their ideas to their Build Knowledge page of their reader's notebook.

Self-Selected Reading

Have children select another informational text from the online **Leveled Reader Library,** or read the **Differentiated Text,** "At the Lake."

LITERACY ACTIVITIES

Have children complete the Literacy Activities on the inside back cover of the book.

❯ STUDENT CHECK-IN

Have partners retell how the people in the text help protect Earth. Then have children reflect using the Check-In routine.

IF children can read *Let's Save Earth* ELL Level with fluency and correctly answer the Literacy Activity questions,

THEN tell children that they will read a more detailed version of the text.

HAVE children page through *Let's Save Earth* On Level and describe each picture in simple language.

- Have children read the selection, checking their comprehension and providing assistance as necessary.

MODELED WRITING

LEARNING GOALS

We can write what we like about panda cubs.

OBJECTIVES

Use dictating and writing to compose opinion pieces that state an opinion about the topic.

LANGUAGE OBJECTIVES

Children will argue by writing sentences using describing words.

ELA ACADEMIC LANGUAGE

• *sentence*

 Writing Practice Display images of panda cubs from the **Literature Big Book** and read the sample sentences on p. 74 of the **Reading/Writing Companion**. Guide children to analyze the first sentence using the Actor/Description routine: *Who is the actor?* (I) *What is the description?* (like that panda cubs look fuzzy and pink) *When are they fuzzy and pink?* (when they are born) Then read the prompt on p. 75, and have children answer it as a group. Write the sentences on the board and have children choral read them. Then ask children to write their own sentences.

 Beginning Have children view the pandas and tell what they see. Use their responses to create a word bank. Help them use the word bank to write.

Intermediate Have partners take turns asking and answering *who/what* questions to create their sentences. Provide a sentence frame if needed.

Advanced/Advanced High Challenge children to include describing words and point them out to the group as they share their sentences.

FORMATIVE ASSESSMENT ❯ **STUDENT CHECK IN** Partners share their sentences. Ask children to reflect using the Check-In routine.

INTERACTIVE WRITING

LEARNING GOALS

We can write about how the Wolong Nature Reserve helps pandas.

OBJECTIVES

With guidance and support, respond to questions and suggestions from peers.

LANGUAGE OBJECTIVES

Children will inform by writing a sentence using a descriptive word.

ELA ACADEMIC LANGUAGE

• *prompt*

 Write a Response: Share the Pen Choral read the sample sentence on p. T428 of the **Teacher's Edition.** Have children analyze the first sentence using the Actor/Action routine: *Who are the actors?* (the people at the reserve) *What is the action?* (help pandas) *How?* (by feeding and protecting the cubs) Then help children complete the sentence frames at the bottom of p. T428, using at least one descriptive word.

 Beginning Help children think of their sentence by providing a visual from the book: Trained people help <u>twin pandas eat</u>.

Intermediate Have partners ask and answer questions from the photographs in the **Big Book** to help them complete the sentence frames.

Advanced/Advanced High Challenge children to think of their own sentences about how the people at the Wolong Nature Reserve help the panda cubs. Encourage them to share their sentences with the group.

FORMATIVE ASSESSMENT ❯ **STUDENT CHECK IN** Partners share their sentences. Ask children to reflect using the Check-In routine.

INDEPENDENT WRITING

LEARNING GOALS

We can write about the texts we read.

OBJECTIVES

Use dictating and writing to compose opinion pieces that state an opinion about the topic.

LANGUAGE OBJECTIVES

Children will identify details in a text to answer a question.

ELA ACADEMIC LANGUAGE

• *environment*

 Find Text Evidence Use the Independent Writing routine. Ask questions to help children orally retell the shared read, such as: *How does Dad help?* (He gets rid of junk at the lake.) *How does the girl help?* (She uses a lunch box.) Then read the prompt on p. 90 of the **Reading/Writing Companion:** *Why is it good to ride a bus? Can a bus take a few people or a lot of people?* (a lot of people) How does this help the environment? (fewer cars)

 Write a Response Write the starter from p. T438 on the board, and read it. Model completing the sentence starter, and have children choral read the response. Then ask children to copy the sentence into p. 91 of the **Reading/ Writing Companion.**

 Beginning Provide a sentence frame to help partners talk about their sentences: I used the pronoun *it.*

Intermediate Encourage children to use the Word Bank to help them spell words as they write, and then help them check this item off the writing checklist.

Advanced/Advanced High Read the writing checklist with children, and have them identify where they used each item in their writing.

FORMATIVE ASSESSMENT ❯ **STUDENT CHECK IN** Partners share their sentences. Ask children to reflect using the Check-In routine.

SELF-SELECTED WRITING

LEARNING GOALS

We can revise our writing.

OBJECTIVES

Demonstrate command of the conventions of standard English grammar and usage when writing.

LANGUAGE OBJECTIVES

Children will inquire about their writing by checking possessive pronouns.

ELA ACADEMIC LANGUAGE

• *possessive pronoun*

 Work with children to revise the group writing activity. Point to each word as you read the sentences. Stop to ask questions, such as, *Is the possessive pronoun used correctly here?* If needed, write a sentence using a possessive pronoun incorrectly, and work together to revise the sentence. Then, have partners work together to revise their sentences before they publish them.

For support with grammar and possessive pronouns, refer to the **Language Transfers Handbook** and **Language Development Card** 3B.

FORMATIVE ASSESSMENT ❯ **STUDENT CHECK IN** Partners tell what revisions they made. Ask children to reflect using the Check-In routine.

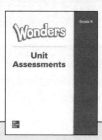

UNIT 10

Summative Assessment
Get Ready for Unit Assessment

Unit 10 Tested Skills

LISTENING AND READING COMPREHENSION	VOCABULARY	GRAMMAR	SPEAKING AND WRITING
• Listening Actively • Details	• Words and Categories	• Pronouns	• Offering Opinions • Presenting • Composing/Writing • Retelling/Recounting

Create a Student Profile

Record data from the following resources in the Student Profile charts on pages 136–137 of the Assessment book.

COLLABORATIVE	INTERPRETIVE	PRODUCTIVE

• Collaborative Conversations Rubrics
  • Listening
  • Speaking
	• Leveled Unit Assessment
	  • Listening Comprehension
	  • Reading Comprehension
	  • Vocabulary
	  • Grammar
	• Presentation Rubric
	  • Listening
	• *Wonders* Unit Assessment
		• Weekly Progress Monitoring
		• Leveled Unit Assessment
		  • Speaking
		  • Writing
		• Presentation Rubric
		  • Speaking
		• Write to Sources Rubric
		• *Wonders* Unit Assessment

The Foundational Skills Kit, Language Development Kit, and Adaptive Learning provide additional student data for progress monitoring.

Level Up

Use the following chart, along with your Student Profiles, to guide your Level Up decisions.

LEVEL UP	If **BEGINNING** level students are able to do the following, they may be ready to move to the **INTERMEDIATE** level:	If **INTERMEDIATE** level students are able to do the following, they may be ready to move to the **ADVANCED** level:	If **ADVANCED** level students are able to do the following, they may be ready to move to **ON** level:
COLLABORATIVE	• participate in collaborative conversations using basic vocabulary and grammar and simple phrases or sentences • discuss simple pictorial or text prompts	• participate in collaborative conversations using appropriate words and phrases and complete sentences • use limited academic vocabulary across and within disciplines	• participate in collaborative conversations using more sophisticated vocabulary and correct grammar • communicate effectively across a wide range of language demands in social and academic contexts
INTERPRETIVE	• identify details in simple read alouds • understand common vocabulary and idioms and interpret language related to familiar social, school, and academic topics • make simple inferences and make simple comparisons • exhibit an emerging receptive control of lexical, syntactic, phonological, and discourse features	• identify main ideas and/or make some inferences from simple read alouds • use context clues to identify word meanings and interpret basic vocabulary and idioms • compare, contrast, summarize, and relate text to graphic organizers • exhibit a limited range of receptive control of lexical, syntactic, phonological, and discourse features when addressing new or familiar topics	• determine main ideas in read alouds that have advanced vocabulary • use context clues to determine meaning, understand multiple-meaning words, and recognize synonyms of social and academic vocabulary • analyze information, make sophisticated inferences, and explain their reasoning • command a high degree of receptive control of lexical, syntactic, phonological, and discourse features
PRODUCTIVE	• express ideas and opinions with basic vocabulary and grammar and simple phrases or sentences • restate information or retell a story using basic vocabulary • exhibit an emerging productive control of lexical, syntactic, phonological, and discourse features	• produce coherent language with limited elaboration or detail • restate information or retell a story using mostly accurate, although limited, vocabulary • exhibit a limited range of productive control of lexical, syntactic, phonological, and discourse features when addressing new or familiar topics	• produce sentences with more sophisticated vocabulary and correct grammar • restate information or retell a story using extensive and accurate vocabulary and grammar • tailor language to a particular purpose and audience • command a high degree of productive control of lexical, syntactic, phonological, and discourse features